THE ANCIENT HISTORY OF WESTERN CIVILIZATION

THE ANCIENT HISTORY OF WESTERN CIVILIZATION

ELIAS BICKERMAN
Emeritus, Columbia University
and
Jewish Theological Seminary

MORTON SMITH
Columbia University

HARPER & ROW, PUBLISHERS
New York   Hagerstown   San Francisco   London

Sponsoring Editor: John Greenman
Project Editor: Robert Ginsberg
Designer: T. R. Funderburk
Production Supervisor: Francis X. Giordano
Compositor: Maryland Linotype Composition Co., Inc.

Portions of this text appeared previously, in slightly altered form, in *The Columbia History of the World* edited by John A. Garraty and Peter Gay.

THE ANCIENT HISTORY OF WESTERN CIVILIZATION

Copyright © 1976 by Elias Bickerman and Morton Smith

All rights reserved. Printed in the United States of America. No part of this book may be used or reproduced in any manner whatsoever without written permission except in the case of brief quotations embodied in critical articles and reviews. For information address Harper & Row, Publishers, Inc., 10 East 53rd Street, New York, N.Y. 10022.

Library of Congress Cataloging in Publication Data

Bickerman, Elias Joseph, Date-
   The ancient history of Western civilization.

   Includes indexes.
   1. History, Ancient. 2. Civilization, Ancient.
I. Smith, Morton, 1915-   joint author. II. Title.

CB311.B52   930   75-31639
ISBN 0-06-040668-2

CONTENTS

Preface xi

Chapter 1. WHY HISTORY? 1
Human interest in history (1) the reasons for it (2) history and social solidarity (2) examples of its invention (2) other functions (3) scientific vs. humanistic interest (3) proper subjects (4) "relevance" vs. accuracy (4) difference from the physical sciences (5ff.) consequent uncertainty of results and limited utility (7) recapitulation (8)

Chapter 2. WHY ANCIENT HISTORY? 10
Stability of culture before the industrial revolution, and transformation since (10) divisions within the ancient period (11) continuance of classical influence to present (11) especially because of human uniformity (12) history and humility (12) and objectivity (13) and causation (13f.) dialogue with the past (15) necessary for understanding the present (15)

vi CONTENTS

Chapter 3. MESOPOTAMIA 17
　History and prehistory (17ff.) emergence of agriculture (20) spread (21) development of towns (21) weaving and pottery (22) domestication of man (23) Sumerians (24) technology and agriculture (25) trade (26) cities (27) writing (28) other cultures (28) Sumerian civilization (29) literature, religion, and law (30) kings (31) rise of Akkad (32) political history to Hammurabi (32) Babylonian law and culture (33f.) trade and neighbors (35) Mari, Elam, Assyria (35) diffusion of Babylonian culture, especially literature (36ff.)

Chapter 4. EGYPT 41
　Geography (41) irrigation and population (43) afterlife (44) development of culture, hieroglyphics (44) pharaohs (45) economy (46) trade (47) pyramids (47f.) extension of funerary privileges (49ff.) political history (51) Middle Kingdom, scribes (52f.) portraiture (54) Hyksos (55) New Kingdom (55) cultural changes (56) Ikhnaton (56f.)

Chapter 5. EMPIRES AND THEIR FALL 59
　Syria and its cities (59f.) horses and chariots (61) Egypt vs. the Hittites (61) international culture (62) the Hittites (63) Ramses II (63) iron (64) alphabet (64) Cyprus and copper (65) Crete (65) Mycenae (66) the end of the Mycenaean world (67f.)

Chapter 6. GODS AND MEN 69
　Role of the gods in ancient thought (69) notions of them (70) anthropomorphism (71) history and life of the gods (71) how to deal with them (72) private gods (73) internationalization of the major gods (73f.)

Chapter 7. THE NEW CULTURE 75
　The invasions (75ff.) the political scene after the invasions (77) Assyria (78) the new civilization (79) the heroic (79) Homer and Genesis (80) the "history" in Genesis (80f.) Moses and the Israelites (82) Joshua, tribal heroes and kings (82f.) life in the little city (83f.) the success of the city-state (85) Phoenician trade (86) Greek characteristics (86f.)

Chapter 8. THE GREAT DIVIDE 89
　Increase of wealth (89) social changes, the two patterns (91) the Greek pattern: oligarchy, hoplites (91) constitutional law, lay priesthoods, games (93) nudity, gymnasia, homosexuality (94) population and agriculture (95) colonization (96) the Near Eastern pattern (96) Amos and the Yahweh-alone tradition (97) Amos, Hosea, Hesiod (97f.) Assyria (99)

Chapter 9. THE CENTURY OF THE MINOR POWERS   101
   Fall of Assyria, the four kingdoms (101) international culture and trade (103) wealth, poverty, tyranny (104) purity (105) individualism, eroticism (105f.) Sparta (106f.) Athens (107f.) Athenian government (108) Near Eastern political history (109) Judea and Deuteronomy (110) the exile and Judaism (111) the influence of Deuteronomy, "Second Isaiah" (112)

Chapter 10. PERSIA AND ATHENS   113
   Cyrus, Cambyses, Darius, the Persian empire (113) religion, administration, army (115) history, art (117) subject peoples (117) post-exilic Judea, Psalms, Job, Ionian philosophy, Thales (118) Xenophanes, Parmenides, Pythagoras (119) Doric temples, Persian attacks on Greece (120) Delian League, Athenian empire (121) navy, fortifications, consolidation, Peloponnesian war (122) Athenian culture (123f.) sophistry (124) philosophy, medicine, Socrates (125) drama, histories, Herodotus and Thucydides (126f.) evaluations of Athenian democracy (127f.)

Chapter 11. THE FOURTH CENTURY TO THE
DEATH OF ALEXANDER   129
   Political history of Greece to 362 (129ff.) hellenized barbarian states (131) Greek economic crisis; culture, Praxiteles, Plato (132f.) Aristotle (133) Philip II and Alexander (133f.)

Chapter 12. THE HELLENISTIC WORLD   137
   Division of Alexander's empire, revival of Greece (137) new comedy, philosophy, Cynics, Stoics, Epicureans (139) hellenistic kingdoms, Ptolemaic Egypt (140) Alexandria, Galatians, Pergamum, Rhodes (141) characteristics of hellenistic culture (142f.) science, technology, influence on the Near East (143f.) easterners writing Greek (144f.)

Chapter 13. THE ROMAN REPUBLIC   147
   Rome, entrance into near eastern history (147) origins and characteristics (149) manpower, alliances, expansion, Punic wars (150) provinces, taxation, provincial government (151) domestic government, depopulation, slaves, bourgeoisie vs. senators (152f.) annexations (153) slave revolts, revolt of Italian allies, attempts at reform, the Gracchi, relief and politics, Marius' proletarian army (154) Sulla, Pompey, Caesar (155) Octavian's triumph (156) Roman republican culture: Plautus, Terence, Cicero, Cato, Caesar (156f.) portraiture, architecture, roads, city planning, public entertainment, gladiators, sewers, aqueducts, traffic (158f.) private houses, technology, warfare (160) jurisprudence (161) Roman law (162)

viii CONTENTS

Chapter 14. THE AUGUSTAN EMPIRE 163
Octavian's objectives: the army (163) conquests and frontiers, republican façade, class interests (165) the Roman mob, equestrians (166) the Senate, provinces, religious policy (167) traditionalism, cult of Rome and Augustus, provincial support, the new order (168f.) political history of the principate (169f.) success of Augustus' system, imperial culture, economic progress, cities, amenities (170f.) architecture, trade (172) entertainment, religion, city government, artifacts (173) philosophy, literature, decoration (174f.) changes in social status: women (175) slaves and peasants, religion: oriental cults (176) Judaism: uncertain extent, history (177) varieties, John the Baptist, Jesus, Paul (178f.) early Christianity, organization, relation to Judaism, persecutions (180) Jewish revolts, rabbinic Judaism (181) characteristics and success, Jewish competition with Christianity (182)

Chapter 15. THE LATER ROMAN EMPIRE 185
The crisis of 235–285, its causes (185ff.) economic consequences, recovery, fortifications, reorganized army (187ff.) financial problem (189f.) new tax system, bureaucracy (190) social changes, peasants become serfs, government: senators (191) the imperial council, the sacred emperor, Constantinople (192) the growth of Christianity, persecutions, Constantine's patronage (193) Christian organization (194) Church vs. State, persecution of heretics, the Arian controversy (195) Cynicism and monasticism, Pachomius (196) characteristics of early monasticism, structure of Constantine's empire (197) the army, loss of the west, the situation in the east (198f.) invasions, Justinian and his successors, Phocas and Heraclius, loss of Syria and Egypt (199f.)

Chapter 16. LATE ROMAN SOCIETY AND CULTURE 201
Economic changes: transfer of property (201ff.) consequent social changes, the privileged classes, the peasants (203ff.) alienation of the population, consequent military impotence (205f.) Christian indifference, missions (206f.) suppression of paganism (207) Manichees, Jews, Samaritans (208) penitential discipline, church government, patriarchal rivalries and heresies. Nestorianism, the monophysites (208ff.) cultural changes and survivals: (211f.) church architecture, medicine, law, historiography, philosophy, Plotinus, classical rhetoric, education (212f.) influence on Christianity (213) Christian education of converts, barbarization of imperial culture, failure of the scientific tradition (214f.) decline of mental health, exorcism, magic and miracles, cult of the Virgin (215f.) asceticism (216) extent of the Christian reorientation (217)

Chapter 17. THE CHARACTERISTICS OF
ANCIENT CIVILIZATION   218
    Out-of-door life (218f.) sparse population, room to expand, city/village settlements (219) small cities, closely connected with countryside, seasonal diet, city loyalty (220) egalitarian tendency, class conflict, regulation of private life (221) limited manpower, use of women (222) children, animals, conquest of wild animals (223f.) primitive technology: *medicine*, high mortality, early aging, poverty, family solidarity (224f) *chemistry*, plagues and pests, fertilizers, population control (225f.) *engineering*, rudimentary discoveries, lack of interest (226f.) low productivity, social stability, manufacture by craftsmen (227) local variations, limited travel, importance of local connections (228f.) laxity of central government, unimportance of trade (229) simplicity of life, large empires (230) quiet, importance of song and speech (231f.) importance of cities for entertainment (232f.) lack of good artificial lighting, consequent life by day, importance of celestial bodies and nocturnal ceremonies (233f.) large supernatural population (gods and demons), sacrificial worship, not congregational (234f.) prevalence of magic, frequent communication with gods and demons (235ff.) Greek rationalism and its consequences vs. the stability of Egypt (237ff.) comparative stability of even Greco-Roman society, hereditary determination of most careers, education by apprenticeship (239) lack of glasses, ignorance of the cosmos, expense, inconvenience, and inadequacy of books (240) characteristics of Greek rationalism, parallel phenomena (240f.)

Chapter 18. WHAT HAPPENED IN ANCIENT HISTORY   242
    Human lives, their number (242) private history, major cultural developments: development of tools and techniques, conquest of the environment (243f.) unimportance of political history (244) the Greek revelation, life in fifth-century Athens (245f.) Athens compared with Babylon (246f.) dissemination and stagnation of Greek culture, Roman life under Constantine (247f) causes of this failure, classical survivals, new orientation (248) new religious organizations and new types of careers, the Church-State antithesis as a source of freedom (249f.) survival of the rationalist tradition (250)

Picture Credits   251

Map Index   257

Subject Index   261

LIST OF MAPS

   I   Earliest Egypt and Mesopotamia   18
  II   The Late Bronze Age   60
 III   The Theater of the Invasions   78
  IV   The World of Assyria, Archaic Greece, and Israel   92
   V   The World of Persia and Classical Greece   116
  VI   The Hellenistic World   136
 VII   The Roman World   148
VIII   The End of the Roman World   186

PREFACE

The present work had its origin in the chapters on the ancient Near East and classical antiquity that we wrote for the *Columbia History of the World*. Those were well received and it was suggested that they might be published separately as a paperback. This gave us the opportunity to add the prefatory chapters on the study of history in general and of ancient history in particular, to revise extensively the chapters already written, and to add concluding chapters on the general characteristics of ancient—as opposed to modern—civilization, and on the chief cultural developments that occurred in antiquity.

As the book now stands, Chapters 1–6 are basically the work of Professor Bickerman, revised by Professor Smith; Chapters 7–18 were written primarily by Professor Smith, but they incorporated from the beginning many notes provided by Professor Bickerman and they have been extensively revised in accordance with his observations. For statements of fact, each of us has in many instances relied on the learning of the other; for judgments of causation, value, and the like, each has been the final authority in his own chapters, but it is a pleasure to record that our differences have been few and that we have almost always been able to find expressions to which we could both agree.

It is our mutual hope that the book may help the beginning student of ancient history to escape from the morass of names, dates, and details, to get an overview of the whole terrain, its major divisions and their characteristics, and even to ask himself some of the ultimate questions: Why study history at all? Why ancient history? What of importance really happened in antiquity? What is the importance of the historical process? These are questions we have often asked ourselves and for which we have indicated the answers that have seemed to us most persuasive. For such questions, of course, *quot homines, tot sententiae*—every man has his own opinions. It is at these points that history becomes autobiography, and that we leave it.

Our thanks are due to the many scholars and institutions who made their photographs available to us, and particularly to Mr. Levon Avdoyan for his reading of the proof and preparation of the indices.

ELIAS BICKERMAN
MORTON SMITH

New York, 1975

NOTE: Words followed by an asterisk (*) in the text refer to subjects illustrated in the photographs.

THE ANCIENT HISTORY OF WESTERN CIVILIZATION

1
WHY HISTORY?

HUMAN INTEREST IN HISTORY

A historian should be both scholar and craftsman. As both, he does his job because he likes it. As a scholar he values knowledge for its own sake, not only for its utility. Indeed, history would seem to be, of all studies, the most surely useless. For—one might argue—all other branches of learning help man to affect his future, but history deals with the past, something man cannot affect because the past no longer exists.

Nevertheless, men have always busied themselves with their past. Long before there were books, there were tales and songs about the men and gods of old. Mortals, says Pindar, are forgetful, but remembrance is carried on by the sounding stream of song. Thus the historian, as a German romantic author put it, is a prophet looking backward. But why look backward? "Let the dead bury the dead." Why did and do men care for the past which, as the Greeks said, even the gods cannot alter?

Briefly, the Greeks were wrong. The past is what we make it.

Most men, admittedly, make little of it—except for that brief, immediate past which they, themselves, experienced. For a man who fought in the Second World War, his experiences and image of that war are unforgettable, but for men born after Pearl Harbor the war means little—it preceded their life. The Roman poet Lucretius, seeking to free men from the fear of death, tells them to look back to the past before they were born: As this means nothing to them, so the future, after they are dead, will mean nothing.

THE FUNCTIONS OF HISTORY

But while individuals are ephemeral, groups—human families, nations, churches—can live for millennia by renewing their members. The present Pope is reckoned the 264th Bishop of Rome. Conversely, the survival of identity depends on the survival of a group. Even a pyramid will not preserve the memory of its builder unless some group able to tell its story or read its inscriptions also survives.

To acquire new adherents who will make it last, an association must inspire them with faith in its future. But the future, as Aristotle says, is the complement of the past, thus any group working for a common future is likely to create for itself a common past as well. Mao's slogan, "Let the past serve the present," derives from the intuition that human societies need histories in order to survive. Conversely, as Chinese history before Mao shows, the present serves the past, as present societies are subjected and directed by the influence of the traditions alive in the minds of their members. For those who share them, such traditions are important bases for common judgments and purposes; thus belief in a common past strengthens even the most revolutionary community. For the Christian Church, the Incarnation opened a new aeon, but the same Church claims to be the only true Israel, heir of the patriarchs and prophets of the Old Testament.

Greek philosophers asked how a city, constituted of different elements (old and young, rich and poor, and so on) could survive. Their answer was by "blending" these ingredients. This blending depends on the feeling of community and this feeling results not only from present association but also from hope for a common future and belief in a common past. History provides the common past. Of history, therefore, the philosopher will say, as Voltaire said of God, that if it does not exist, it must be invented.

Accordingly, the new states of Africa are already fabricating histories for themselves, to produce common feeling and develop pride among the tribes of which they are composed. In Ghana, murals were painted to show that the alphabet and the steam engine had been invented in Ghana. Similarly, under Ataturk, Turkish children learned that the Turks were akin to the ancient Sumerians. Almost every group that rejects its past immediately adopts a new one. Pagans converted to Judaism or Christianity threw over the pagan past and taught a new history which began with the Old Testament. In turn, Biblical heroes were replaced by classical ones in the historical speeches of American revolutionaries, and American leftists now replace the American revolutionary leaders, Washington and Jefferson, with Mao and Che Guevara. Henry Ford, who reputedly said that history was bunk, founded an automobile museum—he needed a history in which he would be the hero. Those American Negroes who refuse to accept American history as "theirs" put themselves in the tragic position of a people who have lost their past, and go vainly in search of it to the ports of West Africa. The universal longing for a history, even, if needs be, a fictitious one, proves the importance of history for societies. Even primitive societies, by teaching myths that form a pseudohistory, train their members to hold those beliefs about the past which give cohesion to the group and create trust in its future.

Accordingly, accounts of the past change with a society's changing needs. Until the end of the eighteenth century, history dealt mainly with the mighty—conquerors, kings, and popes. Then, at the height of the French Revolution, the philosopher Condorcet proclaimed that history should no longer deal with exceptional men or events but with the ordinary lives of "laboring families." He was a marquis later driven to suicide by his revolutionary protégés, but neither of these inconveniences discredited his democratic dogma. In the spirit of Condorcet, therefore, the historiography of the past two centuries has created a historical past, first for the middle class, and then for the proletariat, thus contributing to the cohesion of these newly powerful groups.

Indeed, the formation of a group and the formation of its past are often complementary processes. As the body of Roman citizens was extended to include natives of many Italian cities, a legendary history of Italy was invented to link these cities by common derivation from the heroes of the Trojan War. Sometimes, a powerful past will evoke new political groups to claim it, as the story of the Holy Land called forth Zionism and the State of Israel. Thus to shape the past is to shape men's expectations and ideals, and, as Orwell's dictator in *1984* says, "He who controls the past controls the future."

We must, however, consider the other values of history. It not only helps hold groups together, but has humanistic value. It preserves knowledge of what men have thought and done that was true, beautiful, and noble. It inculcates morality by preserving the good or evil actions and characters of the past for admiration or contempt. The Roman historian Tacitus, in one of his rare moments of optimism, thought it restrained vice by threatening posthumous infamy.

Apart from its moral value, history is of scientific interest as a record of past events and their connections and the problems they raise, though it differs from the physical sciences in many respects. Above all, we are apt to participate imaginatively in the events studied. We can record the movements of atoms or stars and the lives of insects without feeling love or hate for them or attempting to relive their experiences, but in history we have the opportunity, as Gibbon says, and therefore the temptation, to "climb the Alps with Hannibal." The Roman dramatist Terence put it more generally in his famous declaration, "Because I am a man, I think nothing human is of indifference to me." The most difficult aspect of the historian's work is to share this universal concern and to recreate imaginatively the history he attempts to understand (for it cannot be understood unless it is recreated) yet always to distinguish his imaginings from the preserved evidence, and never to distort that evidence to serve his wishes or fit his theories.

THE SUBJECTS OF HISTORY

Of the secondary functions of history, the scientific was perhaps performed as well by middle-class and proletarian history as by the history of rulers. The humanistic and moral values of history, however, suffered. Detailed study of the material conditions of peasants and slaves is not likely to reveal much worth knowing for its own sake. The advice of St. Paul, "Whatever things are true, worthy of reverence, just, holy, pleasant, well spoken of—anything that demonstrates virtue or deserves praise—think of these things," will generally lead the historian to the "great historical" figures and documents. The traditional choice of material reflects the judgments of many generations and much wisdom.

"RELEVANCE" VS. ACCURACY

The relevance of history to society does not mean that the historian should be a time server. Scientists, too, focus their interests in response to needs of the society. Geologists became attentive to oil in the automobile age; aerodynamics grew with the growth of air travel. Such "relevance" is of course compatible with strict adherence to the truth and may even favor it, since the more important the subject, the more important it is to have an accurate account. A dishonest historian cheats both his readers and himself. Nations have fallen because of historical fallacies. Think of the "Aryan" theory of Hitler's Germany. The nationalistic history prevalent in Europe between the two world wars distorted the picture of the first one by minimizing the importance of American intervention. As a result Hitler and Mussolini, as well as Wilhelm II, reckoned without the United States—and lost. The Marxist misinterpretation of history led the Kremlin to help their "comrades" in Peking make China the most powerful and most dangerous neighbor of the USSR. And better knowledge of history might have prevented that squandering of American wealth on the third world which has left the United States without a single friend there. The great German statesman Bismarck had already observed that "Liberated peoples are not thankful, they are demanding."

HISTORY AND THE PHYSICAL SCIENCES

Yet in spite of the importance of history and the true historian's commitment to accuracy, fallacies abound in historical works and even the most careful historians rarely succeed in settling once and for all the questions they treat. Why cannot historical works attain the reliability of books on the physical sciences?

In the first place, the scientist is not identical with the object of his study, but the most scrupulous historian is himself a part of history. He is not only examining the past, he is shaping the future. What he writes, if accepted, becomes a part, however small, of the historical tradition of his society and will therefore influence its policy. Consequently the acceptance of the historian's work does not depend on its accuracy alone; it may be attacked and made "controversial" if it runs counter to policies advocated by any organized group, private or official, that can widely publish its views. Even theories of physical scientists, if related to history, run this same risk. For example, so long as the movements of celestial bodies were believed to be related to the divine government of the world and, thus, to history, society demanded that astronomy justify this belief. Therefore, in the Roman period, the historian Plutarch praised Plato for having shown that astronomy does not lead to "atheism" (by which Plutarch meant, denial of providence). By the same principle, in modern times, the science of genetics has been muzzled in the Soviet Union and is attacked in the United States by various pressure groups. As for history itself, in every totalitarian country it is the handmaid of the government. This does not increase its credibility in free countries, where the friends of totalitarian powers often try to pass for historians. But the totalitarians are not alone. Everyone, to some extent, tailors history to suit himself. Hobbes, writing *On Human Nature* in 1640, recognized two kinds of learning: mathematics, of universal validity, and "dogmatic learning" in which there is nothing indisputable, because it meddles with men, rights, and profits, about which "as oft as reason is against a man, so oft will a man be against reason."

Secondly, in history each event determines the future. Southey's famous sneer at the battle of Blenheim (where the English and Austrians defeated the French in 1704—"What good came of it at last, why, that I cannot tell . . . But 'twas a famous victory") overlooked the fact that this famous victory made it possible for Southey to publish his pacifist poem while England was at war with France. Blenheim demonstrated that a free, constitutional government, England of the Bill of Rights, could withstand the absolute monarchy of Louis XIV. Thanks to Blenheim, James Otis, defending *The Rights of British Colonies,* could declare in 1764 that, "The finest writers of the most polite nations [on the continent of Europe] envy great Britain no less for the freedom of her sons than for her immense wealth and military glory." In history, today is different from yesterday because of all the other days before.

By contrast, the physical sciences (with some exceptions) suppose that the same laws hold at all times; consequently, for scientific purposes an experiment can be repeated exactly, and when describing an event the physical scientist need specify only the three dimensional facts, not the time at which the process took place. History is four dimensional: things worked differently in the past than they do now. Therefore no events, *as historical events,* can be exactly repeated and there are no firm "laws" of history. We cannot cope with four dimensional causality. We have to reckon with "accidents," that is, events we cannot explain. To cite a famous example, if Cleopatra's nose* had been different (for our taste her nose, as represented on coins, appears too long) Antony might neither have wanted her nor, consequently, have lost the battle of Actium, and, with it, his chance to become ruler of the Roman world. Every event is an offspring of innumerable antecedents. For this reason history appears to us, as it did to the Greek historians, to be determined by unpredictable chance, or, as Stoics, Jews, and Christians believed, by inscrutable providence.

Thirdly, the scientist's account of "causation" is ultimately descriptive. When he says, "A causes B," he is describing a regular sequence of events in a standard environment. The historian, too, speaks of "causes." He says, for instance, that in 490 B.C. the Persians invaded Greece and thus caused the Athenians to meet them at Marathon. But the word "caused" here does not refer to a regular sequence of events, and the environment cannot be recreated. Since each historical event is unique, we can never be sure just why it happened as it did. For instance, choice is always incalculable. The Athenians could have chosen to submit to the Persians, or to fight at the gate of Athens, or something else, and each alternative decision would have changed the course of history. Therefore the historian must "understand" (not simply describe) the causality he suggests. He must also be aware of, though

---

* For items marked with asterisks see the illustrations.

he cannot account for, "negative causality"—the absence of obstacles. Cleopatra's nose would have had no importance for history had she died as a baby. But why did she not die as a baby? Here history gives up.

One of the most common historical fallacies is neglect of the distinction between the necessary and the sufficient conditions of change. As Lenin wrote in 1920, it is not sufficient for revolution that the "exploited" demand change—to his mind, the "necessary" condition—it must also happen that the "exploiters" are not able to rule as before; unless this occurs the "necessary" cause is not also "sufficient." But again, the events such causes should produce sometimes occur without them, so the most common of all historical fallacies is the supposition of any absolutely necessary causal relation between an antecedent and a subsequent event. The Marxist interpretation of history, for instance, is based on this fallacy. Certainly, men may rebel when they are exploited, but they may also rebel when they are not exploited. And why do the exploiters sometimes yield to the rebels, sometimes not? Why did the mutiny of the garrison in Petrograd in 1917 overthrow the Russian government, while the more extensive mutiny of French troops in that same year did not destroy the French Republic? By neglecting negative causality, historians often represent as necessary what was in reality accidental. But recognition of it entails the recognition that all historical accounts of causation are to some extent hypothetical and therefore always open to revision.

Moreover, they are always being revised because the historian is a part of history and his interpretations must therefore change with time. The view of Plato's *Republic* taken by a historian in 1976 cannot be the same as that of a historian in 1776, because the *Republic*, between 1776 and 1976, has continued to influence the course of history. This does not mean that historians should read modern ideas into ancient documents. It is ridiculous to see Plato as a "communist" or a "fascist." But his dialogues did in some measure influence both fascist and communist theories; therefore our experience with those can help us understand Plato better. Like the action of gravity, Plato's *Republic* has remained the same, but our understanding of it in the past two centuries has changed because of new observations.

Even in the natural sciences, as soon as the dimension of time has to be considered (in geology, medicine, the theory of evolution, or the movement of electrons), the relations between cause and effect are no longer constant—the same cause can produce various effects in various circumstances. Moreover, the observer becomes an important factor in determining the result of an experiment—as he is in the study of history. It is strange that many historians do not consider these scientific developments, but still model history on Newton's mechanics. Marx' theory of history antedates not only Einstein, but even Darwin, and has been superannuated by both. We need new concepts of the historical process.

The limitations that prevent history from attaining the certainty and finality of the physical sciences also prevent the historian from foretelling future events with the assurance possible to a physicist or a chemist; thus they limit the utility of history. But utility is not the historian's primary concern. As a scholar he studies the past out of curiosity, for the sake of knowledge. As a craftsman, like any cobbler, he should stick to his last. The attempt to be timely is characteristic of the conceited. The pursuit of the relevant too often deprives those who practice it of the greatest delight of research: the discovery of the unexpected. As the Greek philosopher Heraclitus declared: "If you do not expect the unexpected, you will not find it." For this reason, historical research must be untrammeled by social demands. The historian must be free to find what he finds, and he has no obligation to demonstrate the utility of his findings. For society, the Greek maxim elegantly rendered by the eighteenth-century philosopher and statesman Lord Bolingbroke, "History is philosophy teaching by examples," still stands. But the error of Bolingbroke and his Greek predecessors was to believe that the historian had to formulate "the lessons of history" as pills for the ills of society. The historian, as such, cannot perform this task and should not claim this honor. He should leave to philosophers, sociologists, and statesmen the opportunity of learning from his learning, according to their needs and capacities.

SUMMARY

Let us recapitulate. History deals with something that no longer exists—the past. Yet it is necessary to man who is the only historical animal. The knowledge of the past is relevant to the human society which (unlike, say, a swarm of bees) is not a biological unit from which there is no escape, but an ideological association against which the individual members can and often do rebel. This association exists in a continuum of change, for the present, as the Stoic philosophers saw, is only the meeting point between past and future. Thus, to persist, the constantly ephemeral society must have a firm hope of a common future, nurtured by knowledge of a common past. This need for a past often leads to manufacture of a pseudopast, a lie apt to ruin the people who believe it. The task of the historian is to discover the real past of his society. The discovery remains imperfect because the historian himself is a part of his society, because history is four dimensional, involving time as well as space, and because the past continuously influences the present and thus looks different to every succeeding age. These imperfections limit, but do not destroy, the utility of history; they deny to the historian's work that finality the physical scientist may hope for; but they promise the pleasure said to have most delighted the Athenians, that of always discovering something new.

FOR FURTHER READING

H. Meyerhoff, ed., *The Philosophy of History in Our Time*
A. Momigliano, *Studies in Historiography*
F. Stern, ed., *The Varieties of History*
C. Wedgwood, *The Sense of the Past*
M. White, *Foundations of Historical Knowledge*

2
WHY ANCIENT HISTORY?

THE DIVISIONS OF HISTORY

Some 10,000 years have passed since the development of agriculture. Of this time span, roughly 5,000 years belong to Prehistory, 3,600 years to Ancient History, and the remaining 1,400 to Medieval and Modern History, as these subjects are taught in our schools and universities. As usual, the conventional teaching conceals the basic facts. The facts are that from the development of agriculture until the industrial revolution man's world remained essentially the same. And the industrial revolution, though its beginnings can be traced to the eighteenth century, did not really start to produce a new type of society until the middle of the nineteenth century. It was only about 1850 that in England, at that time the most industrialized country of the world, the urban population came to outnumber the farming population. But the branch of industry most important in 1850, the manufacture of textiles, still depended on agriculture for raw materials: "King Cotton", wool, linen, and silk. Of the technological devices that condition our life today, none was of major importance in the beginning of our own century. The telephone, the electric light, and the automobile became common during the first decades of this century, the radio and phonograph for private entertainment in the 1920s, airplanes for public transportation in the 1930s, oil heating for private residences about the same time; Franklin D. Roosevelt never saw television. Above all, medical science was almost as helpless in the time of Queen Victoria as it had been in the time of the Roman emperors. The modern age begins not with Columbus or George Washington but approximately in the time of Lincoln. The labor of a single farmer in America in 1820 normally sufficed to support four people (including himself); in 1970 it sufficed to support forty-five. The first major military conflict of which the course and result were determined by an engine was the American Civil War. By contrast with the industrial age everything earlier is Ancient History.

On the other hand, within the preindustrial millennia, different ages have different claims on our interest. Prehistory has the charm of all beginnings, and it laid the foundations of all later occidental societies, but most of the evidence for it is lost. Building on prehistoric foundations, the cultures of the Bronze Age produced much basic technology and many patterns that would persist, especially in religion and law, but as cultures they were overwhelmed, in part by the barbarian invasions of the twelfth to tenth centuries B.C., in part by the new Greek culture of the early Iron Age. Only the excavations of the past and present centuries have brought them back to light. Now we can reconstruct their histories, and sometimes their buildings and languages, but the languages are alien to us, the symbols on the buildings are often of uncertain significance, and the histories are strangely bodiless—lists of names and dates for which, often, we cannot imagine the people or the events. It is only with the coming of the Israelites, Greeks, and Romans that we find ourselves in a world we know from within, as parts of it, because from our childhood on, elements of its literature have been part of us.

ANCIENT HISTORY AND MODERN CIVILIZATION

Using the discoveries of the Greeks, and eventually incorporating Israelite tradition, the Roman Empire created a civilization which in many respects remained unsurpassed until about the middle of the nineteenth century and even then shaped the succeeding culture of the industrial age. The gauge of our railways is that of a Roman cart. In 1842, the commission appointed to improve the sanitary conditions of London studied the installations of the Roman Colosseum. The Romans built the first permanent bridges over the Rhine; after Roman times, the next was built at Cologne—in 1859. In most Roman cities pure water was piped to fountains and cisterns, to baths and public buildings, and sometimes to private houses. In New York, as late as 1860, drinking water was bought from horse drawn carts for a penny a pail.

Accordingly, until the First World War (1914), the classics of Greek and Roman literature shaped man's thought, and even technical works of classical civilization were of direct practical use. Until Napoleon, works on Roman tactics were basic to military education. In the age of Washington, Roman agricultural works were translated for the use of American farmers. Galen, who wrote in the second century A.D., was still, in the first decades of the nineteenth century, the great authority in medicine.

Thus the history of Greece, Israel, and Rome is our own past. And within our past, knowledge of antiquity is prerequisite for any serious work on the intellectual history of the Middle Ages, the Renaissance, or the modern world, whether of the Near East, Europe, North Africa, America, Australia, or any other country which has derived most of its present culture from the Arabic and European heirs of Greece, Rome, and Israel. To put it in a nutshell, the Greco-Roman civilization shaped the agricultural civilization of the following centuries, of which our industrial civilization is the direct continuation. The industrial and scientific revolution has now displaced much of the pretended science of the preindustrial age, and therewith the religion, philosophy, and literature dependent on prescientific notions of the world have been discredited more or less, according to the extent of their dependence. But there has been no industrial revolution in the nature of man.

The human body, except for such secondary traits as weight and height, has not changed during the fifty thousand years of *homo sapiens*' existence. Likewise, man as an intellectual, moral, and social animal, seems to have changed little or not at all between the discovery of fire and the discovery of atomic energy. Such constants as sloth and stupidity, curiosity and ingenuity have remained the determinants of history, though mostly overlooked by historians.

The devaluation of ancient technology, from military machines to medicine, and the permanence of ancient wisdom, due to the constancy of the human condition, explain the two faces of Ancient History: it is strange, but familiar; it is alien, but it is ours; we can stand apart from it and study it with detachment, yet it speaks directly to us about some things that concern us most.

HISTORY AND HUMILITY

One of these is humility. All historical thought is a reminder of mortality. From Homer on, it has contributed to literature a series of poems and essays on the "where are" theme (Where are the snows—

ladies, rulers, gods, whatnot—of yesteryear?). The thought of human transience should do something to correct not only self-importance, but also the more subtle self-centeredness that commonly deforms our thought. Natural egotism has led men, in theology, to create god(s) in their own image (animism, anthropomorphism, anthropopathism), in poetry, to attribute their own emotions to physical objects (the "pathetic fallacy"), in astronomy, to suppose themselves and their earth the center of the universe, and in history, to think themselves the final figures of all time and therefore to designate preceding events as "important" or "unimportant" insofar as their consequences do or do not affect the present. The study of history—and especially of Ancient History, because it stands furthest from our own—enables us to overcome, momentarily, this myopia, to see things as they were to their own times, and to learn modesty, even if we cannot consistently practice it.

HISTORY AND OBJECTIVITY

We cannot consistently practice it because we have our own lives to live. As Hillel is said to have said, "If I don't look out for myself, who will look out for me?" Another consequence to be drawn from human mortality is that the dead are dead, and anything now important must be so to the living. Therefore, even Ancient History is studied ultimately because of its importance to our own world. Israelites, Greeks, and Romans still have their passionate defenders, and the events of their history (for instance, the Romans' loss of Palestine to the Arabs in A.D. 636) lead directly to events of our own time (for instance, the conflict in the Near East). Yet, for all this, the two or three thousand years of time that separate us from ancient events enable us most often to view and evaluate them with some objectivity. Even if we were to say, with Voltaire, that the philosophers of Athens, Miletus, Syracuse, and Alexandria made the Europeans (and thus the Americans) superior to other men, our statement would reflect not only our prejudice about ourselves, but also our objective judgment about the difference between Greek thought and that of earlier civilizations.

HISTORY AND THE CONCEPT OF CAUSATION

This difference began with the question "Why?" The knowledge of earlier civilizations was technical; it was knowledge of "How." The technician is one who knows how to do something, how to repair a typewriter or to reconcile a man with his god. The Greeks asked "Why?" and thus created science. The scientist begins with what the Greeks called *aporia*, that is, man's discovery that he does not know. Learned stupidity stifles research, but the ignorant man, as Aristotle says, furthers it, because in his ignorance he asks "Why?" All western science is fundamentally Greek, be it practiced in New York or Teheran, or Tokyo.

For those who would ask the "Why?" of historical events, Ancient History is particularly instructive. First, its scene is reduced. The available body of material can often be surveyed without help of computers and statistical techniques, but is sufficiently large and complex to yield reliable answers. And even the tiny states of classical Greece may provide miniature models of typical historical situations and sequences. An example may illustrate this point. Our political life, and perhaps human life itself, depends on the "peaceful coexistence" of the atomic superpowers. This type of historical situation was observed and explained 2,400 years ago by the Greek historian Thucydides, who then remarked that uncertainty about the future is the surest reason for preserving peace. When neither the justice of a cause nor the apparent strength of either side can assure military success, enemies will cling to a precarious truce, fearing the inscrutable.

This observation illustrates a second important characteristic of Ancient History—for the most part it rests on a scientific tradition. Greek historians and their Roman disciples asked "Why?" Their works offer us an extended series of questions and answers, the like of which is not to be found elsewhere in historiography before Machiavelli's essays on the first ten books of Livy (essays showing that Machiavelli had learned well from his Latin master the art of asking "Why?").

Of course the philosophy, or, if one prefer, the sociology of history suggested by ancient historians may not always be to our liking, though it nurtured the thought of the founding fathers of our own republic. But just because their views are often different from those modish and modern, they often compel us to ask "Why?" For instance, a mediocre Greek historian of Rome states that "democracy" led to civil strife because the more powerful men, each seeking primacy for himself and bribing the poor, turned everything upside down. Was Dio Cassius prejudiced? Or did he describe what we see going on at present? Let us discuss the eternal problems of leadership and following, of the relation between freedom and political structures, of the position of woman, and so on, with the Greeks and Romans at hand to present the classical evidence and the theories by which this evidence was originally understood.

HISTORY AS A DIALOGUE WITH THE PAST

Thus, in Ancient History we do not simply draw materials from our sources; rather, we are in a constant dialogue with our own past, that is, with the past relevant to us. The demand for "relevance" is not new. The Greek historian Plutarch already spoke with disdain of "useless history," but to him it was what we call "social history," that of "classes," economics, and so on, which was useless. The history he wanted was that of individuals, to provide models for man's behavior. Some 250 years after Plutarch, another Greek author denied any value to chronology. What does it matter, he said, whether the battle of Salamis was fought in early fall or at some other date? The historian would reply that, first of all, being human, we are curious, and since curiosity is one of the most valuable and important of human motives, it should be licensed to seek satisfaction. But, as we have seen, the essential function of the past is not merely to exercise curiosity, nor yet to provide examples for our imitation; it is rather to strengthen the identity of a given society, be it a nation or a society of would-be revolutionaries. Therefore, as Americans we have a proper and peculiar interest in the history of Europe, from which the American colonies were founded, in the history of Greece, Rome, and Israel, whose science, literature, law, and religion shaped European civilization, and even in the history of the more ancient Mediterranean and Mesopotamian world from which Greece, Rome, and Israel emerged. These are our spiritual ancestors, whatever our biological backgrounds. By contrast, even the history of China, which now begins to be interwoven with ours, is not our history. Despite some contacts with Rome, despite Marco Polo and China clippers, despite silk and gunpowder and tea, the path of Chinese history is outside our historical cosmos. But the Ancient History of the Mediterranean world is our history. We can understand Ancient History without knowing American or, say, Russian, history. But we cannot understand Russian, or American, or Arab history without knowing Ancient History.

FOR FURTHER READING

C. Bailey, ed., *The Legacy of Rome*
G. Highet, *The Classical Tradition*

R. Livingstone, ed., *The Legacy of Greece*

B.C.	All dates on this page are approximate. In some the error may be ten percent or more.
10,000	Wooden reaping knives set with flint blades used in Palestine
9000	End of the Ice Age
8000	Domesticated cereals in the north Tigris Valley
7500	Extensive settlement at Jericho, weaving, fortification, remains of cultivated cereals
7000	Pottery begins. Domesticated sheep and cattle in the north Tigris Valley
6700–5700	Çatal Huyuk in Turkey; obsidian mined for tools; fertility cult indicates use of domesticated cattle
6500	Copper used in Turkey for trinkets
6250	A dugout canoe used in Holland
6000	Farming in Macedonia, pottery plentiful
5000	Use of copper in Mesopotamia begins
3500	Agriculture reaches Ireland and China
3200	Writing begins in Sumer; wheeled vehicles and wheel made pottery, sailboats and animal drawn plows in Sumer
3100–3000	Invention of hieroglyphic writing in Egypt; Sumerian fashions prevalent in Ashur
2700	Royal inscriptions appear in Sumer; Sumerian script used in Akkad; Sumerian fashions prevalent in Mari
2500	Cuneiform writing in Assyria; keeping of daily accounts in Sumer; the Great Pyramid completed
2400	Cuneiform writing in Mari
2350	Sargon I of Agade, first known empire
2300	Copper common in Sumer; writing in the Indus Valley (local script)
2250	Fall of the dynasty of Sargon
2100–2000	Supremacy of Ur in lower Mesopotamia
2100	The laws of Ur-Nammu of Ur, the earliest preserved lawbook
1750	Hammurabi of Babylon rules most of Mesopotamia; financial transactions in Sumer and Akkad now commonly in silver
1600	Fall of the dynasty of Hammurabi

3
MESOPOTAMIA

HISTORY AND PREHISTORY

History begins in the Near East. The cradle of humanity probably lay elsewhere, but the slow biological emergence of *homo sapiens*, the sort of human being we are, precedes history, and the greater part of the existence of *homo sapiens* also ran before the beginning of history. The essential difference between "prehistory" and "history" is mental. "History" means the conscious and intentional remembrance of things past, in a living tradition transmitted from one generation to another. For this there must be some continuous organization, be it the family of the chieftain in the beginning, or the school today, which has reason to care for the past of the group and has the capacity for transmitting the historical tradition to future generations. History exists only in a persisting society which needs history to persist.

But a continuous and persisting society was late in coming. It came into being first in the Near East, and thus the historical tradition of Babylon and Egypt became the fountainhead of our historical memory. Many of our fairy tales may go back to the imagination of men who lived long before the foundation of Babylon or in the regions,

18 MESOPOTAMIA

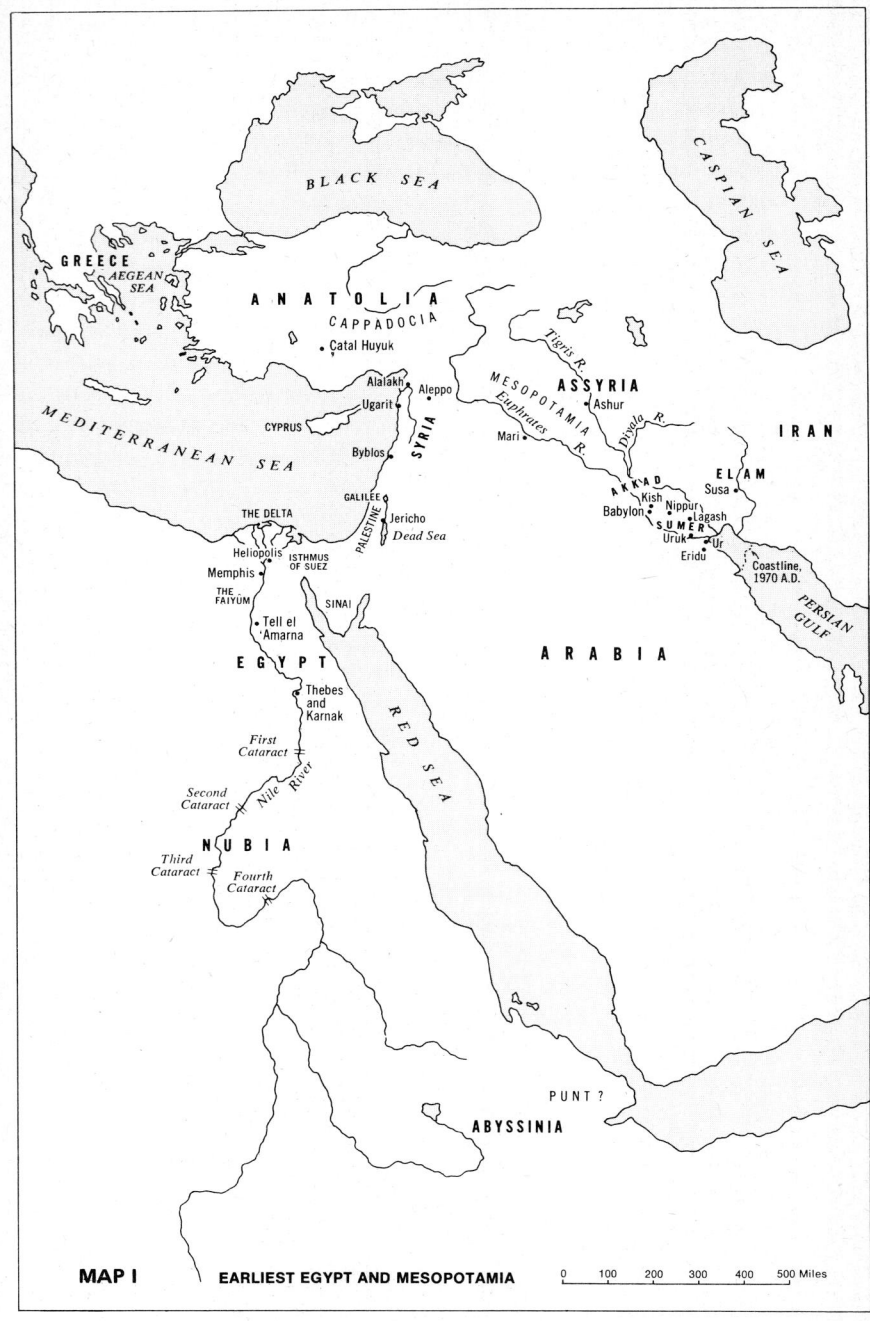

MAP I   EARLIEST EGYPT AND MESOPOTAMIA

such as north Europe, which remained outside the historical tradition that began in the Near East. But no living memory links us with the inventors of fire, with the masters who some 15,000 years ago painted walls of caves in France and in the Ural Mountains, or with the builders who, perhaps about 2000 B.C., began to erect the monoliths at Stonehenge in England. These men left signs, and they knew what those signs meant, but since no tradition has enabled us to read those signs their meaning is lost to us.

The pyramids,* however, not only astonished every generation which succeeded their builders, but every new generation also learned that these gigantic edifices were royal tombs; Cheops, the name of the pharaoh of the Great Pyramid, was known to the Greek historian Herodotus, who lived midway between his time and our own. The ancient Egyptian language can still be heard daily in the Coptic churches, and the word "Coptic," through the Greek word *Aiguptos*, comes from the Egyptian name of Memphis, the first capital of the land on the Nile. "Babylon" has been a byword for four millennia, and some of the first pages of the Bible echo the voices of storytellers who instructed or amused their audiences on the banks of the Euphrates 5,000 years ago. For this reason, the archeologists' discoveries of a forgotten kingdom or of an unknown language in the Near East fall within the scheme of our historical tradition. For the same reason, in the Near East, history imperceptibly leads back to prehistory. Therefore the historian has to go back to the beginning of the stable societies in the Near East where the idea of history was born.

As long as *homo sapiens*, like his near-man ancestors and predecessors, was solely hunter, fisher, and collector of wild fruits and vegetables, there could be no persisting society. Like the other predatory beasts, man needed an enormous space for maintenance. English prehistorians believe that at this stage the total population of England and Wales amounted to no more than three or four thousand souls. This sparse population consisted of very small groups, a few families living together. To the present day some food collecting bands in the Amazon basin comprise about twenty persons each, including children. Such groups were unstable biologically and socially. It appears from skeletal remains that two-thirds of the new-born died as babies, that at least a third of those who survived infancy died before the procreative age, and that almost all adults died before fifty. Like wild animals, men rarely lived beyond the age of fecundity.

This brevity of human life, together with a very high infant mortality, casts doubt on the common explanation of the origin of agriculture as a result of the need of an increasing population. Perhaps food production should be connected with the domestication of animals, which may often have been attempted before it eventually succeeded. Dogs may have been tamed already by hunters in the food gathering period. (Yet no bones of dogs have been found in the earliest—ninth to seventh millennium—sites in Palestine.) Domesticated cereals seem to have been known east of the upper Tigris about 8000, domesticated sheep appear there in the eighth millennium, domesticated cattle by 7000. But the relation of the domestication of animals to that of cereals is enigmatic, and the latter remains a problem. Cultivation of cereals could originate only in a territory where these plants grew wild and man already reaped them. Why should he sweat to cultivate what he could get without any preparatory work? The Hazda, a tribe of some 800 persons, who only ten years ago still lived as hunters and food gatherers in East Africa, roaming an area of more than a thousand square miles, spent more time in enjoying leisure, particularly gambling, than in obtaining food.

THE EMERGENCE OF AGRICULTURE

Abel, the shepherd, was a child of nature. The farmer forces nature, and the history of our civilization begins with Cain, the first farmer. Agriculture, whatever its origins, made a stable society both possible and necessary. Husbandry not only provided more food and did it more reliably, but above all it furnished a sort of food, grain, which could be stored in pits for a long time to tide the society over those months when nothing else was available. And the development of agriculture made possible an increase in livestock, too. Cattle and poultry require cereals. It takes $2\frac{1}{2}$ pounds of feed to produce a pound of chicken, 8 for a pound of beef. Consequently, the ancients could not often afford meat. (Steak was so rare in classical Athens that the city still observed a religious ceremony in expiation of the first "murder" of an ox and told a myth to excuse the crime—the animal had eaten a sacred cake.) Thus agriculture became and remained the foundation of civilized life.

The change to agriculture meant also a mental change. Man began to correct nature, and he did so with his eye on the future. Every skill, as Aristotle says, requires the idea of a result before that result can be achieved. The men who learned to fell trees in the forests which began to cover the temperate regions of the Northern Hemisphere after the Ice Age, say after 9000, were no less ingenious than the first agriculturalists. In a modern experiment more than one hundred birch trees were felled with one polished stone ax, made and sharpened in Denmark about 4,000 years ago. However, the agriculturalist worked not for today, nor even for tomorrow, but for a distant and uncertain objective which was very remote when he planted a tree. The future had become for him a far-off yet foreseeable time. Symmetrically, the past became valuable. It was, as the Sumerians used to say, "the seed of (present) days." Today was now a station on the long road from the past to the future.

The archeological evidence, as well as the distribution of wild species of the earliest known domesticated plants and animals, points to the region from Turkestan to Palestine as the laboratory of the incipient agriculture and, thus, the birthplace of stable society and historical memory. It was a long process which probably began in the ninth millennium, of selection of seeds, of learning the elements of sowing, tending, and reaping cereals, of inventing and improving tools. For instance, the reaping knife set with flint blades was used in Palestine about 10,000, if only for cutting wild grass. The earliest known remains of cultivated cereals date from the eighth millennium: einkorn and emmer, two varieties of wheat which are no longer cultivated, and a type of barley. Our bread wheat is first attested somewhat later in Asia Minor. Goats and, probably, pigs were soon added to farm animals bred by man. At Çatal Huyuk in central Turkey, by the middle of the seventh millennium, people were worshiping a fertility goddess whom they represented in the act of giving birth to a man, a bull, and a ram.

We do not know why agriculture began in the Near East, rather than elsewhere, but it did so, and from here the art of farming spread to the four corners of the world. It reached Crete, Greece, and the Balkans about 6000. By about 5000, it had spread to Mediterranean France, by 4200 to England and Denmark. It began in Ireland by 3500 and in China about this same time. For the civilized peoples of the Near East, nomads were now barbarians "who knew no grain."

CONSEQUENCES OF AGRICULTURE

The increased supply of food made the expansion of mankind possible. In Palestine we find the earliest human settlement of some size. The site of Jericho covers about ten acres (equal roughly to a square 650 feet on a side); the inhabitants had domesticated barley and sheep before 7000. In this and other comparatively large and stable settlements of the new age—Çatal Huyuk, destroyed about 5700, had been inhabited without interruption for at least a thousand years and had grown to cover 32 acres—men went on to discover new components of civilized life and to develop chance discoveries (which may have been made many times before) into techniques, and to perpetuate them by regular practice as part of the cultural tradition. The wealth of Çatal Huyuk depended on mining the black obsidian in the neighboring volcanic mountains. (As before, weapons and tools were made of stone, bones, and wood; copper was used already in the seventh millenium, at least in Turkey, but only for trinkets.) Other sites owed their importance to agricultural wealth. It was a prodigal spring, which still produces a thousand gallons of water every minute, that for ten thousand years attracted men to the plain of Jericho. Until the invention of watertight (plastered) cisterns, permanent settlements were possible only near springs, lakes, or rivers.

POTTERY

The first of the major new techniques were probably weaving* and pottery making. The earliest known woven fabric was apparently of hemp, which began to be worked in the eighth millenium. The invention of pottery by itself is not so important; men could use stone vessels or baskets as well. Yet pottery could be placed on the fire. This changed the character of cooking. Previously, raw food had to be held over the flame directly or cooked on a thin stone. Above all, potter's clay—a combination of earth, water, and some ingredient to prevent cracking (grit or straw)—was the first artificial material manufactured by man. Its production required know-how. To make a pot and bake it hard required more know-how. Consequently, the art spread slowly. The invention was made somewhere in the Near East, probably around 7000. By 6000, pottery was already plentiful at Çatal Huyuk as well as at a farming settlement (Nea Nicomedia) in Macedonia. But some centuries later, pottery was still unknown at Jericho and at sites in Phoenicia. Only gradually, during the sixth millenium, did its use become practically universal in the Near East; in North Africa (outside Egypt) it begins about 3500. Since styles of decoration and of manufacture (the make-up of clay, the shapes of the vessels) varied at different manufacturing sites and changed in the course of time, and since potsherds were neither easily destroyed nor worth carrying off, the remains of pottery have become the most important tool of the archeologists for dating finds and ascertaining cultural contacts.

Pottery soon began to be painted with crescents, circles, and other motifs. Some designs imitated basketwork, others reproduced human faces. Here, for the first time, decoration expresses an abstract thought: though not a basket, nor a head, this pot is *like* a basket, or a head—or, conversely, somebody's head is like this pot, or should become so. The purpose behind such decoration may sometimes have been magical.

GOVERNMENT

While men were domesticating animals and learning the techniques of agriculture and manufacture, they were also domesticating their children and learning the techniques of government. For any society to be stable it is necessary that the average member should behave regularly and predictably, and should do what the group expects him to do according to his status and to the circumstances. He should respond willingly to recognized words of command from recognized leaders, just as other trained animals do. He should, in one word, be domesticated.

The domestication of man by his group preceded settled life, but was intensified in agricultural societies which demanded collective work and, thus, spiritual unity. Each social group developed a technique of pressure to modify individual behavior. Respect for tradition, that is, for the past, is, as we have seen, the main means to perpetuate a group, each new member learning to follow the traditional rites and customs. A Sumerian poem mirrors this training by the group. Enkidu, a wild man who lives with beasts and as a beast, is seduced by a girl from the city of Uruk. Now the animals abandon him, and he learns the customs of her group, from the manners of eating to friendship and to fighting for the city.

The result of such integration is that the great majority obey a few, who explicitly or tacitly establish the rules of behavior. Why do the majority accept such leadership and cling to it, so that, even though rules and rulers from time to time are overthrown and replaced by new ones, the new followers will be no less thoroughly domesticated than the old, and even when the revolution is carried through in the name of tolerance the new believers will be intolerant of disagreement with the new faith? Why is there no anarchic society? The answer is twofold: A group could not exist if everyone were free to think and do as he chose, and man could not live if his freedom of choice were not limited. He would be lost in perpetual conflicts with the other members of the group and with himself. As man's intellectual capacity frees him from the fixed stimulus-response chains in which the other animals are bound, he must accept external control of his liberty to prefer and to decide. Observing the manners and customs of his society is like following a road, it enables man, by accepting an established pattern, to arrive more quickly at the individual goals he freely chooses. Therefore men demand and follow social roadmakers, to spare themselves trouble and, above all, thought. They leave group decisions to the leaders. Bands of food gatherers in the Brazilian Mato Grosso follow the leader whose person unites the group. He walks ahead on the warpath, he organizes the hunting and food collecting. He has to exert himself without end, and his sole privilege is to have a couple of young girls as bedmates and assistants. He rules by tacit consent. If he fails in his task another leader appears, or members of the group join other bands. Thus even the most primitive society requires leadership, but the need is far greater when the society comes to depend on agriculture, which necessitates persistent, organized work: "In the sweat of thy face shalt thou eat bread." The first and main purpose of every developed society is to compel its members by one means or another, by whip or by advertising, to do more work than they need to keep soul and body together. An African chieftain told a French missionary, "Apes can speak, but they won't speak, because, if they did, the French would make them work." All animals are playful, lazy, and stupid, but only man is so stupid as to talk.

THE SUMERIANS

Perhaps in the early fifth millennium, when the benefits of farming were already recognized in the whole Near East and the techniques of pottery and weaving were in general use, some adventurous and imaginative men dared to colonize a country about the size of New Jersey between and around the lower courses of the Tigris and Euphrates rivers. They did not come from the piedmont zone in the north (Assyria) which, fertilized by bountiful rains, was already tilled in the sixth millennium; they came from Iran or from the Persian Gulf through the estuaries of the Tigris and the Euphrates.

We do not know who these pioneers were nor whether they came all at once or in successive, perhaps unrelated, waves. Later their neighbors in the north called them Sumerians; they called themselves "the darkheaded." Skeletal remains show that most inhabitants of Sumer were heavily boned, short men with long and narrow heads. Yet their sculptors represented them as round-headed.* Their agglutinative language is not related to any other known tongue. Many geographical names in Sumer as well as many words relating to farming and other skills appear to have been borrowed by the Sumerians from some other language, perhaps that of a preceding wave of immigrants from the Zagros Mountains (the border country between northern Iraq and northern Iran).

Sumer was a flat land of brown dust and mud, swept by stormy winds (the Babylonians believed that the sky had been forced apart from the earth by the wind) and devastated by unpredictable inundations of the rivers, most often the Tigris. In Mesopotamia the flood, which punishes sinful men, was first experience and then myth.

The first settlements of the colonists were huts in marshes alongside watercourses of the lower Euphrates. A Babylonian myth recalls how, in the primordial time, a god constructed a reed frame on the face of the waters and, pouring mud on it, made the floor of a hut. Had the Sumerians failed, they would have remained marsh dwellers like the present inhabitants of the same swamps, who still live in reed huts where the miry floor often oozes water at every step.

Through relentless toil guided by imagination, the Sumerians slowly transformed their perilous land into one of milk and grain, of date palms and sesame. A Sumerian myth preserves a memory of the introduction of cereals from the eastern mountains. But in Sumer the poor wild barley became our barley which bears six rows. This was the staple food of the working man. He added to it sesame oil and some greens. In the second millennium, dates, which are very nutritious, also became a staple food and diarrhea became endemic. The exploitation of date palms demands knowledge of artificial pollination and also the gift of anticipatory patience. The farmer, who erected a mud wall around his trees, had to tend them five long years before they began to yield fruit. But his knowledge enabled him to double the crop of an area by eliminating all the male trees (which bear no dates) except for the one or two needed to fertilize some hundred female, fruit bearing trees.

The land had no stone and no metals. By firing clay at a temperature of 1,200 degrees, the Sumerians fabricated clay blades which could be used as sickles. They also substituted the plough (the picture of which appears in the earliest writing) for digging sticks and hoes. Happily, their alluvial plain required no water-raising devices except along the Tigris, where such machines are first attested in the eighteenth century.

The farmer, according to a Sumerian myth, was "a man of dikes and canals." He did not depend on rain, therefore he did not fear drought. As modern experience of the Near East shows, he could feed ten times as many people as the farmer on an equal plot in the lands dependent on rain. The canals served as waterways and fishponds (fish, mostly carp, was the main protein food); they irrigated palm groves and rich grasslands which furnished feed for sheep and cattle, and grain fields of fabulous fertility, reportedly reaped thrice a year. Herodotus heard that in Babylonia grain yielded two and three hundredfold; in fact, the average yield was ten- or fifteenfold. Barley production made possible the feeding of sheep and cattle during the unbearably hot summer. The main crop of cereals came in the spring and that of dates in the fall. With the products of their husbandry the Sumerians paid for the raw materials which were wanting in Sumer. In a Sumerian saga, a king of old gives grain to a ruler in Iran, but demands in return precious metals, gems, and building stone for the temple of his goddess.

DEVELOPMENT OF TRADE

Thus the earliest well-known agricultural civilization depended on trade. It could not exist without foreign raw materials, be it basalt for pestles or lapis lazuli from Afghanistan, copper or tin for making bronze, and so on; and it had to export finished goods to pay for imports. In a Sumerian saga, the legendary hero not only plunders a city in the east, probably in Iran, but also carries away its craftsmen with their tools.

The trade, in turn, depended on middlemen. It took months for donkey caravans to carry, say, tin from eastern Iran to Susa, Babylonia, and then to Mari. Therefore the wares changed owners at each great trade center. The original owner could not wait for payment until his merchandise reached its final destination; he had to sell to a middleman, who bought to resell. Thus merchants of Ashur in the nineteenth century bought wool clothing from Babylonians and sold it in Cappadocia for about three times its price in Ashur; it had been carried over six hundred miles by a donkey caravan. Such caravans—which could carry up to twelve tons—also transported much copper, tin, and lead, again purchased and resold in transit by middlemen.

These middlemen, on whom the trade depended, had to have credit, and credit means interest. Banking had already begun in Mesopotamia, because of the need for security. Temples offered security, so people deposited gold, silver, and grain in them, and paid for the privilege as we do for a bank vault. Now, given the increase of trade, and the facts that the medium of payment (silver) was rare, productivity low, and risks very high, the creditor became a usurer. Further, this credit system could not function without state protection and, often, state participation. (As late as the 950s King Solomon's ships traded in the Mediterranean and the Red Sea.) Accordingly, kings protected merchants (creditors) abroad and at home. The laws gave a preference to the claim of a creditor on the property of his debtor. In this way, these little agricultural communities, who fought with their neighbors for irrigation canals, created a privileged class of international merchants and "bankers," whose trade stations formed a net of interrelated social groups outside the agricultural communities, a net which in the second millennium covered the whole Levant. Assyrian traders of this period even invented a sort of bill of exchange—a promissory note without the name of the creditor, which could therefore serve as a means of payment.

CITIES

This trading network, however, was derived from and built on the individual communities, and these were cities. Long before the appearance of the Greek city, the civilization of Mesopotamia was urban. The seat of political and economic power and the home of the ruling class was the city and not the manor or, as in Egypt, the royal residence. In lower Mesopotamia, the city territory coincided with the land fed by the irrigation canals controlled by the city. The city had its council of elders, popular assembly, and some jurisdiction. Yet the city was apparently not walled before about 2700.

Eridu, the southernmost city of Sumer, "situated on the shore of the sea" (the Persian Gulf) was also, according to tradition, the earliest; its foundation antedated the end of the fifth millennium. The first Sumerian cities were small mud settlements of fifteen to twenty square acres each. (A square acre is about 210 feet on a side. The Great Pyramid would later cover more than thirteen acres.) Soon house walls were made of mud bricks joined by bitumen. As the Book of Genesis says of Babylonia: "They had bricks for stone and slime had they for mortar." When the settlers became richer, they built shrines on platforms made waterproof with bitumen. Raised higher and higher, the terraced, multistoried temple towers ("ziggurats")* appear in the Bible as "the tower of Babel" challenging the heavens. As with medieval cathedrals, the Sumerian temples, soon separated by enclosing walls, dominated the city and proclaimed its power and wealth.

WRITING

In this age of the first cathedrals, probably around 3300, the Sumerians made their greatest contribution to the advance of civilization: the invention of writing. Many primitive peoples, such as the American Indians, have used pictures to convey messages, for instance a call to a raid. But the pictures necessarily referred to some concrete and particular fact. The Sumerian writing differed qualitatively from pictographs of primitive peoples. The schematic representations of objects (head, fish, and so on) here denoted species, and the signs, thus, were valid permanently. The Sumerians had different words for woman and her pudendum. But in writing, the representation of the latter stood for a woman. The picture of a foot came to connote such different words as "to stand," "to go," and "to bring."

Using such pictorial symbols, a scribe could record "52 head of cattle." More complex ideas were expressed in the fashion of rebus: the combination of signs for "woman" and "mountain" denoted a female slave. (Slaves were bought from the mountain peoples around the valley.) The system was adequate for its original purpose: business accounting of temples.

Then the Sumerians (and only a little later the Egyptians) made the decisive advance. They realized that the same syllabic sounds could appear in different words, so that the picture of fish, *ha* in Sumerian, could also indicate the syllable *ha* in other words. Since the Sumerian language consisted of unchangeable and variously combined monosyllables, a syllable became a writing unit, other signs were added to represent syllables for which there were no words, and Sumerian writing came to consist chiefly of three sorts of signs—syllable signs, word signs, and signs that could stand for either syllables or words. The Sumerians, having no cheap writing material but clay, wrote with a reed stylus on unbaked clay tablets. The end of a reed can easily be pressed into soft clay so as to make a wedge-shaped mark. Thus, the originally pictorial signs were reduced to mere wedges and combinations of wedges. Accordingly, we call this script "cuneiform,"* from the Latin word *cuneus*, meaning wedge. A sun dried clay tablet is not likely to be destroyed, so an enormous quantity of records (close to half a million tablets) has come down to us in the ruins of ancient buildings.

WRITING AND HISTORY

The Sumerians and the Egyptians were not alone in the forefront of civilization about 3000. During the third millennium, other "irrigation" societies flourished also on the Indus and southeast of the Caspian Sea, and societies based on the use of metals prospered in Palestine and Asia Minor. Pictographic script was employed in the Indus Valley between about 2300 and 1700. Did the city of Susa in Elam, which also had a pictographic script in the third millennium, invent syllabic writing? We do not know.

The historian should not confuse facts and their recording. The earliest written reference to a boat comes from Sumer. However, a dugout canoe discovered in Holland was constructed about 6250, that is about 3,000 years before the invention of writing in Sumer. In this way archeological discoveries supplement and correct written sources. Yet these discoveries are accidental. The earliest extant musical instruments come from royal graves in Ur. This surely does not mean that men did not play harp, lyre, and oboe before 2500. Above all, objects are mute; they have to be interpreted with the help of written sources. The use of writing changed the mode of historical memory. Thereafter, until our age of audiovision, eye, and not ear, counted. What had not been written down was lost forever. According to a later story, Enmerkar, a legendary ruler of Uruk, had to drink foul water in the nether world because he had not left a written record of his victories for the instruction of future generations.

Our narrative must willy-nilly follow the course of written tradition which links us with the Sumerians, the Egyptians, and their heirs, while neglecting peoples who were often no less gifted in other respects but remained illiterate.

SUMERIAN CIVILIZATION

By 3300 B.C., when writing began, the Sumerians already used sailboats, wheeled vehicles, and animal drawn plows. They invented the first industrial machine providing continuous rotary motion; the potter's wheel which spins the clay as the craftsman shapes it. From Sumer this device invaded the whole Old World. In the third millennium technological and economic advances continued unabated. The walls of Uruk, built about 2700, were eighteen feet thick and had a circumference of about six miles, so the city was roughly two miles across; from any place in it you could walk to the walls in fifteen minutes. The enclosed area provided a refuge to men and cattle from the whole territory of the city, but it was not solidly built up, it included gardens and even fields. Metal tools became common: Copper and bronze objects have been found in about fifteen percent of the graves in Ur dating about 2800, and in eighty percent of the graves of three centuries later. By 2300 a Sumerian could buy a copper ax for two sheep. A yoke was invented for harnessing draft animals, and shadoofs for raising water helped the gardener. Sumerians had the means for distilling barley beer; they also knew how to prepare medicinal drugs and cosmetics, and they could manufacture imitation precious stones.

The artisans' skills, taught orally and by imitation, were immediately usable for tanning hides or carving a statue. Reading and writing by themselves enabled the learner only to read and write. The essential problem of liberal education was and is: What to read? Nevertheless, the method of writing was so complex that merely to learn to read and write demanded a long and arduous training. This divided a small "white-collar" class of scribes from the mass of illiterate workers. School and apprenticeship, head and hand, now became separated. As a Sumerian text says, a son sent to a scribal school did not learn to plow his father's field. The function of the scribal school was rather to furnish secretaries, accountants, revenue officers, and other functionaries. This self-perpetuating bureaucracy produced an enormous quantity of written tablets. From about 2500 there were daily accounts, and monthly and yearly summaries of these accounts which carefully distinguished between food given to pigs and that given to piglets, and so on. Toward the end of the third millennium the standard unit of work—a "man-day"—appeared for calculating payments to unskilled workers. Such "paper work" was needed to keep the complex economy going. Without a scribe counting every bunch of vegetables that left the temple stores there would soon be no food for daily rations of cattle and of dairymen. Soon archives became libraries and book catalogs were required and compiled. Royal inscriptions began about 2600; the earliest yet known law book was promulgated by Ur-Nammu, a king of Ur, about 2100. Between these two dates the scribes recorded the first literature, ranging from epics to love songs. Yet they did not completely monopolize learning. A daughter of Sargon I, about 2350, wrote religious hymns. She is the first known authoress. Even some artisans seem to have had a little knowledge of cuneiform writing.

These books reinforced the cultural unity of Sumer: the same books were read in Ur and in Nippur. However, in a civilization where reading and writing were so rare that some kings boasted of their mastery of these skills, the oral lore must have remained of great importance in shaping men's minds. The story of creation, recited during the Babylonian New Year's feast, ends with the appeal to the faithful to recite and impart to their sons the fifty names of the god Marduk which expressed his various powers. Yet the oral tradition has been lost and, except for the buildings and works of art, we see Sumer only as it appears in the writings of the Sumerian scribes.

Sumer consisted of about two dozen small cities with their respective territories. From Eridu one could see Ur. United by language, custom, and some common gods, united also in contempt for the barbarians of the western desert and of the mountains to the east, these independent cities were in eternal conflict one with another for fields and water rights. As a proverb put it: "You go and take the field of the enemy; the enemy comes and takes your field."

RULERS AND WARS

Although each city was ruled by an absolute monarch, absolutism did not mean despotism. As Athens was the city of Athena, the boundaries and fields of Lagash belonged to the god Ningirsu to whom Lagash had been assigned by the supreme, fate-determining deities. The ruler served as a bailiff of the gods, bidden by them to promote the weal of the city. He represented the community before the deity, but not the deity before the community. He had to consult the elders and the popular assembly. He had to observe the recognized rules of behavior and compel recalcitrants to do the same. Maintaining justice in the land, he saw to it that children supported their aged parents and he supervised weights and measures. The rights of private property, the only sure foundation of civil liberty, were sacred. The king himself had to pay for the land he wanted. A little man no less than a magnate had his rightful place in the city. Men were created to toil for the gods, and the professions were usually hereditary. There were no estates in the body politic. Accordingly, the rulers proclaimed that powerful men should not oppress widows and orphans, nor should a "man of one shekel" fall a prey to a man of many shekels. Slaves, mostly prisoners of war, were mainly used as household servants.

Royal despotism was also restrained by the economic power of the temples. Sacred land was inalienable; thus, with every generation, the temples became richer. In the twenty-fifth century, at Lagash, the ecclesiastical landed property amounted to perhaps a third of the territory of the city. A part of the sacred land was exploited directly by the temple; the rest was either given to temple personnel to supplement their food rations, or rented to sharecroppers. The temples had also their own craftsmen, from jewelers to carpenters, from fishers to merchants, and employed slaves in temple shops, particularly slave women for spinning. The sacrificial system was of particular importance because sacrifices were the main source of protein food (meat and fish). Since almost all our documentation comes from the temple archives, the role of secular property in Sumerian society must remain hazy for us. The rulers tried to obtain control of the sacred estates. They appointed themselves and members of their families high priests of the main temples. But the temples persisted while the rulers were mortal.

The king had to build temples and canals, but from the beginning he was also a war leader, at first represented as conquering enemies and killing lions single-handed.* By the middle of the third millennium, however, victory had come to be conceived as a result of collective action. A single stele from Lagash shows both the king leading his troops into battle* and the god throwing a net over the enemy. A plaque from Ur* pictures the king receiving the booty captured by his soldiers.

The army consisted of chariotry and infantry. The solid-wheeled chariots* were drawn, it seems, by a now extinct species of asses. A warrior in each chariot hurled javelins into the enemy's ranks. The heavy infantry* marched in several files; all soldiers wore the same uniform and carried the same weapons: short spears in Ur, heavy pikes and axes in Lagash. Were these disciplined battalions the king's retainers or the city militia? We do not know.

The battles pictured on Sumerian monuments and described in royal inscriptions were caused by squabbles between neighboring cities about irrigation, or by raids of barbarian tribes from the mountains of Persia in the east and desert nomads from the west. But in the meantime, the populations to the north, from modern Baghdad up the two rivers, passed from barbarism to civilization. These men called their land *Akkad* and spoke a Semitic language, that is, a language of the great family to which Arabic, Hebrew, Phoenician, and most of the languages of the Near East belong. The Akkadians had long been in contact with the Sumerians: Akkadian Babylon was only ten miles from Sumerian Kish and slightly to the north of it; about 2700 a king of Kish dominated the Diyala Valley, from fifty to a hundred miles north of Babylon. There was a steady infiltration of Akkadians into Sumer; they soon became captivated by the Sumerian way of life. As far north as the city of Ashur, from about 2800, and as far northwest as Mari, on the middle Euphrates, from about 2600, men and gods lived in Sumerian fashion and were portrayed as if they were Sumerians.

The Sumerians had not yet extended their political power far to the north, but the Akkadians and their relatives to the north and west were busy protecting their cities from nomads and mountaineers, and colonizing the affluents of the twin rivers. Meanwhile they eagerly took over the cultural achievements of the south, thus developing their own power, and eventually became strong enough to turn on their teachers, as America and Russia have turned on western Europe, and as the non-industrial world may eventually turn on Russia and America.

Toward the middle of the twenty-fourth century, Sargon I, from Agade, near Babylon, an Akkadian minister of the Sumerian king of Kish, subjugated Sumer and founded the first known empire. It extended from the Mediterranean to the Persian Gulf. Sargon's inscriptions were written in both Sumerian and Akkadian. Enlil, the supreme god of Sumer, made him without peer and gave him Elam, in the east. But in his western campaigns he knelt to the Semitic god Dagon, who gave him the "Upper Land." For later ages, Sargon became the prototype of the emperor. An Akkadian poem about this "King of Battle" was still read a thousand years after his death.

His grandson Naramsin was the first ruler who proclaimed himself the lord of the world ("King of the four regions") and put the cuneiform sign of divinity before his name. On a relief, he, much taller than the other figures, is represented as fighting alone. His soldiers follow him in a loose formation. They have axes and spears, but the king shoots arrows. The use of bows in warfare and the breaking of the solid ranks of the Sumerian phalanx go together. The power of the Sargonid dynasty was based on the loyalty of its household troops: 5,400 men who ate bread daily before Sargon.

In a civilization where donkeys were the fastest means of overland transport, empires broke up and local powers survived. About 2250, the house of Sargon was swept away by barbarians from the east. At the end of the next century, the rulers of Ur, adopting the new title "Kings of Sumer and Akkad," reunited Mesopotamia from the Persian Sea to the

Zagros Mountains. Some 18,000 records from local archives show centralization of government and economy under the new rule: 21,799 men were mobilized and received food rations for harvesting fields around Nippur. Centralization of the economy led to road building. A king, who compared himself to a swift horse, spoke of the highways he straightened and the stations he built on them.

The supremacy of Ur lasted 108 years. Then Ur was sacked by the Elamites and the other cities regained their independence until, two centuries later, in the 1700s, Hammurabi of Babylon imposed his power on the land down the stream. Thereafter, Babylon was the hub of the world. Akkadian became the language of administration and business; the importance of Sumerian cities decreased and the Sumerian language died.

SUMERIANS VS. SEMITES

No natural frontier separated Sumer from the Semites, north and west. Semites had probably joined the Sumerians in their original colonization of Sumer, and they continuously immigrated into Sumerian land. Akkadian words appear in the earliest Sumerian texts. Sumerian was intelligible only in Sumer while Akkadian, a Semitic dialect, was understood from Babylon to Egypt. The Sumerians, an exotic minority at the southern end of Mesopotamia, could preserve their separate nationality and impose their isolated language only so long as they enjoyed the monopoly of learning. Having taught everything they knew to the Akkadians, they were absorbed. The title "King of Sumer and Akkad" was still held by the Assyrian kings a thousand years after Hammurabi. But Hammurabi's fourth successor spoke of his subjects as "Akkadians and Amorites," the latter being Semitic invaders and immigrants from the western countries.

Yet the Babylonians won and kept their preeminence only by becoming Sumerians spiritually. They studied Sumerian without end, and in the scribal school a student who had learned Sumerian well boasted that he was a "Sumerian" and looked down on his less learned Akkadian fellows. A student who could only use syllabic signs was called a "Hurrian," that is, a half-barbarian. Only with the help of Sumerian grammars and lexicons compiled in Akkadian by the Babylonians is it possible for us to read Sumerian texts. (Akkadian texts* were deciphered by analogy from the other Semitic languages.) Sumerian texts mostly come down to us in copies made by Babylonian scribes, just as we know Latin authors mainly through medieval manuscripts.

In fact, Babylonians and Assyrians identified themselves with the vanishing Sumerians. About 1800, an Assyrian king built a temple in an Assyrian city to his "Lord," Enlil, the supreme god of the Sumerians. Some decades later, Hammurabi called his subjects "the black-headed," the name that the Sumerians used for themselves. The Sumerians conquered their conquerors.

THE AGE OF HAMMURABI

Our documentation for the period of Hammurabi's dynasty (eighteenth to sixteenth centuries) is abundant but again lopsided. Unlike Sumerian documents, which come from temples and palaces, it mainly concerns private persons. Hammurabi's laws also concern private persons. (Constitutional law was generally unwritten, as in modern England and Czarist Russia.) Still copied a millennium after his death, they constitute no systematic code. The 282 preserved articles of his collection, though many of them reproduce earlier enactments, presumably deal with those legal questions which required regulation in his time.

In pre-Hammurabi laws a bodily injury was compensated by the payment of damages; sixty shekels for a lost eye, and so on. In the laws of Hammurabi the system remained the same for a *mushkenum*, a free man of lesser degree, but if a "gentleman" blinded an eye of another "gentleman" the principle of exact retaliation was applied: an eye for an eye, a tooth for a tooth. Hammurabi does not say anything about the bodily injury inflicted on a "gentleman" by a *mushkenum*, but we can be sure it brought dire consequences. Hammurabi's point of view was pragmatic. The bodily integrity of a rich man was worth more than that of a poor man; conversely, a rich man could afford bigger medical expenses. Thus, the legal fee for an eye operation on a "gentleman" was twice as much as the fee to be paid by a *mushkenum*.

The principle that social status determined one's rights and obligations also applied to slaves and women. The slave's function was to work for his owner. A citizen who blinded the eye of a slave paid a half of the latter's value to the owner. But except for his relation to his owner, a slave remained a person. He could engage in litigation, and so on. He could marry a free woman, in which case their children were treated as free. Our term "slave" is actually a misnomer for him. He was rather a perpetual servant. The same Babylonian word that meant "slave" also meant a king's "minister."

The function of a wife was to provide her husband with legitimate sons. Therefore, the adulterous wife and her paramour were both drowned. (But men could have secondary or temporary wives and slave concubines.) In all matters unrelated to their wifely functions, however, women were independent. They could own, buy, and sell property, lend and borrow money, and so on. A childless widow was free to remarry.

In the farming society of Mesopotamia, barley functioned as money. Hired hands (who appear about 2000) generally received most of their pay in rations, men receiving twice as much as women since they were bigger, did harder work, and ate more. The sign meaning "price" and "buying" originally contained the picture of a grain measure. Silver, an imported material, mainly served to pay for other imports. All merchants, however, based their accounts on silver, and by the time of Hammurabi, virtually all business transactions were evaluated in silver (not in "money," for the silver was not coined). Artisans were paid in silver, shepherds in barley. But even hired hands commonly received some payment in silver, besides their payment in kind, to enable them to make purchases.

The silver economy favored the capitalist. (The economic use of our word "capital," from the Latin *caput*, meaning "head," goes back to a Babylonian term which also meant "head" and had the same economic significance.) A bushel of seed yielded a harvest of some ten to fifteen bushels. Thus, in a normal year, a debt in barley could easily be repaid in kind at harvest time, although the customary interest amounted to 33⅓ percent. But if a debt and its interest had to be paid in silver, the case was altered. The price of barley went down at harvest time, when farmers' loans usually came due. Yet, to repay his silver debt, the farmer had to measure out barley "on the threshing floor" according to the current rate of exchange, as the loan contract stipulated. He was now at the mercy of the money market. A son who had borrowed seventeen shekels to redeem his father from bondage had to sell himself because "he had no silver." A ruler of Uruk, in the nineteenth century, boasted that his reign was a time of such abundance that one shekel of silver bought three times as much barley as usual.

Hammurabi decreed that the "merchant"—that is, the professional moneylender—must accept payment from ordinary borrowers in grain and other commodities even for a silver loan, at a rate of exchange set forth by the royal ordinance. On the other hand, loans between merchants, even of commodities, had to be repaid in silver. A century later, a successor of Hammurabi, proclaiming a general cancellation of debts, significantly excluded commercial loans. Thus, Babylonian documents illustrate the view of the Federalist Papers that the conflict between landed and moneyed interests "grows up of necessity in the civilized nations" and that the regulation of such conflict forms "the principal task of the legislator."

The hegemony of Babylon was as short-lived as that of the Sumerian cities. Hammurabi dominated the south and conquered Mari on the middle Euphrates only in the last ten years of his forty-two-year reign. Thereafter, the Babylonian realm began to shrink, and Hammurabi's dynasty ended 125 years after his death when a Cassite chieftain from the Zagros Mountains seized Babylon. The Cassite dynasty allegedly reigned for 576 years, but Babylon was no longer a great power and the little land between the twin rivers lost its leadership.

DIFFUSION OF AKKADIAN CULTURE

Ancient Mesopotamia was rich only in cattle, sheep, wool, and agricultural produce. There were only two ways to acquire gold and silver: foreign war and foreign trade. A Babylonian story credits King Sargon with an expedition to protect merchants in Asia Minor. According to another text, Marduk, god of Babylon, spent twenty-four years in Asia Minor establishing caravan traffic between that country and Babylonia. In fact, Mesopotamia necessarily depended on waterways for transporting its bulky agricultural surplus, and the influence of Mesopotamian cities followed the course of the Euphrates. About 2500 a king of Ur sent gifts to a king of Mari, a city some 500 miles upstream. Yet farther north, east of Aleppo, the river flows only a hundred miles from the Syrian coast. Though Babylonian agents in the eighteenth century penetrated as far as Hazor in Galilee, such cities as Mari and Aleppo effectively cut off the Mesopotamian cities from the west. There is no reference to Egypt in Mesopotamian texts before the Egyptian conquest of Syria in the fifteenth century.

In the east, the Mesopotamians intermittently succeeded in extending their power as far as Susa, to which they sent wares via the Persian Gulf, but the Elamites in turn raided Mesopotamia.

Up the Tigris, the Assyrians protected Mesopotamia, but also isolated it from the barbarian north. Whatever may have been the success of Sargon or of the god Marduk in Asia Minor, "Akkadian garments" were sold there by Assyrian traders, not Babylonians. In the nineteenth century, Ashur established trading stations in the rich copper belt of Cappadocia. Donkey caravans going west carried tin, which was rare, expensive, and necessary for the production of bronze, a harder alloy of copper. They also carried standardized pieces of cloth and other commodities. They took home to Assyria not only copper and bronze, but also lead, gold, and silver. Above all, one people after another appropriated the secret of Mesopotamian success: the art of writing. Rulers of Mari already used cuneiform writing about 2500, and the Assyrians followed a century later; Elamite was written in the same script before 2200. By 1800 Akkadian was a common language of chancelleries in Syria. In Asia Minor the Hittites used Akkadian in the seventeenth century, and soon adapted the cuneiform script to their own language. With the script went the knowledge recorded in writing. Students at Susa, probably from Iran, about 1700, not only learned mathematics but solved problems "according to the Babylonian method."

Mesopotamian techniques of predicting the future were also used in Susa, in Syria, and by the Hittites. The Sumerians had invented office equipment, a necessary tool of bureaucratic organization. They "filed" tablets in baskets by content and labeled each basket accordingly. In the eighteenth century, the kings of Mari used the same device for sorting their profuse correspondence. The exercise of statecraft was no longer possible in the Levant without the assistance of scribes. At Alalakh cuneiform tablets in Akkadian appeared toward the end of the eighteenth century when this little town of the kingdom of Aleppo became the seat of a semi-independent dynasty.

Simultaneously, the practical knowledge of Mesopotamian artisans was diffused through the adjacent lands. The spoked wheel, the plow with a seeding attachment, and sewers under street pavements entered into general use. An eighteenth-century ruler in Mari had storage facilities for ice (probably brought from the Zagros Mountains) to cool the drinks of gods and princes. Glazed earthenware was already being made at Alalakh by the sixteenth century.

While Mesopotamia became the southernmost province of the world united by the cuneiform script, it also became more and more remote from the mainstream of history. Copperwork was of great importance in the Mesopotamia of the third millennium; the ore came by the sea, probably from Oman. In the beginning of the second millennium extremely rich sources of this metal, which then was essential for civilized life, began to be exploited in Asia Minor and particularly in Cyprus. Our word "copper" comes from the name of this island. The new sources of wealth were Mediterranean and shifted the center of economic and manufacturing activity away from Mesopotamia.

It is symbolic that toward the middle of the seventeenth century a Hittite king raided Babylon. Soon afterward, the axis of history ran across the Mediterranean from the Hittite capital, near the Black Sea, to the Egyptian Thebes, some thirteen degrees west of Babylon. The Babylonians had become great as the first disciples of the Sumerians; now the peoples of the Mediterranean lands had learned from the Babylonians.

DEVELOPMENT OF LEARNING

The scribal art diffused from Mesopotamia was a skill like that of a smith. Scribal schools prepared technicians for government, church, and business. Babylonian scribes boasted of their ability in calculating payrolls, delimiting fields, and so on. Just as smiths did not need to know the laws of natural science to perfect the fabrication of daggers, so a scribe learned merely from practice how to balance accounts, write down the meaning of an omen, or choose the appropriate clause of a contract from a convenient list of legal formulas. There were numerous reference works: vocabularies, mathematical tables, lists of animals, plants, stones, drugs and corresponding ailments, medical instructions arranged according to symptoms or parts of the body, collections of texts concerning the techniques of divination and worship, and so on. To lighten their work the scribes, by 2400, had invented stamps. Later these even had mobile signs; they could be used to stamp the same long text, with appropriate minor variations (e.g. the proper names of the parties concerned in each instance), on a great number of bricks or other clay objects. The device was also used for magic formulas. The same principle was in common use for seal impressions and, almost two thousand years later, came to be used for coinage. Later yet, similar stamps were used by the Romans on bricks and on papyrus. Children, as today, learned the alphabet by combining isolated block letters, and Augustine said that letters are the "elements" of language. We seem on the threshold of printing. Yet Europe had to wait almost four thousand years for the first printed book. Why? History, being a mirror of life, must be no less irrational and capricious than its original.

Although basic principles and major possibilities were thus alike neglected, yet centuries of practice, with observation of the results, brought considerable progress. Babylonian physicians prescribed effective potions, ointments, and plasters mainly made of herbs, though the patient more often than not also sought the help of the exorcists and their spells. By 1900, Babylonian scribes handled mathematical operations which in our terms would be cubic equations with two unknowns. They already knew the result of the "Pythagorean" theorem, but no systematic and didactic book like Euclid's *Elements* has been found—no book, that is, which taught the science instead of teaching the problems. A typical Babylonian mathematical exercise would both state a problem—say the calculation for the construction of a dike—and demand its solution, specifying every step. Much later, probably in the fifth century, Babylonian scribes began to develop a very sophisticated theory of lunar phases which was necessary for calendar reckoning. Neither in astronomical texts nor elsewhere does there ever appear an idea of a general proof demonstrable by arguments. There is never any theoretical statement, and no divergent opinion is ever recorded. Yet there must have been some discussion before this or that hypothesis or process was accepted as authoritative. A Mari text of the nineteenth century mentions sending a physician to examine some healing herbs.

But the tradition of the scribal school hid from the uninitiated the controversies and adventures of learning. As far as the written sources go, science in our, that is in the Greek, sense did not exist in Mesopotamia or generally in the ancient Near East.

Similarly, literature was produced for some practical purpose. A poem about the rage of the god Era was used as a charm against pestilence. There are love songs of which the first lines sound as though they were written for a hit parade: "I'm crazy with love for you." Their frankness leaves nothing to imagination, for they belonged to a fertility rite and were written for the sacred marriage between the ruler and the life giving goddess of love.

Most of the literary texts have come down to us on school tablets. The students copied classics to learn spelling and style. The adventures of King Gilgamesh of Uruk were read at the Hittite court as well as in Megiddo in Palestine. On the Nile and in Elamite Susa, scribes copied the myth of Adapa-Oannes, the wisest of men, who had ascended into the heavens yet failed to attain immortality. The role of Sumer in this school tradition is evidenced by the fact that almost all gods, heroes, and men of Akkadian classical literature are Sumerians. But how can we explain that the Sumerian heroic sagas concerned Gilgamesh and other kings of the first dynasty of Uruk, who were supposed to have lived, not in the dim, heroic beginnings of history, but recently, in the twenty-seventh century according to our reckoning?

Since we do not know the authors, places, and times of composition of all these works, we are unable to understand them in their historical contexts. The modern reader discovers the quest of immortality, or the tones of wanton pride, in the epic of Gilgamesh, and compares him with Faust. Yet the earliest reference counts him among the gods. In a Sumerian myth, the goddess of love is a younger sister of her enemy, the goddess of death. Was there a streak of romanticism in the Sumerian soul? Does the juxtaposition of love and death express some eternal truth hidden in our unconscious?

The practical purpose of the scribal craft also explains why there was no writing of history in Mesopotamia. Rulers, dedicating objects to gods, referred to their deeds of piety, which included wars, as reasons for expecting divine blessing, but these ephemeral events were of no interest to posterity. When a king of Uruk, writing to the king of Babylon about 1800, mentioned the dispatch of Babylonian auxiliaries as something which had happened "two or three times" in the past, he did not quote the annals, but referred to conversations with his father and grandfather. What we have as Sumerian and Babylonian historiography are lists of kings which, in later compilations, briefly record some victories of old.

FOR FURTHER READING

Cambridge Ancient History, 3 ed., Vols. I–II

W. W. Hallo and W. K. Simpson, *The Ancient Near East*

S. Kramer, *History Begins at Sumer*

J. Mellaart, *Early Civilizations in the Near East*

O. Neugebauer, *The Exact Sciences in Antiquity*

4
EGYPT

GEOGRAPHY AND ARCHEOLOGY

Egypt was, as the Greeks said, the gift of the Nile. Like a gigantic snake (720 miles from the first cataract to the sea), the Nile slithers through the desert which isolates its green valley. Eastward the desert continues to the Red Sea and, beyond it, into Arabia; westward lies the Sahara. When, about 2000, an Egyptian force marching to the Red Sea had to cross some ninety miles of the desert, donkeys carried spare sandals for the soldiers walking on the burning sand. Southward, the cataracts prevented any large invasion until about 730 B.C., when a powerful kingdom had developed in the Sudan. Nobody before Napoleon succeeded in conquering Egypt from the Mediterranean. In Mesopotamia mountaineers from the east and the nomads west of the Euphrates could enter the sown lowland at will. Asiatic enemies could invade Egypt only over the narrow Isthmus of Suez; this happened in the eighteenth and in the seventh and later centuries B.C.

The Nile valley is so narrow that from the banks of the Nile one can sometimes see the desert cliffs on right and left. Thus, though modern Egypt is as large as Texas and New Mexico together (386,000 square miles), 99 percent of the population crowds some 13,000 square

B.C.	Dates before 2500 are approximated to the nearest century, thereafter to the nearest quarter-century.
3100–3000	Egypt unified under a single pharaoh; beginning of the Old Kingdom; appearance of writing
2700	Copper in common use in Egypt; pictures used in graves as part of funerary arrangements
2600	Egyptian conquest of Nubia; the pyramids begun (Fourth Dynasty); the potter's wheel in common use
2130	Beginning of the Middle Kingdom (Eleventh to Fourteenth Dynasties)
1825	Egyptian influence dominant in Byblos
1750–1550	Hyksos in Egypt (Fifteenth and Sixteenth Dynasties)
1550–1200	The New Kingdom (Eighteenth to Nineteenth Dynasties); wheeled vehicles become common, as does the use of bronze and labor saving devices (bellows for blacksmiths, the shadoof for watering gardens); chickens introduced
1375–1350	The Amarna Age; Ikhnaton's religious reforms

miles of the "black land" (as the ancient Egyptians called their country). The rest is the tan desert.

Villages clustered along the margins of the cultivated land and during the annual flood* stood out of the water like islands in the sea, as the Greeks used to say. The prevailing wind facilitated navigation upstream, and the current carried the vessels northward. An energetic ruler could easily dominate the whole valley. Territorial unity was normal in Egypt and exceptional in Mesopotamia.

Last but not least, the rivers of Mesopotamia led to the Persian Gulf, the backwater of history. The Nile poured its waters into the Mediterranean world of the future.

Swollen by the rains in Abyssinia, the Nile begins its rise in the middle of August in Cairo and attains its maximum height in the beginning of October. Thus, the flood comes after the harvest and moistens the earth parched by the summer heat that kills weeds and aerates the ground. (In Mesopotamia, the floods come in the spring; summer evaporation makes the ground saline and thus, in the end, unproductive.)

The brown water of the flood leaves behind a deposit of silt rich in organic matters which renews the topsoil. The modern dam, disturbing the ecology, deprives the cultivated land of a part of this silt. The Egyptian needed no more than a wooden hoe to till the muddy ground capable of yielding, if watered between floods, two crops in the year. Greek authors spoke with envy of the farmers who without effort collected the bounty of the Nile.

In fact, however, it was backbreaking work that sustained the agricultural civilization of Egypt through six millennia. The sand blown in from the desert encroached upon the cultivable land. Dikes and canals which regulated the flood and extended its benefits had to be built and reconstructed after each inundation. In fact, some fourteen percent of the cultivated land in Egypt is still today occupied by irrigation works. At the dawn of history, the Egyptians already marked the height of the successive rises of the river. Even the Nile could default; the seven lean years which Joseph predicted to his pharaoh could become dire reality. As soon as man's effort slackened, the population dwindled. It totaled 8,000,000 under the Romans in the first century A.D.; it was only 2,000,000 at the beginning of the nineteenth century, under Turkish rule.

The crowding of population in the irrigated land determined the nature of the evidence available to us. Since the Egyptians wrote on sheets made out of stalks of papyrus* (our word "paper" comes from the Egyptian name of this plant), humidity and time destroyed their archives. The mud brick buildings also disappeared, since the Egyptians did not use baked bricks. But graves built at the desert's edge remained. In the delta, however, the distance made desert burial impracticable. Hence, almost no evidence comes from the delta, and our reconstructions of the Egyptian past must be unbalanced and unreliable. Moreover, the Egypt that we know is mainly an Egypt of the dead. The pyramids are tombs. To understand the life of ancient Egypt we have first to know the world of the dead.

The Egyptian hereafter was unique. In the Mesopotamian underworld pale shades ate bitter bread and drank foul water. The mighty hero Gilgamesh could only become their shadowy ruler. Man's sole hope was to bribe the powers of the underworld by sacrifices and gifts. In Egypt death led into an afterlife where the gods assigned to the deceased the due portion of water for the cultivation of his field. As long as the corpse, or at least a material image of it, subsisted, life continued. Hence, the careful burial in dry tombs which preserved the corpse. Mummification was already known at the beginning of the third millennium. The abundance of funerary imagery in burial chambers served the same purpose. Palaces and shrines were built of sun dried mud bricks; the first known Egyptian building of limestone was the pyramidal grave of a pharaoh. For the Egyptian, as an Egyptian formula says, the grave was "the eternal home." And it is this "eternal home," its inscriptions, statues, reliefs, paintings,* furniture, and so on, which tells us about the past of ancient Egypt.

Proverbial wisdom instructs us that only good words are to be said about the dead. The Egypt of the dead is peopled by well-fed men, and ladies who are young and good-looking. The pharaohs are benevolent, officials efficient, the lower classes busy and satisfied. Even the slave woman who grinds grain* sometimes looks optimistic. The funerary texts give only isolated bits of evidence, and the historian must strive to elicit meaningful and correlated information from the eulogies.

DEVELOPMENT OF CULTURE

The first agricultural settlements on high ground along the Nile and the Faiyûm, probably established in the sixth millennium, reveal no surprises. The villagers cultivated barley of the Mesopotamian type, emmer, and flax. They raised livestock and used pottery, flint tools, and some copper articles. Life of the same kind continued in Nubia as late as the third millennium, but in Egypt two new powers appeared around 3100–3000 which for the next 3,000 years determined the style of Egyptian life: the pharaoh and hieroglyphs.

In predynastic times pictorial representations of hunt and battle show warriors who are equal. Then, suddenly, representations appear in which a giant bestrides his own men and his adversaries, single-handedly destroying the enemy or digging a canal. He is the pharaoh, and his name is written alongside the picture in hieroglyphs. For instance, the images of fish and of chisel, read in Egyptian as Nar-Mer,* give the name of a pharaoh. Yet, the impression that the hieroglyphs and the pharaoh emerge together may be erroneous, since the texts of the same period written on papyrus have disappeared and the prehistory of Egyptian writing remains unknown.

The hieroglyphic signs were and remained pictorial: A man leaning on a walking stick meant old age. Then some of the pictorial signs came to have consonantal values; for instance, the picture of the mouth (*ra*) came to stand for the sound *R*. Various supplementary signs made hieroglyphic writing capable of expressing any thought. Egyptian writing, like Hebrew and Arabic, did not indicate vowels, so we do not know exactly how the words were pronounced. Different scholars have had different theories and in accordance with these have inserted vowels in Egyptian names for the convenience of modern readers; thus it is not uncommon to find in different texts quite different spellings of the same name.

At a very early date, by grouping 24 of their one-consonant words, the Egyptians created an alphabet. But this discovery was not exploited; the alphabetic signs were merely used to complement the pictorial signs. Likewise, as we saw in Mesopotamia, peoples using syllabic and, later, alphabetic writings never fully realized the potentiality of their achievements for the development of printing.

The first representations of the pharaohs show them wearing, now the white crown of the south, now the red crown of lower Egypt. It seems that the ruler of the south conquered the delta. Thereafter there was in principle only one pharaoh. (This term comes to us through the Bible; it meant "palace" in Egyptian.) The history of Egypt became the story of the pharaohs. Its three millennia are divided among thirty dynasties, the last of which reigned between 378 and 342 B.C. The first two dynasties laid the foundation of the pharaonic civilization. The third settled in Memphis, near modern Cairo, immediately south of the delta, and here, about 2600, the kings erected the famous pyramids.* (There are many others, monuments of earlier and later pharaohs, strung along the Nile as far south as Nubia.) For the whole period of the Old Kingdom, from the unification of Egypt to the last pharaoh of Memphis (Eighth Dynasty), the Egyptian king lists counted 955 years.

During this millennium the pharaohs reclaimed brackish lagoons in the delta and papyrus swamps in upper Egypt, where the rich hunted aquatic birds.* About 2600, a royal officer founded twelve villages in the delta. Storehouses where grain was laid up for use in lean years covered the land. Barley or emmer bread and beer from barley remained the basic foods. ("Barley and beer" often meant any kind of salary.) Vegetables, particularly onions, supplemented the diet. Grapes and wine* are first mentioned under the Second Dynasty (twenty-ninth to twenty-seventh centuries). Some 300 years later, under the Fourth Dynasty, there were five varieties of wine from the delta, several sorts of beers, and some twenty bread products. A repast found in the grave of a noble lady of the Second Dynasty consisted of eight courses, from barley porridge to fresh fruits. Agricultural techniques remained simple. A wooden hoe was sufficient for the muddy ground and a small plot. From the Second Dynasty on, a light plow* drawn by cattle aided the farmer. The houses were built of mud bricks, although those of the wealthy must have been quite comfortable. As early as the Second Dynasty, tombs were equipped with bathrooms for the next life of the owner.

ECONOMY AND TRADE

Egypt abounded in excellent stone, from limestone, the building material of the pyramids, to porphyry and granite. In the first centuries of the third millennium the manufacture of heavy vessels made of hard stone was prodigious both in quantity and in workmanship. We still cannot understand how an Egyptian craftsman with his flint-pointed drill could hollow out rock crystal to make jars with sides as thin as paper. The use of stone for building was apparently more difficult. The tomb of the last pharaoh of the Second Dynasty was the first entirely lined with limestone. Stone vessels were for the wealthy, but the common use of the potter's wheel from about 2600 made pottery available to all. In the pit burials of the poor a clay cup for water and a dish for bread comforted the dead. The Egyptians imagined that the god Khnum fashioned men on a potter's wheel. Thus a technical device, introduced within the historical period, could become the material for a myth.

The use of copper became more and more widespread during the third millennium. Toward the end of it the payments to workers, besides food and linen, often included copper utensils. From about 2750 copper tools, hardened by skillful hammering, facilitated quarrying and the use of stone for building. Copper points for arrows were in use by 2100.

However, flint tools and weapons, which could be easily and cheaply replaced, continued to be employed well into the second millennium. Flint was a native material; copper had to be brought from faraway lands. For the same reason, bronze, which required tin as well as copper, was not used for weapons and tools before the sixteenth century, a millennium later than in Mesopotamia, though the alloy is stronger and easier to cast than copper.

It seems that the pharaohs intentionally isolated the valley of the Nile and endeavored to make its economy self-contained. Cultural influence of Mesopotamia and Syria-Palestine was tangible in the predynastic times and under the first pharaohs, about 3000. The Sumerian motif of entwined monsters appears on Narmer's palette. But when Egypt became powerful, the pharaohs preferred domestic development to trade, and during the Old Kingdom foreign elements remained few. Under military protection, the Egyptians exploited malachite and turquoise veins and, perhaps, copper mines in Sinai. About 2600, the pharaohs conquered Nubia to the south of the first cataract; near the second cataract they established foundries for working Nubian copper.

As a matter of fact, Egypt, the richest agricultural country of the ancient world, could well dispense with foreign trade, which mostly brought in objects of luxury. When an Egyptian author described a time of calamities, he mentioned the lack of cedar wood from Byblos usually used for expensive coffins. When, in the beginning of the fifteenth century, Queen Hatshepsut sent a trade expedition to the land of "Punt" (probably the Somali coast), an event commemorated in the reliefs of her funerary temple, the main product brought back by her five ships was incense for temple service. She sent her vessels in order to eliminate the middleman and to bring living incense trees which were planted as "a Punt" in her capital. Elizabeth of England could not have been more mercantilistic in the sixteenth century A.D. The economic isolation of Egypt, where seagoing ships were constructed in the manner of papyrus skiffs* on the Nile, was also expressed in her exchange system. Goods were disposed of by barter; for instance, beads were exchanged for onions or cakes. Yet, to quote Aristotle, how can one find the number of sandals equivalent to a meal? Therefore, as the philosopher says, the invention of money, a universal standard of value, was a work of justice and equality. The Egyptians did not invent money, but they used copper, grain, silver, and gold as common denominators of value. Yet, as late as about 1170, a sarcophagus valued at about 5 pieces of copper was purchased for about $2\frac{1}{2}$ pounds of copper, 1 hog, 2 she-goats, and 2 sycamore trees. By contrast with Mesopotamia, the self-contained economy of Egypt remained primitive.

PYRAMIDS*

The pyramids express the self-confidence of self-centered Egypt. The Great Pyramid, built in the middle of the twenty-sixth century, covers more than thirteen acres and remains one of the largest buildings in the world. For almost 4,500 years it was also the tallest (over 480 feet). It was erected without machinery or scaffolding by the sweat of perhaps 100,000 workers and the ingenuity of Egyptian engineers who used levers and ropes. Men drew sledges up brick ramps to make a pile of some 2,300,000 limestone blocks weighing about two and a half tons each. The sides of the pyramid were oriented according to the four cardinal points, and the maximum error was about one-twelfth of a degree. Each side was to be 756 feet long at the base, and the maximum error was only a few inches.

Some 2,100 years later, Egyptian priests told Greek travelers that Cheops, the pharaoh of the Great Pyramid, reduced the people to misery for his project. In fact, the annual working season for the building of the pyramids was presumably the late summer, when the Nile flooded* and farming stopped. At that time the stones could be carried over water to the site of the pyramid. Since the mobilized peasants were paid in kind, the building of the pyramids was also a kind of relief work system. Modern man may ask whether the capital and labor extended in erecting the royal pyramid and enormous funerary complex centered on it could not have been better devoted to low-cost housing. The same question can be asked about Gothic cathedrals or the Temple of Jerusalem. To each question the builders would have answered that these structures were needful and proper for the service of the gods, and only the proper service of the gods would secure prosperity for the country. We might add that the labor kept the workers quiet and the economy stable. As Adam Smith wrote, "The desire of food is limited in every man by the narrow capacity of the stomach," but the desire for "conveniences and ornaments" is unlimited. When Smith wrote (1776), conspicuous consumption was, perhaps, the main stimulus of surplus production. As he put it, for most rich people the chief enjoyment of wealth consisted in the parade of riches. But he wrote at the dawn of the industrial revolution. In earlier and poorer societies religion provided the incentive for works of economic supererogation; it raised common labor to the dignity of a ritual gesture. The Sumerian king is represented carrying on his head a basket with bricks for the foundation of a temple—of course he did not carry many bricks, but his example gave some respectability to those who did. When the men of Lagash had to repair a canal, it was the canal of their god Ningirsu. This belief did not make them like the work, but it did ease the burden. Their myths told them that they had been created to free the gods from toil. Much as they might hate it, they had to perform the functions to which their god, through his priests, had assigned them. Kings and canal-diggers were alike his slaves and each had to carry whatever load was laid on him. Determinist mythology, whether Sumerian or Marxian, helps men to accept the unavoidable and go on living.

In Egypt, the pharaoh,* a god himself, linked mortal men to the eternal. He was represented on the temple walls worshiping the gods and associating with them, "the servants of the god" (priests, in our terms) were his delegates, and none of his subjects was ever pictured in association with a deity while alive. The common people needed the pharaoh for eternal salvation, since the offerings without which the deceased could not exist were officially the pharaoh's gift: he alone had the key to the afterlife. His eternal life in the pyramid, thus, was directly related to the well-being of every Egyptian. Princes and courtiers were entombed around the royal pyramid, and images of their tenants and servants appeared on the walls of these tombs, so that their names, too, were "established forever." It has been thought that, through this chain of hope, the humblest worker on the Great Pyramid expected to participate in the pharaonic immortality, just as men who raised the Gothic cathedrals labored in the hope of eternal reward for their pains.

In due time the incarnate god became a corpse, and magic formulas were necessary to make the motionless body living in the hereafter: "This king Phiops dies not." Another set of charms was read by the mortuary priest in the tomb of a private man. A royal prince, in the twenty-fifth century, to ensure the continuance of oblations and liturgies after his death, endowed his tomb with twelve villages.

DEMOCRATIZATION OF THE AFTER-LIFE

By the latter half of the twenty-fourth century it became clear, however, that even a pharaoh could not be sure of perpetual repetitions of charms which had to be spoken daily to restore his body to life. The relevant texts began to be inscribed on the walls of his burial chamber so that, if necessary, the deceased himself would be able to speak the formulas of revivification.

In the middle of the twenty-third century these formulas began to be reproduced in the burial chambers of members of the royal family and of nobles who thus usurped the unique privilege of the pharaoh. As one of them boasted: "I know every secret charm of the palace." By the end of the millennium anybody could copy this or that part of the royal liturgy in his tomb.

After his death, the pharaoh joined the immortal gods in the heavens. But since his subjects after their deaths continued to exist in the nether world, the deceased pharaoh became identified with Osiris, the king of the dead. Thus the same pharaoh, in the hereafter, was enthroned in heaven and was also "Osiris, Lord of the Lower World."

The pharaoh, being of divine essence, obtained eternal life as his right. His subjects had to prove that they deserved it. They needed the intercession of the pharaoh with the god Anubis, who led the dead into the other world. From about 2600, the titles and merits of the deceased were inscribed on the walls of his tomb. He did "what the pharaoh praised," whereas his "beloved wife" stated that she was held "in honor by her husband." In the course of time, these eulogies became more prolix. The deceased, for instance, said that he had taken swimming lessons with the royal children or had given bread to the hungry and clothing to the naked. The latter statement not only attests that the lord who speaks was wealthy and fulfilled his duty to his villagers, "so that I might become greater than the great ones," it also shows his duty was thought to include care for the poor.

Besides his own merits, the dead man needed the sympathy of the living to ensure his existence in the hereafter. By the middle of the twenty-fourth century, in the parts of the tomb accessible to visitors, " those who love life and hate death" are entreated to make an offering or, at least, to wish that the deceased might be blessed with "a thousand of bread and beer." In making this appeal to the passerby, the dead man naturally stresses that he did "what men love and gods praise." He also promises to intercede for his helper with the powers of the other world. Yet, despite the belief in the nether world, the tomb remained the "eternal home" of the dead. From the days of the pharaohs to the age of the Caesars, perennial graveside dialogue took place between the living and the dead. In the twenty-second century a son wanted to be buried in the tomb of his father so that he might see him every day. In the same period the Egyptians began to deposit letters to the dead in their tombs. For instance, a widow asked her dead husband to rescue her and their baby from servitude to his relatives. In the thirteenth century a widower who could not overcome his grief complained to his dead wife that she prevented his heart from being happy. It was not only the hope of personal survival that confirmed the Egyptians in these beliefs about the future. The assurance of life to come was also a source of present satisfaction. A low born man was not a person of any consequence except in death, which required people to take notice of him. But anticipation of the future could give him a little present self importance.

His hope might be the greater because, in the realm of the shadows, neither one's merits nor the assistance of the living could be as potent as the arts of magic. As we have mentioned, ordinary men usurped the charms composed originally to help the pharaoh. From the beginning of the second millennium every dead man affluent enough to obtain the advantages of mummification was identified with the ruler of the underworld as "the Osiris So-and-So." His wooden coffin was inscribed with spells to help him overcome the hazards of the journey

Stela of Eannatum
Lagash c. 2400 B.C.

2 Palette of Narmer of Egypt c. 2900 B.C.

Eannatum leads the first known "regular" troops, with standard equipment, apparently drilled, moving as a unit. He may be the same size as his men (above) or a giant (below), for artistic convenience. The Pharaohs are usually symbolic giants. Narmer's name appears in hieroglyphs beside the captive's head.

3 The Nile in flood

4 "The Mosaic Casket of Ur" c. 2400 B.C.

The Nile's floods (ended by Nasser's dam) not only fertilized but made the outer fringe of the land accessible by water for heavy transport, via such little branches as this old photograph shows. The desert begins below the pyramid. The inlaid plaque from Ur shows the first tanks—battle wagons with four solid (!) wheels and high front and side walls, pulled by four ponies;

5 The Lion Gate, Mycenae c. 1300 B.C.

6 The Ziggurat, Tchoga Zambil c. 1240 B.C.

probably valued for prestige and protection. Ancient near-eastern cultures evoked different developments: in Elam (Tchoga Zambil) even Mesopotamian ziggurats were imitated; Mycenae learned fortification and also produced Europe's first monumental sculpture.

7 A fertility-goddess, Jerusalem c. 700 B.C.

8 Aphrodite, after Praxiteles c. A.D. 100

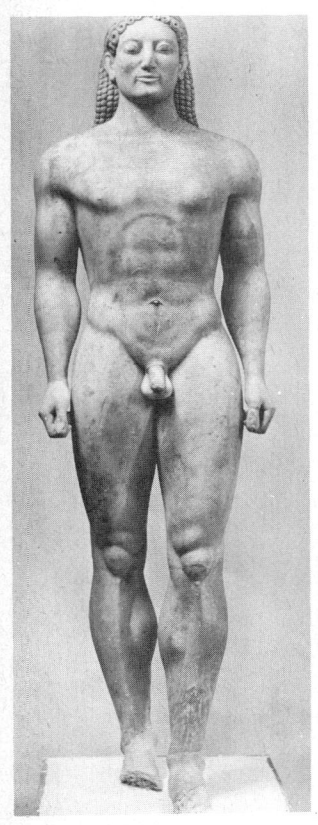

10 A Greek youth from Anyvassos c. 540 B.C.

9 Pharaoh Mycerinus and his Queen c. 2600 B.C.

Photographs 7–14 show how differently the near east and Greece treated figures of their common heritage. Notice the Greek feeling for reality—what the physical forms actually are—and muscles—even Aphrodite's! Idealization (Zeus and Demeter are middleaged but unwrinkled) must observe these limits: Zeus has a better body than Baal, but no third arm. Near-eastern

11 Baal hurling thunder, Ugarit c. 1400 B.C.

12 Zeus hurling thunder, Dodona c. 475 B.C.

13 A seated goddess (?), Ugarit c. 1400 B.C.

14 "The Demeter of Cnidus" c. 150 B.C.

schematism and exaggeration show less interest in figures for their own sakes than as expressions of ideas. Hence less concern for craftsmanship, except in Egypt. These differences long endured: Mycerinus c. 2600 B.C.; Aphrodite c. A.D. 100, but from a fourth century B.C. original.

15 Sowing, The Tomb of Nakht, XVIII dynasty

16 Winnowing, The Tomb of Nakht

Nakht, a scribe of the temple of Amon in Thebes, died about 1425 B.C. His tomb's paintings were to provide him forever the services and property represented. They picture the agricultural techniques that supported the Egyptian Empire, the largest state of antiquity prior to Persia. Cheap labor and ideal conditions compensated for primitive techniques, e.g. oxen yoked by their

7 Fowling, fishing, and vintage, The Tomb of Nakht

horns. The plough was wood. Egyptian art, though conventional, loves "human" details—the harvester drinking from the waterskin in a cool tree—and abandons convention in lower-class figures: the winnowers are in true profile. Its palette was exquisite: peacock blue, green, yellow, tan, black.

18 Egyptians weaving, figurines from a tomb

19 Egyptian woman grinding grain, VI dynasty

Besides paintings, Egyptians furnished their tombs with models of houses, etc., equipped with statuettes of slaves and spells to make them serve hereafter. Most such "doll houses of the dead" come from the Middle Kingdom; no. 19 is unusually early. Herodotus (II.35) cited the difference between Egyptian and Greek weaving in contending that Egyptians do everything

20 Greek women spinning and weaving, c. 560 B.C.

21 Roman grain mill, turned by a donkey

backwards. Spinning, weaving, and cooking were women's work; "the slave woman behind the flour mill" was the lowest social figure (Exodus 11.5). She was liberated by donkey, wind, and water mills of hellenistic and later times, among the most important mechanical advances of antiquity.

22 Greeks gathering olives, c. 510 B.C.

23 Greek woman fetching water, c. 525 B.C.

Greek agricultural work was done by men. Few things took women out of doors. One was the endless labor of getting water. City fountains were therefore centers of gossip; Athenian dinner parties provided material. Attic black figure vase painting represents such everyday scenes for their beauty and charm; contrast the magical intent of Egyptian tomb paintings and models

24A and **24B** Greek dinner parties, early and mid fifth century B.C.

25 An Egyptian fishing skiff, c. 2000 B.C.

26 Greek boat arriving at shore, c. 570 B.C.

(like this boat) made to be buried. Greek aesthetic feeling also shaped their cities—the fountain house, the lion's head spout. Also Greek is the boat specialized for warfare, with long, narrow hull and crew of athletic oarsmen.

27 Tiglath Pileser III (744–727 B.C.) besieging a city

28 Scenes from an Assyrian army camp, c. 860 B.C.

As against Egyptian and Greek art, Assyrian palace friezes were primarily neither magical nor aesthetic, but narrative. Adapting history to propaganda, they showed important visitors the Assyrian army, its victories, technological advances (battering rams, moveable walls to protect archers), and severity. Here a city is trying to surrender, but one Assyrian who has scaled the

29 Troops of Ramses III (1198–1166 B.C.) on a hunting party

30 The guards of the Persian King, c. 490 B.C.

walls beheads a suppliant, another kills men thrown down. Impaled in the background are men caught earlier. Pictures of cook's tent and stables recognize their military importance. By contrast the light armed Egyptian troops seem boy scouts, the stiff Persian guardsmen, parade soldiers.

31 Combat on a gold ring from Mycenae, c. 1500 B.C.

32 Sleep and Death carry off a Trojan hero, an Athenian vase of c. 515 B.C.

Battles in antiquity were mainly hand to hand combats. Their violence and pathos are concentrated on the Mycenaean ring and reflected in Homeric verses. But when these are again reflected in vase painting, death is romanticised by epic reminiscences. Similarly, ancient kings were supposed to kill lions. Originally functional, the role became symbolic, so Assyrian kings

3 Ashurnasirpal II of Assyria (883–859 B.C.) killing lions

34 Darius I of Persia killing a lion, c. 500 B.C.

35 A Greek footrace, Athens, late sixth century B.C.

had lions rounded up and released for killing. Darius of Persia succeded to Assyrian pretension, and had himself represented in the traditional role. Both king and lions seem stuffed. Contrast the Greek athletes in their actual, nonheroic contest; though not quite accurately seen, they are vividly alive.

36 Plan of an Egyptian temple (XX dynasty)

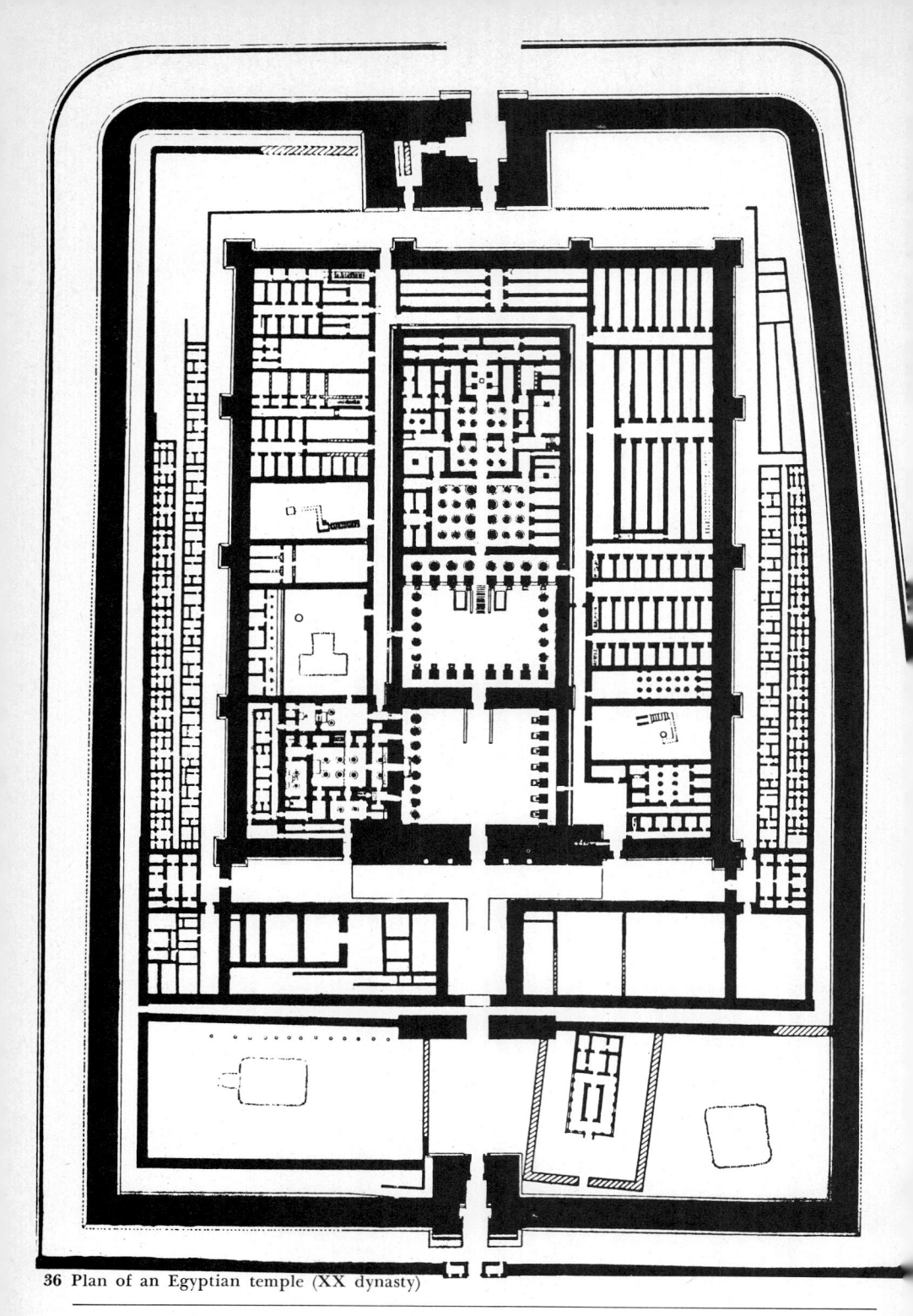

The plans of Egyptian temple and Parthenon indicate differences of priestly staff and social cost. Note the beautiful proportions of the Parthenon and other Acropolis buildings (completed in 405 B.C.) to the hill and to each other. Trade payed. Coinage for trade began c. 600 B.C. with tiny electrum pieces; Croesus, c. 550 B.C., issued this gold (actual size); Darius' gold

37 Athens, The Acropolis from the southwest

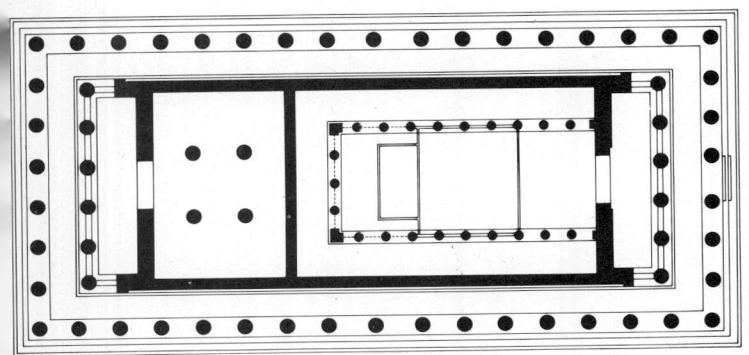

38 Plan of the Parthenon (447–432 B.C.)

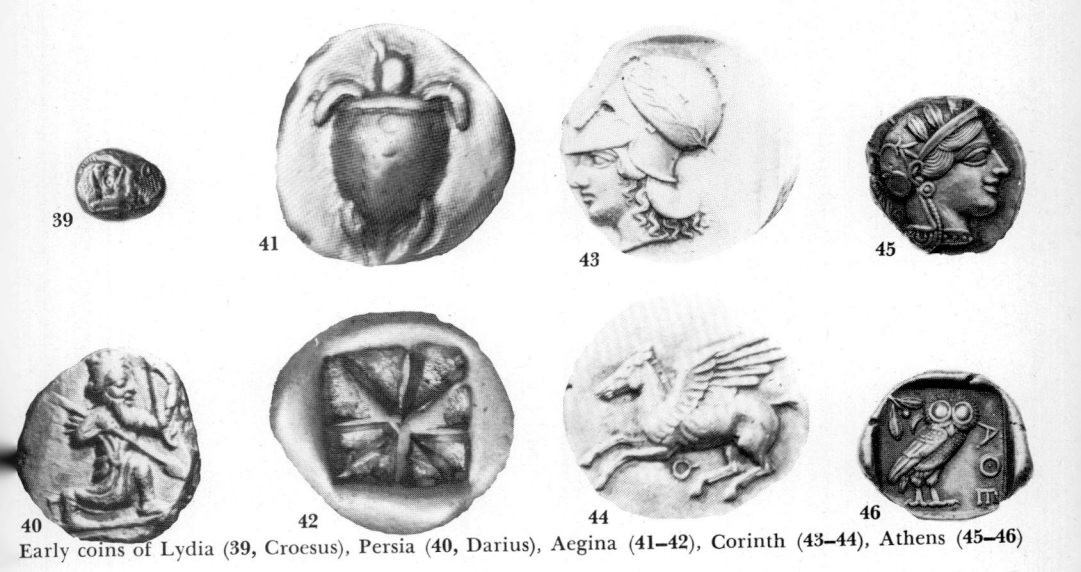

Early coins of Lydia (**39**, Croesus), Persia (**40**, Darius), Aegina (**41–42**), Corinth (**43–44**), Athens (**45–46**)

"Daric" spread coinage through his empire; Greek silver, through the Mediterranean. The reverses of very early coins, like 42 (c. 550 B.C.) show only the mark of the punch; soon the punch end was engraved, producing double-faced coins like these of Corinth (c. 325 B.C.) and Athens (c. 475 B.C.).

47 A cuneiform tablet with a note in alphabetic Aramaic, 423 B.C.

48 Egyptian writing on papyrus, XVIII dynasty

49 ALPHABETS

Phoenician	Old Hebrew	Greek
✡	✡	A
9	9	B
1	1	Γ
◁	◁	Δ
∃	∃	E
Y	Y	
I	I	Z
⊟	⊞	H
⊗	⊗	Θ
⁊	Z	I
↳	↳	K
⌐	⌐	Λ
⌐	⌐	M
⌐	⌐	N
╪	╪	Ξ
O	O	O
⌐	⌐	Π
⌐	⌐	
P	Φ	P
9	9	Σ
W	W	T
+	X	Y
		Φ
		X
		Ψ
		Ω

Note the simplicity of Aramaic alphabetic writing (47, top line) vs. cuneiform (the rest, here inverted). Clear, elegant Egyptian hieroglyphics cost long training—and these are "cursive," i.e. simplified! Greek adapted Phoenician by reversing the direction of writing and letters, taking out two signs and reusing them at the end for Greek sounds, dropping one sign and adding

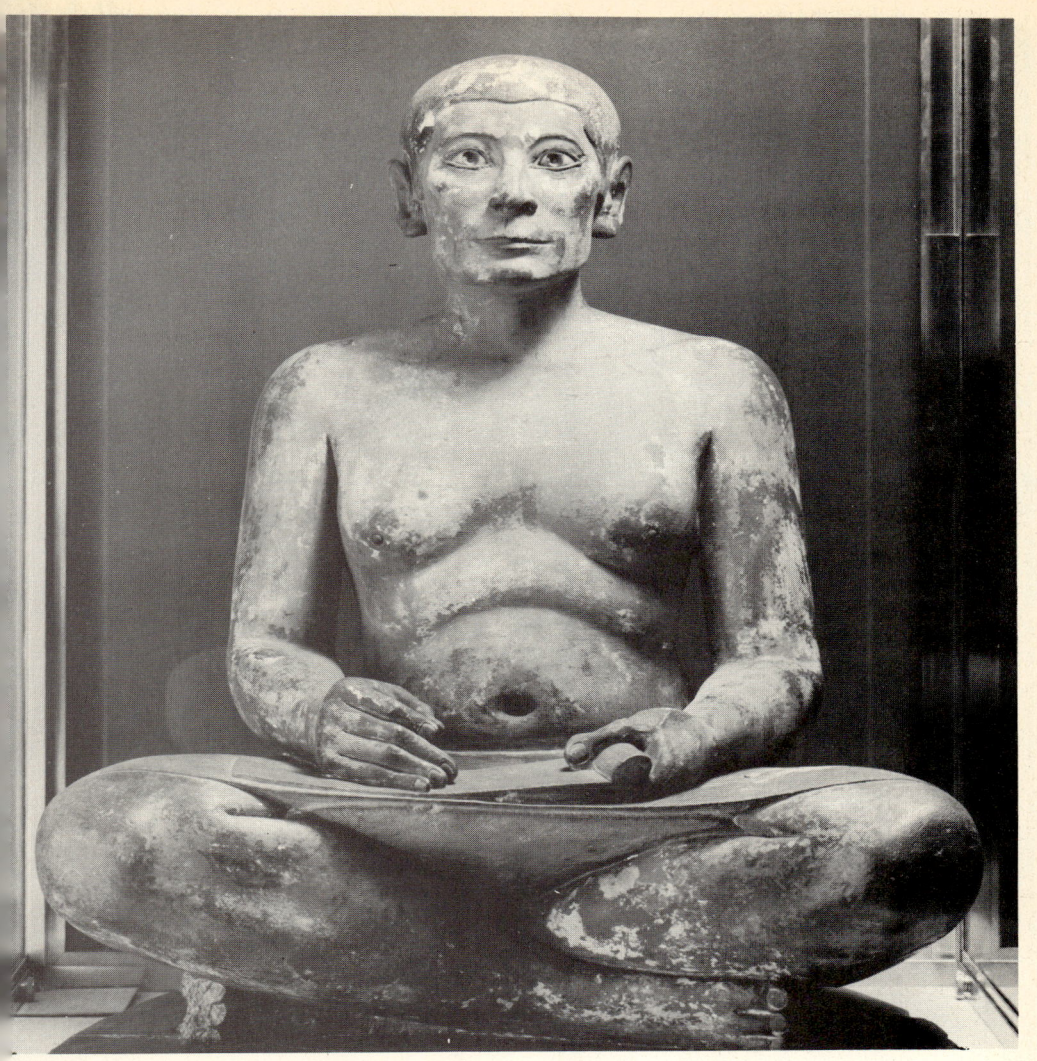

50 An Egyptian scribe, V dynasty (c. 2450 B.C.)

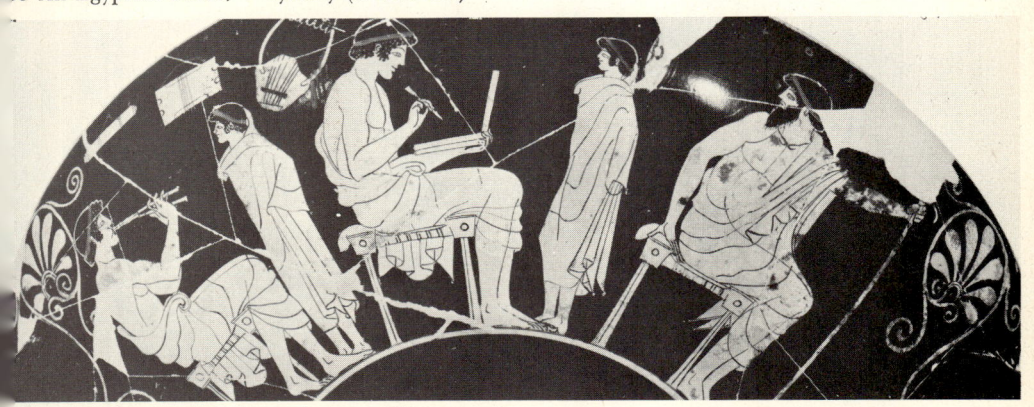

51 Greek boys with their teachers, c. 480 B.C.

three. Position for writing changed with wealth; the great Egyptian scribe sat on the ground, the Greek elementary teacher had a stool. But papyrus was still an Egyptian monopoly, so the "paper" was a wax tablet, written with a stylus. The third man was the slave who chaperoned the boys.

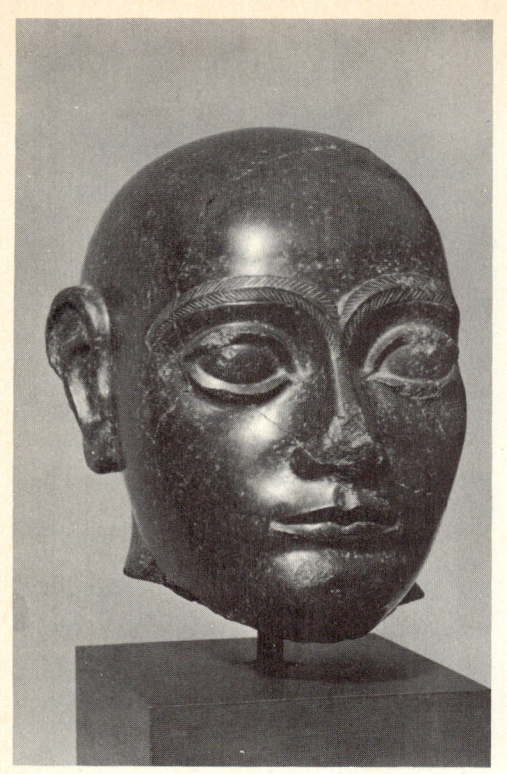

52 Gudea, ruler of Lagash, c. 2150 B.C.

53 Alexander the Great 336–323 B.C.

54 Socrates, executed in 399 B.C.

55 Euripides, died 406 B.C.

Cleopatra VII, 51–30 B.C.

57 Octavian, later Augustus, 43 B.C.–A.D. 14

The Lighthouse of Alexandria protected by Isis

59 The Temple of Janus in Rome with its doors closed

Both Gudea and Alexander, being rulers, are idealized, but how different the stolid Sumerian stylization from the Greek suggestion of inspiration and individuality! Greek also is the respect for philosophers and poets that has preserved (or created?) their portraits; these Roman copies reflect fourth century B.C. originals. Near-eastern portraits (other than funerary and votive) are of rulers. Darius used coinage for self advertisement, then Alexander, thenceforth most monarchs, e.g. Cleopatra and Augustus. Coins were also used to advertise tourist attractions—the Alexandrian lighthouse—and royal achievement—Nero's peace with Parthia in A.D. 63. (The temple of Janus might be closed only when Rome was wholly at peace.)

60 The Roman aqueduct at Segovia, first century A.D.

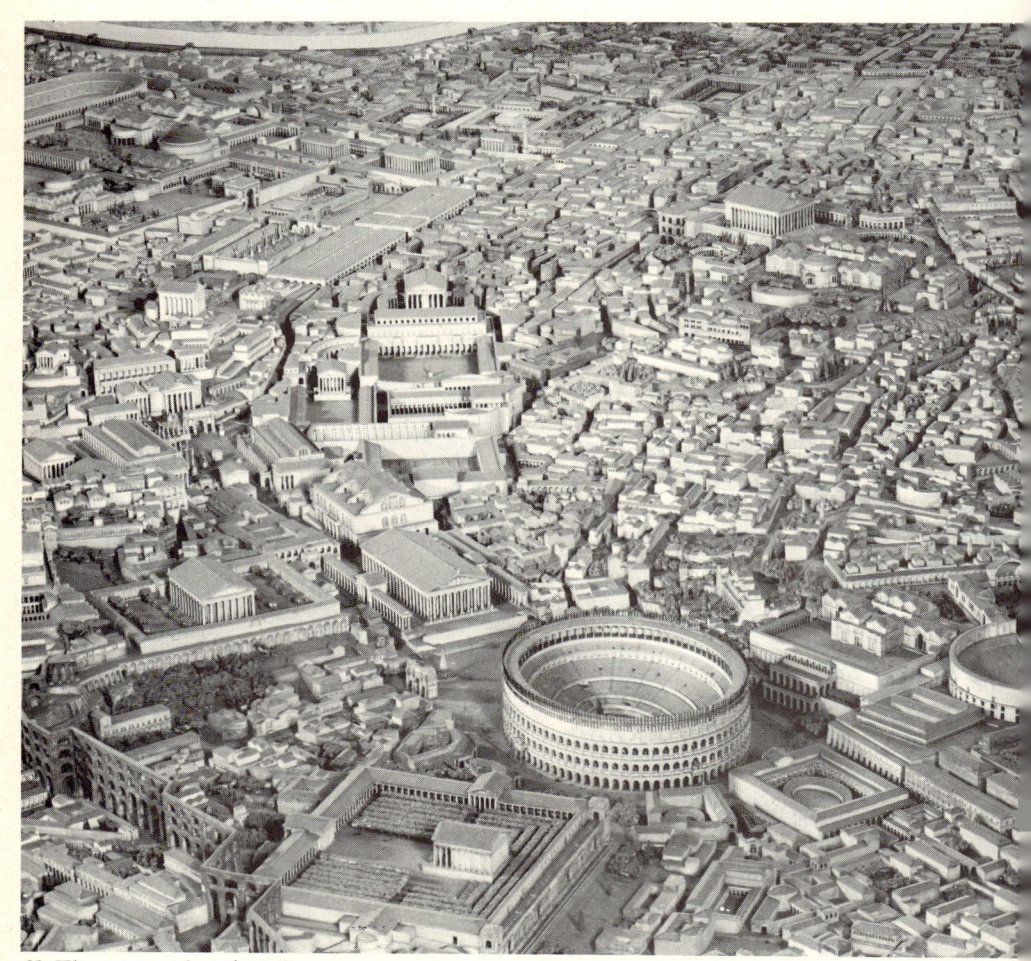

61 The center of ancient Rome

Monuments of Roman peace, power, and architectural genius were mostly practical, like the aqueduct at Segovia (still functioning), but theaters and temples attest cultural concerns. The theater of Timgad, in southern Algeria, seated 4000. It is in shadow in the foreground of 63; to its right, the forum, then the street to the triumphal arch, beyond which the markets; left

2 The Roman theater at Timgad, second century A.D.

3 Timgad, a Roman provincial city

center the capitol (state temples), left foreground, a bath (the city had thirteen). In Rome (61) left foreground, Nero's aqueduct leads to the palaces; behind them, the Capitol; center, forum of Trajan; foreground, Colosseum; right of it, baths of Titus. And so on—this shows only the center.

64 Ostia, the port of Rome, c. A.D. 65

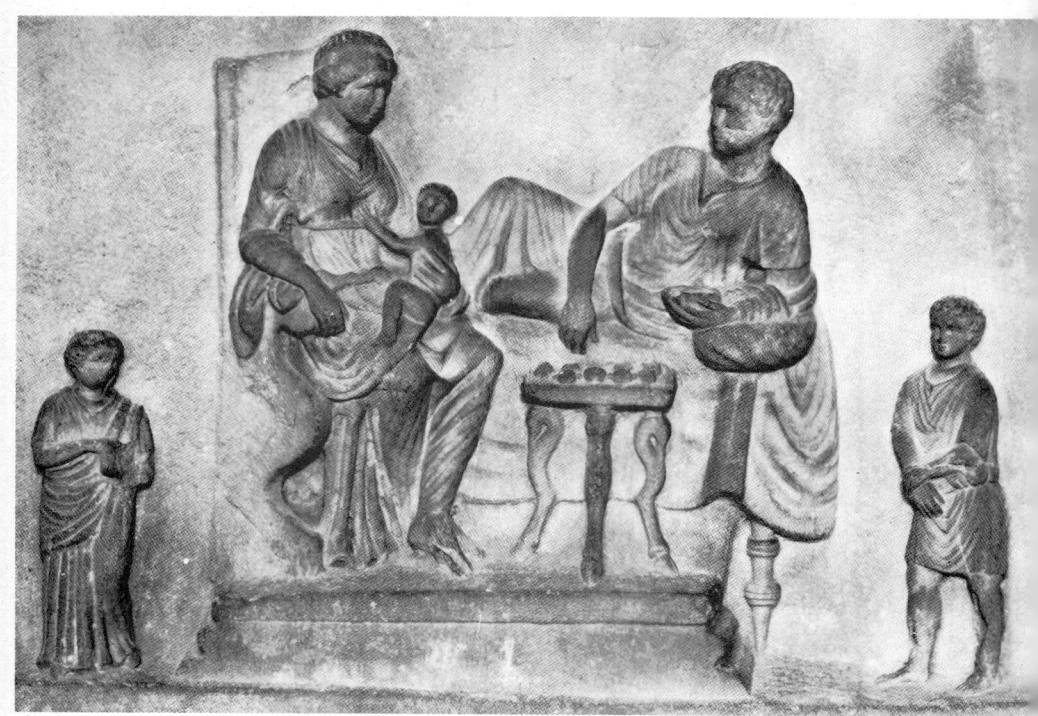

65 A provincial family at dinner, Avignon, first century B.C.

Rome was fed by sea; overland transportation was dear. Nero's coin (64) celebrates a new port, a 3000 foot basin accommodating over 200 ships; the colossus doubles as lighthouse. Such imperial harbors indicate the Mediterranean's importance as the empire's central transport route. Trade homogenized Greco-Roman culture: The family on the Greek tombstone from

66 A baker's tomb, Rome, c. 25 B.C.

67 Gladiator at work, Córdoba, first century A.D.?

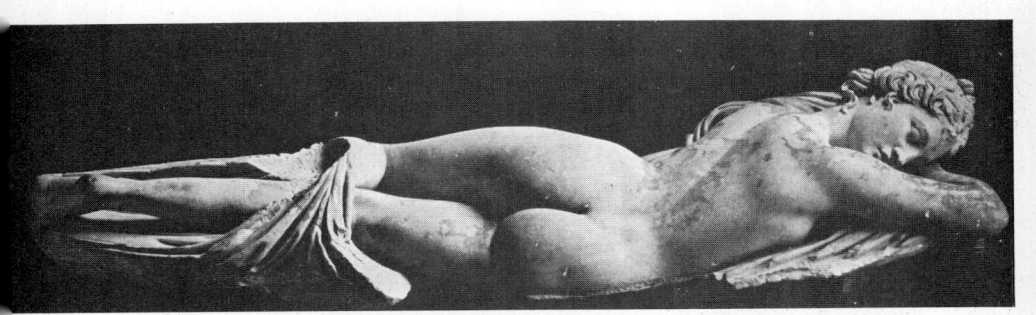

68 Hermaphrodite at rest, first/second century A.D.

69 "Know yourself"—a skeleton, second century A.D. mosaic

south France have Roman names. Mercantile mentality—a baker's million-dollar tomb shows piled-up grain measures. Gladiator and male prostitute (copied from a hellenistic original) recall the grim pleasures of this mercantile world. The skeleton with the Greek proverb "Know yourself" was a popular reminder to enjoy life now.

70 Roman soldiers attacking a Dacian fortress, A.D. 106

71 A Roman emperor kneeling to a Persian king, A.D. 260 or later

Trajan's conquest of Dacia (A.D. 101–106) marks almost the peak of Roman power. His column in Rome, whence this relief, shows barbarians fighting Romans with similar weapons, armor, stone fortifications. Romans won by manpower and organization. Then came plagues and revolts. By A.D. 260 Sapor I of Persia had captured the emperor Valerian. No. 71, supposedly Valerian's

Nero, A.D. 54–68

74 Diocletian, A.D. 284–305

Trajan, A.D. 98–117

75 Constantine (or Constantius II?)
A.D. 306–337 (or 337–361)

submission, may be later, but demonstrates the new situation and Persian propaganda. Concomitant internal changes surface in imperial portraits, Nero's extravagance, Trajan's "classic" grandeur. The crisis leads to hardheaded Diocletian, then the swollen head (five feet high) and apostolic pretensions of Constantine (or Constantius?), a masterpiece of mummified mystique.

76 A businessman of Pompeii, first century A.D.

77 A rich man of Ephesus, fifth century A.D.

78 A hellenistic philosopher, second century B.C.

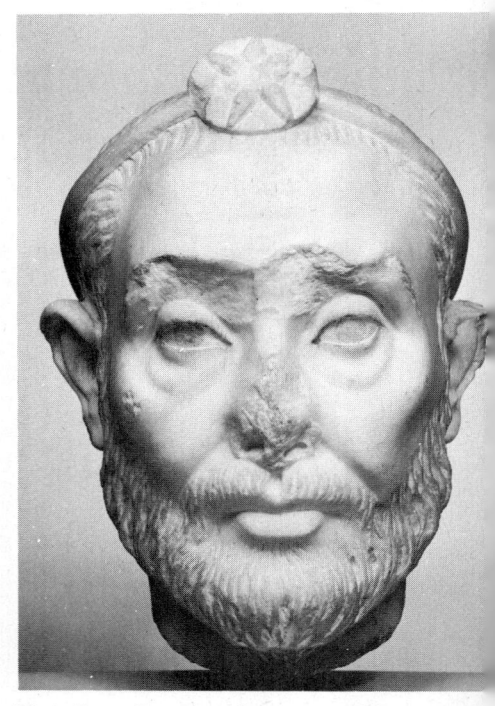

79 A Greco-Egyptian theosopher, third century

People changed, too. The early empire businessman is an optimistic egotist; the fifth-century millionaire (if correctly identified) is a gloomy aristocrat who probably made his money in imperial administration and certainly expects the worst. The hellenistic philosopher had an observing, inquiring, *thinking* mind; the theosopher with his astral paraphernalia (one need

A country house in N. Africa, fourth century A.D.

The palace to which Diocletian retired

not think him a priest) views the outside world with walleyed indifference and does not **think**, he *meditates*. But life in the later empire had its good sides, among them delightful country estates, the mosaic art that pictured them, and the unequalled magnificence of the palaces, above all Diocletian's.

82 The goddess Isis nursing her son, Horus

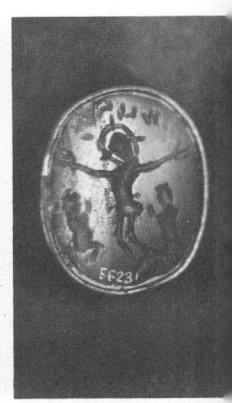

Magical amulets: **83** Egyptian gods; **84** Iao-Abrasax; **85** Moses with the Law; **86** the crucifixion

In this hellenized, first century A.D. Isis only horns and crescent (broken) identify the goddess; Egyptian majesty is sacrificed to universal appeal. More Egyptian is 83, to cure hysteria: Anubis, the serpent Chnum, and Isis stand on a womb. Of other near-eastern deities who spread through magic, the rooster-headed god is most often labelled IA(O), the Greek name of

87 Mary the Mother of God nursing Jesus

Late Roman coins: **88** Angel holding the globe; **89** Justinian (A.D. 527–565); **90** Heraclius (A.D. 610–640) and his sons; **91** the Cross

the Israelite god. Moses, too, appears with a rooster's head. Mary nursing seems modelled on Isis; this fifth century example, among the earliest, is Egyptian. Byzantium similarly converted the goddess Victory to an angel. With Heraclius and the "true Cross" which he recovered from Persia in 628, the Middle Ages are at hand.

92 The Church of the Holy Wisdom (St. Sophia), Constantinople, interior

93 St. Sophia, cross section

94 St. Sophia, exterior

St. Sophia's was dedicated in 537. The central dome (diameters 230 x 250 feet) collapsed in 558 and its rebuilding entailed minor changes, but the plan is substantially intact and is revolutionary in its use of domes to create a vast, interior world. Turkish bricabrac and external accretions must be overlooked.

to the other world. The felicity of the Osirean realm was now accessible to the common man. "I live, I die, I am Osiris . . . I grow up as grain . . . the earth has concealed me. I live, I die, I am barley, I do not pass away. . . ." We remember Paul's argument for the bodily resurrection: "That which thou sowest does not sprout again except it die" (I Cor. 15:36). In Egypt, and only in Egypt, the living, the dead, and the gods were three species of the same substance. Again, only in Egypt, a murdered king, victim of his evil brother, not only became a god after death, but by his death assured the personal immortality of his devotees. Similar ideas would later appear in Jewish, Christian, and Muslim hopes of future life. But meanwhile, outside Egypt, for two thousand years death led only to a dismal existence among the shades, and a blessed immortality was a miraculous gift of the gods to an exceptional man or to the recipients of a peculiar initiation. Thus in Greece the chorus of deceased initiates in Aristophanes' *Frogs* can sing, "Only for us is there sun, and the light is pleasant, we who have been initiated" (in the mysteries of Eleusis), but in spite of these Eleusinian claims Homer had already told of how the gods rewarded Menelaüs—they carried him off to the western Islands of the Blessed, where he lives forever with Helen as his bride.

POLITICAL HISTORY

The evolution of Egyptian ideas about the hereafter paralleled changes in this world. Pictorial representations began to appear in the graves about 2700 when the deceased was represented as receiving the offerings due to him. At this time, the "great ones" were officers of the pharaoh, and the vizier was always a royal prince. By the middle of the third millennium, the vizier was a superbureaucrat heading several departments. By about 2300, local governors obtained the vizier's title so that they became equal to the chief of the central administration. Careers were opened to men of talent. One man who began as a "herdsman of cattle" and later served in 26 different offices died about 2350 as a director of royal works. Successful officials acquired wealth: about the middle of the twenty-sixth century one of them boasted that 2,500 asses were needed to carry away the sheaves of his fields. Rich and influential officials naturally desired to hand over their lucrative offices to their sons. Toward the end of the Old Kingdom, a son regularly took the place of his father. Sometime later a governor boasted that he had been appointed to his office as an infant "of a cubit in height." The pharaoh was god; his high officials felt themselves demigods. By 2500, they were pictured in their tombs as masters of their estates,* and on the walls of their graves they towered over the retainers and villagers. The noble whose ancestors had asked the favor of burial near the pharaoh and at the pharaoh's expense now built his tomb in his hereditary estate, "through love of the district where I was born." He prided himself on furnishing water to his city and being beloved by "my entire city."

After Pepi II, who allegedly ruled ninety-four years and lived to be a hundred, a succession of short-lived pharaohs at Memphis lost control over the local viceroys. Of course these kinglets soon became involved in wars one against another. At last, about 2130, the governor of Thebes prevailed over his rivals. His dynasty (the eleventh) and the two following reunified Egypt and kept law and order for some 400 years. We call this period the Middle Kingdom.

THE MIDDLE KINGDOM AND THE SCRIBAL CLASS

The task of the new pharaohs was not easy. Amenemhet I, the founder of the Twelfth Dynasty who about 2000 had overthrown the last king of the Eleventh Dynasty, was murdered, twenty-nine years later, in a palace conspiracy. The local governors continued to behave like monarchs. One of them in his tomb pictures his subjects, including priests and military, dragging his colossal statue (some twenty feet in height) to his mortuary temple. "Their hearts expanded when they saw the monument of their lord."

In these circumstances the new pharaohs appealed to popular feeling for support against the local magnates. Like simple mortals, they chose names expressing personal piety. For instance, the name Amenemhet put its bearer under the protection of Amun, the patron god of Thebes. The same pharaoh circulated tracts representing himself as the saviour of Egypt predicted by a seer of old. The praise of Sesostris I was attributed to a political refugee who had foolishly run abroad at his accession, but later returned to enjoy his benevolence. The importance thus given to propaganda was one thing that led to a great increase in the importance of the scribal class.

The economy demanded more and more scribes,* and the profession was open to talent. A man without a high-sounding title could send his son to the scribal school among the children of the "great ones." Toward the beginning of the second millennium, the scribes became a proud body. In tomb pictures of daily life of the Old Kingdom, the scribe is often represented as attending his lord, who is carried in a litter for inspection of his fields, but the paintings of the Middle Kingdom represent the scribes by themselves in the exercise of their profession, or as overseers of the workers in the field.

The officialdom of scribes was the mainstay of the unity of the

Two Lands. As in Mesopotamia, every governmental transaction was recorded in writing. In the temples, by 2400, the month was divided for accounting purposes into three ten-day periods; the presence or absence of the personnel was recorded daily, payments (in kind) had to be made on the first day of each month, and so on. Scribes accompanied marching soldiers, scribes counted crops, scribes recorded monthly inspections of sacred utensils in every temple and registered wicks (made of rags) for work inside royal tombs. The higher officials untiringly admonished the lower scribes to work with utmost zeal. Thus in the third quarter of the fifteenth century an order was dispatched to an official with the stern warning: "Don't take things easy, for I know you are sluggish." The letter was found 3,300 years later, still unopened.

In the Old Kingdom, the scribe was often a son of a noble, on rare occasions even of a pharaoh, and received his education from his father and a tutor. Professional requirements compelled even a highborn youth to start at the bottom of the bureaucratic ladder. The aristocratic architect who built the pyramid of Pepi I (about 2300) began his career by carrying his "scribe's palette," helping with the measuring rod, and so on, until he became royal builder. Consequently he knew how to deal with the workmen: "I never left anybody angry with me when I went to bed."

It is noteworthy that a man who wrote propaganda for Sesostris I also wrote a book warning the students of writing schools that all manual occupations were demeaning. The scribe alone never lacked sustenance from the pharoah; he alone was always an important official. "Nothing surpasses scrolls." No wonder that this scroll was copied without end in scribal schools. The new government appealed to the professional pride of the imperial bureaucracy. But this propaganda activity also attests a new understanding of the power of the pen. As a scribe of the twenty-second century wrote, "speech was mightier than any fighting." Sesostris I could, perhaps, believe he had been chosen as pharaoh, when still unborn, by the sun god, but he knew and said that the only king who does not die is one whose name is remembered on account of his work.

In the eyes of the scribe the social pyramid was a part of the world order. As soon as man comes from his mother's womb he runs to his master. The scribal idea was one of conformity to this natural principle. A good man listens to his superior; he is neither a talebearer against his colleagues nor deceitful toward the Palace. He must be a paragon whom everyone would wish to be like, yet not be overbearing. He makes "Egypt work with bowed head" for the pharaoh, but should not misuse his power. In this world view the washerman who refuses to carry the laundry and the female slave who talks back to her mistress appear as symptoms of revolution and become figures of the Egyptian apocalypse. Yet, when the officials in their funerary inscriptions stress their sinlessness: "I did not rob the poor," "I have not taken away a man's daughter, nor his land, either," they suggest that their colleagues were more rapacious. No independent evidence about the behavior of the officials of the Middle Kingdom has come to light as yet. But toward the end of the twelfth century, a scribe freed a tomb robber for a bribe. The gang repaid the loss to its unlucky member and continued its operations undisturbed.

Our perspective of the Middle Kingdom may, however, be distorted, since we lack comparable material from the Old Kingdom. Posterity regarded the language of the Middle Kingdom as classic. When it became fashionable to place scrolls in coffins as a kind of viaticum, these classics accompanied the dead, and in this way, and also in school copies, some writings of the Middle Kingdom have come down to us. On the other hand, from Old Kingdom literature, the later scribes appreciated and copied only advice given to budding bureaucrats. Thus, some views expressed by the authors of the Twelfth Dynasty may have been taken from older books now lost, and, therefore, may have been less startling to their contemporaries than they are to us.

It seems that the new feature of the Middle Kingdom was its emphatic style. The kings and their generals not only boasted of victories, but swore that their reports were true. A king erected his statue in conquered Nubia to mark the new boundary. He says that the statue was made in order that "you might prosper because of it, and fight for it." Statues of this period are often colossal, more than fifty feet in height, but the faces are grim and sad. We can even see the bags under the eyes. To please his patrons, the artist stressed the fatigue and worry of the pharaoh, worn down by his responsibilities. The sculptors of the Old Kingdom,* no less masters of their craft, were more reserved. They, and their pharaohs,* knew more of kings and kingship than they chose to express.

Nothing succeeds like success. Toward the middle of the nineteenth century the pharaohs could suppress the "great chiefs," and the whole land was now administered direct from the palace. The pharaohs extended their power up to and beyond the second cataract. Egyptian influence was consolidated in southern Syria; in the last decades of the nineteenth century the rulers of Byblos used hieroglyphs and Egyptian titles.

The affluence of the river lands, in Egypt as in Mesopotamia, attracted the hungry dwellers of the deserts bordering the streams. A document of the nineteenth century mentions some Bedouin offering "to serve the pharaoh" since "the desert was dying of hunger." The Egyptian border post in Nubia turned them back. No unauthorized Nubian was permitted to go downstream; when Nubians came down for trade, they were sent back next morning to the place whence they had come. A system of fortresses with ditches, ramparts, and bastions from which the archers could shoot arrows in three directions, controlled the southern entrance to Egypt.

A more or less similar control was exercised at the Isthmus of Suez. But the bedouin from Palestine were not excluded from Egypt. When the famine was sore in his land, Abraham went down to sojourn in Egypt. Egyptian texts about 2000, and again in the thirteenth century, state that Asiatic herdsmen "as a favor" were permitted to enter Egypt, "to keep them and their cattle alive."

After the middle of the eighteenth century, the "wretched Asiatics" somehow succeeded in conquering lower Egypt. Following Egyptian tradition we call these invaders Hyksos, that is, "rulers of foreign lands." In the same period, before or after the Hyksos, native princes seized control of the territories south of Elephantine. Even in many districts of upper Egypt power was seized by local magnates. At last, toward the middle of the sixteenth century, the princes of Thebes undertook a patriotic war against the Hyksos and their Egyptian allies who "had forsaken Egypt their mistress." The Hyksos were driven out, Nubia was reconquered, and Thebes again became the capital of a united Egypt. The "New Kingdom" began.

THE NEW KINGDOM

The New Kingdom (about 1550–1100) was a period of military expansion, that is, of enrichment. War was, until the industrial revolution, the fastest and the most direct way of capital accumulation. Booty and, afterward, the tribute of conquered lands stimulated the economy. The skill of captured and enslaved craftsmen sustained the economic growth. That the pharaohs extended the boundaries of Egypt in accordance with the command of gods was not surprising. The pharaoh Sesostris I, in the twentieth century, said of the sun god of Heliopolis: He makes himself rich when he makes me conquer. The great hall of the Karnak temple, a forest of 144 stone shafts, each fifty feet high, cool on the hottest day, the two colossi of Amenhotep III, almost seventy feet high, the treasure of the tomb of Tutankhamen, and the mighty obelisks of Thutmoses III that now stand in Istanbul, Rome, London, and New York, thus fulfilling his hope that his name might endure forever and ever—all these wonders were paid for with the plunder of Nubia and Syria. The simplest soldiers profited from a successful campaign. They were "drunk and anointed with oil every day as at a feast in Egypt."

We do not know how much of the new wealth percolated to the

nameless toilers of Egypt who had no means to erect tombs. But documents show that the bastinado and the shout of the taskmaster, "The rod is in my hand, be not idle!" were only a part of the real life. For instance, an official reported about 1230 that three peasants of a royal domain ran away after having been beaten by the manager, and now there were none to till the royal land. The workmen at the royal tombs lived in pleasant two-room houses which were gaily decorated (dancing girls, protective spirits), and at least some of them read the perennial classics. They received decent salaries in kind, had a lunch break, three days of rest monthly, plus many days off on the occasions of festivals: they rejoiced until sunset at the accession of a new pharaoh. Disputes among them were settled by judges from their village. They even went on strike, "because of hunger and thirst" when rations were in arrears. And they had their own burial chambers in the mountain near their village. But they were a privileged, hereditary group.

Yet these glimpses of real life are rare. Equally rare is evidence about technical advances during the New Kingdom: the yoke resting on the necks of the cattle (it was previously lashed to the horns), wheeled cars, shadoofs for watering gardens, bellows for blacksmiths, the introduction of a new breed of rams and also of the chicken, "a bird that gives birth every day," and so on. Our sources, the eulogies of the dead and the self-praises of the pharaohs, speak to posterity and hence are not directly concerned with the routine of life.

For the same reason we know little about the meanings of changes which suddenly become visible. Experience taught the Egyptians that even pyramids cannot protect the corpse; therefore—many concluded —let us eat, drink, and be merry. But why did a scribe of the New Kingdom, like Horace and Horace's imitators in later ages, proclaim that literary works outlive the pyramids? In the sixteenth century Egyptian scribes began to visit ancient monuments as sightseers. One scribbled on a wall: "I have visited the pyramid of Zoser. It is beautiful." Why was he so much concerned about antiquities? The increase of interest in the past is an important novelty. Again, we can understand that affluence brings self-indulgence. Women in diaphanous dresses and unclad dancing girls people the decorations of the tombs in the fourteenth century. Yet in the no less affluent thirteenth century scantily clothed girls disappear from the walls—in one reused tomb such figures were repainted to show them decently dressed—and funerary subjects replaced the scenes of eternal happiness. The deceased now was not enjoying a festival in his garden, but praying prostrated under a palm.

How are we to understand the strangest figure of Egyptian history, the Pharaoh Ikhnaton, who about 1370 undertook to reform the religion of Egypt? Some fifteen years later, after his death, his memory was damned, his residence city, which we call Amarna, about 160 miles south of modern Cairo, abandoned, and the old faith restored. The artificialities of Amarna art, which appeal to modern taste, and the anachronistic interpretation of Ikhnaton as a forerunner of Jesus, have made the name of this deformed and sullen pharaoh well known. He is described as the first monotheist. In fact, he proclaimed the solar disk as his own deity. Ikhnaton means, "Serviceable to the sun disk." He addresses the disk as, "Thou sole god, like to whom there is none other." In the language of polytheism this would mean that the god in question was the preferred one, but Ikhnaton eventually came to worship no other god. Moreover, he claimed that he alone knew the god and was its sole representative on earth. In the private houses and tombs at Amarna, paintings and reliefs expressed the new "Doctrine of Life": Ikhnaton and his family prayed to the sun. Its rays blessed them. His subjects prayed to him. The reform was not monotheistic but egocentric, although its intolerance resembled that of monotheism. Throughout Egypt the names of the other gods were obliterated. According to Egyptian belief the destruction of the name destroyed the person. We need not wonder why Egypt did not revolt. The army remained faithful to the legitimate pharaoh.

The natural path of Egyptian expansion lay up the Nile. Between 1550 and 1450 the pharaohs of the New Kingdom, following the steps of their predecessors, colonized and Egyptianized the gold producing land of Nubia, advancing the frontier to the fourth cataract. The savages to the south could not endanger the pharaonic forces. Despite some setbacks, Egypt held the greater part of Nubia securely almost to the end of the second millennium, and when the southern province finally became independent its rulers remained the devoted protégés of Amon-Re of Thebes.

FOR FURTHER READING

Cambridge Ancient History, 3 ed., Vols. I–II
J. Černy, *Ancient Egyptian Religion*
W. Emery, *Archaic Egypt*

A. Erman, *The Ancient Egyptians: A Sourcebook of Their Writings*
A. Gardiner, *Egypt of the Pharaohs*
W. W. Hallo and W. K. Simpson, *The Ancient Near East*

B.C.	Dates are approximated to the nearest decade
1550	Hyksos expelled from Egypt; new model Egyptian army using chariotry and composite bows
1525	Thutmoses I claims Syria to the Euphrates; consequent war with Mitanni intermittent until 1410
1500	Invention of alphabetic writing in Syria
1400	The palaces of Crete destroyed; Mycenaean Greeks dominant in the eastern Mediterranean
1375–1350	The Amarna Age; Ikhnaton's religious reforms; Egypt paralyzed by internal problems; Hittite expansion destroys Mitanni
1300	Egyptian revival; wars with the Hittites for Syria
1270	Peace between Ramses II and the Hittites
1230	Egypt invaded by the "sea peoples"; Troy destroyed by the Mycenaeans
1200	Iron begins to come into common use; the palace of Pylos burned; beginning of the breakup of Mycenaean power
1190	The Philistines (one of the "sea peoples") settle along the Palestinian coast
1100	Egypt loses Nubia; camels in common use in north Arabia; use of lime plaster to make watertight cisterns opens dry areas for settlement

5
EMPIRES AND THEIR FALL

SYRIA AND ITS CITIES

Syria and Palestine differed greatly from Egypt, although the Egyptian influence was here recognizable as early as 2700. Cities like Byblos and Ugarit were older than Memphis and on a level with Thebes as centers of civilization. Ugarit (modern Ras Shamra) on the Syrian coast opposite the easternmost cape of Cyprus controlled more than eighty towns and villages lying in a territory of about forty square miles. The city could equip 150 seagoing ships for a trading expedition. Seven languages, from Cypriote to Sumerian, and five scripts occur in Ugaritic documents of the thirteenth century. The legal system was highly developed, for instance Ugaritic texts distinguish between the service to be rendered to the king by an official owing to his rank, and his duties as a grantee of royal land. The Ugaritic language is akin to Hebrew, and the texts written in this language illustrate a civilization closely akin to that of Canaan (Palestine) on the eve of the Hebrew settlement. The mythological tales of Ugarit narrate deeds of Baal* and other gods whom the Hebrews rejected. On the other hand, Ugaritic documents mention names and

MAP II
THE LATE BRONZE AGE

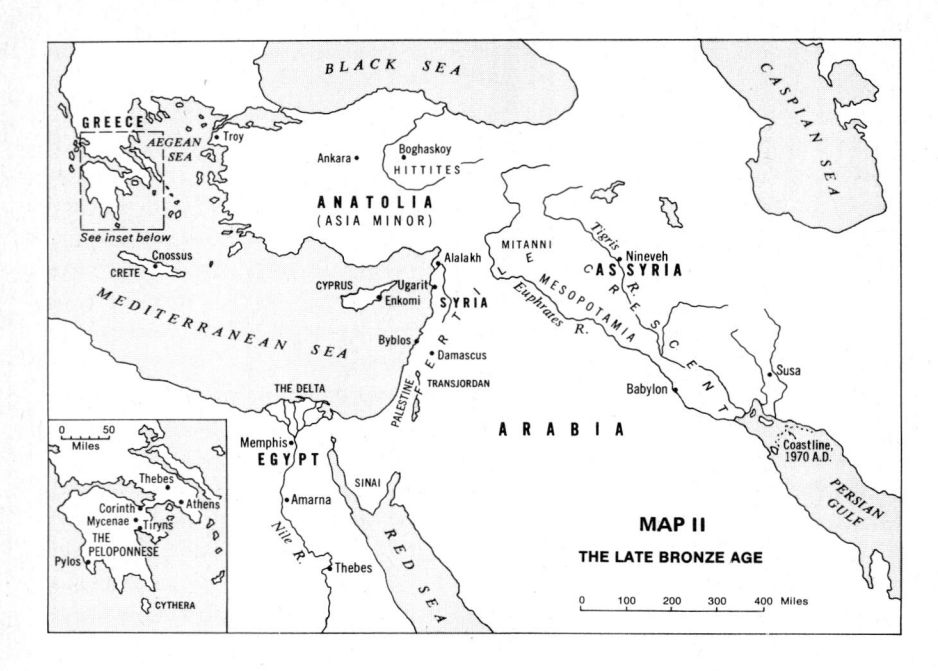

details that also appear in Biblical narratives, for instance, Abraham, or the adoption of a grandson by the grandfather, a legal act also reported of Jacob with regard to Ephraim and Manasseh (Gen. 48:5).

By contrast to Nubia, Syria remained to a considerable degree culturally independent of Egypt and indebted to Babylon. Even in the days of Egyptian supremacy the chieftains of Syria salaaming before the pharaoh ("Seven and seven times I fall at the feet of my lord") did so in the Babylonian language. During the New Kingdom, the worship of Syrian gods became popular in Egypt. The pharaoh Ramses II named his favorite daughter "Daughter of Anath" after the Semitic goddess of war also worshiped in Ugarit.

The pharaoh Thutmoses I, about 1525, announced by anticipation that his empire extended from the third cataract of the Nile to the "inverted water" of the Euphrates, which unlike the Nile, runs from north to south. Afterward he actually reached the Euphrates. Two of his successors in the fifteenth century repeated the same feat. Well into the thirteenth century the pharaohs dreamed of the Euphrates frontier, and in the meantime tried to control as much of Syria as they could.

HORSES, CHARIOTS, AND BOWS

The conquest of Syria and her wealth began in earnest when the pharaohs mastered the instrument that made this task realizable: the horse. Horses were known in Mesopotamia as early as the twenty-first century: a Sumerian king proudly compared himself to a swift horse. On the upper Euphrates and in Asia Minor in the eighteenth century the horse was often harnessed to vehicles. But a longer time was needed for adapting the horse to the needs of warfare. The animal was really a pony, about fifty to sixty inches in height.* Moreover, these horses were not gelded—a mare in heat could stampede a whole camp. Hence until the thirteenth century horses were rarely used for riding. But two ponies harnessed to a light wooden chariot could transport a driver and a rider,* who shot arrows from a composite bow that had an effective range of more than 600 feet. For the first time men possessed a mobile missile force which could destroy the enemy swiftly and definitively. The pharaohs now boasted of their knowledge of horseflesh and prowess in archery and other sports, while pictures in tombs represented the owners transported in horse drawn vehicles to their estates.

The new weapon was very expensive. A horse cost as much as several slaves. Fine materials and perfect craftmanship were necessary for making chariots and composite bows. A pharaoh tried 300 bows before selecting his own (which nobody but he could bend, just as no other man could draw the bow of Odysseus). Only rich and industrially advanced states could afford chariotry.

Unfortunately for the pharaohs of the New Kingdom, the sight of their chariots on the Euphrates was bound to provoke other great powers. Here again, to use Napoleon's maxim, geography explains history. Desert separated the Mediterranean coastlands of Syria from Mesopotamia, except in the north where the Euphrates linked them. Northern Syria also offered the best passage between Asia Minor and the lands to the south. The copper of Cyprus reached the continent through the ports in the same region. As long as the pharaohs remained below Byblos and Damascus, they did not threaten the security of the powers outside Syria. But Egyptian control of the hub of communication lines in northern Syria hurt the cities of this region and the interests of such powers as the Mitanni beyond the upper Euphrates and the Hittites in Asia Minor. These potential adversaries also had chariots and archers. A poet of Ugarit described the invention of the composite bow and said the goddess of war killed the inventor in order to appropriate the weapon. At Ugarit not only the crew of a chariot but sometimes the horses were clad in mail. The

Hittite kings used chariotry as early as 1600, and their chariots in the fourteenth century held a crew of three. The pharaoh and his rivals in Syria fought with the same weapons, and no victory was ever final.

THE INTERNATIONAL CULTURE

The struggle for Syria continued for almost the whole third quarter of the second millennium (1500–1250). Between the campaigns, the courts entertained amicable relations; rulers on the Euphrates and in Asia Minor exchanged gifts and letters with the pharaohs. The king of Babylon, when he fell sick, expected to receive the pharaoh's condolences, and the statue of the goddess Ishtar traveled from Nineveh to Thebes to help an ailing pharaoh. The Asiatic kings sent their daughters with fitting retinues (for instance 317 girl servants) into the pharaoh's harem. But a king of Babylon was curtly rebuked for asking for an Egyptian princess in exchange. (He then begged the pharaoh to send him any good-looking Egyptian girl with a big dowry: who would dare to say she was not a princess?) Marriages were a form of international trade. And international trade, like domestic, was not above bazaar tricks and bargaining. A king of Mitanni discovered that statues of gold sent him from Egypt were of gilded wood.

These transactions, the diplomatic correspondence, and the intermittent wars exemplified the interdependence of the lands of the Levant. It was the first international age of the Near East. The courts from Susa to Thebes corresponded in the same Babylonian language, and from the Black Sea to Nubia chariotry dominated the military art. The use of this weapon required professional soldiers, and the new military technology changed the social structure. In Asia Minor and Syria the chariot warriors received fiefs in return for military service. In some Syrian cities they formed a kind of nobility, membership in which was conferred by the ruler. One of these feudal lords of Ugarit possessed 2,000 horses. Even in Egypt the military,* enriched by the wars, came into the forefront of the society. The pharaohs now affected uniform. When the Eighteenth Dynasty became extinct, three generals in succession ascended the throne, and the last of them founded the Nineteenth Dynasty. One of these crowned generals says that he gave the temples of Egypt priests chosen from the pick of the army. In other words, the military appropriated the choicest tidbits of the Egyptian economy.

THE HITTITES

The other phenomenon of the new Levant was the emergence of a new great power. The troops fighting the Egyptian armies in the fourteenth century were directed from a faraway capital near the Black Sea, and when the peace came, it was followed by marriage between a pharaoh and a Hittite princess from Asia Minor.

The Hittite capital was Hattushash, modern Bogazköy, some 110 miles east of Ankara, the capital of Turkey. Thousands of clay tablets inscribed in cuneiform characters from the royal archives were found here. The grammatical structure of the Hittite language relates it to the Indo-European group, but the vocabulary is mainly that of the non-Indo-European indigenous peoples of Anatolia. The Indo-European invaders had completely forgotten their ancestral gods, and the civilization of the Hittites was essentially derived from Mesopotamia.

From their capital the Hittite kings with varying success extended their supremacy over a great part of Asia Minor. They preferred indirect domination: a conquered country or city became a vassal of the Hittites. About the middle of the fourteenth century, having destroyed the kingdom of the Mitanni in northern Mesopotamia, they took over its Syrian dependencies and its role in the struggle with Egypt. About 1270 the struggle ended in stalemate. Ramses II made peace with the Hittites, who preserved their sphere of influence in northern Syria.

RAMSES II AND THE SEA PEOPLES

Ramses II was the last imperial ruler of Egypt. His fame reached Greek tradition and, through it, English poetry. He is the Ozymandias of Shelley. He fathered 162 children during his reign of 67 years, raised some of the more colossal colossi (his statue at Abu Simbel is about 66 feet high), and covered the walls of his enormous temples* with vainglorious pictures and inscriptions. "Look on my works, ye Mighty, and despair!" Today the tourists view his legless statue, 34 feet long, lying in the sand near Cairo, and stare at his mummy in the Cairo Museum. "Nothing beside remains."

Unknown to Ramses II and his Hittite rival, movements and inventions of little men were soon to end the might of the Hittites and to make the splendor of Egypt obsolete. About 1230, five years after Ramses' death, the "sea peoples" began to descend on Egypt. For some fifty years the pharaohs had to fight off migratory invaders by sea and by land. We do not know who these peoples were or whence they came, nor are we sure how much they had to do with the collapse of the Near Eastern empires that began during the time when they were active. We do know that the Hittite empire fell shortly after 1200, and we may guess that it was the "sea peoples" who at about this time destroyed the cities of Syria and Palestine (which received this name from the Philistines, one of the "sea peoples" who settled there). Egypt survived but lost her empire in Asia.

TECHNOLOGICAL DEVELOPMENTS, IRON AND THE ALPHABET

Then, about 1100, the pharaohs lost Nubia, and for some four centuries Egypt, torn by internal dissensions, did not count in world politics. Blessed by the Nile, Egypt could afford to stand still while camel, lime plaster, iron, and alphabet changed the mentality of men and the equilibrium of political forces in Asia. By the end of the twelfth century men had trained camels to work for them, and camel caravans crossing the sand wastes changed the life of the countries around the Arabian desert. About the same time men learned to store rain water in cisterns lined with the new waterproof lime plaster. Much arid land now became habitable.

Iron, if fortified with carbon, is stronger than bronze, but its smelting demands special knowledge and it has to be shaped by hammer at red heat. Knowledge of how to smelt it was probably acquired about 2500 in Asia Minor, but only about 1400 did smiths learn how to produce (by repeated hammering and reheating at temperatures of 900 to 1400 degrees centigrade) a form that was less breakable than bronze. By the tenth century, iron plow tips made tilling of heavy soil possible in Palestine and elsewhere. As heavy soils give better crops than light soils, iron raised food production and thus stimulated the growth of the population. The main advantage of iron, however, was the wide distribution of iron ore, which is 500 times more common than copper. Even a small, low-grade iron deposit in the neighborhood was sufficient to free a city or tribe from dependence on distant sources of copper, tin, and lead.

The creation of the alphabet* was the most important advance in the transmission of knowledge between the invention of writing and that of printing. After 1500, scribes in Syria, trying to invent a script for their Semitic dialects, hit on the device of a consonant alphabet. Hieroglyphs indicated sometimes sounds, sometimes words, sometimes general notions; the cuneiform script was mainly syllabic and equally complex. But the inventors of the alphabet used signs to represent the ultimate particles, the "elements," as Augustine says, of writing, the single sounds of which syllables and words are built. In Ugarit an alphabet of 31 characters was already in use about 1400, and the scribes arranged the signs in essentially the same ABC order* as the letters of our alphabet. About the same time there appeared the first predecessors of the Phoenician* alphabet from which, via Greece and Rome, our alphabet has descended. The knowledge of hundreds of signs was necessary for both the hieroglyphic and the cuneiform script; this limited literacy to trained professionals. No great effort was needed to memorize two or three dozen alphabetic characters; now anyone could learn to read and write. The alphabet is democratic.

CYPRUS AND THE AEGEAN, CRETE, MYCENAE

Our survey of the Bronze Age has centered on the Levant, particularly Egypt and Babylonia, two main sources of civilization. Now we must sketch the role of the Aegean region, the future Greek world, which in the Bronze Age was the outer province of the Levantine civilization, and our sketch must begin with Cyprus and Crete, as well as mainland Greece and the Aegean islands.

Cyprus lies only 43 miles from Asia Minor and 76 from Syria. The north wind, as Homer says, carried a sailing ship from Crete to Egypt in five days, and chains of small islands linked Crete with Asia Minor and the mainland of Greece. About 6000 the art of farming reached Cyprus and Greece; 500 years later came pottery making. Corinth and Athens were settled before Babylon and Memphis. The Stone Age settlements in Greece and in the Aegean Islands lay mostly on or near the eastern coast, and Greece always turned eastward. Yet, for a long time, the Aegean peoples remained behind the advance in the Levant. Copper appeared in the Greek world only in the first, and bronze only in the last, centuries of the third millennium. But then, about 2000, the whole Aegean region became involved in the Levantine economy. Texts from Mari mention copper from Cyprus and imports from Crete. By the beginning of the sixteenth century, pupils in Egyptian scribal schools learned Cretan names. In the fifteenth century inscribed cylinder seals from Babylonia reached Thebes in Greece. The architecture and the frescoes of Cretan palaces imitated the arts of the Levant and were themselves imitated in Syria and Egypt.

These palace complexes appear in Crete about 2000 and some centuries later in Greece, where, until about 1400, the Cretan taste prevailed alike in feminine fashions and the form of shields. The unity of civilization in the future Greek region is striking in religion: there were no temples; the deities, foremost of whom was a great goddess, were worshiped out of doors or in house chapels and caves. Yet, in several respects the "Minoans," as we name the inhabitants of Crete after their legendary king Minos, and the "Mycenaeans," as the inhabitants of Greece are called after Mycenae, the city of Homeric Agamemnon, were different nations. The ideal Minoan was a lithe and slender person. Men shaved. The golden life-size masks of the Mycenaean rulers show large, bearded faces. The Cretan palaces were originally protected by bastions, but soon the fortifications disappeared, and Cretan art shows society life, acrobats, and the beauty of nature, from bull to octopus. The Mycenaeans liked to represent battle scenes* and hunting, and many of their palaces were built as parts of enormous fortifications which, like the acropolis of a Greek city, served as a refuge in time of war. Crowned by a relief of two heraldic lions protecting a column, a symbol of the palace, the gate of the acropolis of Mycenae* is the earliest historical relic of Europe: Agamemnon—if there was an Agamemnon—passed through this gate to make war on Troy. Cretan rulers were mummified in Egyptian manner, but built no pyramids. The enormous royal tombs of the Mycenaeans—the so-called Treasury of Atreus in Mycenae has a dome 43 feet high and 46 feet wide—were unknown in Crete.

A profusion of gold and silver objects found in these tombs, and the splendor of the palaces discovered in Crete and at Pylos, at the Bay of Navarino in the Peloponnese, evidence the wealth of the Aegean rulers in the second millennium. Some of this wealth percolated down to their subjects. Houses in the Cretan village were even furnished with clay pipes for sewage. But we do not know how this wealth was procured. Neither Greece nor Crete had natural riches. It seems that in the second millennium Greece and Crete carried goods between Europe and the Levant. The same neck rings were used from Syria to Scandinavia. Amber beads from the Baltic Sea reached Greece via the Adriatic. Fourteenth-century faïence beads, originally fabricated in Egypt, but probably imitated and certainly traded by the Mycenaeans, have been found as far afield as England and the Caucasus. An Egyptian list compiled about 1400 mentions Knossus, Cythera (an island between Crete and the Peloponnese), and Nauplia, the ancient port for Mycenae. It is hardly by chance that Knossus, the greatest Cretan settlement, faced Greece.

The Aegean peoples who colonized Cyprus were also craftsmen. An industrial city, Alasia, protected by a stone wall, flourished in copper-rich Cyprus (at modern Enkomi) in the second half of the second millennium. A ship wrecked off the southern coast of Turkey about 1200 carried ingots and metal implements from Cyprus.

In the fifteenth century the Mycenaeans, for unknown reasons, got the upper hand. (Perhaps most Minoan centers were ruined by earthquakes.) In Egyptian texts the term for Cretans disappeared. Between roughly 1400 and 1250, Mycenaean pottery was popular from Italy to the Turkish coast; potters in Crete and Cyprus imitated the new mode.

From this "all-Mycenaean" period we have texts we can understand. Writing appeared in Crete as early as the beginning of the second millennium, and the earliest signs are already simplifications of pictograms. Neither this writing nor that used in Cyprus has been wholly deciphered. But Michael Ventris (1922–1956), an English amateur, decoded the syllabic script of some ninety signs used in Greece and in Crete (Knossus) in the fourteenth and thirteenth centuries. The deciphered language was pre-Homeric Greek. Except for some words incised on seals and vases we know this language only from inscribed clay tablets that were preserved because they became baked in conflagrations. The unbaked tablets as well as any texts written on perishable materials (papyrus, leather, wood?) have disappeared without a trace.

About two-thirds of the signs we read are proper names, among them the names of gods, which are Greek: Zeus,* Poseidon, "the Mistress Athena,"* and so on. The rest of the words are mostly names of objects and crafts. We learn what we already knew or could surmise: the Mycenaeans had chariots and smiths. The interpretation of terms referring to social relations, for instance to landholding, remains tentative. Yet the tablets show the working of a bureaucratic apparatus similar to that of Sumer. Again tablets were "filed" and labeled according to content, and the condition of every chariot wheel in the stores was recorded.

Clay tablets inscribed with signs similar to the earliest Sumerian script have been found also in Rumania. The use of clay tablets indicates a Mesopotamian model. Yet, the Creto-Mycenaean script owes nothing to the cuneiform. It does not fit the Greek language either, and for this reason the meanings of many words remain unknown or doubtful. The script was probably borrowed from some people of Asia Minor. The tablets show that in the second half of the second millennium the Mycenaeans spoke Greek. In the absence of earlier texts, however, we cannot know how old was the use of Greek in the Aegean world.

Empires and civilizations are sometimes short-lived. Prosperous and apparently secure about 1300, the Mycenaean world disintegrated before 1100. The palace of Pylos was burned about 1200, but the palace of Tiryns near Mycenae existed well into the twelfth century, and the citadel of Mycenae may have burned only toward the end of that century. The acropolis of Athens continued to be inhabited without interruption. Numerous sites were abandoned or lost their former importance, but other cities often rose in the neighborhood. Argos inherited Mycenae. When Alasia (modern Enkomi) in Cyprus, a center of bronze industry, declined in the eleventh century, perhaps because of the silting of her harbor, her role was immediately taken over by the neighboring Salamis. When Salamis was destroyed by earthquakes in A.D. 332 and 342, it was rebuilt as Constantia. When Constantia was destroyed by the Arabs in A.D. 647, the city was succeeded by its old rival, Arsinoë, the medieval and modern Famagusta, two miles off. It is true, however, that no palaces of the post-Mycenaean period, or other evidence of wealth, have yet been found in the Aegean region. For three or four centuries our evidence is essentially limited to pottery shards. When the "Dark Age" ends, in the eighth century, the Aegean region is Greek, and only the sagas of Agamemnon, of Nestor, and of the "Homeric" heroes preserve for the Greeks the memory of the proto-Greeks who built the palaces of Mycenae and Pylos.

FOR FURTHER READING

J. Chadwick, *The Decipherment of Linear B*
O. Gurney, *The Hittites*
R. Higgins, *Minoan and Mycenean Art*
N. Platon, *Crete*
L. Woolley, *A Forgotten Kingdom*

6
GODS AND MEN

THE ROLE OF THE GODS IN ANCIENT THOUGHT

The preceding survey would have disappointed a Babylonian or an Egyptian scribe and, probably, a Mycenaean Greek. They would have said that it ignored the real causes of events: the gods.* When the supreme god is angry with a land, says a late Egyptian sage, he exalts its humble people and humbles its mighty people. If the city of Ur was destroyed by barbarian invaders about 2000, it happened because Enlil, "the lord of all lands," sent the "evil storm" against the city. The gods sometimes acted arbitrarily, but generally they rewarded piety and punished evildoers. Men believed in the premise, without which no society can endure, that good men prosper; and goodness was equated with piety. Therefore, an illness or a defeat was a punishment for sin. The loser had offended the gods. When the glorious dynasty of Sargon was overthrown by the barbarians, the reason for the catastrophe was obvious to Babylonian scribes: Enlil, the god of Nippur, had punished the land because Naram-Sin, a king of Sargon's line, had sacked Nippur. Encircled by the enemy, Ramses II appealed to Amon, his divine father. "Has a father forgotten his son? Have I ever disobeyed your command? Have I not filled your temple with my booty? Can Amon care for the wretched Asiatics who do not know god. . . ." And Amon saved the pharaoh. "Worship your god daily . . . sacrifice prolongs life, and prayer expiates guilt." As Voltaire (speaking of the Jews) acutely observed, this view saved the self-respect of the loser. Even more, it encouraged him to hope for revenge.

This conception mirrors the reign of justice within any organized human society. The phenomena of nature—the alternation of seasons and rhythm of stars—were unrelated to man's deserts. Social life alone presupposed and expressed a moral order. Man did not learn the idea of law from nature, but imposed it on the forces of nature and on the gods whom he invented to control these forces. Man was not yet interested in any causality that he was unable to influence. A weak link in the chain of beings, terrorized by lion and wolf, snake and scorpion, he regarded beasts as his peers and rivals. To set himself above them he relied, among other things, on his knowledge of the past which enabled him to face the future with courage and intelligence. King Naram-Sin allegedly described one of his wars in order to teach future rulers not to become pusillanimous in the face of a barbarian invasion.

Happily for the godly man, the gods would indicate his future in dreams, and also by oracles, prophecies, and signs. Thus, in Babylonia, history was the servant of prognostication. From the twenty-fourth century on, the scribes collected and transmitted omens and their consequences. For instance, the lungs of a victim sacrificed by King Ibbi-Sin of Ur, about 2000, were deformed. Later the land rose against the king. A new occurrence of the same sign would foretell the same kind of trouble. There were also other kinds of omens which were derived from behavior of animals, from dreams, and so on. The idea that gods "write" their message on the liver and other organs of a sacrificed animal was an Akkadian concept which later, via scribal schools, reached Greece and Italy.

Enlil was the god of storm and Amon-Re the sun god. A god was a doer, who did this or that. In Sumerian Lagash, in the twenty-second century, theologians invented second-class gods to work for the great god, Ningirsu: one shepherded his asses, another took care of water levels in the city's canals, and so on; he had a complete staff of divine domestic servants, and public officials, since each human profession and office needed its patron deity. As nature and mentality were essentially the same from the Indus to the Nile, the same functions were attributed to gods who bore different names according to the languages of their worshipers. The Hittites named the storm god Teshub; Arinna was their sun goddess, and so on. This does not mean that the pagans worshiped the phenomena of nature. A would-be reformer like Ikhnaton might limit his devotion to the sun disc itself, but most men of the ancient world believed that, beside the physical object, there was a "personal" deity, usually—except, perhaps, in Egypt—conceived as human in form. The anthropomorphic personification, to use our language, made the driver responsible for the good and evil that his car—the sun or storm—might do. By thus understanding phenomena in anthropomorphic terms, men tried to deal with what they could not control. From our point of view it is ridiculous to say that Amon saved Ramses II in the battle at Kadesh. But our explanations are often no less metaphoric. For instance, scholars say that after 1200, the "dynamic power" of Egyptian civilization was dead. One advantage of such circumlocutions is that they mean nothing and for this reason do not prevent further search, whereas reference to Amon made the explanation final. Another is that Amon required a priesthood and tangible sacrifices; "dynamic power" requires only sacrifice of the intelligence.

A Greek philosopher of the sixth century B.C. observed that if cattle and horses could make images they would represent their gods as cattle and horses. Aristotle noted that men imagine not only the forms of the gods but their ways of life to be like our own. Long before Aristotle the cities of men had become models for the heavenly city of the gods, who were thought of as superkings.

THE HISTORY AND DAILY LIFE OF THE GODS

According to Sumerian and Babylonian belief men were created to free the gods from work. A story, originally Sumerian, told of a time when the lesser gods had to toil on earth, digging canals and so on for the sustenance of the great gods in heaven. At last, the lesser gods refused to work and burned their tools. So the great gods manufactured men who now work for both the great and the lesser gods. But after making men the gods began to suffer from "noise pollution." Men were so noisy that "the land was bellowing like a bull" and the great gods could not sleep. The gods, therefore, destroyed mankind by a flood. But then there was no one to offer sacrifices and the gods, lacking sacrifices, went hungry. So they allowed a man who had been saved from the flood (the Babylonian "Noah") to restore the human race. Although by making some women barren, others nuns, and by sending demons to make babies die, the gods limit the multiplication of the human species, they do permit some men to live, so that the service of the gods can be maintained.

Like a king, a god lived in his palace, "the house of the god," which we inexactly call a "temple." Like the royal palace, the house of a god was not accessible to a common man. "The servants of the god," whom we call "priests," fed, clothed, amused, and otherwise took care of their masters. It was easy to understand the behavior of deities. A Hittite instruction for temple officials puts the doctrine neatly: "Are the minds of men and of the gods different? No. If a servant stands before his master he must be clean and attentive, and when the master has eaten and drunk, he is relaxed and kind. But if the servant is negligent, the master will punish him and his kin. Likewise, if a man angers a god, the god will destroy him, his kin, his cattle and crops. Hence, be very reverent as to the words of a god." Accordingly, we can understand the flood story. On the other hand, when Era, god of pestilence, ravaged the land, making no distinction between good and evil men, he was stopped at last by the other gods, because, without their subjects, whence would they get their food offerings?

THE COMMON THEOLOGY OF THE ANCIENT NEAR EAST

The anthropomorphic view of the divine world united the religious thought of the ancient Near East. Consequently its theological material exhibits one overall pattern.

Prayer is the link between worshiper and deity. The prayer praises the god to whom it is addressed: He is the greatest of gods, nay, the only (true) god. Thus, he can and, therefore, must help the worshiper. The petitioner's claim may be supported by reference to his need: "O Amon, give ear to one who is alone in the law court, who is poor.... May it be found that the poor man is vindicated. May the poor man surpass the rich," prays an Egyptian of the thirteenth century. About 1300, a Hittite queen prayed to the sun goddess, the divine protectress of her land: "Among men there is a saying: 'To a woman in travail the god grants her wish.'" Since the queen is (soon to be) in travail, the sun goddess must grant life to her sick husband. Ramses IV petitioned Osiris to grant him high Nile floods so that he might make offerings to the gods and preserve his country: Osiris made the people and cannot abandon them. A god must help because he is father and king of his people; he cleanses sin, comforts the afflicted, and punishes evildoers. In short, he is both feared and loved. Thus, the workers on the royal tombs at Thebes prayed to Amon the "beloved god who listens to humble requests"; they knew that "though the servant was disposed to evil, yet the Lord [Amon] was disposed to be merciful."

Like a king, the god would punish men who offended him and would reward those who did what he wanted. Men placated him by sacrifices and gifts, but also by their righteousness. Although arbitrary and often immoral rulers, the gods, like earthly kings, insisted on the observance of law and order by their subjects. The rules of morality being virtually the same in the whole Levant, the list of sins was the same in all religions: taking the life or wife of another, false accusation, not giving water to one who asked for it, and so on. Except for the prohibition of the worship of other gods and the interdiction of idolatry, the Ten Commandments had been repeatedly prescribed in teaching—and broken in practice—ages before Moses. And several centuries before Jesus a Babylonian sage wrote down the rule: "Requite with good the man who wrongs you."

The more the gods became a sort of corporate directorate, the more an individual believer needed a "customer's man," a god for himself alone, to whom he paid constant devotion and from whom he expected personal attention. In twenty-first century Lagash, children were named after the goddess Bau three times more often than after her august husband Ningirsu, the city's chief god. The Babylonian often carried a seal showing him introduced to a high god by his personal god or some other minor deity. King Adadnirari of Assyria (810–782) proclaimed: "Trust Nabu, do not trust another god."

In this way, what we call personal piety was born. The mother of Nabonidus, the last Babylonian king (556–539), was a devotee of Sin and three other gods of the city of Haran. From her childhood she sought after them. When Sin was angry with his city and went off to heaven, so that Haran was destroyed, she laid hold on the hem of his robe. Day and night she prayed for his return, she fasted, wore a torn dress, and praised Sin. After fifty-four years of desolation, Nabonidus, her son, restored the temple of Sin. Now, at the age of ninety-five, she prayed to Sin for her son: "Let him not offend thee." (But she added, "Endure not his wickedness.")

The essential unity of theological thinking made unification of the pantheon possible. About 2100, in Sumerian Lagash, all local gods were considered members of the family or staff (musician, architect, and so on) of the principal god Ningirsu. Gods of different cities were similarly coordinated. The theologians of Memphis declared that Ptah of Memphis had created all and had brought the other gods into being; Horus, Thoth, and Atum (the principal god of Heliopolis and, in an earlier theology, creator of the world) were forms of Ptah. The same tendency operated on the international level. Arinna was not only "the mistress of the Hatti lands," but also "the queen of all the countries." "In the Hatti country thou bearest the name of the Sun-goddess Arinna, but in the land which thou madest the cedar land [Syria], thou bearest the name Hebat." At least the main deities became international. In the middle of the twelfth century, according to an Egyptian report, the prince of Byblos recognized that the Egyptian Amon provided for all lands. As early as 2000, worshipers were called upon to proclaim the greatness of this or that god everywhere. When Ramses II appealed to Amon for help he exclaimed: "What will men say if even a little thing befall him who bends himself to your advice?" The gods had to pay a decent respect to the opinion of mankind.

FOR FURTHER READING

H. Frankfort, et al., *Before Philosophy*

7
THE NEW CULTURE

THE INVASIONS

If the history of the ancient world were divided by content rather than convention we should recognize only two periods, the first from the appearance of writing to the invasions of 1200–900 B.C. which broke up the ancient Near East, the second from 1200 B.C. to the invasions of A.D. 400–700 which broke up the hellenized Roman and Persian empires. Of these periods the first, with the Neolithic which preceded it, saw the development of the physical and social techniques basic to human society—agriculture, pottery, metalworking, glassmaking, the domestication of animals, and the organization of men. The second saw an enormous increase of the civilized world in area, population, and equipment, important technical advances (glass blowing, concrete), and, more important, a profound change in the direction of human concern, from the mastery of the physical world to the discovery of the intellectual and spiritual life.

The great invasions which destroyed much of late Bronze Age civilization came from two directions. From the northwest a variety of tribes,

B.C.	All dates are approximate, at best to decades.
1250	Israelites beginning to invade Palestine
1230	Destruction of Troy; "sea peoples" invade Egypt
1200	Mycenaean palace of Pylos burned; the Hittite empire and Syrian coastal cities destroyed, perhaps by the "sea peoples"; beginning of the Iron Age
1190	The Philistines settle on the Palestinian coast
1130	Mycenae destroyed
1100	Dorian invasion of Greece; Arameans using camels invade the Fertile Crescent
1075	Collapse of Assyria
1000	David rules most of Palestine and Transjordan
925	Death of Solomon, separation of Israel from Judah
900	Revival of Assyria, important artistic and military developments (siege warfare, battering ram) through the following century; King Asa of Judah acts against the worship of gods other than Yahweh; development of heroic legend in Greece and among the Israelites; biography of David, Hebrew historiography

called by the Egyptians the "sea peoples," began raiding the eastern coasts of the Mediterranean in the late thirteenth century. In 1200 the Hittite empire was destroyed and Cyprus raided. Invaders then came down the coast of Syria, destroying the cities there, but were stopped at the entrance of Egypt. Some of them, the Peleshet, whom the Greeks were to call "Philistines," settled in Palestine, which gets its name from them. The rest dispersed; traces of them may be found in many regions around the Mediterranean. In Greece it was probably they who burned the Mycenaean palace at Pylos before 1200. During the next century new waves of barbarians, the Dorian Greeks and the "northwest" Greeks, overran the mainland (except Attica and Arcadia). Mycenae fell about 1130, and the Dorians pushed on through the southernmost islands as far as Crete and Rhodes, while the Greeks who had been displaced by these invasions themselves overran the central Aegean islands and, about 1000, the western coast of Asia Minor.

While these invasions from the northwest swept over Greece, Asia Minor, and the Mediterranean coasts, other invaders came from the southeast, from the fringes of the Arabian desert, where the seminomads, mostly Aramaic speaking, began first to infiltrate and then to conquer the countries around the Fertile Crescent—Palestine, Syria, northern Mesopotamia, and Babylonia. The movement began early: the Israelites were already in Palestine before 1230. Farther north it seems to have become serious only after the fall of the Hittite empire in 1200. To the east it was delayed yet longer by the resistance of Assyria, which wore itself out in a generation of wars against the Arameans around 1100. But about this time the Arameans gained enormously in wealth, mobility, and striking power by their increased use of camels, hitherto rarely domesticated in north Arabia. Therefore, in the two centuries after 1100, they were able to drive the Assyrians back to the walls of Ashur itself, while in the south they were raiding Babylonia from the eleventh century on, and their kindred, the Chaldeans, infiltrated the country after 900 and secured the throne of Babylon in the centuries following.

Nowhere through the arc of the Mediterranean coast from Greece to Egypt, or through the arc of the Fertile Crescent from Palestine to Babylonia, was the change uniform. Each little city and each little band of invaders was a law to itself. In this valley the city would drive off the invaders; in the next, it would be destroyed; in the third, invaders and city dwellers would live side by side. In Palestine as in Greece, in Mesopotamia as along the coasts of Anatolia, what we find by the year 1000 is a patchwork. One city or tribe might temporarily conquer its neighbors and enjoy a few decades of more extensive rule, but such exceptions did not alter the overall picture. Egypt and Assyria had, indeed, escaped complete conquest. But both had lost much territory

78   THE NEW CULTURE

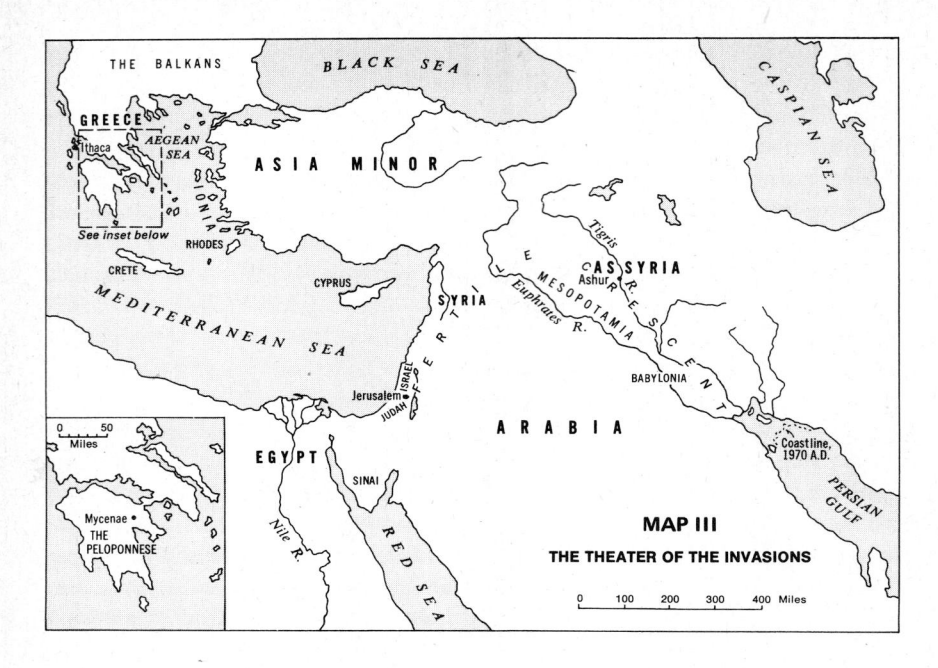

MAP III
THE THEATER OF THE INVASIONS

by infiltration, and even in Egypt fragmentation prevailed. The land was dismembered by mutually hostile princes, priests, and leaders of military clans of Libyans, who had been brought in from the western desert as mercenaries and remained to become rulers. Assyria too, though it regained control of the neighboring territories in the late 900s and began a policy of expansion to secure the trade routes along the Tigris and across northern Mesopotamia, was in reality no exception to the particularism of the time. It was primarily the territory of a city state, Ashur. In a world of warring cities and tribes, the Assyrians were the most warlike and one of the biggest. Consequently, whenever they were at peace with themselves they could overrun their smaller neighbors, who could oppose them with only makeshift alliances. But the particularism which made possible Assyria's conquests prevented it from assimilating the cities and tribes it conquered. It only collected booty, imposed tribute, and appointed puppet rulers from and for the conquered peoples. As soon as the Assyrian armies* were withdrawn the peoples were ready for revolt; the puppets had either to lead the revolts or be overthrown. Then the Assyrians would return. They used dreadful punishments to discourage revolts. But pillars of skulls erected in front of rebellious towns, captives impaled on stakes* around the fortifications, prisoners burned alive and variously mutilated, failed to perpetuate submission. Thus the political history from 1150 to 750 remains essentially one of petty states, without major governmental developments. And even when the Assyrians developed a more coherent imperial organization after 750, the petty state remained the most stable form of ancient society. As a Greek poet said after the fall of Assyria, "A little city on a crag that lives in good order is stronger than the folly of Nineveh."

Culturally, however, these four centuries show both general advance and a number of important achievements by particular peoples. The general advance was the rebuilding of civilization after the barbarian invasions. In Greece and the Greek islands, in Asia Minor and coastal Syria (except for the Phoenician cities), in Palestine and many places along the Fertile Crescent, even the art of writing had been lost, almost all large buildings had been destroyed, houses had been replaced by huts. The pottery had declined in technical skill without introduction of radically new forms—presumably the invaders had no forms of their own to introduce. There must have been an enormous destruction of tools and other artifacts, animals, and men. Evidently few survivors had the skills needed to replace what had been destroyed. The replacement therefore required the slow civilization of the barbarians, which was the great achievement of these centuries.

THE NEW CIVILIZATION

The new civilization differed widely from the old. Even in Egypt, Assyria, and Babylonia, where the chief cities and temples escaped destruction and Bronze Age culture lived on, men felt the change outside. An Egyptian romance tells of a priest of this time who had to go to Phoenicia—once an Egyptian dependency—to get cedar for the god's boat. The story tries to describe the new, dangerous world of the barbarians and to prove that even there the gods of Egypt protect their worshipers.

The traditions of the new peoples perpetuated the ideals of their former barbarism; in literary terms, they were "heroic." They reflected, not the hierarchy of the Bronze Age imperial administrations, but the chaos of the invasions, in which a man's standing depended mostly on his abilities. The pharaohs, high priests, and scribes of the former civilization were replaced by the warriors who stormed their cities, the sheiks who pastured their flocks along the edge of the Fertile Crescent, the prophets who led their tribes in desert wanderings and local wars. Ancient Near Eastern literature had dealt with gods, kings, and cities; the stories of Genesis and of the latter part of the *Odyssey* give us family history in a landscape almost pastoral—cities are there, but in the background. Whence came this new literary style? We do not know, but we can recognize the sort of society it reflects. This primitive society admired especially stature and strength (Samson, Ajax), the physical beauty of men (Absalom, Achilles), masculine friendship (David, Patroclus), skill in deception (Jacob, Odysseus), hospitality to strangers (Abraham, Menelaus), wisdom in dealing with men rather than book learning (Nestor, the older stories of Solomon), and, above all, the friendship and personal guidance of a god (Moses, Odysseus). Given these good things a man could do well in life—acquire property, a wife, and children, die at a ripe old age, and be given a magnificent funeral. These were the legitimate goals of human endeavor.

THE HOMERIC POEMS AND THE OLD TESTAMENT

During the years from 1100 to 750 this heroic ideal must have been embodied in many poems and legends. Of these we have two incomplete collections—the Homeric poems and the early material (with many later additions) in the books of the Old Testament from Genesis through II Kings. The histories of both these collections are matters of such dispute that it is difficult to determine even "the common opinion." The following account, however, is defensible.

The Homeric poems—the *Iliad* and the *Odyssey*—were put into much their present forms in the central Aegean area during the eighth century. They incorporate earlier elements of various dates, but have not been much interpolated and therefore present us with a relatively uniform body of the literature which was sung for entertainment in the courts of the petty kings and the festivals of the little towns of the Ionian Greeks during the years from 1150 to 750. Unfortunately, both poems deal chiefly with minor elements of the story of Troy (destroyed about 1230) and therefore offer little direct information about the later history of Greece.

The material collected in Genesis to II Kings did not reach its present form until the end of the fifth century. Beside the legends, the collection contains fragments of law codes, historical works, imaginative literary compositions (notably the Joseph romance), borrowings early and late from Mesopotamian mythology, and many minor elements. Most of these have been worked over by three or four editors and augmented by editorial additions. The collection now begins with the creation of the world, which it dates about 4000 B.C., and contains a history of mankind from creation to the building of "the tower" of Babel, a genealogy of the Semites from the flood to Abraham, and a history of Abraham and his descendants down to 560 B.C. Of the elements which here concern us, the legends, there are six main groups: those dealing with (1) creation and the early history of mankind, (2) the patriarchs, (3) Moses, (4) the "judges," (5) Saul and David, and (6) the prophets. Almost no one claims historical value for the creation stories and their like.

The "essential historicity" of the legends about "the patriarchs" (Abraham, Isaac, and Jacob) is defended by determined believers, but a stronger case can be made for the view that these were legends about the founders of Palestinian shrines whom the Israelites, after their conquest of Palestine, adopted as ancestors. According to the present story, Jacob's children had to be driven by famine into Egypt so that the Israelites, arriving from Egypt "470 years" later, could be represented as his descendants. (Similarly, the children of Hercules had to be banished from the Peloponnese so that they could lead the later Dorian invasion.) Once Jacob and his children have settled in Egypt the Old Testament knows practically nothing of their stay—no continuous tradition connected the "patriarchal period" of the 1700s with the exodus, which by Biblical chronology occurred about 1270. (It was forty years prior to the conquest, and an Egyptian inscription tells us the Israelites were in Palestine about 1230. The year 1270 saw the height of the power of Ramses II, who certainly did not drown in the Red Sea. His government dominated Palestine for the next fifty years, but Old Testament tradition knows nothing about even the presence of Egyptians in the country.) Furthermore, after the exodus, the people are always "the children" of "Israel," not of "Jacob," and Jacob has to be identified with Israel by the story that his name was changed. Near Eastern genealogies of this period commonly go back to fictitious "eponymous ancestors" whose names are those of all their descendants—thus Kar was the ancestor of the Karians, Dorus of the Dorians, and so on. The eponymous ancestors of the Israelite tribes, however, (Reuben, Simeon, Levi, Judah,) are not the patriarchs, but the children of "Israel," and the names of the patriarchs do not recur in Israelite names. Moreover, tradition connects the patriarchs with northeast Syria, but the language of the Israelites (Hebrew) is closer to Arabic than to Aramaic (the language of ancient Syria). The god of the Israelites, YHWH (probably "Yahweh") was unknown to the patriarchs (Ex. 6:3) and his "holy mountain" was somewhere in Sinai or northwest Arabia (I Kings 19). The Israelites came into the country mainly from the southeast, and their closest relatives, according to their own tradition, were their southeastern neighbors, the Edomites, Moabites, Ammonites, and Ishmaelites (Arabs). The Israelites practiced circumcision, as did northwest Arabs and Egyptians, but not Syrians and Babylonians. So it seems the patriarchs were, as the Old Testament says, founders of Palestinian shrines established long before the Israelite conquest. The Israelites took them over as ancestors when they took over the shrines and the country.

These facts help to explain the peculiar literary character of the stories about the patriarchs. Like the Romans, the Israelites were newcomers among the peoples. But while the Romans, like the Greeks and the ancient Near Eastern peoples, told their prehistory as a story of gods, kings, and heroes, of wars and crimes, the Old Testament tells of three generations of shepherds, like the Israelites. Sarah is fair as Helen and kings desire her, yet she is not an adulterous queen but a selfish mother. Except for two adventitious episodes, the patriarchs are not involved in wars, and, unlike real wars, the two episodes have no political consequences. Unlike Greek heroes, the patriarchs do not become kings in the land (when they are called so, it is flattery). They found or acquire holy places—the cave of Macphelah, the well of Beer Sheba, the altar of Bethel; but the Israelites' title to the land as a whole is not based on their possession of it. Yahweh is said to have given them the land, but they never take it; it is promised to their descendants, but these turn out to be "the children," not of Abraham, Isaac, or Jacob, but of Israel, and their title to the land is finally based on their own conquest of it. The patriarchal stories have thus been made over by subordination to the national legend. They survive as unique literary curiosities, stripped of their original environment but not fully integrated into that of the new conquerors, who remembered them as alien, but claimed them as their own.

Native Israelite tradition, of quite different tone, begins with the children of Israel in Egypt. Its hero is Moses, a prophet of YHWH. From here on the tradition seems to be, in outline, historical. The details, however, are fantastic; not only minor episodes but major ones like the covenant at Sinai may have been invented to provide Israelite origins for Canaanite ceremonies. (The covenant is to obey the law, said to be "the law of Yahweh"; but the law now attached to the story is certainly descended, although remotely, from Canaanite material.) For "historical outline," thus, not much is left: some Israelites escaped from Egypt under Moses, picked up adherents in the wilderness, fought off attacks by other tribes, were driven out of southern Palestine, and eventually conquered the western edge of Transjordan, where Moses died. The historical connection of Moses with Joshua is uncertain, and the legends of the Joshua cycle have suffered badly from later accretion; they contradict both archeological evidence and each other.

But the Israelites did establish themselves in Palestine during the thirteenth century. For two centuries thereafter they fought with neighbors and rival invaders; legends from several tribes about the heroes of these local wars have been collected and elaborated in the book called Judges. Eventually central Palestine was subjugated briefly by the Philistines. A new cycle of legends told of the resistance to them, first under Saul and his son Jonathan, whom the Philistines eventually killed, then under David, who with his band of "mighty men" (at first fellow outlaws, later mercenaries) captured Jerusalem, made it his capital, and about the year 1000 created a sizable kingdom in Palestine and Transjordan. (Significantly, in his time heroic legend is displaced as the main element of the Biblical account by historical narrative, though popular imagination continued to produce heroic legends about both the kings and the wandering prophets of Yahweh, and later compilers made use of these.) Solomon, David's son, squeezed enough out of his father's kingdom to build in Jerusalem a palace for himself and a temple for Yahweh, to fortify some strategic cities, and to maintain a luxurious court. At his death, about 925, the northern Israelite tribes understandably revolted and set up a separate kingdom. Presently the subject peoples also revolted and the area returned to the pattern of petty tribal states characteristic of the age.

We have described the Israelite legends because of their importance for medieval and modern thought. From A.D. 391, when Christianity became the official religion of the Roman Empire, until 1859, when the credibility of the creation story was destroyed by Darwin, the Old Testament was the official authority for ancient history. Before the triumph of Christianity a similar, though less official, authority was enjoyed throughout the Greco-Roman world by the Homeric poems, which became the basic texts of elementary and secondary education. At first, however, both in Israel and in Greece, the legends were less important as accounts of past events than as pictures of ideal figures and adventures, which influenced the life of the new age.

CITIES AGAIN

The theater of this life was the city, from which, at this time, the village is hardly to be distinguished. Generally speaking, a place is called a city if it both is the permanent residence of a considerable number of people and has a government of its own and a territory over which its government exercises legal control. Most or all of this land is commonly owned by residents of the city. Various amenities later thought essential —a city wall, a public water supply, a bath, and the like—may be lacking: Sparta's wall was not completed until 184 B.C. On the other hand, all these urban luxuries and more—including local self-government by elected officers, local courts and finances, and so on—are eventually found in some villages. Again, cities in the territories of major powers were commonly garrisoned and subjected to royal governors, sometimes stripped of their territorial jurisdiction, and occasionally denied any self-government, but none the less remained cities. In districts where there were no preponderant centers of population, where tribal feeling remained strong, and where the adult males of the tribe met for governmental purposes two or three times a year at some rural sanctuary, all the residential centers may be described as villages, but their cultural development generally followed, albeit somewhat slowly, the same lines as that of the cities of more heavily settled areas, and as tribes settled down their territories commonly broke up into city states. Accordingly we shall discuss the development of the new culture in the city state and shall neglect the village as generally the hanger-on and eventually—to the best of its ability—the imitator of the city.

Within the tiny area of the city state, the city itself was infinitesimal, often no more than a couple of hundred yards from wall to wall. It was usually ruled by a hereditary king, who was the leader in war, the judge in peace, and the high priest at all times. This economy in administration was dictated by poverty as well as tribal tradition. Trade was negligible and confined to luxuries. The city lived on what it could grow in its fields, supplemented by fishing and hunting. Agriculture, however, was primitive; half the land was left fallow every year to prevent its exhaustion. The plants available for cultivation were little removed from their wild forms and yielded meager harvests. Consequently, given the small size of the city's territory, there was almost no surplus to support unproductive labor. Large priesthoods were out of the question. The new culture was at first spared their conservative economic, political, and cultural influence. Temples, too, were luxuries rarely possible. No large ones appear in Greece until the eighth century. In Israel, David's military success made possible Solomon's buildings, but their cost led to revolt.

Poverty also delayed the development of specialists. The ideal man, like the small farmer, could do everything for himself: the tradition pictured Odysseus, king of Ithaca, building his own house, Saul leaving his plow to lead an army. But some specialists there were. Divination, thought to result from possession by a spirit, was always a specialty of persons psychologically liable to such seizures. Another specialty was that of the metalworkers. Their secret craft was now more important because it included more feasible ways of working iron. Iron increased the productive capacity of the workers, and with better tools the craftsman became an object of more value and more political importance, especially since he was part of a small political unit, a city or a tribe, to which the gain or loss of a single skilled man was important. Concern for the individual is consequently an important characteristic of the Homeric poems, the legends of the Old Testament, and the western civilization which derives from them.

Because the typical city was so small, everyone in it was aware of all details of the life of his neighbors. The clearing house for gossip was the gate of the city. Here sat the old men of the city, the heads of the principal families, who were both the king's council and the local archives. To make a contract or record a sale, one "declared before those who sat in the gate." In such a small society, reputation became a matter of life and death. Acute concern for honor is characteristic of heroic legend. To revenge an insult, Achilles would imperil the whole Greek army; David, for the same reason, was ready to wipe out the household of Nabal, man, woman, and child (I Sam. 25:34). This concern for honor was an important motive for achievement—for bravery in warfare, but also for skill in speaking (the public assembly is, for Homer, "where men get honor"), and for skill in any kind of craft, even the humble arts of domestic service (*Odyssey* XV.320). Since the city needed the work of every man and woman, it praised or blamed each one according to the quality of his work. The slacker could not escape censure, nor the incompetent, worse than censure, ridicule.

Therefore, during the years from about 1100 or 1000 to 750 the cultural level of the newly occupied areas steadily rose. Poverty remained general, but when the political configuration changed momentarily, permitting a ruler to draw income from a larger area, sufficient wealth could be raised to finance monumental building and works of art. The greatest examples of these are the palaces of the Assyrian kings, which contained a new style of historical art—low reliefs of exquisite clarity* narrating the rulers' triumphs. The figures of these reliefs are often masterpieces, combining stylized treatment with vivid, lifelike effect. The tradition thus established was continued to the end of the Assyrian empire in 612. As the palace art of the greatest military power and wealthiest court of the age, it exerted a wide influence. The great reliefs were too costly to be directly imitated by lesser states, but their details and their vigorous treatment of animal figures* were copied on minor works of art all around the Mediterranean.

REVIVAL OF TRADE

In Greece and Phoenicia, hemmed in by mountains and warlike neighbors, the cities turned to the sea to supplement their incomes. Here the arts served commerce—in Greece, metalworking and pottery, in Phoenicia, ivory carving, silverwork, and the manufacture of colored

86   THE NEW CULTURE

glass and fine fabrics, especially admired for the "Tyrian purple" dye. Beside these luxury products, slaves (often kidnapped along the way), ores, and smelted metal in ingots were staples in this gradually increasing trade. Piracy and exploration went with commerce. The Phoenicians sailed south to Egypt, thence west along the African coast, finally through the Straits of Gibraltar to the Atlantic coasts of Africa and Spain. The Greeks in the west sailed along the Balkan coast, thence to Italy and Sicily; in the east they penetrated the Black Sea and discovered the Russian rivers. Neither Greeks nor Phoenicians kept out of each other's territories. Homer sings of Greek voyages to Egypt and of Phoenician traders in the Aegean. Several cities in Greece claimed Phoenician founders. Cyprus, where the copper mines were still important, kept its Mycenaean settlements and received new settlers from Phoenicia. Greek pottery appears in the earliest level at Carthage.

The Phoenician traders carried their alphabet* wherever they ventured. To the traders the alphabet was merely a convenience for keeping records, but it was to become the shaping instrument of the literature, learning, and science of the western world. Nor was it alone. Mesopotamian weights, measures, and techniques of divination, the lunisolar calendar, and a host of decorative motifs and artistic and architectural techniques were taken over by the Greeks and contributed to the rapid growth of Greek civilization.

CHARACTERISTICS OF GREEK CULTURE

But this growth cannot be explained solely by Oriental influences or economic opportunities. A most important factor was the peculiar genius of the Greeks. Consider only two examples, their language and their love of beauty. Among the languages of the ancient world Greek is outstanding for its wealth of means to express *precisely* the relations between the subjects discussed. Where other languages simply string together clauses with a few all-purpose conjunctions, Greek always makes possible, and often requires, a detailed analysis of the complex of ideas to be expressed. A page written in some Semitic language, or in early Latin, is to a page of classical Greek as a brick pile is to an arch. Along with this amazing sense for linguistic and intellectual structure, the Greeks had an equally amazing sense for visible beauty, particularly that of the human body.* If a sinner is a beautiful man, says Plutarch, the gods deal gently with him. But here an amazing exception must be noted. All the Mediterranean is beautiful and Greece outstandingly so. It is plausible to suppose that this magnificent landscape nurtured the Greeks' sense of beauty. But classical Greek art and literature shows almost no interest in landscape. What little there is, is practical, not aesthetic. Rich fields, good harbors, and good hunting grounds are praised, but not splendid peaks or romantic cliffs. Rivers are gods of considerable importance, mountains are not. The Greeks seem to have taken the beauty of their country for granted, as children do the virtue of their parents.

A consequence of the Greeks' acute sense of human beauty was their concern for youth. Man is afraid of death. The Greeks added fear and hatred of old age. In Babylonian myth, the hero Gilgamesh, who had received from the gods the plant of life, lost it to the serpent. The Greeks told the same story, but said the divine gift was youth. Men grow old, but the serpent, having carried off the charm, remains ever young by shedding his skins. In the voluptuous "Homeric" hymn to Aphrodite we hear that a goddess obtained eternal life for a mortal lover, but forgot to ask for eternal youth and so, when his first grey hair appeared, she abandoned him and later put him in a locked room where he now babbles endlessly. In art, gods like Apollo appear as youths whose beards have not yet grown. Youth is desired not only for itself, but also as the necessary condition for love. An old man, says the poet Mimnermus, is hateful to women and to boys—and without love, he goes on to say, life is not worth living. No one in the ancient Near East had attributed such importance to sex; the Greek exaggeration marks the discovery of romantic love and consequently of the despair latent in it (the frustration of the attempt to possess completely another person, the hostilities thus generated, and so on). Such themes were unknown in the Near East, where only the external difficulties of love-making are described (mother prevents girl from meeting boy in an Egyptian love song). Henceforth, the psychological tension between lover and beloved remains a major theme of world literature. But even love and youth derive their power from beauty, which is the *summum bonum*. When the Hebrews said that God, on viewing creation, saw that it was *good*, the Septuagint translators—though they tried to translate literally—felt compelled to say, "he saw that it was *beautiful*." For in Greek, they knew, "beautiful," not "good," was the common term of approval. The attitude lasted down to Christian times and spread, with Greek culture, throughout the Roman Empire. Both Augustine and Gregory of Nyssa, rejecting Greco-Roman values, argue that Jesus must have been ugly or the crowd would not have ill-treated him. No other literature of the ancient world even remotely approaches Greek in feeling for physical beauty and intellectual structure. With these peculiar gifts, the Greeks set out on their course.

FOR FURTHER READING

N. Fustel de Coulanges, *The Ancient City*

G. Kirk (ed.), *The Language and Background of Homer*

D. Moscati, *The World of the Phoenicians*

H. Rowley, *The Growth of the Old Testament*

R. de Vaux, *Ancient Israel*

8
THE GREAT DIVIDE

THE INCREASE OF WEALTH

The accumulation of men and belongings during the years from 1100 to 750 was neither uniform nor uninterrupted. The Assyrian conquests, in particular, so gutted northern Syria that it remained unimportant during the next four hundred years. Everywhere, the rate of progress was retarded by endemic wars between neighboring cities or tribes. These wars had their root in poverty and were primarily fought for control of land since, given the size of the cities' territories and their total dependence on local agriculture, even a small strip of land could make a perceptible difference in diet. The wars left grudges, perpetuated the heroic ideal which led to war as a means to honor, and perpetuated poverty which led to war as a form of honorable theft.

But these wars were not very destructive—the Assyrian achievements were unique. Most buildings were of stone; fire only burned off the roofs. Killing, like everything else, had to be done by hand; therefore mortality was usually low. Nobody knew much about siege warfare* (except, again, the Assyrians, who developed a good battering ram* as early as the ninth century). The soldiers were farmers who had to get back to put their

B.C.	Dates ending in zero are approximate.
780	Alphabetic writing begins in Greece (Phoenician alphabet)
776	Traditional date for the beginning of the Olympic games
760	First Greek colony on the Italian mainland (Cumae)
750	Large temples begin to be built in Greece; Amos' denunciation of the rich, Yahweh a god of justice
750–700	The *Iliad* and the *Odyssey* reach approximately their present forms
744	Accession of Tiglath-pileser III, reorganization of the Assyrian army and empire, beginning of the great century of Assyrian conquests, building, and historical art
740	Hosea's denunciation of the Israelites for their worship of gods other than Yahweh
722	Assyria destroys the kingdom of Israel
714	Sargon II of Assyria reduces Urartu
710	Sargon takes Babylon
700	Hesiod denounces the rich, Zeus a god of justice; development of hoplite tactics in Greece; monarchies in Greece giving way to oligarchies
690	Scythian invasion of Armenia; Cimmerian invasion of Asia Minor
672	Esarhaddon of Assyria controls western Media
671	Esarhaddon takes Egypt
663	Ashurbanipal of Assyria resubjugates Egypt
646	Ashurbanipal conquers Elam
640	Ashurbanipal destroys the Cimmerians

fields in shape for planting before the autumn rains fell, so victors had little time to do damage. Consequently, in spite of wars, the period from 1150 to 750 saw a great increase of population and wealth, and these brought with them diversification of culture.

Previously, small cities and tribal kingdoms were alike made up of large families, not to say clans. The heads of these families were the king's influential advisers, in effect, "the royal council." When quarrels arose, opponents could not easily be eliminated—they were too important to the state; nor could their power be broken and the victor's power greatly increased by economic reprisals—there was too little property to make much difference. With wealth came the possibility of decisive change. When the city had men enough, opponents could be exiled; when it had wealth enough, the victor could use their property to hire supporters and make his victory permanent. Therefore, both in the Near East and in Greece, political patterns changed as one side or the other, the king or the council, gained the advantage.

THE TWO PATTERNS OF SOCIAL CHANGE

The changes were uniform through large areas. In Greece the councils won; the kings were reduced to officials; the government became an oligarchy. In Anatolia outside the Greek cities, in Cyprus, Syria, Palestine, and the Fertile Crescent, the kings became absolute, the heads of families lost their conciliar rank, and the royal council came to be made up of the king's great officers, appointed by him and often of no distinguished ancestry. No doubt the monarchic tradition of the Near East was influential in this development. It is dangerous to talk of ethnic character: the Greek cities of Cyprus became kingdoms on the Near Eastern model, as did the Phoenician coastal cities, but Carthage, equally Phoenician, became an oligarchy on Greek lines.

One important factor in the Greek development was the discovery of a new military technique, the use of a solid line of heavily armed spearmen (hoplites). The success of this technique in Greece, a rugged country ideal for light infantry armed with bows, is a mystery. But succeed it did; it saved Greece from Near Eastern domination, and tactics developed from it eventually enabled the Greeks to conquer the Near Eastern world and impose on it their culture. Classical Greek art, literature, and philosophy could be produced, preserved, and propagated only because the Greeks made themselves individually the best soldiers and collectively the greatest military power of their age.

Their new technique, developing about 700, required men who could afford full armor and time for practice. So the wealthy men and their sons became the cities' crack regiments. No Greek city king could

MAP IV

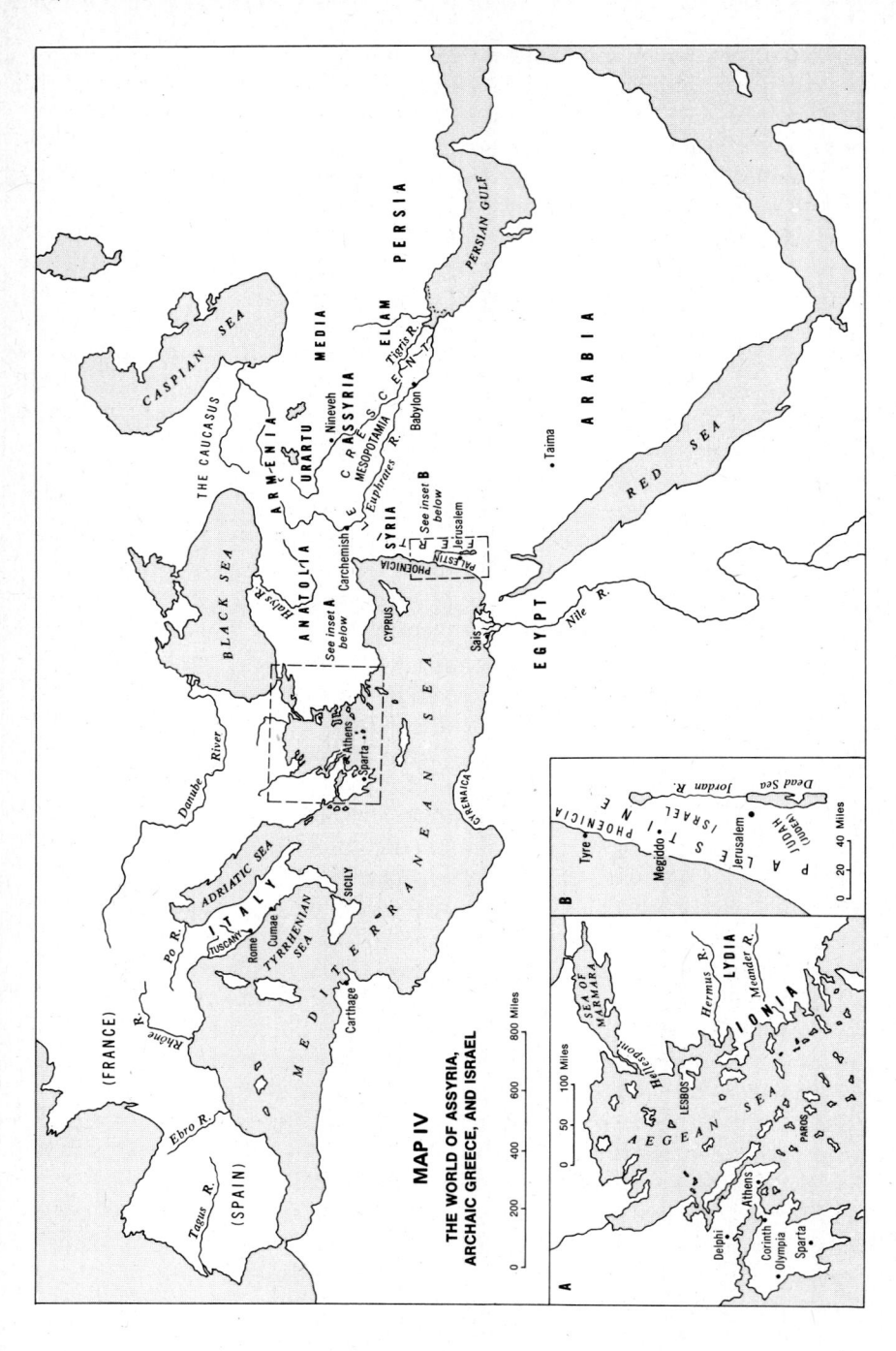

THE WORLD OF ASSYRIA,
ARCHAIC GREECE, AND ISRAEL

afford a hoplite force of his own; that required a large taxable area for its support. The fragmentation of Greece by mountains, which made it difficult for a state to expand, was thus a factor in the triumph of the oligarchies. In the Near East, perhaps because the land was less fragmented, the kingdoms grew larger, the kings could afford mercenaries and so became absolute rulers.

This political differentiation accompanied a sharp cultural change. The Greek oligarchs were united in military cliques whose members had to hang together to preserve their military efficiency. Brought up on the heroic poems, they were intensely concerned about honor. Since they had to govern by mutual consent it became customary to pass the city offices around, by election, from one leading family to another. Hence in every city grew up both the custom of elections and a set of conventions as to what should and should not be done—an unwritten constitution. This is the background of later Greek constitutional law, almost unparalleled in the Near East. Not only the civil offices, but the chief priesthoods became elective, for the kings of the invaders had also been priests and had commonly assumed the chief priestly functions in the conquered cities. When they were forced out, these offices, like the rest, fell to members of the oligarchy. Therefore Greece, unlike the countries of the Near East, has no priestly caste, nor even a priestly class. In many places, every man could offer his own sacrifice, there was no mediator between him and the god, and a priesthood was a civic honor to which he, too, might aspire.

Concern for honor and, even more, for wealth and mutual protection led the oligarchs to marry women from the ruling families of other cities. Consequently the ruling families became an international clique. The members of this clique gathered to see their in-laws and display their wealth at the festivals of the great religious centers. Most centers had cults of local heroes who were thought to protect the land and assure its fertility. The cult of these heroes commonly involved military and athletic contests; the Greeks were outstanding among the peoples of the ancient world for their love both of contests and of athletics.*
In 776, we are told, the athletic and military games for the festival of Zeus at Olympia in the western Peloponnese were organized as a contest recurrent every fourth year. Eventually victory in these games became one of the highest honors of the Greek world. Other religious centers followed suit. Song and dancing were parts of the worship of many Greek gods. Contests in music and poetry were held at the shrine of Apollo in Delphi. Civic festivals with "games" were similarly developed, notably the festival of Athena at Athens. And all these contests were means of gaining honor.

Athletic and military concern alike focused attention on the male body. Since every citizen from his twenties to his forties, if not a cripple, was liable to military duty and might have to stand in combat every few years, most cities prescribed athletic training as a form of military preparedness. A fine body was a means to honor and a source of pride. The Dorians, the most warlike of the Greeks, expressed their pride by exercising naked. Soon the gymnasium, "the place where men go naked," became throughout Greece the center in which upper-class citizens passed their leisure time. Male nudity* became a major concern of Greek art. Above all it contributed to the development of sculpture and the sense of space, that is, the gift of seeing objects three dimensionally, which is distinctive of Greek as opposed to Near Eastern sensibility. The extraordinary tactile awareness of muscles and movement,* the consequent power and presence of Greek statues, derive directly from the military and athletic tradition. By putting a premium on exercise and consequent bathing, nudity made the Greeks the cleanest and longest-lived people of their times.[1] In the gymnasium, too, arose the discussions from which philosophy and political theory would grow, as well as the friendships that rapidly became homosexual love affairs.*

Discussion produced an intellectual environment in which new ideas could secure acceptance, by contrast to the older cultures of Egypt and Mesopotamia where the traditional wisdom, fixed in written texts inherited from the Bronze Age, was something to be learned, not discussed. It was the Greeks' lack of a classical culture that enabled them to create one.

Homosexuality occurs all over the world; Greece was unusual in honoring it. Even in Greece, however, there were limits; homosexual intercourse was commonly prohibited by law. But such laws were more honored in the breach than the observance, and in many Greek cities the lover came to have a recognized part in the boy's education. He was the model and guide who introduced the boy to the world of men. (The relationship might continue into young manhood, but homosexuality between elder men was thought ridiculous.)

These developments did not occur in the Near East, where games were for children, singing and dancing were the work of professional entertainers, nudity was a disgrace, traditional wisdom was not open to discussion, and homosexuality was a capital crime.

Even in Greece, presumably, sexual relations were most often marital. On the Athenian stage, Andromache, widow of the heroic Hector, speaks of "the insatiable lust of the bed," which "infects" women even more than men, but which women conceal. (Prostitutes did not, and were popular.)* Plutarch admonishes his newly wedded friends that,

---

[1] By modern standards their cleanliness left much to be desired. A king of Sparta, while performing a solemn public sacrifice at the country's principal shrine, was bitten by one of his lice.

while the works of Aphrodite can cure any marital quarrel, disagreements that originate in bed are not easily settled elsewhere. In defense of homosexuality it was said that love of a wife kept her husband home, but commonly it did not. The man's world lay outside the house, the woman's, within it; his duty was to acquire goods, hers to preserve and distribute them. This role helped satisfy her need to be needed. Wives did not appear at men's gatherings but, describing one of them, Xenophon imagines that, after seeing a lascivious pantomime, young men decided to get married and married men hurried home to their wives. In Aristophanes' ribald comedy (*Lysistrata*) the husband hates the thought of returning to his home while his wife is absent. Without her, even the meal is no longer pleasant. The magic sadness of Attic grave stones representing wives who had passed away attests the conjugal affection which Aristotle, a contemporary of these works of art, expects in marriage. But this conjugal affection often coexisted with homosexual passion; in Xenophon's *Symposium* it is a newly married man who gives the most outspoken account of his devotion to his lover (IV. 10ff.).

Shortage of land and decline of grain production may have been among the reasons for the popularity of homosexuality in Greece, where the tiny, infertile valleys were already overpopulated. The country has little rainfall and only a quarter of its territory is arable. There is plenty of fine stone and good clay, but no metal in any quantity except for silver. Nature destined the land for sculpture, pottery, and poverty. Even where the soil is good, it is better for olive trees* and vines than for grain. Trees and vineyards take time—olives, five years—before they begin to bear, but once they do they pay better than grain; the yield of an olive yard was four times the value of the grain that might have been grown on it. Consequently, as the Greeks got richer and more men got enough money to convert their fields into olive yards and vineyards, the country's production of grain declined. The resultant shortage led to legislation prohibiting the export of grain—e.g., by Solon at Athens in 593—but this lowered the price of grain and consequently encouraged the conversion of yet more land to olive yards. Less food became available and there were always more mouths to feed—hence both homosexuality and the practice of abandoning unwanted babies. But these did not suffice to check population growth.

Overpopulation and the desire for a better life led to emigration, both by individuals and in colonies, but they also led, if emigration proved inadequate, to revolution. (Without industrialization, chemical fertilizers, and the like, the modern alternative—to raise domestic production—was not available.) Civil oligarchies understandably favored emigration, the more so as the rising standard of living increased potential discontent. Also, cities now had the money and manpower to organize mass emigrations for the foundation of colonies. When a city wished to send out a colony, it would usually consult Apollo of Delphi. With his approval and prudently obscure advice, a leader and lawmaker would be appointed from one of the city's distinguished families, ships provided, and a body of colonists made up; sometimes even outsiders would be invited to participate. Choice of the location might be guided by the advice of traders as well as that of the god, whose priests heard the reports of visitors from all parts of the world.

Before 750 there was a Greek colony at Cumae (north of Naples), and by 550 colonies were thick around south and southwest Italy, Sicily (except for the western, Phoenician tip), south France and east Spain, the north shore of the Aegean, the Hellespont, Sea of Marmora, and Black Sea, and the promontory of Cyrenaica on the north African coast. They vastly expanded the markets of Greece. They imported manufactured articles, wine, and olive oil; and they supplied raw materials—metals, grain, wood, tar, salt, fish, hides, and slaves. By relieving the population pressure and stimulating economic growth they made possible the glorious cultural achievements of Greece. Colonization also made the Greeks aware of the great world, its variety of peoples and customs—whence philosophic problems as to right and wrong. It confronted them with different environments, exercised their adaptability, developed their practical intelligence. The necessity of founding cities trained their founders in urban and in social planning. It made them legislators—and philosophers. Plato's *Republic* reflects the experience of colonization. The colonies were a frontier from which the Greeks derived awareness of new possibilities, willingness to experiment, and "philosophic" detachment from established customs and ideas. Greek colonization was not paralleled in the Near East except among the Phoenicians, of whose intellectual history, unfortunately, we know almost nothing.

Oligarchy, priesthood of the laity, hoplite military tactics, athletics, homosexuality, colonization, and consequent intellectual attitude—Greece between 750 and 650 distinguished itself from the context of the eastern Mediterranean world. There absolute monarchies reigned, supported by hereditary priesthoods and mercenary armies, and ruling through councils composed not of men of wealth and stature but of royal appointees in charge of the branches of the government—the mercenaries, the corvée, the secretariat, the palace, and so on. With this return toward the ancient Near Eastern type of monarchy went related developments. Growth of royal income financed growth of the professional clergy. In spite of the alphabet, the scribal class lived on as royal secretaries and administrators. As their efficiency (in tax collection) and the luxury of the courts increased, the small farmers were squeezed harder. Their reaction can be heard in the denunciations of the rich by the Israelite Amos (about 750), a prophet of Yahweh, convinced that his god would soon destroy the oppressors of the poor.

That Amos' prophecies have survived is surprising. For the most part we know of ancient history only from the upper classes—it was they who ordered inscriptions and had books copied. When, occasionally, we hear a lower-class comment it is thanks to quotation by a wealthy author or to chance discovery of some poor man's papyri. But Amos owes his preservation to a different sort of accident.

ISRAELITE RELIGION

Yahweh, the god whose worship the Israelites seem to have learned from Moses, was a desert divinity, good in razzias, but no farmer. Hence when his people conquered Palestine and needed help to farm it, they began to worship the gods of the land, a family of fertility deities* known from Ugarit—Father El and Mother Ashera, with their children Baal* and Anath, Baal ("husband, master, owner") being the most popular. But this produced a reaction. Whether it came from the upper-class invaders who may have wanted, for military purposes, to keep their followers separate from the Canaanites, or from the lower, who may have wanted to keep themselves distinct from the peasantry; whether it expressed the revulsion of the desert people from the drunken Palestinian fertility rites, or the jealousy of the prophets of Yahweh at their new competitors, at all events, the claim was made that all Israelites were obligated to worship Yahweh and *only* Yahweh. They were his people, his "private property"; to worship any other god was an offense against him.

Just when this notion arose is uncertain because the later editors of the Old Testament have constantly written it into the early stories. Here our concern is not with its origin, but with its acceptance in the historical period. We first hear of royal action against the worshipers of gods other than Yahweh in the reign of Solomon's great-grandson Asa (913–873?). By the middle of the ninth century there was an active "Yahweh-alone" party of prophets led by Elijah and Elisha. The party is credited with having inspired a revolution in the northern Israelite kingdom about 840. Shortly thereafter the priest of the temple of Yahweh in Jerusalem organized a revolution there. But the movement was not able to impose its will on the country as a whole; indeed, it soon lost control even of the courts. As a minority, it turned to the discontented for support—hence its adoption of the works of Amos, who probably had not been part of it. Had he thought the worship of other gods important he would have given the practice a more prominent place in his list of the sins which Yahweh will punish. How party members felt on the subject can be seen in the tirades of Hosea (about 740). For him, Israel was wedded to Yahweh; to worship other gods was to commit adultery. With Micah and Isaiah at the end of the eighth century, the themes of Amos and Hosea are fused and the principal traits in the party's picture of Yahweh are fixed: he is a jealous god, who will not tolerate his peoples' worship of any other divinity, and he is a just god, vigilant to protect the poor.

AMOS AND HESIOD

The same concern for justice appears half a century later (about 700) in Greek literature. As Yahweh called the shepherd Amos to prophesy, the Muses told the shepherd Hesiod to sing of the things to come, and those that had been, and of the eternal gods. Hesiod's attempt to organize the deities genealogically wasted the time of Greek theologians to the end of paganism. At least the worshipers of Yahweh alone were spared this. Hating all other gods, they cut down mythology to stories of creation and of Yahweh's interventions on earth. On the other hand, paganism, starting from the premise that the number and natures of supernatural beings are not fully known to us, is able to take the religious intuitions of other peoples seriously; it has a potentially experimental and ecumenical attitude toward religions, easily degenerating into superstition, as the exclusive and intolerant attitude of monotheism naturally inclines to dogmatism. But in spite of these differences in their backgrounds, Hesiod and Amos agreed about the deity's present role in human society. Zeus, like Yahweh, was the ruler of the world and the god of justice; he punished the unjust, and the oppressors of the poor. Amos was more concerned about justice *for the poor*, Hesiod, about justice. Amos expected the immediate destruction of Israel. Hesiod thought that men were going from bad to worse and would eventually be destroyed, but that meanwhile the righteous would be rewarded by peace and plentiful harvests, the wicked would be visited by plague, famine, and the disasters of war. The genuine prophecies of Amos were predictions of doom, but Hesiod offered practical advice: The wise man will be a careful farmer, so he can afford to be just; the rules for farming follow. Hence his work was preserved. It not only gives us an invaluable picture of Greek village life, but by its concern for justice it stands beside the prophecies of Amos in the intellectual and moral history of its time and of western civilization. Again the difference between Greek and Israelite culture is indicated by the different histories of these similar authors. Both Amos and Hesiod wrote in verse and claimed to be prophets, but Amos is remembered as the first in a line of prophets whose work becomes more and more prosy, Hesiod as the second of a line of poets whose work soon loses any serious pretension to prophetic powers.

THE REVIVAL AND RULE OF ASSYRIA

These theological developments, and everything else in the Near East, were overshadowed in their own time by the revival of Assyria. Tiglath-pileser III,* who seized the Assyrian throne in 744, transformed the old kingdom into the first empire with a provincial organization. Instead of merely looting territories and leaving them under native rulers to rebel, he made frequent use of the practice, hitherto rare, of deporting part of a conquered people and replacing them with others, thereby splitting the territory politically. He cut territories into small provinces, usually under foreign governors. To keep these governors in touch with the capital he instituted the first official postal service. He built a standing army to support the governors; no longer would the imperial government have to rely on peasants anxious to get back to their farms. Full-time professional troops drawn from diverse peoples formed a military machine able to survive the loss of Assyria itself. Thus, though the new Assyria was still unable to win over the peoples it conquered, it was able to split them up and to enlist some of their members in its service.

With this power Tiglath-pileser III resumed the Assyrian program of conquest—south to Babylon, north to Urartu, east to Media, and west to the Mediterranean. His successors pushed it farther than ever before. They destroyed the northern kingdom of Israel in 722, reduced Urartu to unimportance in 714, and recaptured Babylon in 710; Esarhaddon extended Assyrian control into Media before 672 and into Egypt in 671; Ashurbanipal resubjugated Egypt in 663, and pushed beyond Babylon to subdue Elam about 646.

With military expansion went an enormous expansion of wealth. The brilliant tradition of Assyrian art was resumed, with increasing naturalism, in pictures of military campaigns* and court ceremonies. A library of 1,200 tablets of cuneiform texts, collected at Ashurbanipal's orders, preserved most of what we know about ancient Near Eastern literature—a dismal picture. The largest group of texts are interpretations of acts thought ominous; the next largest, dictionaries—so cumbersome was cuneiform writing; and the third, magic spells. The few literary texts are not Assyrian compositions, but copies of older ones. From royal correspondence, historical inscriptions, and treaties we see a different sort of mind—vigorous and matter-of-fact. But the aristocracy was a small group occupied by war, administration, and trade. Their educational tradition was dominated by the study of classical texts notable for their linguistic difficulty and their intellectual poverty. Hence, perhaps, the paradox of Assyrian civilization—the contrast between its magnificent achievements in art and architecture, military technique and administrative organization, and its utter literary insignificance.

FOR FURTHER READING

J. Boardman, *The Greeks Overseas*
———, *Pre-Classical*

M. Smith, *Palestinian Parties and Politics that Shaped the Old Testament*

9
THE CENTURY OF THE MINOR POWERS

POLITICS AND CULTURE AFTER THE FALL OF ASSYRIA

To meet the threat of the new Assyrian empire, traditional enemies united—for instance, the Israelites, the Phoenician cities, and the Aramean kingdom of Damascus. Such local leagues were unsuccessful. Next came what may be called national states among ethnic groups threatened by Assyria, like Egypt, Babylonia, and Media. In Egypt the Assyrians helped by killing off the local rulers except for one, Necho, whom they chose as their agent. Thus Necho's son, Psammetichus I, could unify the country in the 650s. The Assyrians also cleared the way for union of the Median tribes in the 650s and of southern Mesopotamia by the Chaldean kingdom of Babylon about 625. Assyrian defeat of the Cimmerians about 640 enabled the kingdom of Lydia to expand into central Anatolia. These kingdoms allied against Assyria and fomented rebellions among Assyria's subjects. Moreover, a new horde of nomads, the Scythians, had come through the Caucasus in the 690s and thereafter threatened Assyria from the north. Nineveh, the greatest Assyrian city, fell to the Medes and Babylonians in 612. The Assyrian army was broken up in 609. The Scythians were eventually—in the 590s—driven

B.C.	Dates ending in zero are approximate.
650	Egypt united under Psammetichus I; Media united in reaction to Assyrian pressure; Archilochus of Paros, lyric poet
646	Ashurbanipal's conquest of Elam
640	Assyrian defeat of Cimmerians opens central Asia Minor for Lydian expansion; Lydians begin coinage
625	Rise of the Chaldean kingdom of Babylon
621	The Deuteronomic law code found in the Jerusalem temple; King Josiah's religious reforms; publication of the laws of Athens by Draco
612	Nineveh falls to the Medes and Babylonians
609	Necho II of Egypt conquers Palestine-Syria; Battle of Megiddo; death of Josiah
605	Battle of Carchemish; Egyptians, defeated by Babylonians, retreat to Egypt
600	Circumnavigation of Africa by Phoenicians; Sappho of Lesbos; Corinthian pottery predominant in Greek trade; Greek monumental sculpture developing
593	Solon's reforms in Athens
590	Scythians driven out of Armenia by the Medes
587	Destruction of Jerusalem by Nebuchadnezzar II of Babylon; the prophets Jeremiah and Ezekiel
585	Battle between the Medes and the Lydians for control of central Asia Minor, the Halys fixed as boundary
560	Pisistratus tyrant of Athens; Athenian black figure pottery becomes the most popular Greek ware
550	Cyrus of Persia gains control of Media
540	"Second Isaiah," author of Isaiah 40–55, denies the existence of gods other than Yahweh; Xenophanes' philosophic monotheism

back into Russia, presumably by the Medes. By 585 the Near East was divided into four kingdoms: the Lydians controlled western and central Anatolia to the Halys, the Medes, everything from central Anatolia through the mountains around the Tigris Valley to southern Persia; the Babylonians held Mesopotamia, Syria, and Palestine; the fourth kingdom was Egypt.

All these kingdoms were absolute monarchies. The king's power rested on his control of the army but also, now, on ethnic feeling. Of the Medes we know little. The Lydian and eastern Greek cultures were closely related, but not identical. To the Greeks the Lydians represented Oriental luxury. Some important cultural innovations, notably coinage,* are said to have come from Lydia. In Egypt and Babylon ancient traditions were revived, ancient literature copied, and new works of art created, following ancient fashions but displaying a new technical skill and calculated simplicity. In particular, the Saïte art of Egypt (so called from the new capital, Saïs, in the Delta) produced among its many masterpieces a series of heads which seem to show the first true portraiture since the Amarna Age.

The new Mediterranean states imitated the fashions of the Near East. The lions, rosettes, and palmettes of Assyrian and Phoenician decoration were perpetuated on the "orientalizing" pottery of Corinth, popular all around the Mediterranean. Statues of Greek youths* show Egyptian postures and wigs. The Etruscans, a mysterious people who gave their name to Tuscany (the region between Florence and Rome), incorporated so many Near Eastern elements in their art and religion that they were thought immigrants from Asia Minor, as perhaps their rulers were. The Etruscan kings grew rich from the copper and iron deposits of north Italy; their twelve cities ruled Tuscany, planted settlements in the Po Valley and controlled western Italy down to Cumae; their shipping gave its name to the Tyrrhenian Sea, and their trader-pirates were active even in the Aegean.

ECONOMIC DEVELOPMENT AND POLITICAL CONSEQUENCES

All these countries were much concerned with trade. Nebuchadnezzar II (604–562), the greatest of the kings of Babylon, besieged Tyre for thirteen years, hoping to control its far-reaching trade (described in Ezekiel, ch. 27). Nabonidus (555–539), the last of the Babylonian kings, established himself at Taima in the west Arabian desert to control the incense trade between south Arabia and the Mediterranean. (Incense, now fashionable as an offering to the gods, contributed enormously to the wealth of south Arabia, wealth which seems to have produced nothing worth mention.) The Saïte pharaohs drew support from Greek mercenaries and merchants; a tyrant of Corinth named his son for Psammetichus. Necho II (609–594), Psammetichus' successor, tried to cut a canal from the Nile to the Red Sea, and sent a Phoenician fleet around Africa. The Lydians' invention of coinage* is evidence of their economic interests; the wealth of the Lydian kings was fabulous—"as rich as Croesus." Greeks now rivaled the Phoenicians as the principal carriers of the Mediterranean.

Trade both required and produced both markets and goods. Markets were found in the growing colonies and the swelling populations of the old countries. Goods were supplied by increased agriculture, mining, and manufacturing. Corinth, with its florid pottery and metalwork, became a great city. Phoenician glass, dyed fabrics, and ivory, Arabian perfumes, Egyptian linens and faïence, amulets,* and papyrus* scrolls, were money making luxuries. Slaves and metals remained major cargoes, though wine and oil perhaps took first place, and there was even shipping enough for trade in grain.

Profits from commerce and manufacturing produced a new rich class, distinct from the old, landed, oligarchic families, and jealous of the oligarchs' control of the government. But the increase of wealth also produced a new poor. Wealth could be lent. Money* made lending easier, especially when, in sixth-century Greece, coins of small denominations were introduced. High rates of interest led to default, seizure of the debtor's land, and enslavement. Slavery meant competition for the artisan and the small farmer. As colonization fell off after 600, when the best places had been taken, the cities filled up with dispossessed and embittered men. A further cause for bitterness was injustice: the law, traditional and unwritten, could be shaped by the judges in favor of their fellow oligarchs. Therefore the late seventh century saw in Athens and Israel, and presumably elsewhere, the promulgation of written law codes.

Where law codes did not satisfy, the poor found leaders—men from the new rich or mavericks from the oligarchy—eager to overthrow the oligarchs and rule alone. Such a sole ruler the Greeks called a "tyrant." The word originally was not pejorative, but rapidly became so in the upper-class literature. Tyrants usually expropriated the property of their opponents, giving some to the poor, more to their mercenaries and friends. They also used the money of the rich for public buildings (which provided employment) and for religious festivals and games. They were therefore popular. The oligarchs who escaped found support in neighboring cities, normally hostile and glad to make trouble. Hence came attempts at counterrevolution, new murders, flights, and counterplots. Either counterrevolution or the initial threat of revolution might lead to an absolute ruler who represented the interests of the rich, but who would equally—qua absolute—be called a "tyrant." These developments, frequent in Greece, were not unparalleled elsewhere, for instance in the careers of Amasis of Egypt (568–526) and Nabonidus of Babylon (555–539).

THE BREAKDOWN OF STANDARDS AND INDIVIDUALISM

Tyranny was the extreme example of the breakdown of standards, now everywhere evident. Here again the Greeks were the leaders. Before 650, the poet Archilochus of Paros sang of his escape from battle at the cost of abandoning his shield—traditionally the ultimate disgrace. His poems set a fashion among poets, if not soldiers. The Greeks are the first people to produce individuals who are not afraid of going counter to common opinion, not because of some supposed revelation, but just because they want to, *and* of celebrating the fact. This new, open defiance of laws and standards reflects the diffusion of authority in Greek society, where every city made its own laws and individuals could move freely from one to another. But the change was not limited to Greece. Everywhere trade and travel sophisticated the travelers and shocked the stay-at-homes; to every country came aliens with outlandish ways and opinions. These aliens were "impure"—they did not observe the local purity laws—and might pollute others. So all around the Mediterranean we find an increase of concern about "purity," a matter hitherto taken for granted. Apollo at Delphi was busy prescribing purifications, and Greece swarmed with less authoritative purifiers, many claiming to use the spells of the legendary Orpheus. Entire cities were "purified," among them Athens. In Babylonia, the Judeans, deported from Jerusalem in 597 and later, were exposed to all sorts of impure contacts. Therefore Ezekiel was a fanatic about impurity, to which he gave far more space than any previous prophet. The priestly lawmakers of his time were also more concerned with it than were the earlier legislators. But both Ezekiel's polemics and the mixture of Judean and Babylonian names in later business documents show that many Judeans were neglecting purity rules, breaking away from their communities, and becoming unattached individuals.

In Greece this growth of individualism produced a new literature—personal lyric poetry. Lyrics, anonymous and often intended for use in rituals, had hitherto been concerned with common experiences. Now, along the Ionian coast, appear poets who tell us their names and sing of themselves, their political and military adventures, their travels and homesickness, poverty and drinking parties, hates and loves. No earlier literature exists in which love plays so large a part. Significantly, the greatest of the new love poets, Sappho of Lesbos (c. 600), is the first woman whose fame as a writer survived to modern times. Love is the easiest adventure for the individualist; for the respectable woman, in this period, it was the *one* adventure. Her home was her realm—she would be angry if her husband stayed home and meddled in her business. Accordingly, Sappho's poems celebrated that love between women which was the obverse of Greek male relationships, but plays almost no part in later Greek literature, perhaps because that was mostly written by and for men. Why?

With such eroticism and, for men, the related interest in athletics, goes the development of Greek sculpture and drawing already mentioned. The first major works of sculpture—beginning before 600—are statues of naked youths,* often memorials of individuals. The nudity probably comes from athletics; women are shown clothed. These statues were painted, but the colors, and the Greek sense of color, are lost to us. Other factors in the new art were delight in elaborate linear patterns, seen in Ionian statues, and equal delight in simplicity, seen in the Doric temples of the following age.

Of these many changes—increase in population and trade, extension of monetary economy, breakdown of standards, and development of individualism and of the arts—the political concomitants differed somewhat in each city. Generally, trading cities had tyrants early and often —so Corinth and the big cities of the Ionian coast and Sicily. Many small, out-of-the-way places never had them: their oligarchs stayed in power. For later history the developments in Sparta and Athens were of greatest importance.

SPARTA

In Sparta the Dorian invaders, much taller than the other Greeks, made the natives serfs ("helots" was the local word). They also conquered all the southern Peloponnese. With 600,000 acres of arable land, capable of supporting 30,000 warriors with their dependents and helots, they could afford to neglect colonization, keep their population at home, and become the greatest military power in Greece. Their worried neighbors backed a helot revolt in the mid-seventh century, which almost ruined the Spartans. Since they could not do without the helots, who did the agricultural work, they reorganized their state as a military camp. Helots were prohibited even from carrying their masters' weapons. (Aristotle remarked that those who carry the weapons decide the form of the government.) Citizens were forbidden to engage in agriculture or business; their lives were devoted to military duties. The most difficult but most important duty was suppression of personality, for the decisive factor in battles was the discipline of the hoplite line; every man must keep his assigned place and do exactly as ordered. To foster esprit de corps, boys were taken from home at twelve and brought up in troops, trained in military exercises, music (besides battle songs, they memorized and sang their laws), concern for what people thought of them, respect for elders, obedience, endurance, and silence. As youths they went into the secret police, to ferret out and murder potentially rebellious helots. As adults they went into the army. Luxuries were prohibited, domestic life reduced to a minimum; a soldier ate with his fellows in the mess hall. One visitor, after tasting the food, said, "Now I understand why the Spartans do not fear death." Rewards were honors which made life less comfortable: victors in the Olympic games were assigned to the front rank in battle. Sparta became a military machine devoted to perpetuating itself. The soldiers were buried in their red uniforms.

The rest of Greece admired Sparta, partly because of its military success, more because Spartan life was a training in "virtue" in the "good old-fashioned" sense, the sense inculcated in children by adults, who want of children respect, obedience, endurance ("Stop crying!"), and silence. But the most important of the Spartan virtues was the men's willingness to die in defense of their country and in obedience to their laws—a virtue without which no country in a competitive world can long endure. The Greek admiration for Sparta was rooted in common sense. But it had another root in the irrational. Self-inflicted suffering satisfies deep psychological drives and is therefore prominent in primitive religions. Greek religion had little of it, and the growth of individualism and rationalism diminished what little there was. Repressed drives found prudential justification in the example of Sparta; what could not be excused as superstition was admired as wisdom. Sparta also inspired the Greek philosophical imagination: it showed what could be achieved by lawgiving—the imposition of a "rational" pattern on the life of an entire city. Lycurgus, the supposed "lawgiver" of Sparta, became the great legendary representative of a class whose first real members had been the lawgivers of colonies; the recognition of the importance of the "lawgiver" and the ideal of "the city with good laws" were probably derived from colonization. Sparta did not reciprocate the philosophers' admiration. It wanted unanimity, not speculation, and banished philosophers because they disagreed. But many philosophers (who would have liked to banish one another) were not thus deterred. Sparta became the chief historical source of the ascetic and authoritarian ideals at work in Plato's *Republic* and its philosophical followers (including contemporary totalitarians).

ATHENS

Athens did not subject its neighbors; instead it gave them citizenship. By the end of the eighth century it had united Attica, a territory almost half the size of Long Island. Therefore it, too, at first had no need to colonize or trade. With economic change, the oligarchs gave way gradually. The law began to be published shortly before 621. Solon, in 593, abolished some debts, prohibited enslavement for debt, encouraged manufacture and trade, and reportedly so reformed courts and elections that the poorer citizens could restrain the oligarchy. The development of trade enabled the landowners to use their ground for olive groves, which paid four times what they could earn from grain. Cheap grain could now be imported from the plains around the Black Sea. Some thirty odd years after Solon, Pisistratus became tyrant, but followed the usual policy of tyrants with unusual moderation and success. He preserved the external forms of government, improved the lot of small farmers, won Athens a footing on the Hellespont (securing the route for the grain trade), built up the city, and died peacefully in 527. The relative tranquillity of his reign went with its prosperity, to which an increase in Athenian trade also contributed. Important exports were olive oil and a new style of pottery, called "black figure"* because of the elegant silhouettes of men and animals cavorting on its orange-red ground. This black figure ware outsold Corinthian pottery all around the Mediterranean—a success deserved by the vigor and variety of its decoration.

Two sons of Pisistratus continued his rule in Athens until 514, when one of them was murdered. The survivor's reprisals increased and united his opponents. He was driven out in 510. An alliance of oligarchic and democratic elements then established a new constitution, a compromise in which the *demos*—practically speaking, the majority of the citizens—had the ultimate say.

The resultant democracy was not a government by elected representatives, of the sort familiar in the modern world. Instead it was a direct government by the citizen body, which formed the controlling assembly and decided even technical questions like the disposition of troops before a campaign. To assure that all the citizens had equal likelihood to hold office, officials came to be chosen by lot rather than elected; thus every citizen not mentally incompetent had a chance, and at some time would probably have an obligation, to participate at some level in the work of government, normally a nuisance and a bore. The system must have been particularly onerous because the minor towns and territories had their local governments, on the Athenian model. To get attendance for the Athenian assembly police had to noose the marketplace with a red powdered rope and herd the citizens in—those who got marked were fined. The assembly's control over officials was secured by limitation of their terms to one year, at the end of which they were called to account before a court. But the citizen body which controlled this democracy was composed only of adult, free, native-born males— about six percent of the population; women, children, slaves, and aliens were excluded. To be granted citizenship was a rare honor. As always, however, the quality of the government depended less on its form than on the character of those in power. In Athens, the *demos* exhibited surprising moderation, the fruit of the oligarchic tradition of mutual forbearance, essential for the working of a democracy. Each side must be confident that the other will not push its victories too far; awareness of common interest must be stronger than mutual distrust. In Athens this awareness was intensified by the hostility of their neighbors and the threat of a return of Pisistratus' family. Another factor was the discovery of large deposits of silver, shortly after 490. Silver built a big navy, which produced employment, prosperity, and civic pride.

THE POLITICAL HISTORY OF THE NEAR EASTERN KINGDOMS

The political fortunes of the great Near Eastern kingdoms from the fall of Assyria in 609 to the rise of Persia after 559 need not long detain us. The first part of the period was dominated by the alliance of Babylon and Media that had brought down the Assyrians. Cemented by marriage of the daughter of the Median king to Nebuchadnezzar II, it enabled both states to turn their forces against their other neighbors. Babylon attacked the Egyptians (who had invaded Syria), drove them back to Suez, annexed Syria and Palestine, and between 600 and 573 suppressed several revolts along the coast and forced its suzerainty on Tyre. The Medes extended their rule northwest through Armenia, presumably drove the Scythians into Russia, and penetrated Anatolia where they came into conflict with Lydians who were expanding eastwards. The war ended on May 28, 585, when an eclipse of the sun during a battle frightened both sides so badly that they made peace and accepted the Halys as their common boundary. The agreement was confirmed by marriage of the daughter of the King of Lydia to the heir of the Median throne. After Nebuchadnezzar's death in 562 and the overthrow of his son in 560, Babylonian relations with Media deteriorated and subsequent Babylonian rulers expanded their territory in the northwest, taking Harran and campaigning in Cilicia. But the last of them, Nabonidus (555–539) was apparently more anxious to control the trade between southern Arabia and the Mediterranean. He also had domestic difficulties with the priests of Marduk in Babylon. The Egyptians, meanwhile, after standing off the Babylonians at the Suez in 601, struck back by fomenting revolts in Palestine and encouraging the resistance of Tyre. They also subjugated Nubia and attempted to subjugate Cyrene. This attempt came a cropper in 568 and touched off a domestic revolution in which a major factor was hostility to the Greek mercenaries and merchants who under royal protection had permeated the country. The new dynast (Amasis, 568–526) limited Greek traders to the port of Naucratis but did not give up his Greek mercenaries and was able to annex Cyprus. Lydia, after making peace with the Medes, turned westward and subjugated, one by one, most of the Greek cities of the Asia Minor coast.

JUDEA AND THE DEVELOPMENT OF JUDAISM

The territorial consequences of these border wars were presently wiped out by the rise of Persia, but one minor state, overwhelmed by the Babylonian expansion, was meanwhile shaping the literature that was to shape the religion of the western world: the history of the tiny kingdom of Judah ranks in importance with those of equally tiny Athens and Sparta.

All over the Near East "nationalistic" reactions against the Assyrians had been associated with the cults of "national" gods: Nebuchadnezar II's enormous expenditure for the temple of Marduk in Babylon is a conspicuous example. So Judea saw a revival of the cult of Yahweh. Since Yahweh was now protector of the poor, this revival was associated with demands for legal reform. About 630, when Assyria was losing her grip, a lawyer in Jerusalem produced a new code as a program for future reforms, including the prohibition of the worship of gods other than Yahweh, and relief of the poor. He drew on older "Yahweh-alone" traditions, common usage, and ancient taboos, but his work was organized by his own thought, replete with his own invention, and cast in his own style. He represented it as "the law of Yahweh" and—probably—as the work of Moses, and he arranged to have it "found" by the high priest in the Jerusalem temple in 621. It was taken to King Josiah, authenticated by a prophetess, and accepted. Most of it is preserved, with minor interpolations, in chapters 12–26 and 28 of Deuteronomy. King Josiah tried to enforce it, but he also tried at Megiddo to stop Necho II's invasion of Syria and so met his end in 609. His defeat seems to have been taken as proof of the error of his ways; the later prophecies of Jeremiah and Ezekiel show polytheism back in practice.

But the "Yahweh-alone" party held to the Deuteronomic code, and the code reshaped the party. Like the laws of Sparta, it was to be learned by heart, repeated morning and night, an everpresent monitor of its people. The central act of religion became the learning of the Law, and this it remains for most of Judaism. Moreover, the Deuteronomist inspired a school of followers, recognizable by their imitation of his style, who augmented his code with a "historical" framework eventually extended to include earlier collections of legends and court records. These they reworked to make one great "history," teaching that only when Israel worshiped Yahweh alone did it prosper, and whenever it worshiped other gods it was punished. Thus the "historical" half of the Old Testament began to take shape. Other writers of the school collected, edited, and improved the works of the "Yahweh-alone" prophets. To prevent worship of gods other than Yahweh, the Deuteronomist had proposed to limit sacrificial worship to Jerusalem. Consequently, when the Judeans were carried off to Babylonia, those who held to the code developed a new, nonsacrificial form of worship, which eventually became prevalent in Judaism and Protestant Christianity.

The party's position was strengthened by the fall of Jerusalem. Since Nebuchadnezzar's defeat of the Egyptians and takeover of the Syro-Palestinian coast (605–603), the city had been subject to Babylon. Popular, nationalist feeling encouraged revolt by the claim that Yahweh would defend his city. The "Yahweh-alone" prophets, on the contrary, maintained that Yahweh, angered by the city's apostasy, would prolong its servitude; accordingly they were pro-Babylonian. When Nebuchadnezzar, irritated by repeated conspiracies, plundered the city in 597 and destroyed it in 587, the party was able to say, "We told you so."

Moreover, among the exiles in Babylonia, whither Nebuchadnezzar deported most of the upper-class Judeans, the party had a strong position. Their nonsacrificial worship—prayer and praise (psalms), sometimes with reading and exposition of the Law—was inexpensive by comparison with sacrifice. It required no special clergy, equipment, nor temple, only a "meeting place" (Greek: *synagogue*). This became characteristic of "Judaism"—the name later given to the religion of the Judeans (whence the English "Jews"). Another new characteristic was isolation. Observance of purity laws and the refusal to worship any god save Yahweh had been merely punctilious in Judea; in the "diaspora"— the "scattering" of Judean settlements outside Palestine—this behavior cut the observant off from the life of the world around and made them a peculiar people. It also gave the party coherence, while the Law's concern for the poor (a sign of its times) gave them the strength of mutual support, which must have won over many of their fellow exiles. Eventually they would return to Jerusalem and gain control of the restored temple. Deuteronomy would then become the basis for an official legal tradition. In yet remoter time its prohibition of the worship of any god other than Yahweh (an offense it would punish by death, Deut. 12–13) was to be a factor in the hostility between the Jews and the Romans and was to be taken over from Judaism by Christianity and Islam—a major element in the tradition of intolerance from which the western world has suffered much. It was not, however, the only element. Most ancient cities prohibited worship, or at least, public worship, of deities whom the city had not officially accepted. On this ground the charge of "not worshiping the gods that the city recognizes, but other new divinities" was included in the indictment that led to the execution of Socrates. Rome repeatedly prohibited the practice of alien cults within the city limits and expelled, or even executed, their worshipers. Deuteronomic legislation may be seen as an extreme case of this general practice. But in the pagan world such laws were commonly neglected and popular foreign deities commonly won official acceptance, so the influence of the Deuteronomist made the Jews, and later the Christians, peculiar.

Not all Judean exiles in Babylonia, however, were followers of the Deuteronomist. The prophet Ezekiel had a different style and vocabulary, and different legal opinions. Akin to him in these matters was a group of priestly collectors, editors, and inventors of ancient traditions, particularly of legal material, to whom we owe compositions so diverse as Leviticus and the superb creation story in Genesis 1. The notion of Yahweh as creator is also important in the greatest writer of the exile— and one of the greatest writers of all time—the so-called Second Isaiah, author of Isaiah 40–55, whose lyrical expressions of joy and hatred, release and revenge, are of unmatched power. But most powerful and magnificent of all is his concept of Yahweh, throned on the enormous circle of the heavens, declaring, "I am the first, and I am the last; and beside me there is no God." All gods of all other nations are mere idols which can neither hurt nor help. The religious conceptions of all other peoples are worthless.

FOR FURTHER READING

A. Andrewes, *The Greek Tyrants*
G. Glotz, *Ancient Greece at Work*
M. Noth, *A History of Israel*

M. Rostovtzeff, *Greece*
M. Smith, *The Ancient Greeks*

10
PERSIA AND ATHENS

THE PERSIAN EMPIRE, ITS RISE AND CHARACTERISTICS

Cyrus the Great began his career about 559 as a kinglet in southwestern Persia. He won over the Medes about 550, defeated Croesus of Lydia in 546, and then subjugated Asia Minor. Next he descended on Babylon. King Nabonidus, at odds with the clergy of Marduk, chief god of the city, fell in 539. Cyrus then turned to northeastern Persia and was killed there about 530. His son, Cambyses, settled that frontier, then conquered Egypt in 525. After his death in 522, the throne was seized by Darius* who put down revolts all over the empire and set about organizing what Cyrus and Cambyses had hastily conquered.

The organization he created was the largest empire the world had seen. It initially included Asia Minor and adjacent islands, Armenia, Azerbaijan, Syria, Palestine, Egypt, northern Arabia, Mesopotamia, Persia, Afghanistan, Turkestan, Uzbekistan, the Tadzhik and part of the Kirgiz Soviet Republics, and western Pakistan. To these Darius himself added the rich Indus Valley and Thrace. Macedon and Cyrenaica submitted to him but remained self-governing. The size of this empire gave it a military advantage: its enemies on opposite sides were too far apart for effective military cooperation.

B.C.	
c. 585	Thales of Miletus, beginning of natural philosophy (physics)
561	Pisistratus becomes tyrant of Athens
c. 550	Cyrus of Persia conquers Astyages of Media
546	Cyrus conquers Croesus of Lydia
c. 540	Xenophanes, philosophic monotheism; "Second Isaiah," nationalistic monotheism
539	Cyrus conquers Nabonidus of Babylon
525	Cambyses, Cyrus' successor, conquers Egypt
c. 525	Pythagoras, the philosophic life; the Doric temples of southern Italy and Sicily
c. 525–400	Athenian red figure pottery at its best
522	Darius begins reorganization of the Persian empire
510	Pisistratus' family expelled from Athens
499	Ionian cities, aided by Athens, revolt from Persia
490	Battle of Marathon, Persian expedition against Athens beaten off
480	Xerxes, Darius' successor, invades Greece; Battle of Salamis, Xerxes' fleet crippled; Carthaginian invasion of Sicily defeated at Himera
479	Battle of Plataea, Xerxes' army destroyed; Battle of Mount Mycale, Xerxes' Aegean fleet destroyed; Persia loses Macedon, Thrace, and Cyrenaica
478	Athens creates the Delian League for liberation of Greek cities from Persia
c. 475	Parmenides' opposition of reality (changeless) to appearance (changing); Pindar (lyric poetry)
458	Aeschylus' *Oresteia*; beginning of Pericles' power
457	The "long walls" secure Athens from attack by land
454	The treasury of the Delian League moved to Athens
449	Athens makes peace with Persia
447	Beginning of the Parthenon, work of Ictinus
c. 447	The Sophists (argument and rhetoric); Sophocles (tragedy); Herodotus (history); Phidias (sculpture)
431–404	The Peloponnesian War, ending with destruction of the Athenian fleet, the long walls, and the Delian League; Socrates (moral philosophy); Hippocrates (rational medicine); Democritus (atomic theory); Aristophanes (comedy); Euripides (tragedy); Thucydides (history)
c. 405	Egypt revolts from Persia

The ruler of this empire, "the King," as the Greeks called him, was absolute. As usual, his power rested on control of the army and was exercised through his appointees. Nevertheless, this empire differed radically from the earlier empires of the Near East. The river valleys were no longer the centers of power, nor were the Semitic-speaking peoples the rulers. The Persians spoke an Indo-European language and ruled principally from Susa in Elam and Ecbatana in Media. They also had their own religion, in which an important element was the teaching of Zoroaster, a perhaps early-Iron-Age prophet of some east Iranian cattlemen, who had worshipped especially a god called Ahura Mazda, "the wise Lord." Inspired by Ahura, Zoroaster had denounced the fertility cults of the settled peasants and had promised to give his followers "the Kingdom." Nevertheless, Darius protected and sometimes financed, sometimes taxed the temples of his settled subjects. But the priesthoods of the river valley temples now declined sharply in power, less sharply in wealth. The cultural traditions of which they had been centers declined with them. The new ruling class was a very small group. Seven great families, intricately intermarried, held most major court positions, military appointments, and governments of the "satrapies," the twenty administrative districts into which the empire was divided. Below these families, many Persians and Medes, although not strictly members of the ruling group, became officers of the crown and were felt to be aliens by the subject peoples. Ahura had given the kingdom to "the King," not to the Persians—so, at least, the royal inscriptions said. Persians and Medes were privileged subjects, but still subjects. On the royal reliefs they, as well as the conquered peoples, carry the throne of "the King."

The great size of the satrapies may have been dictated by the small number of family administrators. Both invited rebellion. Therefore the satraps (governors) were not given control of the army corps in their domains; legal cases could be appealed to the King; an efficient courier service and chains of fire signals kept the court in touch with the satrapies. Special inspectors, "the King's ears," reported on local conditions. The few high officials relied on a numerous bureaucracy united by the use of Aramaic, which in Assyrian times had become the lingua franca of business and had begun to be used in the government. Aramaic now became, even in Persia itself, the common administrative language, although the Persian rulers spoke Persian to one another and royal inscriptions were commonly in Persian with translations in the local languages of the satrapies. (In Egypt, hieroglyphics were simplified for rapid writing in a script called "demotic.") The international bureaucracy was matched by an international army of which the core was 10,000 Persian spearmen* and the Median cavalry, then the mercenary troops and levies from the satrapies. To these unifying forces should be added the royal gold currency* and the traders for whom the imperial

116 PERSIA AND ATHENS

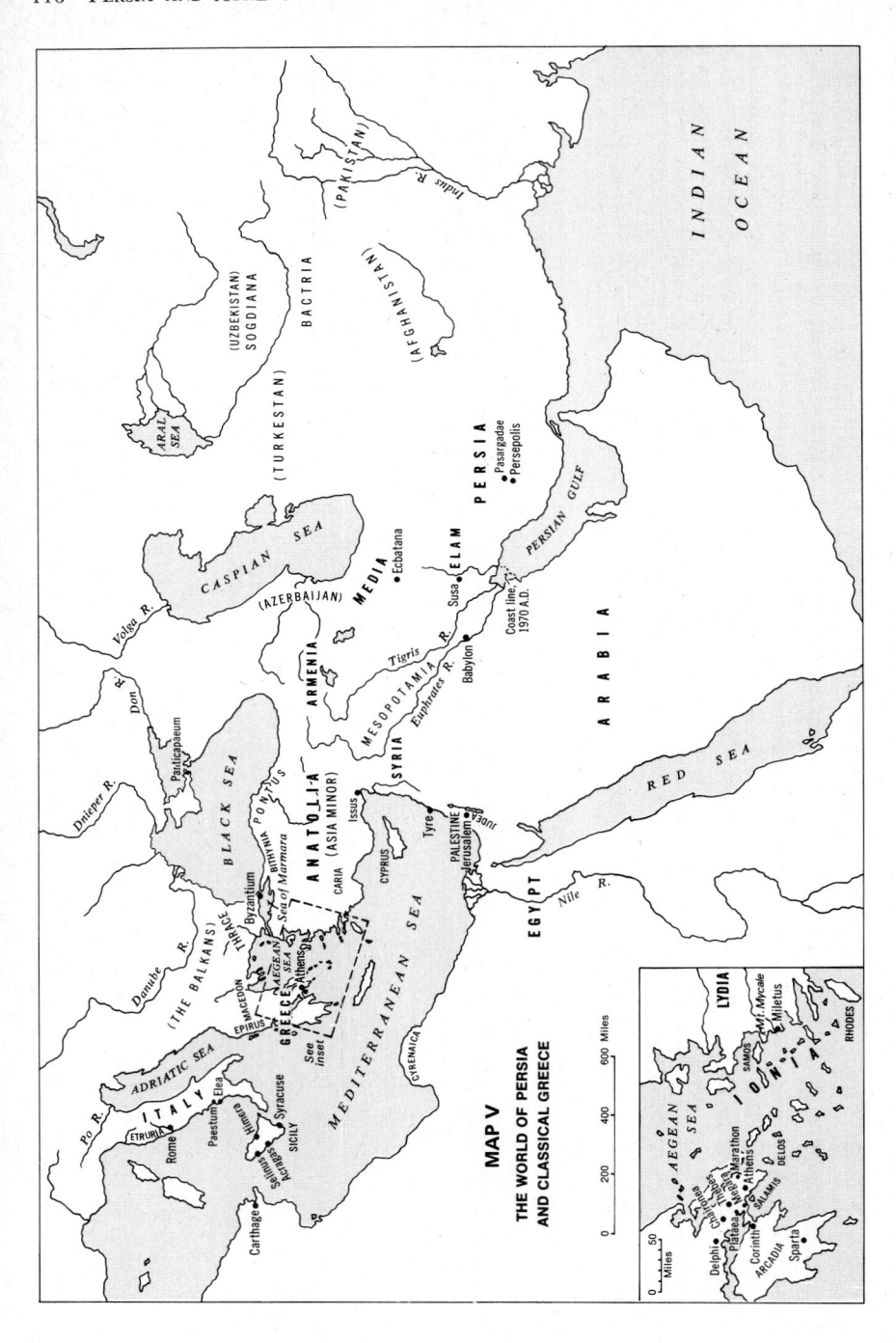

and satrapal courts provided markets, while the extent of the empire made for greater freedom and security in transport of merchandise than ever before.

These bonds held the empire together for 200 years in spite of repeated crises. The death of each monarch touched off a contest for the throne and revolts in the provinces. Xerxes, Darius' successor, lost much of his fleet and army in his attempt to conquer Greece in 480–479. Macedon and Cyrenaica then broke away, and the Persians were driven out of Thrace and the coastal cities of western Asia Minor, but eventually regained the cities. The Indus Valley was lost. Later on, satrapies became hereditary, the satraps built up private armies, and this led to revolts by which Pontus, with some adjacent territory, was lost. Egypt broke away from 405 to 342. Cyprus was long fought over. But in spite of peripheral losses, harem intrigue, and bureaucratic inefficiency, the empire held together. The Persians never went beyond the Assyrians in the art of winning over the peoples they conquered. Like the Assyrians, they deported large groups and so created minorities dependent on them for protection. They also enlisted many in their army and bureaucracy and so won over some. The prevalent attitudes of the subject peoples remained temporary subservience and latent hostility, but for the Persians, subservience sufficed.

The ruling class had a taste for magnificence. Artists from many subject peoples were employed to decorate palaces of which Susa, Pasargadae, and Persepolis have yielded sumptuous remains. Their sculpture shows the court on parade;* the subject is stodgy, the technique brilliant; Greeks and Lydians were the stonecutters. Many elegant vessels of gold and silver survive; the goldsmiths were Medes and Egyptians. And so on, for the other artifacts. When we ask what the Persians themselves did, the answer is: They ruled. Ruling is a skill, like cello playing or baseball, that children can learn from their parents. It is commonly passed on from father to son so long as a ruling class survives.

DEVELOPMENTS IN SUBJECT COUNTRIES:
EGYPT, JUDEA, IONIA

The subjects of the Persian rulers were left free to follow their own traditions. In Egypt and Judea national tradition was compounded by wishful thinking. As the struggle against external domination became more difficult, men found consolation in fancy, retelling their "histories" with less concern for fact or spinning out legislation for imaginary states. Plato's *Republic* and *Laws* show the same reaction in Greece after the failure of Athens.

In Jerusalem, whither Cyrus reportedly permitted the Judeans to return, cult and temple were reëstablished and writers of the priestly and levitical schools gave the Genesis-Kings collection approximately its present form. The prophetic books also continued to grow, mostly by interpolation. But prophecy was dangerous in the Persian empire and declined, as men, despairing of immediate changes, turned either to the past or the far-off future, to daydreams rather than prophecies. Stories of the good old days and collections of pious sayings and of lamentations were rivaled by accounts of the good time to come, when Yahweh would make Jerusalem the capital of all the earth.

Meanwhile the immediate concern of most men turned, as in Greece, to private life and public rituals. Hence the Psalms, a collection of songs which became for at least 1,600 years the daily devotional reading of pious Jews and Christians. Perhaps no other book has done so much to shape the western mind. The collection contains a few songs from preëxilic times, imploring Yahweh's blessings on the king (21, 46, etc.). A few retell the Mosaic legend in the spirit of postexilic times (105, 106, etc.). Yet more reflect the cult of the restored temple (134, 135, 136, etc.). But the main concern of the book is the private life of the righteous man—his determination to follow the law of Yahweh, his failings, appeals for mercy, fear of his enemies, and hope in Yahweh. Like the Deuteronomic Law, these poems were to be memorized. They picture the real world as a world of enemies from which the righteous man should turn to conversation with Yahweh, i.e., to schizophrenia. The conversation repeatedly comes to the question: "Why do the righteous suffer?" To this the answer is, "Trust in Yahweh and you will be saved."

For some, this assurance was not enough. The author of the poem in Job 3–26, perhaps the greatest intellect in the Hebrew tradition, stated the problem of evil with relentless clarity. What answer he came to, if any, will never be known. An editor has substituted a pious conclusion: God is incomparably great, therefore it is useless to question his doings.

In 546 the Persians subjugated the Greek cities along the west coast of Asia Minor. Intellectually, this had been the foremost area of the Greek world. Here the Homeric poems had taken shape, the lyric poets had sung. Here, too, philosophy had begun about 585, with the speculations of Thales as to the possible origin of all things from some single element. This element, he thought, was water. That he was wrong is trivial. The important thing was his attempt to conceive nature as an intelligible order, a "cosmos," and to explain this order by reference to observable processes (the solidification and vaporization of water) so that the explanation could be refuted and replaced. The Egyptians and Babylonians, too, had supposed the world emerged or was made from water, but for them the water was a goddess, so the production of the world could not be investigated. Myths are irrefutable, but lead to nothing. Thales' demonstrable error, because demonstrable, led to the physical sciences.

GREEK PHILOSOPHY AND SCIENCE

It did so because the Greeks were on hand to follow the lead. The source of Greek science was, as Plato said, their "passion" for "wondering," for asking "Why?" Hence their "love of wisdom" (in Greek, *philosophia*), their willingness to question accepted ideas and to follow fearlessly to their arguments' conclusions. (Contrast the Israelites, for whom the first principle of wisdom was "the fear of Yahweh.") Greek intellectual daring was, in Ionia, fused with the new idea of individualism, that a man does well to disagree with common opinion. A philosopher says, "I have sought out for myself"; a historian, "The stories told by the Greeks are many and ridiculous; I write what in my opinion is true." And Sappho, "Some say one thing is most beautiful, some another, but I say it is what you love."

From Ionia the spirit of inquiry spread abroad when the Persian conquest produced a wave of emigrants. South Italy and Sicily became centers of philosophic thought. Xenophanes, who emigrated about 545, argued that the primary substance must be single, eternal, unchanging, conscious, controlling all things—in a word, God. (Some of his arguments have recently been repeated, perhaps independently, by Heisenberg.) Thus physics led to theology. The contrast is striking between this monotheism and that of Second Isaiah, roughly contemporary. Second Isaiah's monotheism is a product of wishful polemic. Yahweh must be able to rescue the Israelites; therefore he controls the world; therefore the other gods are mere idols. Yahweh remains a person, distinct from his creatures. Xenophanes, led by philosophy to hypothecate an omnipresent, primary substance, sought to make this substance acceptable by calling it "God." Both lines of thought led to attacks on idolatry and on popular notions of the gods.

Xenophanes' thought was carried on by a school at Elea where Parmenides (c. 475) demonstrated the contradictions between the notions of being and of change—that is, between metaphysics and common sense. Maintaining that we should not trust the senses, but judge by reason, he chose metaphysics and conceived of reality as changeless being. Back in Ionia, Heraclitus took the other horn of the dilemma and insisted that reality is constant change, like a fire, of which all things are but brief configurations. Meanwhile Pythagoras, a Samian aristocrat who had emigrated to south Italy about 530, founded a brotherhood to practice a peculiar way of life (observing many taboos) and to reform society. Soon his followers were involved in philosophic problems and his way of life became a "philosophy." Within a century revolutions destroyed his brotherhood, but in the new world, with its growth of private life, political exiles, and *deracinés*, the notion of a society to practice the philosophic life lived on. It inspired Plato, influenced monasticism, and has continued, since, to find followers.

Intellectual and political ferment in south Italy and Sicily accompanied economic and artistic development. The Doric temples of Selinus, Paestum, and Acragas (Agrigentum)—wonderfully calm, simple buildings—stand as monuments to the genius of their architects and the wealth of their cities. "The men of Acragas," said one visitor, "dine as if they expected to die tomorrow, and build as if they expected to live forever."

THE PERSIAN ATTACK ON GREECE, AND THE DELIAN LEAGUE

The Greeks were attacked by Persia and Carthage early in the fifth century. Darius sent spies to the western Mediterranean and two exploratory expeditions to Greece, the first shipwrecked in 492, the second beaten off by the Athenians at Marathon in 490. The main attacks, Persian and Carthaginian together, came under Xerxes in 480. They failed. Xerxes lost much of his fleet at Salamis; the Carthaginians were annihilated at Himera. Next year the rest of Xerxes' fleet was destroyed at Mount Mycale, and the land army he had left in Greece was wiped out at Plataea. The Greeks had solid body armor, longer spears, and better athletic training. To the Persians these defeats, though serious, were peripheral; they did not damage the main structure of the empire. But to the Greeks, victory was all-important. Even Marathon was a cause of enormous pride to Athens; her friends claimed it was the first time Greeks had stood up to Persian troops. When the new Athenian fleet played the leading part in the victory of Salamis, Athens could claim to have been the savior of Greece; the claim was to be a factor in building her empire. Another factor was the instability of Sparta, where the upper class opposed foreign campaigns because they increased the powers of the kings. Accordingly Sparta left the liberation of Greek cities around the Aegean to the Athenians.

For this task the Athenians were well equipped. The cities were almost all seaport towns, and the coast was deeply dentelated; thus a naval force had a tactical advantage. Many of the cities were Ionian; so were the Athenians. They were familiar with the Aegean because of their trade; trade and democratic government had given them businessmen-politicians skilled in negotiation, aware of economic interests, and able to draw an advantageous contract.

Such a contract created in 478 the Delian League, which met and stored its money on Delos, the Ionian island shrine of Apollo. (Sanctuaries were customarily treasuries, the god being guard.) The contract bound the signatories to follow a common foreign policy and to contribute ships or money. Athens commanded the fleet. The League's minor members paid, in assessments, enough to maintain about a hundred ships. These ships Athens provided, gaining military experience while the allies learned how to pay taxes. Besides these, Athens contributed about a hundred ships of her own and the other major members, taken together, about the same number; in all, 300 ships and 60,000 men. This force freed the Greek cities around the Aegean; the liberated cities joined the League. Others were forced to come in. Athens also conquered islands held by non-Greek peoples, sold the inhabitants as slaves, and settled their lands with Athenian colonists. When members tried to withdraw from the League, they were conquered and forced to remain. Thus the Delian League became practically an Athenian empire. Athens intervened in her allies' domestic policies by supporting democratic parties and setting up governments similar to her own. These parties and governments were usually loyal to Athens, but the people of the allied cities never thought themselves Athenians. They knew that legally they were not Athenians and could not normally become so; they also knew that Athens exploited them economically and stifled their trade. (Their pottery disappeared from foreign sites, replaced by Athenian.) As in other Near Eastern empires, one political group dominated its neighbors but was unable to assimilate them. Like the Persians, Athens had contingents furnished by subject states in her military forces and so secured the loyalty of some. She went beyond the Persians in securing the support of a party in each subject city by political affiliation—"political ideology" now appears as an important factor in alliances. But she remained, in relation to her subjects, an alien ruling power.

ATHENS' POLITY AND POLITICS

Athens' empire abroad and democracy at home were complementary. The empire paid directly for about a hundred of the city's ships; indirectly, as a trading area (soon required to use the same coinage* and measures as Athens) it paid more. This money paid the citizens who participated in Athens' assemblies and the jurors who served in her courts. Without pay the poor could not have attended to these offices.

Above all, the navy had to have oarsmen, and oarsmen had to be paid.[1] The wages of 36,000 oarsmen (for 200 ships) came from the empire. Since the oarsmen were the poor, the poor favored imperialism. Since the poor—as always—were the majority, democracy perpetuated imperialism. Such domestic opposition as there was came from the landed aristocracy and the middle-class farmers who together furnished the best troops of the army. But in the 460s there were only 300 cavalry and about 10,000 hoplites. Further, in 457 a pair of "long walls" connecting Athens with its harbor, was completed. The Greeks had little skill in siege warfare. With these walls Athens could not be conquered, for she controlled the sea and could not be starved. The navy could now dispense with the army.

The democrats, however, had got involved in central Greece and needed the army to hold it down. Also they were backing an Egyptian revolt against the Persians and that took a large force. It was no time to alienate fighting men. Therefore, Pericles, the new leader of the democratic party, moved slowly. Defeats abroad forced him to make peace with Persia in 449 and with the powers of mainland Greece in 446. Thus the army's importance was minimized, but the navy remained essential to control the overseas League. Naval employment was rivaled by a building program, of which the Parthenon* is the masterpiece, financed by the League's treasury. This was supplemented by economic measures: The coinage of most League members was replaced by Athenian issues. Law cases were made transferable to Athens, assuring a steady flow of visitors, business, and bribes. Resultant rebellions by League members were profitably suppressed. Colonization was pushed and an expedition sent to the Black Sea, whence Athens imported its grain and much of its protein food (salt fish), and where it sold much wine, pottery, metalware, and oil. Cheap food was a mainstay of democracy. These measures kept Athens relatively prosperous, but ruined the other cities of the League. The eclipse of the Ionian coast, begun by Persian conquest, was finished by Athenian liberation.

Moreover, Athens' prosperity frightened her enemies. Thebes, the main city of central Greece, remembered Athens' attempt to dominate the district. Megara's trade was ruined by Athenian rivalry. Corinth also felt the loss of trade and was angered by Athenian interference with her colonies. Sparta felt her position as leader of Greece was threatened. The resultant "Peloponnesian War" broke out in 431, two years before

---

[1] Sailing boats were for trade. Ships fought by ramming each other; in such a fight a sailboat had no chance against a more maneuverable oared ship.* Moreover in summer considerable areas of the Mediterranean are often becalmed. Only oared ships had the speed and reliability required by war. Consequently they dominated the Mediterranean as late as the sixteenth century.

Pericles' death, was interrupted by a truce from 421 to 413, and ended in 404. Its upshot was the ruin of Athens, which had lost between a half and two-thirds of her citizens; her territory had been plundered annually for eighteen years; about 500 warships had been lost; her people were starving. She surrendered to the Spartans; the long walls were pulled down, the fleet and the overseas territories were given up, and the Delian League was dissolved.

ATHENIAN CULTURE

The Athenian "empire" was the shortest-lived of all Near Eastern empires, and the smallest; at its peak it encompassed only Attica, most Aegean islands and the coastlands on the north and east, a sprinkling of strongholds around Greece, southern Asia Minor, and the Black Sea, and one colony in Italy. But the cultural development of Athens, in this brief period, transformed western history.

Novelty in human institutions is always a matter of degree. There had previously been big cities and influential bourgeoisies. But about 50,000 Athenian citizens governed an empire. Of these, perhaps 15,000 were well-to-do. They constituted a new kind of market and power. The art created for them is radically different from that created for the rulers of Egypt, Assyria, and Persia, because, by comparison with those rulers, even the wealthiest Athenians were almost indigent. Alcibiades, one of the richest men in the city, had an estate of less than 75 acres. Another very rich Athenian had a fortune, mostly in land, valued at 90,000 drachmas—the yearly income of 600 manual laborers. He might have had an income equal to that of 60 workers, minus a heavy tax load. (Consequently, most rich men put their money into "invisible" property such as precious metals rather than the more easily taxable sort—land, shops, ships. As usual, poverty discouraged economic development.) The high officials of the state and its guests dined at the public table; the *pièce de résistance* was a barley loaf with goat's milk and cheese. On festival days there was meat, the loaf was wheat, and there might be a sesame cake. Austerity transformed art; limited means necessitated simplicity. To simplicity, already characteristic of Greek elegance, Athenian art added delicacy of feeling, a lighter touch, and an interest in sentiment. This more economical and appealing art, for these reasons, became "classic."

This bourgeois restraint also affected Athenian architecture. Earlier empires produced palaces; Athens, public buildings: colonnaded markets, dockyards, gymnasia, law courts, assembly places, theaters, music halls to seat thousands—all unknown to pre-Greek building. Some structures we should think necessary were little developed. Sewers were rare; many houses kept a sheep or a pig as a dispose-all. These animals were commonly driven out to the country for pasture; one might meet a herd of them in a narrow street and be knocked down and run over. But along with this indifference to rudimentary physical conveniences went extraordinary attention to buildings of cultural value. Even temples were designed less for the service of the gods than for the delight of citizens. Religious services remained simple. The priesthoods were elective offices, sought as public honors. The ground plan of the temples* remained that of a hut with a porch in front, a storage room behind, and sometimes a surrounding colonnade. But the structure was now of marble and the proportions a wonder to the world.* In place of the squat, bulldog strength of old Doric temples, the new Doric style was higher and lighter; even more so the Ionic, now adopted. The figures represented in architectural sculpture, too, became lighter. Decoration increased but was kept subordinate to structure and was extraordinarily delicate in detail. Bourgeois mentality appeared in naturalism, present even in figures of the gods; bourgeois morality restrained this naturalism by reverence and by the common-sense notion that art "should" represent and produce beautiful things. For private life, therefore, Athenian artists and artisans (in popular thought two groups almost identified) now produced utilitarian objects of unusual beauty. Domestic architecture, pottery,* furniture, even tools of this period are characteristically elegant in their lines, proportions, and decorative details. Nowhere else has the luxury of living with beautiful things been so generally available.

The intellectual interests of this Athenian bourgeoisie were also practical. Hence reading, writing,* and basic arithmetic were taught to all boys and even to girls. Next came rhetoric. To speak well was requisite for power in the assembly. In a law court it might be a matter of life or death. One had to speak for oneself, and the jury might number several hundred. Traveling teachers known as sophists ("men who make you wise") taught, besides rhetoric, "how to do well in life." They specialized in devising plausible arguments for any claim—hence the term "sophistry." One even tried to cure sorrow and other psychological disorders by rational persuasion. Sophistry contributed to the breakdown of moral standards and the danger of lawsuits. The man who could not afford to be trained by a sophist needed a professional speechwriter. Such writers wrote sample speeches to demonstrate their powers. Some had admirers who carried around and repeated their masterpieces. Speeches became a form of the new prose literature of entertainment. Since these professional writers often demonstrated their skill by arguing against common opinion, their work also contributed to the breakdown of traditional standards and consequent development of moral philosophy.

Athenians had little tolerance for philosophic teaching without practical application. Therefore the major developments in speculative physics were still made in Ionia, where Democritus (c. 430) anticipated nineteenth-century physics by adding, to Heraclitus' continual change, the specification that what is changing is a congeries of atoms. Scientific medicine also began in Ionia with Hippocrates, who argued that to understand an illness one must take into account the whole patient and his environment and must base one's treatment on experience of similar cases. From such *systematic* thinking came the Greek idea of scientific progress, by contrast to the fixed, traditional wisdom of the Near East, which considered progress mere improvement of technique. The Greek physician Ctesias boasts that the medical use of hellebore "was unknown to our fathers and grandfathers." It was a new discovery. Yet such scientific discovery was based on animism. We try to explain society in terms of mechanical causality; the Greeks explained nature in the anthropomorphic terms of society. Health is democratic—the equality of different forces in the body; a disease is produced by the "monarchy" of one element. All things must make reparation to one another if they overstep their limits. The lot of the Persians was the land; they tried to conquer the sea, and were punished. "Nothing overmuch" is the principle of an equalitarian and poor society.

SOCRATES

In spite of the scientific preëminence of Ionia, Athens became the center of the philosophical thought of the western world. Socrates,* an idle stonemason, made it so. He drifted around the city with a circle of rich or beautiful young men, entangling respectable citizens in arguments about "justice," "bravery," "piety," and the like, and making them look foolish. In 399 various victims accused him of corrupting the youth and introducing the worship of new deities. He was found guilty and executed. We must guess at his teachings from his pupils' reports, but some results of his work are certain. He changed the main concern of philosophy from physics to ethics. He developed the question-and-answer method of treating problems and so contributed to the discovery of logic. He created the private "philosophic life" devoted to intellectual investigation and indifferent to surrounding society. Finally, he formed a circle of disciples who propagated his teachings. His death made many of these disciples enemies of democracy; western philosophy inherited from them a tradition of separation from government and an affectation of superiority to public officials.

ATHENIAN LITERATURE

The condemnation of Socrates was in contrast to the freedom allowed Athenian dramatists. Oligarchic Greece had honored the gods with contests in athletics and lyric poetry, chiefly at rural shrines where the rich and their followers were the principal audience. Democratic Athens made these contests part of its civic festival of Athena and added to them, for its festivals of Dionysus, contests between dramatic poets and teams of performers. Elsewhere the lyric continued to flourish; Pindar, its greatest master in the fifth century, died in 438. But for bourgeois Athens, drama added to the lyric more naturalistic presentation, portrayal of human problems and passions, philosophic argumentation, cross-questioning, confrontation of personalities—in a word, the life of the city. As in the life of the city, almost anything might be called in question, particularly in comedy which had behind it a tradition of ritual abuse in the Dionysiac festivals. During the Peloponnesian War, Aristophanes produced plays attacking the ruling demagogues of the war party, lamenting the losses and advocating peace. He was equally free in ridiculing at least some of the gods, and even in tragedy critical discussion of generally accepted standards was common. Any radical idea attributed to Socrates can be matched in the tragedies of Aeschylus, Sophocles, and Euripides,* but the dramas always ended with virtue vindicated. This dubious virtue should not conceal their importance as the first examples of a new form of entertainment, more popular, thought provoking, lyrically beautiful, and profoundly moving than the world had heretofore seen.

Even more important than the drama, in the long run, was the development of a prose literature read for pleasure. Speeches have already been mentioned. The greatest works, however, were the histories, of which Herodotus' and Thucydides' are preserved. Herodotus' is an account of the eastern Mediterranean world from the beginning of the last Lydian dynasty (c. 672) until the ruin of Xerxes' expedition in 479. Thucydides' is a history of the Peloponnesian War. History had been written before (brilliantly, for instance, by the author of the life of David in I and II Samuel); it appeared independently in different civilizations and with different values. The specific value of Greek historiography is to ask questions. The authors did not begin from knowledge but from inquiry; our word "history" is a transliteration of the Greek word meaning "inquiry," and this sort of inquiry the Greeks invented. They set out to discover something. Herodotus asked the cause of the Persian war and found it, not in any particular fact, but in the panorama of Greek relations with the Near East.

The great thing about Herodotus' history is the scope. A Greek from Asia Minor, won over by Athens, he reflects the trading tradition

behind Ionian thought and its interest in geography. He
traveler, curious about all the sights, customs, and legends of
he visits. Why do they do this? How do they explain that? A
Egyptian priest once said, "The Greeks are always children." In Herodotus we glimpse the delight of these grown-up children in the extent and variety of the world. But, as a traveler, he is always an outsider; he has never seen a great government from the inside and has no clear knowledge of how one works.

Thucydides, by contrast, when he set out to discover why the Peloponnesian War had gone as it did, had a good notion of the likely reasons. He had been a member of the board of generals which controlled Athens. The great contribution of his work, therefore, is the conception of history as a concatenation of specific causes with specific results. He is remarkable, too, for his capacity to view a long series of facts as a single process, or reduce a complex of events to a single pattern. Thus, and by his sardonic picture of human behavior, he has been the teacher of rulers and has shaped history by shaping the beliefs of those who studied him. His own beliefs, and those of Herodotus, had been shaped by Homer. Both thought of war as the proper subject of history. But each strayed from the Homeric theme to indulge his own interests, Herodotus in foreign lands, Thucydides in Athenian politics.

In this respect, Thucydides represents the interests of the Athenian bourgeoisie, Herodotus of the uprooted. For the man who stayed in his own city, politics, business, and agriculture were the major concerns, and it was now settled, at least in Athens, that business and agriculture were beneath the dignity of literature. The political achievement of Athens, therefore, is the most specific record of its culture. That record is double.

ATHENS AS EXAMPLE

On the one hand Athens is the classic example of successful democratic government. Its democracy was strong enough to survive the debacle of 404, throw off a tyranny, and maintain itself, in spite of interruptions by outside powers, to Roman times. Moreover, democracy was not merely a political peculiarity; it stood for freedom in private life, an approach to equality in opportunity to hold public office, and an education which sought to produce adaptability rather than to perpetuate a pattern. For democracy thus conceived as a way of life, the great speech written for Pericles by Thucydides (II.35 ff.) is evidence, exposition, and apology.

On the other hand Athens was also the classic example of the failure of democracy. Her rule had ended in tyranny abroad and demagoguery at home. Abroad she subjugated her allies, looted them, and imposed on them, in the name of democracy, rulers from the lower classes who could hold their positions only with her help and would therefore be her spaniels. At home the courts were often grossly unjust; the assembly repeatedly refused to recognize unwelcome facts, make necessary sacrifices, and reward and punish justly. When the Spartans took the city, survivors and exiles joined in pulling down the long walls to the sound of flutes, "believing that day was the beginning of freedom for Greece." These words were written by Xenophon, an Athenian.

FOR FURTHER READING

J. Boardman, *Greek Art*
C. Bowra, *Ancient Greek Literature*
V. Ehrenberg, *The Greek State*
R. Frye, *The Heritage of Persia*
W. Jaeger, *The Theology of the Early Greek Philosophers*
E. Porada, *The Art of Ancient Iran*
A. Zimmern, *The Greek Commonwealth*

11
THE FOURTH CENTURY TO THE DEATH OF ALEXANDER

GREEK POLITICAL HISTORY, 404–330

From the fall of Athens to the fall of Persia the military and political history of Greece is complicated but trivial. Sparta declared the Greek cities on the mainland and in the Aegean "free"; those in Asia Minor were given to Persia in return for help in the war. Presently they revolted with the connivance of the Persian viceroy in Asia Minor, Cyrus, who was preparing an attack on his elder brother, the King, Artaxerxes II, and wanted Greek support. When Cyrus was killed in the attack (401), the satraps in Asia Minor tried to reconquer the cities; the cities appealed to Sparta for help and got it. This angered Persia, so she financed the rebuilding of the long walls of Athens and instigated an Athenian and Theban attack on Sparta. The Spartans were forced to withdraw from Asia Minor in 394. Their withdrawal was followed by a half-century of intermittent warfare in Greece. First Sparta was cock of the walk for twenty years. Then Thebes developed a new military technique, that of massing troops on the left to break through the opponent's line, which could then be attacked from its unarmed right flank. This technique made Thebes briefly (371–362) the strongest power in Greece.

B.C.	
404–371	Spartan hegemony in Greece
404	Greek cities of Asia Minor given back to Persia
400–394	Spartan intervention in Asia Minor
399	Trial and execution of Socrates
395	Persia finances Greek attacks on Sparta
394–391	The long walls of Athens rebuilt with Persian help
378	Formation of the Second Athenian League
371	Battle of Leuctra, Sparta decisively defeated by Thebes
371–362	Theban hegemony in Greece; Spartan control of the Peloponnese ended; establishment of the Arcadian League
c. 370	The legal and historical books of the Old Testament (except for Chronicles) reach approximately their present form; Plato teaching in Athens; Praxiteles; Isocrates
359	Philip II comes to power in Macedonia
342	Persia reconquers Egypt
338	Battle of Chaironea, Philip II defeats Athens and Thebes and subjugates Greece; Aristotle, Diogenes, Demosthenes
336	Philip II assassinated; Alexander succeeds
334	Alexander invades the Persian empire
333	Defeat of Darius III at Issus
332	Capture of Tyre
331	Foundation of Alexandria by Egypt; defeat of Darius III at Gaugamela; capture of Babylon, Susa, and Persepolis
330	Capture of Ecbatana; death of Darius III
329	Conquest of Bactria
328	Conquest of Sogdiana
327	Invasion of Pakistan
326	Conquest of the Indus Valley
325	Return across south Persia
323	Death of Alexander in Babylon

She set up an "Arcadian League" in the center and southwest of the Peloponnese to keep Sparta down. But while she and Sparta were at war, Athens organized a new league including many of her former island allies and a few on the mainlands. When Thebes collapsed, she emerged as the strongest power in southern Greece. By that time, however, Greek politics was soon to be overshadowed by the growth of Macedon, whose king, Philip II, would appropriate and develop the Theban technique and back it up with cavalry.

THE NEWLY HELLENIZED STATES

The growth of Macedon was the most important example of a phenomenon now going on all around the Mediterranean—the development of large "hellenized barbarian" states in which the culture of the ruling class was mostly Greek, but the population mostly non-Greek—or Greek of such a savage sort that the Greeks would scarcely recognize it. Besides Macedon and Epirus in northern Greece, the old Milesian colony of Panticapaeum in south Russia became the center of such a kingdom. So did the Carians, a people of southwest Asia Minor who now became practically independent of Persia. Although the rulers of the new kingdom of Egypt (from 404 on) continued Saïte traditionalism in their elegant art and official inscriptions, they became dependent on Greek mercenaries, the land was full of Greek traders, and traces of Greek culture were everywhere visible. Egypt's reconquest by Persia in 342 was a blow to Greek economy. Similarly in Carthage, while Punic continued to be used, the form of government, the intellectual life, and the bric-a-brac were alike hellenized. In Sicily Dionysius I, tyrant of Syracuse, built up a kingdom which contained most of Sicily, the toe and heel of Italy, and points along the Adriatic; his court was a center of Greek culture, but his subjects were largely non-Greek and he relied on the non-Greeks to support him against the Greeks. In Etruria the Etruscans, long imitators of the Greeks, were almost ruined by invasions of the Celts in the 380s, but the admiration of Greek culture was implanted in the area, and when Rome grew up it would show deep Greek influence.

These new hellenized states were the results of a long radiation of Greek culture—a new civilizing of the barbarians—which had gone on unnoticed around the Greek colonies. The northeastern and central Mediterranean had been transformed from a world of Greek cities and scattered tribes of barbarians to one of Greek cities and settled states of considerable size with hellenized rulers. This change made the Greek cities second-rate powers. It also ruined their trade. The new countries produced much of their own wine and olive oil and even local imitations of Greek manufactured wares. At the same time the revolts in the western Persian satrapies, the wars between Persia and Egypt and between the Greeks and Carthaginians in Sicily, the civil wars of the tyrants in Sicily and south Italy, and the Celtic invasions in north Italy, all destroyed rich markets. But in Greece the necessity of buying food abroad continued unchanged. The consequent economic crisis led to revolutions and counterrevolutions. These were made worse by the wars in Greece, which disrupted trade, ruined farms, and filled the cities with refugees and exiles whose poverty complicated the social problem.

CULTURAL DEVELOPMENTS IN GREECE; SOCRATES, PLATO, AND ARISTOTLE

Consequently men fled the country. Greeks were already, because of their armor and training, the foremost mercenaries of the Near Eastern states. Now their numbers abroad redoubled and Greece itself filled up with mercenaries. Nevertheless, the century saw major cultural achievements, mostly in Athens and mostly the results of specialization. Specialization in speechwriting and speaking now produced its greatest masters, the writer Isocrates and the orator Demosthenes. Similar specialization appears in sculpture: Praxiteles, the most imitated artist in history, produced the statue sufficient to itself, unrelated to architectural setting, probably devoid of content, a sheer expression of delight in the plastic and tactile qualities of human beauty and in the dazzling technical proficiency of the artist. His statues of nudes* were set up in temples as gods and goddesses. The same development of technique and neglect of consequences appeared in finance, in which banking now became a specialty, newly important because mercenaries had to be paid. And in civic administration the experts on finance were at loggerheads with the newly professional generals, neither group willing to recognize the other's needs. Even the gods specialized: The shrines of Asclepius, a specialist in healing, spread to every part of the Greek world. But the two fields in which specialization yielded its most significant results were war and philosophy.

Socrates had created the philosophic life, but he was not a professional philosopher. A number of his pupils became "professionals" in that they made philosophy the thing they "did." The greatest of these was Plato, who left Athens in disgust after Socrates' execution in 399, but returned about 387, settled in a suburb called Academia, and established a private society for philosophic discussion, probably disguised as an association for the worship of the Muses. This endured until A.D. 529 when the emperor Justinian closed it in the interest of Christian truth. It was perhaps the first example of a privately endowed institution for humane studies.

Just what Plato taught orally is not known, but his published works have influenced all subsequent western philosophic and theological thought. His perfection of Socrates' question-and-answer technique led toward the discovery of formal logic and the rationalistic criticism of common beliefs (important in Hellenistic thought and in Christian polemics against paganism). He gave classic expression to dualism, beginning with the duality in all objects between the form, which can be known and must therefore be permanent, and the material, which is always changing and therefore unknowable. Hence there are two worlds—the world of forms, being, knowledge, light, beauty, truth, the mind, reason, and the philosopher; the world of matter, change, ignorance, darkness, error, falsity, the body, sensation, and the workman. Hence the good life is an escape from the world of the body; asceticism is the handmaid of philosophy and alienation is its goal. Finally, Plato was a superb artist. His style and literary form—the dialogue—became literary models; his myths of creation, the soul, and the afterlife, his imaginative pictures of the ideal state and the idealized Socrates, have been perennial sources of inspiration.

In the long run, even Plato's influence was overshadowed by that of his pupil Aristotle, the completely professional philosopher. His dry treatises deal not only with their professed subjects, but also, incidentally, with the problem posed by the development of specialization: What is the structure of the whole of knowledge wherein each of the specialists' subjects has its place? In other words, how are these subjects related? This problem is basic to systematic philosophy and also to the practical task of organizing the many branches of knowledge for cooperation, as in a university or an academy of sciences. But Aristotle's importance was not at once apparent because he could not fully answer the problem. He laid the bases for an answer by his studies of logic, his classification of the ways in which objects differ (the categories of knowledge), his detailed accounts of a number of fields of knowledge (logic, metaphysics, physics, zoology, psychology, ethics, political theory, poetry, rhetoric), and his creation of much scientific terminology. These were to be the tools of the mind, and eventually the mind would win, but its time was not yet.

THE TRIUMPH OF MACEDON, PHILIP II AND ALEXANDER

At the moment, the Greek world was filled with the consequences of specialization in war. These became fully apparent only when worked out by a brilliant soldier who was also an absolute ruler of a large people: Philip II of Macedon. None of his smaller or less warlike neighbors could stand against him. Striking first on one side, then on the other, making peace with one enemy as a prelude to attacking the next, between 359 and 339 he extended Macedonian control to central Greece and to the Propontis. Goaded by Demosthenes, the Athenians tried several times to stop him. Finally, when they sent their forces to protect Byzantium (Istanbul), Philip marched into Greece, defeated them and their allies at Chaironea in 338, subjugated the Peloponnese, established Macedonian garrisons at key points, organized the Greek cities in a league under his control, proclaimed a general peace, and began preparations for an attack on Persia. In the midst of these he was assassinated in 336.

His son, Alexander,* carried on his policy. After liquidating other claimants to the throne and smashing opponents in the Balkans and Greece, he was able in 334 to invade Asia Minor. He took the cities of the west coast and the center of the country, defeated the Persian King (Darius III) at Issus late in 333, entered Syria, and proceeded down the coast to Tyre, probably intending to cut off the bases of the Persian fleet and prevent its making trouble in Greece. The siege of Tyre—until then an island, he made it a promontory—held him up until August of 332; thereafter he took Egypt. Returning from Egypt in 331 he set out for Persia, where Darius had raised another army. Alexander smashed it at Gaugamela, near the ruins of Nineveh, in October. Babylon, Susa, and Persepolis, with immense treasures, next fell, and Persepolis was destroyed. Thence he turned north to Media, taking Ecbatana in 330, thence east in pursuit of Darius. But Darius was murdered by one of his own satraps. Alexander thereupon declared himself Darius' successor and pressed on to reconquer "his" kingdom. This led him through six years of fighting in Afghanistan, Uzbekistan, and Pakistan, down the Indus Valley and back across southern Persia to Babylon, where (after a year of reorganization and another expedition to Media) he died on June 10, 323, in the palace of Nebuchadnezzar II. He was thirty-two years old.

FOR FURTHER READING

V. Ehrenberg, *The People of Aristophanes*
P. Friedlander, *Plato*
G. Griffith, (ed.), *Alexander the Great*
W. Jaeger, *Demosthenes*
W. Ross, *Aristotle*
T. Sinclair, *A History of Greek Political Thought*
U. Wilcken, *Alexander the Great*

MAP VI

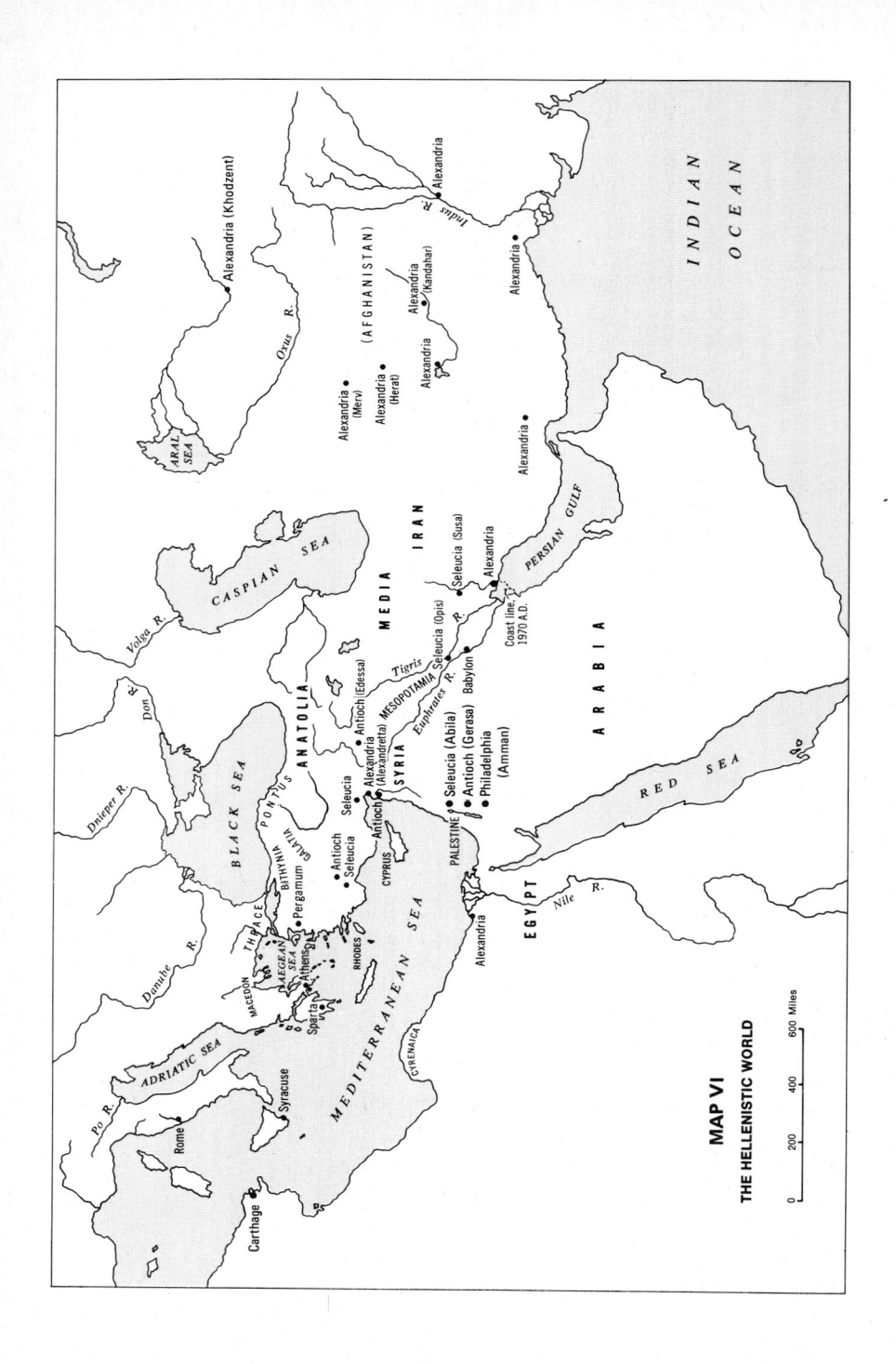

THE HELLENISTIC WORLD

12
THE HELLENISTIC WORLD

HELLENISTIC CULTURE AND PHILOSOPHY

Alexander's generals carved his conquests into kingdoms. When, by 276, their wars of succession stopped, three great powers, ruled by three great families, had emerged: Macedon of the Antigonids; Egypt, with Palestine, Cyrenaica, and Cyprus, of the Ptolemies; and Asia, from Anatolia to Afghanistan, of the Seleucids. In the meantime a fourth great power had appeared in the west. By 268 Rome had won control of all Italy south of the Po Valley. But the courts of Macedonia, Syria, and Egypt paid hardly any attention to the events in Italy, a land as far away from the Greek world in travel time as America was from Europe in the nineteenth century.

The Greek powers sparred with one another, but established peace within most of their territories. At the same time economic changes diminished the bellicosity of the Greek cities. Alexander had coined the Persian treasures to pay his troops; many came home with their gains. Money thus became available to pay for new ships and rebuild ruined farms. Even more important, the opening of the Near East gave jobs to the unemployed and homes to the homeless of Greece. The colonists

B.C.	
323–276	Wars of Alexander's successors, emergence of the three major hellenistic kingdoms: Antigonid Macedon, Ptolemaic Egypt (with Cyrenaica, Cyprus, and Palestine), and the Seleucid empire (southern Asia Minor, Syria, Mesopotamia, Media, Iran, Afghanistan); Menander and the "new comedy" (of manners), Epicurus, Zeno (founder of Stoicism), Theophrastus
c. 290	The colossus of Rhodes
279	Galatians devastate Thrace, Macedonia, and north Greece (some cross to central Asia Minor in 278)
300–215	Zenith of Alexandria as center of the new "hellenistic" culture; Aristarchus, Archimedes, Euclid, Eratosthenes, Theocritus, Apollonius Rhodius, Manetho, and Berossus; development of alchemy and astrology; translation of the Pentateuch into Greek (the Septuagint)
268	Rome in control of all Italy south of the Po Valley
216	Serious native revolts in Egypt begin
c. 175	The great altar of Pergamum

lived better than before. They now could eat white bread; barley was for slaves. They could also afford the products of the old country, their native wines, olive oil, and pottery. Pottery now began to imitate silverware, it was no longer a luxury; the standard of wealth had risen. Goldsmiths copied and developed Persian styles with delicacy and magnificence.

This prosperity was the economic basis of a new cultural flowering in Greece. The center of concern was the everyday life of the well-to-do. Even the manufacture of terra-cotta statuettes was raised to a fine art. Sculptors extended the range of their work, developing new interests in realism, portraiture, and pathos. The comedians, notably Menander, abandoned farce and politics for the intrigues of private bourgeois life. Through their Roman imitators they became the ancestors of modern "comedy of manners" and drama of domestic intrigue. The new schools of philosophy, disagreeing on many points, agreed that the function of philosophy was to secure personal happiness, conceived as psychological equilibrium. They agreed also that the average man could attain this, not by changing the world around him, but by changing himself. So "philosophy" became essentially training to live the good life, conceived as independence both from luck and from the environment, from approval and disapproval, as salvation for the individual alone.

As to the exact nature of the good life, three major schools disagreed. First came the Cynics ("Dogs"), whose founder, Diogenes, had made a name for himself in the mid-fourth century by his caustic wit and utter neglect of social conventions. (When laughed at for masturbating in public Diogenes said he wished he could satisfy hunger by rubbing his stomach.) His successors taught that man was an animal and the good life consisted in satisfying one's animal needs. Since needs cause trouble, the wise man will train himself to have as few as possible and to disregard any convention that might interfere with their satisfaction. A second school, the Stoics, was named from the colonnade (Greek, *stoa*) in Athens, where Zeno, its founder, taught from about 300 to 270. For the Stoics, man is an incarnation of reason, the thinking fire that produces and directs the world. The good life is that which accords with reason; this is also wisdom and virtue; consciousness of his own wisdom and virtue enables the wise man—trained by the practice of asceticism—to disregard public opinion, private misfortune, and even death itself. Virtue is, of course, to be desired for its own sake, and the goal of philosophy is to make man virtuous, but since true virtue is true happiness, the goal turns out to be happiness also. Finally the Epicureans—Epicurus was an older contemporary of Zeno—maintained that man is a temporary congeries of atoms, dissolved at death. The part of wisdom, therefore, is to enjoy life while we have it, and the good life is the untroubled one. "It is not necessary," he said, "to save the Greeks, but to eat and drink." Wisdom is that knowledge and training which keeps men out of trouble. It teaches men to avoid political and emotional entanglements, build up friendships which make them secure in society, live economically, take care of their health, tolerate pain, and have no fear of death. In sum, hellenistic philosophy taught indifference and intellectual arrogance. It inspired much later rationalism and Christian asceticism. Strong personalities are still attracted by the central article of its faith: Man is the master of his fate and captain of his soul.

THE MAJOR HELLENISTIC KINGDOMS

The hellenistic kingdoms differed widely. Macedon was unique in that rulers and ruled were, more or less, one people. This gave the ruling dynasty a firm basis in ethnic pride and loyalty. In the east the Seleucids relied, for control of the native population, on their standing army of Macedonians and Greeks, their bureaucracy, and the network of Greek cities across their domains. Alexander left a string of Alexandrias from Egypt to central Asia as military centers, to protect his conquests and his lines of communication. The Seleucids and other hellenistic rulers followed his example; cities named for various members of their dynasties (Seleucia, Antioch, Philadelphia) were founded everywhere to control the lands around them.

In Egypt the Ptolemies became Greek pharaohs and held the throne for 274 years (304 to 30 B.C.). No prior Egyptian dynasty had lasted so long. They founded few cities, since they did not want their power limited by the right of self-government which went with a Greek city. Instead, both native Egyptians and Greek settlers in Egypt, often military colonists, were governed by royal officials. Legally the immigrants and their descendants remained foreigners employed in the royal service. All economic activity was supervised by the king. The government decided which fields were to be planted and with what; where the crops were to be sold and for how much. It regulated transportation, processing, manufacturing, trade, and banking. Nothing escaped taxation. Even abandoned babies were collected and sold—the proceeds went to the privy purse. Since the government rightly distrusted both taxpayers and tax collectors, this system required endless bookkeeping and an immense bureaucracy, oppressive, expensive, and one of the causes of a series of native revolts beginning in 216. But from about 300 to 215 the system made the Ptolemies the richest hellenistic rulers. Inspired by Greek analytic thought—they set up a separate department for each branch of economic activity—their organization was perhaps the greatest technical achievement of the age. It brought out men of managerial psychology who found their calling in the service of the kings. We have most of the business records of one of them, yet we do not know whether he had a family.

The wealth thus accumulated was lavished upon Alexandria, the greatest city in the world. Legally it was not "in" Egypt, but was a Greek city "by" Egypt. Here hellenistic culture reached its acme. The court attracted brilliant writers. New literary forms—the epigram, the pastoral of Theocritus, the literary epic of Apollonius Rhodius—came to the fore. The Ptolemies turned their genius for organization to the patronage of science and scholarship. A royal institute was founded, legally for the cult of the Muses, whence its name, the Museum. Royal funds provided for buildings, support of members, and accumulation of an enormous library. Alexandria became the greatest center of historical and scientific studies in the Greek world. But this brilliance was paid for by denial of Greek city life to the rest of the country; the hellenization of the Egyptians lagged far behind that of the Syrians.

MINOR HELLENISTIC STATES

Beside the major kingdoms a number of minor hellenistic states grew up, for instance, Pontus and Bythinia in northern Asia Minor. Their most important action during this age was to protect themselves against the Seleucids by inviting into Asia Minor the barbaric Celts (Galatians) who had devastated Greece in 279–278 and now, established in central Anatolia, terrorized the cities along the coast, breaking up Seleucid rule. On the coast the dynasts of Pergamum, with Ptolemaic help, stood off both Seleucids and Galatians and built up an autocratic court supported by a suppressed countryside. The Pergamene sculptors produced the greatest work of the age, a frieze of gods battling giants, to commemorate the Galatian wars. The Pergamene library was second only to the Alexandrian, and the technique perfected there of preparing skins for writing ("parchment" comes from the Latin *pergamena*, "Pergamene") was to save, in the Middle Ages, many texts which would have disappeared had they been written on material more liable to decay. By contrast to Pergamum, Rhodes carried on the tradition of the Greek city-states. The shift of trade to the eastern Mediterranean made it a shipping and banking center. It beat off the Antigonids with the help of the Ptolemies and vice versa. Its fleet restrained piracy; its sea law started an international tradition; the security and freedom of the city made it the home of eminent philosophers and artists. Its colossal statue of the sun god, Helios, was one of the wonders of the world.

"HELLENIZATION" AND THE CHARACTERISTICS OF HELLENISTIC CULTURE

These different states shared a single culture, called hellenistic. This culture was consciously Greek and international, rooted in the common feeling of the Greeks abroad, where differences between Spartan and Athenian paled beside those between Greek and native. A curious consequence of this was that anyone, whether native or Greek, came to be called a Greek if he possessed the culture. It was not linked to any political or religious organization. Superficially it was a matter of costume, language, and technology; profoundly, of the analytic way of thought. Thus, later on, native rulers like the Maccabees promoted hellenization as necessary for power and independence. By assimilation of this culture ambitious natives rose to power in Greek society; the Greeks, by accepting hellenized natives, half-consciously deprived the native masses of leaders. The language of this culture was a new dialect called "common" Greek, an international tongue which was eventually to disseminate Greek philosophies and Near Eastern religions (including Judaism and Christianity).

The Greek elements of hellenistic culture should not conceal its difference from the culture of classical Greece. Classical Greece had been a world of tiny city states with conciliar governments. In the hellenistic world many such cities survived, more were created, and some succeeded in preserving their independence. They were centers from which hellenistic culture radiated, but they did not dominate their culture, nor was their civic life its main characteristic. Hellenistic culture was dominated by the big monarchies and characterized by the life of their capitals. These cosmopolitan cities were new sociological phenomena, far different from classical Athens, not to mention Sparta. In classical Greece the land had been held chiefly by private citizens in small estates; in the hellenistic world the most important holdings were the vast domains of the kings, temples, and great officials. In classical Greece the cults of the city gods had been the centers both of petition and of patriotism; in the hellenistic world patriotism was expressed in the cults of the deified kings, and petitions were more often addressed to deities without political affiliations, like Asclepius, the god of healing. In the classical world, of small economic and political units, private citizens had been of considerable importance, politics had been a major concern of the average man, and the arts and philosophy had been politically oriented. In the larger hellenistic world, private persons were usually of no importance—to be heard, they had to riot. In big cities like Alexandria, street mobs were the counterpart of the royal bureaucracy. Therefore private persons concerned themselves with their private affairs, and so did philosophy and art (except when motivated by political patronage).

Finally, for the same reason, in small cities, both of classical Greece and of the hellenistic age, the civil administration and army (if any) were run by amateurs: the same man was in turn farmer, officer, judge, and so on. Therefore politics was full of factional conflicts. In the hellenistic monarchies administration and army were run by professionals, and the history was one of bureaucratic intrigues and palace revolutions.

The increase in professionalism was characteristic of all fields of activity in the hellenistic world. Its consequences were increased technical proficiency, the collection and systematization of previous knowledge, and the standardization of products, which improved in quality, but lost their individuality and originality. Accordingly the physical sciences flourished. In geography Eratosthenes calculated the circumference of the earth with an error of less than one percent (his estimate was not surpassed in accuracy till the time of Newton); in astronomy Aristarchus of Samos propounded the heliocentric theory of the solar system. This was the age of the botanist Theophrastus, the mathematicians Euclid and Archimedes. On the other hand, pseudoscience invaded medicine, producing an increase in the practice of bleeding, which persisted to the middle of the nineteenth century and probably killed more patients than any diseases except the great plagues. Alchemy was another "discovery"; astrology was taken over from the Babylonians. But in spite of such aberrations the collection and systematization of knowledge in all fields was the greatest achievement of the hellenistic age. The structures of hellenistic learning were to be the foundations of the Renaissance.

A second characteristic of the age was technological advance; the bill of exchange in banking, the water lifting screw, chain pump, and threshing drag in agriculture, the sternpost rudder in shipping, the copying machine in sculpture, even the five-drachma-in-the-slot machine for dispensing holy water in Ptolemaic temples. The new technology much increased human power and efficiency. Indeed, the hellenistic age may be symbolized by one of the most famous of these devices, the first known lighthouse, at the port of Alexandria;* its fire is said to have been visible for 35 miles.

Finally hellenistic culture penetrated and changed the Near East, one of the greatest revolutions in ancient history. It was a slow process. Greek styles in sculpture led the invasion, carried by coinage,* terra-cotta and metal statuettes, and decorations on household objects. These were recommended by their lifelikeness—a virtue often most admired when least mastered. This penetration had begun in the fifth and fourth centuries. With Alexander came the Greek language, Greek business practices and technology, and the experimental, inventive attitude which, for instance, revolutionized the agriculture of Egypt: better breeds of cattle and sheep, new crops, and better seeds for the old ones were introduced; iron at long last replaced bronze for common tools; irrigation was reorganized and greatly extended; more nutritious wheat flour replaced the ancient emmer—at least in the diet of the middle and upper classes. Under Ptolemy II daily rations of wheat or wheat bread were given to government officials and employees, including slaves. Moreover, the survival of the Ptolemaic dynasty enabled these innovations to survive. Hitherto cultural advances had often been obliterated by political disasters. Sennacherib, for instance, about 700 B.C., had acclimatized cotton ("the tree that bears wool") in Assyria, but within a century Assyria was destroyed. In Egypt the government was stable and the culture changed.

Much slower was the spread of Greek civic life. When a city was founded for Greek settlers the citizens had to be given the rights customary in Greek cities—election of magistrates, their own assembly and courts, government by majority rule, a modicum of freedom of speech, freedom from enslavement for debt and from bodily punishment before conviction, the right to public trial, and so on. They also required the amenities of Greek life—a theater* (which might double as an assembly place), an open market (colonnaded if possible), courts and gymnasia.[1] These rights and pleasures of Greek life were long limited to the few "citizens" of the new cities—Greeks without citizenship, natives, and slaves were carefully excluded. But the pattern gradually spread to native Near Eastern cities. And even natives who perpetuated their ancestral political forms were deeply influenced by Greek culture. The conventional image of Buddha is a creation of the Greek artistic tradition. The influence of the Greek cities of Syria and northern Mesopotamia made the later Aramaic (Syriac) culture of those areas the main instrument for the hellenization of Islamic thought. And the hellenization of Palestine by Greek cities shaped both Judaism and Christianity.

Slowest of all was the penetration of Greek literature and philosophy. The Greeks soon found educated natives to explain to them, in Greek, the contents of native traditions. The histories of Egypt and Babylon were even recast in something approaching Greek historical form for the Ptolemies and Seleucids by the third-century Egyptian priest Manetho and Babylonian priest Berossus; the Jewish law was translated into Greek, reportedly at the behest of Ptolemy II who had many Jews to govern. Natives who had learned Greek even tried their hands at original literary compositions in Greek styles on native subjects —we have anti-Greek pamphlets written in Greek by Egyptians, and

---

[1] The gymnasium now changed from a social center for the adolescent and adult to a secondary school. To athletic and military training were attached music, poetry, and rhetoric, the beginnings of "higher education." These became necessary because the children's Greek was corrupted by the native servants. Even girls had to be sent to school.

fragments of a Greek tragedy on the Exodus. Perhaps the prestige of Greek worked against translation and imitation of Greek literature in native tongues. Anyone who aspired to write a literary work of a Greek sort aspired also to write it in Greek. Consequently the native literatures lived on through the hellenistic and early Roman periods mainly by imitation of earlier native forms.

FOR FURTHER READING

R. Forbes and E. Dijksterhuis, *A History of Science and Technology*, vol. 1

G. Grube, *The Greek and Roman Critics*

H. Marrou, *A History of Education in Antiquity*

O. Neugebauer, *The Exact Sciences in Antiquity*

S. Sambursky, *The Physical World of the Greeks*

W. Tarn, *Antigonos Gonatas*

W. Tarn and G. Griffith, *Hellenistic Civilization*

B.C.	
387	Rome destroyed by the Celts
338	Rome in control of Latium
268	Rome controls Italy south of the Po Valley
264–241	First Punic War; most of Sicily taken over (organized as a province, 227)
238	Sardinia and Corsica taken from Carthage
218–202	Second Punic War (218–216 Hannibal's victories); Plautus' plays
204	Death of Ptolemy IV of Egypt
201–198	Antiochus III takes Palestine
200–197	Rome defeats Philip V of Macedon
192–188	Rome defeats Antiochus III, the Seleucid
194–133	Roman subjugation of Spain
184	Censorship of Cato; one thousand talents spent on sewers
167	Roman citizens freed of direct taxation
149–146	Takeover of Macedonia and most of Greece; Corinth and Carthage razed; territory of Carthage annexed as "Africa"
144	High-level aqueduct in Rome; hydraulic cement
135	Big slave revolts begin (in Sicily)
133	Tiberius Gracchus murdered
129–74	Continued annexations: 129, "Asia" (ex Pergamum); 122, the Balearics; 121, Narbonnese Gaul; 105, Tripolitania; 102, west Cilicia; 74, Cyrenaica
121	Gaius Gracchus murdered
107	Marius enlists landless men for the army
91–89	Revolt of the Italian allies (critical period)
87–83	Sulla's subjugation of Greece and Asia (Athens ruined)
81–79	Sulla's dictatorship (death, 78)
67	Pompey suppresses piracy, east Cilicia annexed
66–62	Pompey defeats Mithridates VI of Pontus and Tigranes of Armenia; Bithynia, Pontus, Syria, and Crete annexed
58–50	Caesar's conquest of France, Belgium, and parts of Holland, Germany, and Switzerland; Lucretius, Catullus, Cicero; glass blowing in Syria
48	Caesar defeats Pompey at Pharsalus
48–47	Caesar in Egypt with Cleopatra VII
46	Caesar's calendar reform (solar year)
44	Caesar assassinated; Sallust retires from politics
43	Cicero murdered; birth of Ovid
42	Philippi: Octavian and Antony defeat Caesar's assassins
37	Antony's marriage to Cleopatra
31	Actium: Octavian defeats Antony and Cleopatra

13
THE ROMAN REPUBLIC

ROME. SOME OF THE WAYS IT
DIFFERED FROM GREEK CITIES

In the summer of 204 Ptolemy IV of Egypt died, leaving a five-year-old son. Philip V of Macedon and the Seleucid Antiochus III moved to seize Ptolemaic territories. Antiochus occupied Palestine in 201; after some years' fighting the Seleucids held the country for half a century. Philip tried to take territories controlling the Hellespont. This frightened Athens, Rhodes, and Pergamum, and they appealed to Rome. Rome defeated Philip in 197 and stripped him of his domains outside Macedon. Though she left the Greek cities independent, the war gave her de facto control of Greece. Many Greeks turned to Antiochus for help. Rome then defeated him at Magnesia in 190.

The defeats of Philip and Antiochus began a new era in the political history of the eastern Mediterranean—eight hundred and thirty years of Roman supremacy, from 190 B.C. to A.D. 640 (the Moslem capture of Alexandria). The stability of this power can be matched in western history only by that of Egypt. Moreover, Rome in 200 B.C. had already existed for half a millennium and the Roman government lived on

148 THE ROMAN REPUBLIC

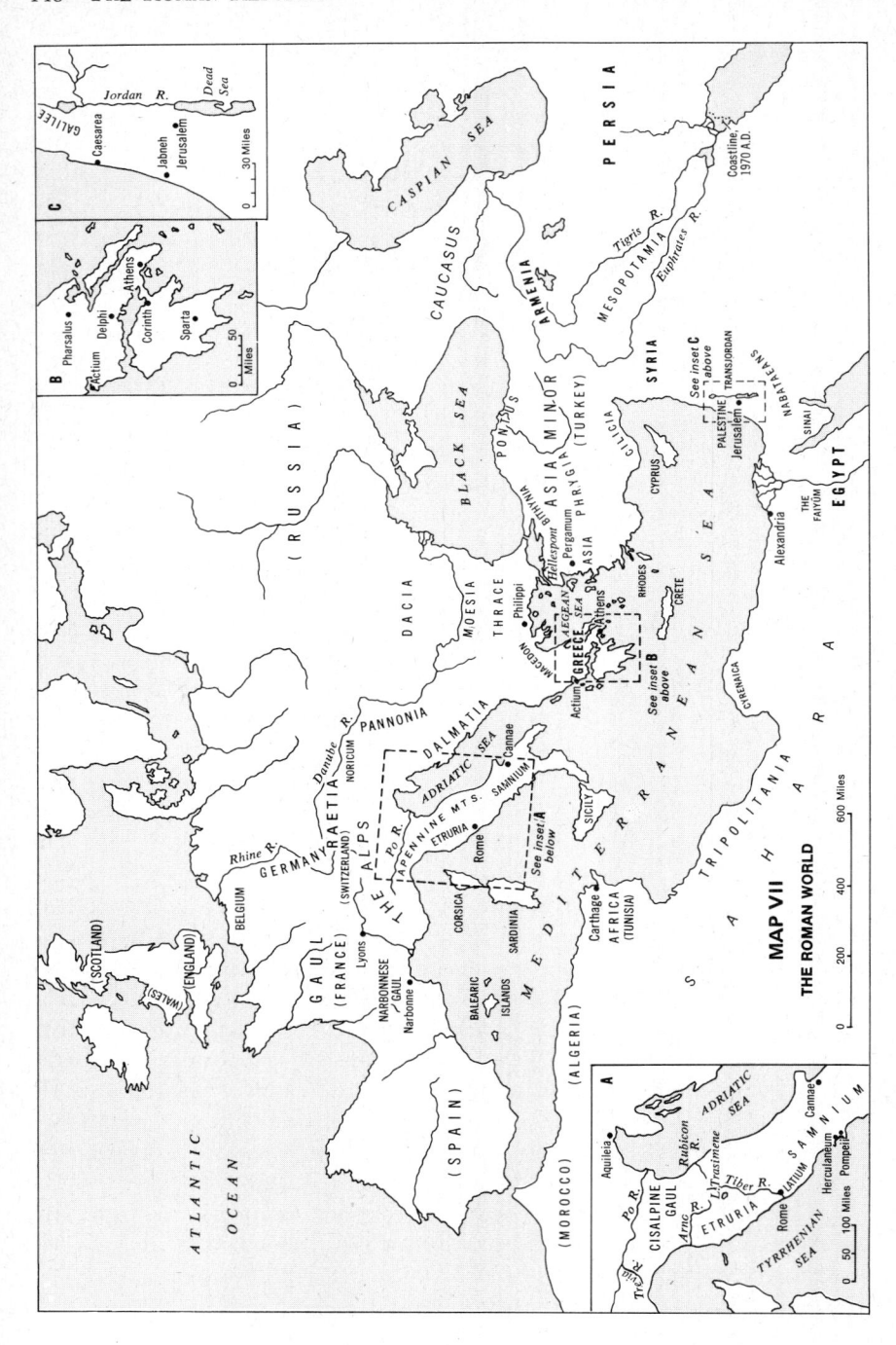

after 640 in the Byzantine empire for eight hundred years. Roman political and legal thought has shaped every subsequent state of Europe or of European inspiration. Therefore the spotlight of western history, hitherto focused on the Near East and Greece, now shifts to the Roman world.

The legends about the origins of Rome, as of Greek cities and Israelite tribes, may to some degree reflect what happened, but the degree is small and not precisely calculable. Whatever the origins, there were settlements on the Roman hills in the eighth century B.C. and the city was there by the end of the seventh. Its early history was distinguished by two characteristics—its willingness to grant citizenship to aliens and its ability to absorb other cities. Hence the manpower which overwhelmed the hellenistic kingdoms and the political stability which carried Rome from the fifth century to the first without a revolution. Greek cities, poor and democratic, could not afford to grant citizenship to large bodies of aliens, since it would carry an important share in the government and a claim on the food supply. In Rome the populace voted by blocks; an additional body of citizens meant only a small fraction of each block's vote, and food, in fertile Italy, was not a critical problem. When a slave was enfranchised in a Greek city he became a resident alien, with no loyalty to the city. He might support a tyrant or an enemy. When a slave was enfranchised in Rome he became a Roman citizen—albeit of the lowest class—and his children would be of higher station. Rome, when it defeated a rival, could afford to take the citizens as well as the land. The manpower would be an advantage in its next war, and the new citizens' loyalty would be won by their profits from the consequent victories. Many of Rome's "allies," too, were acquired by force, like Athens', but, unlike Athens', once in the gang they shared in the loot. Moreover, Rome, itself an oligarchy, supported the local aristocrats, made them dependent on its support, and allied them to its own ruling class through intermarriage. And revolts brought terrible punishments, the more terrible because of Rome's relentless righteousness. The Romans did not resort to war lightly. Unlike the Greeks, they thought of war as an abnormal state of affairs which had to be justified. Not that they normally lived at peace—when a brief period of peace did occur in 235 B.C. it was said to have been the first in almost five hundred years. But they did distinguish between "unjust" and "just" wars, the latter being those waged for "just cause"—to recover property, avenge some wrong, punish a breach of treaty, or the like. This concept of "the just war" was a major development of international relations. It made Rome desirable (but dangerous) as an ally, and formidable as an enemy; both traits contributed to the city's success.

ROME'S RISE TO POWER

In 387–386 a Celtic invasion destroyed the city and its records. Records can hardly have been plentiful; although writing was known in the area from the seventh century, literacy did not become common until late in the third. After the Celtic raid we can trace the areas Rome assimilated or allied to itself. First came the Latin towns south of the Tiber (by 338), then the Samnites of central Italy (by 290), then the Etruscans to the north and the Greek cities of the southern coasts. By 268 it controlled the peninsula south of the Po Valley and the northwestern Apennines, and had tied down its conquests by a network of colonies.

By this time Rome's unite-and-share-the-plunder policy had made it the keeper of a military man-eater which none of its neighbors could defeat, but which had to be fed with plunder if it was not to turn on its keeper. Sicily was the richest country at hand. Since much of Sicily was occupied by the Carthaginians (in Latin, *Poeni*), intervention there led to a struggle with Carthage in two long "Punic" wars, 264–241 and 218–202. Rome's victory in both was due to her superiority in manpower and her ability to hold her allies. In the first war she lost 700 ships (manned by 140,000 men) to the Carthaginians' 500, but nonetheless forced Carthage to sue for peace. In the second war, when the Carthaginian general Hannibal invaded Italy with 26,000 men, Rome had available for service 273,000 Roman citizens and 379,000 allies. Therefore, although Hannibal smashed three Roman armies in succession at Trevia (218), Trasimene (217), and Cannae (216), and although these victories won him support from the Celts of the Po Valley and the Greek cities of south Italy, his invasion finally failed because the bulk of the allies remained loyal to Rome. He never won over enough troops to attack the city. Rome was able to keep one army on his trail and send other armies to conquer Carthaginian Spain, suppress a revolt in Sicily, keep Macedon busy in Greece, reconquer the Po Valley, reconquer south Italy, and finally invade North Africa. And the war with Carthage was so far from exhausting her that after it ended in 202 she was able to defeat Macedon in 197 and Antiochus in 190. (The treaty was not signed till 188.) These victories raised the standard of living of even the poorest Romans. The basic food, formerly emmer, became, by the beginning of the second century B.C., white bread.

CONSTITUTIONAL AND ECONOMIC CONSEQUENCES OF ROME'S SUCCESS

But now the Roman system changed. Big enough to defeat anything in sight, Rome no longer wanted more allies. The more allies, the less plunder per ally. Therefore, beginning with Sicily after the first Punic War, conquered cities were no longer customarily made allies, nor were conquered lands customarily used for the foundation of new colonies in which allies as well as Romans received grants. Instead, the newly acquired territories were organized as provinces. Allies generally contributed military service but were self-governing in domestic affairs, had certain rights guaranteed by treaties in relation to Rome, and were free of tribute; provincials were usually free of military service, but subject to Roman governors, devoid of civic rights, and obligated to pay tribute. The change from alliance and colonization to the creation of provinces was not uniform—almost nothing in the administrative history of the Roman republic was—but it was frequent from 227 on, and after 175 it was general.

This change cut off the largest item in the allies' benefit from the wars—the distribution of land to colonies in which they participated. It increased Rome's profit. The tribute of the provinces was paid to Rome, and Rome farmed to private companies the task of collecting it. These companies raised the necessary capital by selling stock, then recovered their outlay by seizing as "tribute" all they could get. Their rapacity yielded high returns. It also led to innumerable suits between Romans and provincials. Of these, and of many other civil cases in the province, the Roman governor was the final judge. Governors served without salary. (Rome, like most ancient cities, thought public offices honors for which the recipients should pay—a notion that taxed the rich, but kept the poor out of politics.) However, instead of salary, governors got a generous allowance for expenses: the parsimonious but honest Cicero saved the equivalent of $540,000 from his allowance as governor of a minor province for two years. And this was nothing to what a dishonest man could make from bribes. Besides the profits of administration, Rome and her generals got the lion's share of the booty and the cash payments extracted from the defeated; from the Punic Wars on, these payments were greatly increased. Finally, the accumulation of capital in Rome made Romans the principal partners in companies which supplied the needs of the Roman army and navy. In these, and in the tax-collecting companies, the wealthy families of the allies also participated; under Roman protection the Italian allies, particularly the Greeks, took over much of the trade of Greece and Asia Minor, and many of their poor relations were employed as agents of the tax-collecting companies. But most of the poorer citizens of the allied towns were burdened with the fighting and rewarded only with the soldier's miserable pay and trivial booty.

Along with the allies, many Roman citizens were alienated from their government. Rome had long ago gone through the customary evolution from a kingship to an oligarchy of "patrician" families. During the fifth and fourth centuries popular leaders had opened the civic offices and priesthoods to nonpatrician candidates. But here the movement toward democracy had stopped. The final authorities in the state were several assemblies of citizens who voted not by individuals but by companies or tribes. The rulers so gerrymandered these voting units that most could be swung by the few rich voters. Moreover, the wide geographic distribution of the citizens made assemblies difficult to attend and easy to control. And their powers were strictly limited. Bills had to be accepted or rejected without amendment. The presiding magistrate sat, the assembly stood. Control even of general policy by the assemblies was therefore out of the question. But the principal offices of the state were annual, and most could not be held twice. Therefore the officers could not long control policy either. Thus control fell into the hands of the senate, nominally an advisory council composed of the former holders of the four highest offices. Almost all senators came from wealthy landowning families. Their vast profits as generals and governors were invested almost entirely in land, and the price of land skyrocketed.

Small landowners formed the bulk of the army. Throughout the ancient world it was customary to admit to a city's army only men with a minimal landholding. The men had to provide their own weapons, property was a guarantee of patriotism, and only responsible citizens could be permitted in the military organization which controlled the state. During Hannibal's invasion many farms had been ruined by pillage or neglect. The wars threw many slaves on the market, and the exploitation of Sicily provided cheap grain. The soldier returning to his ruined farm found himself facing ruinous competition. (Roman methods of slave management were at this time remarkable for inhuman economy. Even in town houses the slave who was the doorkeeper was usually chained in his place to keep him from running away. On country estates slaves were kept in prisons, treated as animals, and worked, not until they dropped, but until their efficiency dropped. Then they were sold, usually to the state mines, where conditions were harder and the mortality rate necessitated the purchase of the cheapest slaves—the supply of condemned criminals did not suffice.) Given such competition, many small landowners sold out (for the excellent prices their senatorial neighbors offered), went up to Rome, and, when their money was gone, swelled the mass of the unemployed.

Between the small landowners and the senators were the bourgeois families of means. They were not very numerous—in 225, about 23,000 out of 273,000 citizens (adult males). Nor were most of them very rich; anyone who had more than $100,000 capital was included in the class (a fortune of $250,000 was the minimum required for appointment to the senate). But some made huge fortunes in trade and war contracts, and most bought shares in the tax collecting companies. Consequently they were happy to have the tax collecting companies loot the provincials. On the other hand the senatorial families extended to the provinces the policy of protecting the local aristocracies. And some senators, as governors of provinces, were sufficiently honest to provide the protection for which the provincials paid them. Accordingly, as tax collecting companies were sued for extortion or governors for taking bribes, conflict after conflict arose between the senators and the bourgeois. The class feeling of each group was sharpened, and the senatorial families (the *nobiles*—well known) used their influence to prevent outsiders from securing high government offices. This embittered the capable bourgeois, who made fortunes of senatorial size but were excluded from political power and social prestige.

Thus the economic consequences of Rome's success made the allies discontented and envious, ruined the small farmers, and split the ruling classes—business on one side, government and landowning on the other. The ruined farmers became a city mob ready for any violence. At the same time the wars created an enormous population of desperate slaves both in cities and countryside, and the victories surrounded Italy with a ring of provinces in which all Italians were hated, but Romans most.

FURTHER ROMAN EXPANSION

This situation developed slowly while Rome's policy of plunder extended the area of its control. The Punic Wars had brought in Sicily, Sardinia, Corsica, and Carthaginian Spain—a prize because of its silver and lead mines; holdings there were consolidated and extended by continuous wars against the natives from 194 to 179 and 154 to 133. The Po Valley was conquered between the Punic Wars and reconquered after the second; then Roman territories were pushed north to the head of the Adriatic, where Aquileia was founded in 181. Anti-Roman revolts that began in 149 brought the annexation of Macedon, and in 146 of most of Greece; Corinth, which had led the resistance, was destroyed; only a few favored cities (Athens, Sparta, Delphi) remained allies. At the same time Carthage was forced into war and destroyed and its territory annexed as the province of "Africa" (146). In 133 the last ruler of Pergamum left his state to Rome on the condition that she protect its independence; after a revolt in 132 it was made the province of "Asia" in 129. The Balearic Islands were taken in 122, the district around Narbonne in 121, Tripolitania in 105, western Cilicia in 102, the rest in 67, Cyrenaica in 74, Crete in 66.

REVOLTS AND, ULTIMATELY, REVOLUTION

By this time, however, the friction between the parts of the Roman machine had become so great that the whole was about to burst into flame. A series of slave revolts—the first in Sicily from 135 to 132—were inconveniences rather than dangers, for not even the provincials would commonly join with slaves. Indeed, a slave revolt in a province made the provincials sensible of their dependence on Rome for protection. More serious was the revolt of the Italian allies in 91. Rome defeated this by granting most of the allies' demands, notably for Roman citizenship. She began by rewarding those who remained loyal, then won over by generous terms the less resolute of the rebels, finally made examples of the most determined. Divide and conquer had always been her policy. The crisis was past by 89; the fighting went on for a while thereafter.

Rome ceded more easily to the demand for citizenship because her supply of citizen soldiers had continued to dwindle, and her mob of citizens without property, to grow. Of attempts to reverse these changes the most famous were those of the Gracchi brothers in 133 and 123. Relying on bourgeois support, they advocated extension of citizenship to the allies, resettlement of small farmers on public land (hitherto rented to senators at minimal rates), resumption of colonization, and provision of grain at less than market rates to feed the Roman poor, pending their resettlement. The longest-lived of these measures was the last: most of the Roman mob preferred free food in Rome to the hard work of a small farmer, and when one party began to bribe them with public money, the other could not offer less, so cheap grain became free grain, the body of recipients was extended to include persons of middle income, the "temporary relief" measure became the perquisite of a privileged class, and the handouts went on increasing through the centuries until the imperial government broke down.

After the introduction of "relief," the Gracchi's most important achievement was to get themselves murdered by their senatorial opponents. This produced an enduring feud between the majority of the senators and a Gracchan minority supported by the bulk of the bourgeoisie. The majority also had their bourgeois supporters, and both sides, with varying success, bid for the mob. There was no clear-cut class struggle. But the security of senatorial rule gave way to bitter party battles in which anything could happen.

What did happen was that a popular and capable bourgeois general named Marius found a way to raise plenty of troops and good ones—he simply enrolled any men he could get, asking no questions about property and preferring those who looked like good fighters. Such men, largely from the rural proletariat, had little financial interest in the

Roman state and less concern for it. They were not a citizen militia, but a body of professional soldiers, fighting not for Rome but for money. Their pay was minimal, and the senate, with tight-fisted stupidity, did nothing significant to increase it. The state was chronically short of money because the senate would not consent to tax Romans—they had abolished direct taxation of citizens in 167. Nor would they permit the soldier to rise from the ranks—officers must be of bourgeois fortune or better. So pay was fixed. Beyond pay came booty, which depended on victory, which depended on the general. Finally, the soldiers might hope for some special reward provided their general won his war and had sufficient political influence to persuade the senate to grant his soldiers land. Therefore the soldiers were loyal to their generals, not to the senate.

Other generals followed Marius' example. They and their armies were soon fighting for control of the state. Each general, when in power, declared his chief opponents public enemies and put prices on their heads. Fortunately for the senate, the ultimate victor was one of their party, Sulla, who had trained a devoted army in the east. There he had ruined Athens, suppressed a revolt in Asia (the provincials murdered some 80,000 Italian residents), and forced Mithridates VI of Pontus, who had inspired the revolt, back to his own dominions. After returning to Italy in 83, and defeating his opponents in 82, Sulla liquidated his enemies, restored control to the senate, retired to private life in 79, and died the following year without having done anything to alter the basic conditions. The conflicts, therefore, were soon resumed. This time the generals who eventually emerged as leaders were Pompey and Julius Caesar.

Pompey had crushed a Spanish revolt in 72, put down piracy, a pan-Mediterranean plague, in 67, finished off Mithridates of Pontus and Tigranes of Armenia in 66, and in 62 constituted, from conquered territory, the provinces Bithynia and Pontus, and Syria. He brought back his army to Italy in 61 and, after some political haggling, was able to settle it on grants of public land (59).

Caesar, at that time a political ally of Pompey's, was rewarded for his alliance with the governorship of the Gallic (Celtic) provinces in the Po Valley and France. Thence he conquered the rest of France, Belgium, and bits of Holland, Germany, and Switzerland. He then broke with Pompey and, at the end of 50, was poised in the Po Valley, ready to descend on Rome. Pompey's army, meanwhile, already old in 61, had grown eleven years older and was nine years out of training. And Pompey had not reassembled it. When Caesar crossed the Rubicon and invaded Italy, Pompey and the senators fled to Greece. Here they put together an army which was defeated by Caesar's veterans at Pharsalus in 48. Pompey fled to Egypt and was there murdered. Caesar followed him to Egypt and met Cleopatra VII.* She was twenty-two at the time, he, fifty-three. He restored her to the throne; she named the baby Ptolemy Caesar. Caesar returned to Rome in 47, in 46 defeated the senatorial forces in Africa, in 45 the Pompeian forces in Spain. On March 15, 44, he was murdered.

Caesar had not wished to break entirely with the old order and had therefore, on his return to Rome, reconstituted a rump senate of all but his most determined opponents. To this senate the rule of the state reverted after his assassination, but not for long. Caesar's army was waiting to be paid and anxious to avenge him. The senate, desperate to achieve a balance of power, allowed his murderers to take over the governorships of the eastern provinces, where they raised armies. Meanwhile, Caesar's officers, Antony and Lepidus, put themselves at the head of armies in Gaul and Spain; his grand-nephew Octavius, whom he had adopted in his will (hence the change of his name to Caesar Octavian), won the support of his veterans in Italy. By the end of 43, Octavian, Antony, and Lepidus had allied and forced the senate to give them sweeping powers for constitutional reform. The first things swept away were their senatorial opponents, who were proscribed as public enemies and mostly murdered. The eastern armies were defeated at Philippi in 42. Thereafter the alliance degenerated into a rivalry between Octavian, who controlled the west, and Antony, who controlled the eastern provinces and Egypt—he married Cleopatra in 37. (Lepidus retired to the priesthood and to drink.) The resultant war was settled by the battle of Actium on September 2, 31. Antony and Cleopatra committed suicide in 30, and Octavian took over Egypt. Cleopatra had prepared a fleet to take Ptolemy Caesar, now seventeen, to India, but Octavian persuaded the boy to return and had him murdered.

Octavian did not annex Egypt to the territories of Rome, but subjected it to himself. He also took over the remains of Antony's army. Now there was no military force in the Mediterranean world capable of standing against that of which he was the commander (*imperator*, whence the title "emperor"). Legally he was an official of the Roman republic, but in fact the republic had ended.

ROME'S TRANSMISSION OF HELLENISTIC CULTURE

Paradoxically, our intellectual debt to republican Rome is far greater than its intellectual achievement. The early Romans had not been known for refinement. (Reportedly there were no barbers in the city before 300 B.C.) The whiskery old farmers had little respect for literature, art, and science; these were not proper concerns for a Roman gentleman. When they did become fashionable, it was largely through the influence of Greek house slaves, following the conquest of south Italy. Therefore the Greek forms became fashionable; whatever old Roman works there may have been were almost wholly lost. The imitations of Greek works were at first in Greek: Latin was a peasant language with few words for abstract thought: "sincerity," for instance, is properly a quality of honey unmixed with wax; the word *felix* which came to mean "fortunate" originally meant "fertile." But in the theater, to reach a popular audience, Latin had to be used. So the earliest considerable pieces preserved from Latin literature are the plays of Plautus, from about the end of the second Punic War, and these are all imitations or adaptations of Greek comedies. So are those of Terence, a half-century later, who follows Plautus, like a dancing master following a drunken sailor.

Since little is preserved of hellenistic comedy, the works of Plautus and Terence are among the chief sources for our knowledge of the later Greek theater and were the models which inspired the revival of classical comedy in the Renaissance. Similarly in philosophy our most extensive exposition of Epicureanism comes from the Latin poet Lucretius (a contemporary of Pompey), while the philosophical works of Cicero (murdered in 43 on the orders of Octavian and Antony) are one of the best sources for our knowledge of second- and first-century Stoicism. Catullus, of the same generation, shows what Greek erotic poetry must have been for passion and directness. Sallust, one of Caesar's henchmen, gives a fair imitation of Greek historical techniques, and Cicero's speeches are products of Greek rhetoric. This is not to say these authors had no virtues of their own—the peasant vigor of Plautus, the romanticism which breaks through Lucretius' rationalism, the surprising tenderness and feeling for purity of Catullus, the urbanity and worldly wisdom of Cicero are peculiar to these authors, but the major elements in their works are Greek. Their chief contribution to intellectual and artistic history is this transmission of Greek elements to the Latin west, the Middle Ages, the Renaissance, and the schoolboys of all but modern times. Perhaps the most nearly original things we have from the period are Cato's work on agriculture, an unrivaled expression of Latin peasant mentality, and Caesar's report of his Gallic wars, an adaptation of historical form to the needs of political propaganda, written in the terse Latin of a Roman aristocrat and electric with the charge of a great analytical mind. But even these had antecedents in Greek agricultural works and military reports, and if we look for originality beyond personal characteristics, we find little. Cicero does show us a new stage in the history of philosophy—the return of philosophy from the professional philosopher to the man of the world; its practice as part of the life of a distinguished barrister and politician. Here the force of Cicero's example, especially in wedding philosophy to legal rhetoric, was of great importance. So was his development of Latin prose style and vocabulary for the expression of philosophic ideas—whose ideas they were does not matter. Once Cicero had created the language, Augustine could think in it.

ROMAN ART AND ARCHITECTURE

In the fine arts the one great achievement of the republican period was ruthless portraiture.* One look at the stony faces of their funerary statues explains the terrible realism of their foreign policy and slave economy. But in the applied arts few peoples have so distinguished achievements. Their roads, bridges, and aqueducts, some still in use, are masterpieces of functional form and original thought. The arch had been known for millennia, but the Romans were the first to realize its possibilities both for beauty and for utility, first for bridges and aqueducts,* later, especially in and after the time of Nero, for monumental entrances and the creation of vast, open interiors. It was function that the Romans themselves admired. Aqueducts, said Pliny, are more valuable than useless pyramids. But like the pyramids, these great public works were costly: only the enormous capital and cheap labor of Rome made their construction possible. The standard road, for instance, was fifteen feet wide and, with its foundations, four feet deep; each foot of length required sixty cubic feet of construction: first a layer of flagstones, then a bed of rubble, then a layer of concrete, and on top a surface of squared stone or pounded gravel. Moreover, these roads did not follow the previous tracks nor go from town to town. They were laid out as straight as possible across country, avoiding the towns and the traffic in them. To reach a town one turned off on a side road. The main roads even cut across the contours of the country with minimal gradients; this required much cutting, filling, terracing, and bridge building. None of this was absolutely new, but it had never been done before to the same extent. The Roman innovation is reflected even in our vocabulary: our word "street," for instance, comes from the Latin *strata*, meaning "paved." In the hellenistic world there had been relatively few paved roads. The Roman network was built for military movements and official messengers, but, once built, facilitated an increase of trade.

Cities,* too, bear the marks of Roman genius. Roman architects loved balance and grandeur; with the money and labor at their disposal they could cut, terrace, fill, and produce great squares and vistas with monumental buildings on either side, in a fashion far beyond the means of their hellenistic predecessors. The repertory of hellenistic forms—porticoes, temples, and so on—was taken over, the units enlarged, and new forms developed, especially for public entertainment, a major concern of the big cities. The Roman formula for management of the mob was "bread and circuses." The circus, primarily a track for chariot races, became a new architectural form; the earliest, the Circus Maximus, would seat between 200,000 and 250,000. The enlarged theater was no longer a hollowed-out hillside, but a free-standing building in which an artificial hillside of seats confronted a many tiered stage, loaded with architectural decorations, though shallow by modern standards. The first stone theater at Rome, built by Pompey in 55 B.C., seated at most 10,000 (ancient authors said, 40,000); the first live rhinoceros to be seen in the city was shown at its opening. Also at the end of the republic appeared the amphitheater, used especially for gladiatorial games. The largest would be the Colosseum, dedicated in 80 A.D. and seating about 50,000. (The practice of making men fight animals or each other for public amusement was derived from the Etruscans, but developed by the Romans on a scale unparalleled. Large numbers of trained gladiators* were kept by Rome and other cities and by private individuals. Prisoners of war and condemned criminals were used without special training, thus the sadistic side of human nature was gratified in a way that contributed to the maintenance of Roman power and public order. These shows increased in size as the citizens' experience of actual warfare declined; they were the most popular form of public entertainment from the second century B.C. to the third A.D. The tradition survives in bullfighting.) Perhaps the most important creation of Roman public architecture, however, was the sewer. Underground sewage had hitherto been rare. Its development was necessitated by Rome's location (in valleys between a number of sharp hills) and by its great size. Underground sewage made possible the maintenance of larger cities which otherwise would have been decimated by disease. Comparable in importance to the sewers were the aqueducts,* another architectural form the Romans developed far beyond any precedents. They made possible and tolerable the expansion of city populations to numbers hitherto unprecedented. (Not that this was an unmixed blessing. Aristocrats found the city crowds a nuisance. Wheeled vehicles had to be banned from the streets in daytime. One woman of the Claudian clan, whose brother, as admiral, had just lost a naval battle in which thousands of Romans drowned, remarked, when her litter was stuck in the traffic, "If only my brother were alive to command another fleet!" She was fined by the censors.) These great public buildings required expert maintenance. The aqueducts, for instance, raised such problems that Augustus' troubleshooter, M. Agrippa, created a corps of 240 slaves specially trained for their upkeep. These he bequeathed to Augustus, and Augustus to the state. Like all state office holders, they multiplied: Claudius added 460 to the staff.

In private architecture, as in public, the Romans excelled in functional buildings—huge warehouses and towering blocks of one- and two-room tenements, easier to admire than live in. Standard blocks of such tenements appear as part of the city planning of Roman colonies in the third century B.C. Increase of city population in such housing led to new distribution of services. Instead of separate markets and residential districts, small shops lined the ground floor fronts of the tenements, to supply the residents. We know little of the houses of the rich, save that they steadily increased in magnificence—and therefore rapidly became obsolete and were rebuilt. A house which in 78 B.C. was thought the finest in Rome was merely an average house thirty-five years later. Cicero spent about $700,000 for his town house and said one could not live as a gentleman on less than $120,000 a year. Even more magnificent were the country places which, at the end of the republic, began to be surrounded with elaborate gardens. Some, like Cicero's eight, were merely businessmen's playthings of a couple of hundred acres, but others were vast estates, centers of manufacturing as well as farming, dependent on the outside world only for luxuries.

TECHNOLOGICAL ADVANCES

Roman building was made possible by the discovery of cement which would harden under water and was therefore superior to the previous lime mortar. It was perhaps the most important of Roman technological discoveries, though rivaled by glass blowing and the introduction of water mills, windmills, and rotary mills* which made possible the use of animals to grind grain. The senate was concerned about agricultural techniques and in 146 ordered the translation into Latin of a 28-volume Punic work on agriculture. Here both Romans and Carthaginians were indebted to Greek achievements. A debt to Egypt was the solar calendar of 365 days, introduced (and corrected with an additional day every fourth year) by Caesar to replace the Roman lunar calendar with its wild irregularities.

Warfare the Romans themselves revolutionized. For the thrusting spear of the Greek soldier they substituted the throwing spear. After their shower of spears had broken the enemy's ranks they finished the fight at close quarters with a short sword, edged and pointed for both cut and thrust. Spear throwing and swordplay required space, so they abandoned the Greek phalanx and developed an open formation of small groups of men. This had several advantages: Fresh fighters could move up to replace the weary and wounded; forces could easily be shifted sideways; adaptation to irregular terrain was easier.

ROMAN JURISPRUDENCE

Most important of Roman advances in social techniques was the development of jurisprudence, the system of legal interpretation which enabled its practitioners to decide whether and with what effect a general law would apply in a given case. These two questions had always arisen wherever actions were judged in accordance with fixed laws. In Rome, however, their settlement became the province of private individuals called jurisconsults, at first members of senatorial families, who were recognized experts on the meanings of the laws. Their opinions gradually acquired almost the force of law since a judge usually had to choose between the opinions submitted to him by jurisconsults, commonly those consulted by the contesting parties, but often, as well, those consulted by the judges themselves. The chief judicial officer of Rome (the "urban praetor") annually, on entering his office, issued an edict indicating the rules he would apply in court; these rules soon became traditional; many were based on, or shaped by, the opinions of jurisconsults. The origins of this development were two: first, extreme brevity and consequent obscurity of early Roman laws, which necessitated expert interpretation; second, the prestige of the great Roman families, which made the small man seek support by soliciting from one of their members a favorable opinion on his case. But when each party to a case came prepared with an opinion of a noble supporter, the opinion which prevailed would be that of the supporter recognized as an authority on the law. Thus the prestige of learning was distinguished from that of position; it came also to be independent of politics.

The content of this learning was primarily tradition. Laws were to be interpreted as they had been in the past. To learn the tradition one had to frequent the house of a jurist, watch him in action, and talk with him. When Greek philosophy became popular in Rome, particularly in the age of Cicero (who was not a jurist, but a barrister, that is, a pleader of cases), the jurists applied philosophical methods—exact definition, classification, logical inference—to the topics of Roman law and thus transformed the isolated traditions of their predecessors into a legal system. But they shunned pure theory and legal philosophy. They did not question the validity of institutions or established rules. Their concern was to determine how the rules would apply in particular cases. By such determination in many exemplary cases they made the meaning of the law predictable and the same for all. This rivals the political union of the Mediterranean world as the greatest achievement of the Roman republic. (Why did the Romans, not the Greeks, create legal science? We do not know. And the similar but later developments of the Jewish rabbis and the Sasanian magi—the only peoples of antiquity besides the

Romans to develop systematic legal interpretation—are equally puzzling.)

Roman private law, as developed by jurists at the imperial court in the first 250 years of our era, became the model followed by later legal thought of Byzantium, and, through Byzantium, of the Turkish empire. In the west it was partly abandoned by the barbarian invaders but revived in Italian cities toward the end of the eleventh century and later dominated western Europe. Its success was not accidental. The system had been shaped by the classic concern for the rights of the citizen, modified by the philosophic concern for the rights of man, as well as by the increasing importance of the emperor; hence it was ideally suited to the needs of the reviving (German) Roman Empire and the Italian cities in their common struggle against the great nobles and the popes. It also had popular appeal. The emperors often took cognizance of legal questions concerning humble people. The *Digests* (an enormous collection of law cases and legal opinions about them, collected by Justinian) deals with slaves in about 150 cases, in more than 130 of these the case concerns one slave only. (The big landowners, like the big corporations today, rarely needed to go to the court; they had other means of getting their way.) And the jurists commonly decided in the spirit of equity. Thus the tenant does not need to pay his rent if his dwelling (or his field) is ruined or damaged by something beyond his control: bandits or drought or the like. This combination of concerns for equity and for the power of the central government enabled, and still enables, laws of Roman inspiration to replace the native legal traditions of the barbarians throughout the world.

FOR FURTHER READING

T. Frank, *Life and Literature in the Roman Republic*
M. Gelzer, *Caesar*
N. Lewis and M. Reinhold, *Roman Civilization: Vol. I: The Republic*
H. Scullard, *From the Gracchi to Nero*
R. Syme, *The Roman Revolution*
L. Taylor, *Party Politics in the Age of Caesar*

14
THE AUGUSTAN EMPIRE

OCTAVIAN'S PROBLEM AND HIS SOLUTION: THE POWER STRUCTURE OF THE PRINCIPATE

During the thirteen years of war between Octavian's appearance as Caesar's heir and his final defeat of Antony (44–31) his soldiers had repeatedly taken advantage of his difficulties to drive hard bargains. His main concern, therefore, once he got rid of Antony, was to free himself from dependence on the army, without losing its loyalty.

The first step was to reduce its size. After taking over Antony's forces he had about 500,000 men under arms. Of these, he tells us, "I settled in colonies or sent back to their own cities a little more than 300,000, and to all of these I allotted lands or granted money as rewards for military service." The lands and money came mostly from expropriation of his opponents' properties. Since most of the soldiers were Italians and were settled in Italy, their presence guaranteed his security. By the time of his death the army had been reduced to 25 legions (at full strength, 150,000 men), supported by an unknown number of auxiliaries. Legions and auxiliaries together numbered perhaps 275,000, mostly distributed along a frontier of more than 5,000 miles. Pay and pensions,

B.C. 31	Battle of Actium, Octavian victorious
31–A.D. 68	The Julio-Claudian dynasty (Augustus; Tiberius, A.D. 14–37; Gaius, 37–41; Claudius, 41–54; Nero); Vergil, Horace, Livy, Ovid, Seneca, Petronius; Philo of Alexandria "reconciles" Judaism with Greek philosophy
B.C. 28	Purge of the senate; Octavian *princeps*
27	Crisis officially over; Octavian voted "Augustus"
26–A.D. 9	Expansion and subjugation: 26–19, northwest Spain and Portugal; 25, central Asia Minor; 25–15, the Alps, Raetia, Noricum; 29–11, Thrace and Moesia; 13–9, Dalmatia and Pannonia; 10–A.D. 6, southern Asia Minor, Judea; A.D. 6–8, resubjugation of Dalmatia and Pannonia; 9, attempt to conquer Germany abandoned
A.D. c. 30	Jesus crucified
43–85	Conquest of Britain
c. 60	Paul sent to Rome for trial
64	Great fire in Rome; Christians persecuted by Nero
66–73	Jewish revolt in Palestine
69–96	Flavian dynasty (Vespasian; Titus, 79–81; Domitian)
70	Destruction of the temple of Jerusalem; ben Zakkai's court in Jabneh
75–100	The four Gospels written
79	Eruption of Vesuvius, destruction of Pompeii
96–180	"The five good emperors" (Nerva; Trajan, 98–117; Hadrian, 117–138; Antoninus Pius, 138–161; Marcus Aurelius); Martial, Juvenal, Tacitus, Suetonius, Epictetus, Arrian, Plutarch, Appian, Apuleius, Lucian
101–106	Trajan's conquest of Dacia and "Arabia"
113–116	Trajan's conquest of Armenia and Mesopotamia
114–117	Revolt of the Jews in Cyrenaica, Egypt, and Cyprus; Hadrian abandons most of Mesopotamia and Armenia
131–135	Revolt of bar Kosiba in south Palestine
180–192	Commodus, son of Marcus Aurelius
193–235	Severan dynasty (Septimius Severus; Geta, 211–212, Caracalla, 211–217, Elagabalus, 218–222, Alexander)
c. 200	The Mishnah of Rabbi Judah the Prince

both reliable, came from him; the commanding officers were his appointees and were shifted frequently so they could not build personal followings among the soldiers.

This army was kept busy. Following a principle of the republican senate—to have no dangerous neighbors—Octavian set out to consolidate Rome's territories, extend them to easily defensible boundaries, and eliminate pockets of possible resistance within these boundaries. He completed the subjugation of the Iberian peninsula by conquering the northwest corner in bitter campaigns from 26 to 19. Campaigns in 25, 16, and 15 secured the Alps. The year 15 also saw the takeover of the lands from the Alps north to the Danube (ancient Raetia and Noricum, parts of modern Bavaria and Austria). At the eastern end of the river, subjugation of the lands to the south had been going on since 29 and was practically completed in 11 by suppression of a rising in Thrace. Finally the lands south and west of the middle Danube (ancient Dalmatia and Pannonia, in modern Yugoslavia and Hungary) were conquered in 13 to 9, then reconquered, after a great rebellion, in A.D. 6 to 8. This gave the empire control of all Europe south of the Rhine and the Danube. Those rivers—whose headwaters are only ten miles apart—formed a defensible frontier. It was a longer and therefore more expensive frontier than Octavian wanted, so he planned to shorten it by conquering Holland and Germany as far as the Elbe. A defeat in A.D. 9 convinced him that the conquest would be too costly; the project was dropped. To the east, central Asia Minor was annexed in 25, giving Rome control of all the western end of the peninsula; the mountains in the south, adjoining Cilicia, were pacified from 10 B.C. to A.D. 6. Cilicia was protected by mountains to the north; on the east it adjoined Syria which had good natural boundaries—the Euphrates and the desert. Palestine (under a client king, Herod the Great), Egypt, Cyrenaica, Tripolitania, and the province of Africa were all bounded by deserts or by peoples so small, primitive, or isolated that they offered no threat to Roman power and required only occasional punitive expeditions to keep them in order. This settlement of frontier and internal problems enabled Octavian to proceed safely with his policy of cutting down the army, and so achieve two of the goals he most desired, independence and economy.

Along with reduction of the army Octavian tried to strengthen his position in other ways. The first was to make his power legal—a matter of great importance to Roman opinion. He had the senate vote him such powers as he needed, being careful to have them covered by republican titles. The "republican" government went on much as before, only the officials were his nominees and did what he told them.

He was equally aware of the importance of practical interests and appealed to those of the Roman mob, the bourgeoisie, the senate, and the provincials.

The mob was venal by tradition, so he could and did try to win support by direct donatives from his spoils and, later, from taxes, to each adult male citizen resident in the city. Over the 45 years from Actium (31 B.C.) to his death in A.D. 14, these gifts amounted to an average of about $25 per man per year. Moreover he reorganized the grain supply, using the grain of Africa and Egypt. Allottments were made to all adult male Roman citizens, of less than bourgeois fortune, resident in Rome. These numbered approximately 200,000. They were listed as recipients and new names were added to the list only as replacements when vacancies occurred. (The ration was about six bushels of grain per month. This would make about fifty pounds of bread, barely enough for one person. Bread was the main source of food, and remained so in Europe until the late nineteenth century. Africa furnished the grain for eight months of the year, Egypt for four.) The water supply, too, was vastly improved by new aqueducts. There were games and other public entertainments and spectacles of unprecedented magnificence, all the more welcome because weekends were not holidays. But almost eighty days a year were given to fixed festivals, and besides these there were often extraordinary festivals financed by Octavian either directly or in the names of other members of his family or staff. An enormous building program beautified the city* and made work for those who wanted it. The public services in Rome included fire and police departments, management of docks, markets, grain and water supply, baths, sewers, street cleaning and lighting, city planning, supervision of buildings to determine their safety, courts, mints, and religious services, including games and theatrical performances (there was no public transportation). Never had a city done so much for its citizens nor required so little of them. But Octavian was too wise to trust to gratitude. His benefactions were backed up by a quadruple set of guards to keep one another, as well as the citizens, in check. There were his own "praetorian" guards (under two commanders) as well as guards of the city, and police and fire brigades—the first such forces Rome had. Finally, to prevent trouble, popular assemblies and elections of officers were reduced to formalities and the choice of candidates was controlled.

The bourgeois were easy to win over. Caesar had been popular with them; Octavian succeeded to his popularity and did much to deserve it. Of Italian bourgeois background himself, he gave many bourgeois, mostly from Italian cities, places in the senate. For many more he created places as financial inspectors or even governors of minor provinces. For the most successful there were the important "prefectures" —praetorian prefect, prefect of the grain supply, or prefect of Egypt (which was always governed by a man of bourgeois rank; no senator was permitted to set foot in it without permission of Octavian).

The senate was the most difficult problem. Many senators resented their loss of real power. Many resented Octavian as an upstart, from bourgeois and Italian, not Roman, stock. Yet if the façade of legality was to be maintained, if his rule was not to degenerate into a tyranny (and, consequently, remain dependent on the army), the cooperation of the senate had to be secured. Votes were no problem. The senate could be—and was—packed with subservient appointees. But the surviving "genuine" senators were men of widely influential families and vast wealth. They could not be ignored. They had to be either conciliated or exterminated.

Since the senators were anxious not to be exterminated, Octavian's policy of conciliation succeeded. He purged the senate in 28 of its "unworthy" members, but at the same time made himself its leader (*princeps*, whence "prince") and made clear that he expected to govern with it, this policy has led scholars to describe as "the principate" the period through which Octavian's system prevailed (28 B.C.–A.D. 235). Here pride and the maintenance of appearances were of great importance. Octavian was careful to treat the senators with extreme politeness and to maintain every detail of the traditional *decorum*—a Roman word and a major Roman concern. He scrupulously consulted the senate about unimportant questions.

Of important questions the most difficult was control of the provinces, since the governors of the provinces commanded the armies there. Provincial governorships had been the most valuable rewards of a public career; the senate would never relinquish them; nor would Octavian relinquish control of the army. The solution was reached in 27 B.C. Octavian retained command of those provinces in which considerable forces had to be stationed, but governed them by delegates whom he appointed from the senate. The remaining governors were appointed by the senate. In gratitude the senate voted him *Augustus*—"the revered."

This was not quite deification. Octavian had had Caesar deified by the senate in 42 and had since been officially "the son of the god"—by adoption. *Augustus* brought him a step nearer deity. He refused official deification—it would have offended the senators, who would have had to participate in the official worship—but he made himself, even for the senate, an object of religious awe. Provincials were permitted to worship him.

For the senate the most important object of religious awe was Rome itself. Augustus* therefore made himself protector of the Roman tradition and above all of religion. Roman religion had always been somewhat impersonal. A superstitious reverence for "the proper way of doing things" was the strongest religious experience of the average Roman. Republican government had been largely a structure of rituals. As any successful revolutionary, Augustus became a conservative; he therefore hoped to revive respect for such rituals—in others. He saw in reverence for the established order a bulwark for his regime. He made himself patron of the old Roman family life* (laws encouraging marriage and childbearing, penalizing celibacy and adultery), traditional class distinctions (laws limiting manumission of slaves, prohibiting intermarriage of freedmen with senatorial families), and ancient religious ceremonies (82 temples rebuilt, old priesthoods revived, cult associations encouraged, domestic worship restored by law). Horace and Vergil were set to glorifying Augustus, the origins of Rome, the simple, rural, Roman life, the pleasures of patriotism, and the propriety of dying for one's country—the great platitudes still necessary for the survival of a great people. Livy retold Roman history in cineramic style. With imperial favor these works became the classics of secondary instruction. It is difficult to estimate their influence on the western mind; they are so much part of us that we take their values for granted and their epigrams for truisms. For Augustus' purpose they expressed the Roman tradition in the Roman language and provided a Roman literature to distract the upper classes from Greek free thought and rally them to the ancient Roman order as represented by his regime. Moralizing as it was, that regime revived the Roman spirit, and enabled it to preserve the *pax romana*—the peace resultant from Roman rule—for well over two centuries.

In the provinces the cult of Rome spread widely, hand in hand with that of Augustus. Nor was it all flattery. The Greeks had long worshipped as powers what we think of as abstractions: peace, fortune, health, and the like. In Greek *romé* means "power," and the rise and rule of Rome would seem the work of a supernatural power which had become, through Augustus, the protectress of the world. The provincials had been almost ruined by the civil wars and therefore saw the maintenance of peace as the greatest of blessings. Augustus was sincerely hailed as "the savior of the world." Moreover, he was interested in the prosperity of the provinces—they were his domain. His bourgeois financial inspectors checked with expert eyes on tax collectors and governors alike. His control of the senate and of elections enabled him to prevent appointment of unsuitable governors even for senatorial provinces, while provinces under his direct control were governed by his own appointees ("legates") whom he held strictly to account. In general his reign marked the beginning of tranquil and comparatively just government for the provinces. Wealthy provincial families had much to gain from social stability and peace. The one protected their land ownership and loans; the other improved conditions for trade. Many already had ties with Roman aristocrats. They backed Augustus. The poor hated the wealthy, the tax collectors, and the foreign officials, and dreamed of a time when they would again be free. But meanwhile they acquiesced.

Thus, Augustus escaped the army's control. The empire had been pacified and its territories secured, the army cut down and split up, and other supports found for his regime in the settlements of his veterans, the Roman mob, the Italian bourgeoisie, the remodeled senate, and the wealthy families of the provinces. But the army still existed. Training and tactical knowledge made it far superior to any citizen force that could be mustered against it. It remained the ultimate basis of the emperor's power, but a constant threat. For should the newly established concord break down, the emperor would be forced to fall back on the army and so would fall again into its control. After Augustus' death this happened from time to time, but the pattern he created survived as the "formal cause" of the empire at least to the fall of the Severan dynasty in 235. Until then political history was one of adjustments as various elements of the complex increased or diminished in power.

THE POLITICAL HISTORY OF THE PRINCIPATE

In outline there were three periods. From Augustus' death until A.D. 96 relations between the emperors and the senate were more or less strained; consequently much administration came to be done by the emperor's secretaries. The senate, denied power, turned to conspiracies, Stoic philosophizing about the natural liberty of man, and vicious gossip about the emperors. This led to executions for treason; many senatorial families were extinguished, the richer bourgeoisie were decimated, the imperial estates increased by confiscations. This policy increased the emperors' dependence on the troops in Rome, especially the praetorian guard, which took advantage of the situation to extort privileges and money. Jealousy of the praetorians and knowledge of the weakness of the emperor's position tempted the frontier armies to revolt. Revolts under Nero* in A.D. 68 ended the so-called Julio-Claudian dynasty (of Augustus' wife's family) and after a year of chaos installed the "Flavians"—Vespasian, a popular general, succeeded by his sons Titus and Domitian. Under Domitian the government again degenerated to a reign of terror.

When Domitian was assassinated in 96 the senate managed to install a candidate of its own, Nerva, who secured his position by adopting as successor a frontier general, Trajan.* Trajan strengthened the imperial office by commanding his troops in person. The conquests of Dacia* (western Rumania) and "Arabia" (roughly, east and south Transjordan, the Negev, and Sinai) yielded enormous loot which financed gifts to the troops and the Roman mob, games (one set ran for 110 days), and a building program, especially of roads. The senate, by intermarriage and imperial appointment, gradually came to be more representative of the wealthy families of all the western provinces; provincial interest strengthened its support for the emperor. The Stoics discovered that true freedom was not political, but moral, and that the emperor was the servant of divine reason to maintain order on earth. The resultant concord survived a serious strain at Trajan's death and lasted through the reigns of his three successors—Hadrian (117–138), Antoninus Pius (138–161), and Marcus Aurelius Antoninus (161–180)—and might have lasted longer had not Marcus' son, Commodus, been an egomaniac.

Commodus' accession was the beginning of a period of almost constant conflict between emperor and senate; his murder in 192 led to a crisis like that of 68. This time the successful general, Septimius Severus, was unable to reestablish good relations with the senate—many senators with provincial connections had backed his opponents and suffered accordingly. Further, he was of bourgeois family and his wife was a Syrian. He replied by packing the senate with appointees from the eastern provinces, hitherto usually excluded; by giving many positions, formerly reserved for senators, to bourgeois, especially easterners; by further welfare measures for the Roman mob; by extension of citizenship or colonial status to many provincial cities, and by showering favors on the frontier armies. The old praetorians were cashiered, and a new and larger praetorian guard was formed from frontier troops. Under his son, Caracalla, the government became openly a military dictatorship. The army's loyalty to the family enabled a couple of juvenile second cousins to succeed Caracalla; then, in 235, an officer risen from the ranks wiped out the family and proceeded to govern with almost no regard for the senate or the traditional civilian order. The Augustan balance of powers was at an end.

CIVILIZATION IN THE ROMAN EMPIRE

From 27 B.C. to A.D. 235, however, the Augustan political structure controlled England, Wales, and southern Scotland, all Europe south of the Rhine-Danube frontier, all Africa north of the Sahara, Egypt, Palestine, Syria, Turkey, Armenia, and districts in the Caucasus and south Russia. Save for the brief civil wars of 68–69 and 193–197, these had been years of peace; rebellions were rare. The provincial aristocracy's loyalty to the emperors made garrisons in the provinces unnecessary. One legion with auxiliaries (about 10,000 men) sufficed for Algeria, Tunisia, and Morocco. There were no Roman troops in the territory of modern France save for the personal guard of the governor at Lyons, 500 men. The army, though its strength gradually rose above 300,000 as barbarian pressure on the northern frontier increased, was hardly 1 percent of the adult population.

CIVILIZATION IN THE ROMAN EMPIRE 171

This freed the national income for extension of cultivated land and improvement of the standard of living. The characteristic forms of Roman civilization appeared everywhere—roads (over 60,000 miles), bridges, aqueducts,* and above all, cities.* Before the great plague of 166 the inhabitants of the empire possibly numbered about 75,000,000. Increase of population produced increase of equipment—houses, tools, domesticated animals, orchards, vineyards, seed—which transformed the economic situation of occidental man. Knowledge also (the most important form of equipment) was increased and disseminated; the greatest wealth of the empire was its population of skilled farmers and artisans whose labor supported the whole. Selective breeding improved the quality of herds and crops. Vines resistant to cold and humidity were developed. After the French language and the Roman legal tradition, French wines are the most important Roman remains north of the Alps. In Africa, Palestine, Jordan, and Syria, Roman irrigation supported cities in areas now desert. Roman building was so solid that many of its structures—bridges, roads, aqueducts, amphitheaters—are still in use.

The characteristic form of this civilization was the small city* of approximately 50,000 inhabitants, a mile or two in diameter. Only in frontier provinces were the new cities walled. Life was secure even in the countryside, where the rich built magnificent villas* on their estates. Money and labor which formerly went into city walls now went into pavement, sewers, water supply, colonnades along the main streets, and public buildings of which the largest were usually those for the pleasure of the citizens: the circus, the amphitheater, at least one theater,* invariably several baths. The Greeks had commonly bathed in cold water; from Augustus' time on, the Romans made the hot bath the center of a free man's afternoon, and architecturally developed public baths into huge complexes—a large cold bath, smaller warm baths, a hot room, dressing rooms, and often colonnades, gymnasiums, lecture rooms, and so on. In Rome the baths of Caracalla covered 45 acres. Even a village might have two or three public baths. The Romans believed that baths relieve worry; for many they provided the relaxation today sought from drugs. Not only were they financed by the imperial government and the cities, but private benefactors gave funds to pay for admission of the poor. Cleanliness, hitherto a luxury of the rich, became common. In a Danubian village three men elected heads of the local government thanked their fellow citizens by building a public latrine and advertised their generosity by an inscription on the edifice.

After these buildings for public relaxation, the next largest were the temples of the gods and the buildings for public business; forums (open squares, usually arcaded), law courts, and markets. Administrative structures, the equivalents of "city hall" and "federal building," were absent—city administration was by locally elected, annual officers serving without salary, and imperial administration in the provinces was limited to the governors and their staffs; when the breakdown came in 235 there were only about 200 civilian officials with direct imperial appointments in the whole empire.

Of the city's industrial establishments, grain mills* with four or five large grindstones, turned by donkeys, were often the largest. Shops were small affairs, most manufacture was by artisan-shopkeepers with a few slaves working under their direction, and most agricultural processing was done in the countryside. As for housing, a few of the bigger palaces had blocks of tenements, six or eight stories high, honeycombs of one-room residences without even kitchens—the inhabitants ate in taverns. Occasionally there were more luxurious "apartment houses." But most private buildings were of one or two stories. The lack of pumping made it difficult to supply water in high buildings or to fight fires in them. After the great fire of 64 had burnt more than half of Rome the city was rebuilt with low buildings and streets were lined with high porticoes so that firemen could get at most structures from above. The poor lived in blocks cut up into two- or three-room cubbyholes. The middle-class house would have a central courtyard giving light and air to small rooms opening onto it. The rich multiplied courtyards and added cloisters, mosaic pavements, fountains, and even private baths. In Africa houses were sometimes constructed underground as refuges from the heat; the northern provinces had houses with central heating. Even lower-class buildings, in many cities, had running water somewhere, piped in from the municipal aqueduct which also supplied public fountains. (The pipes, especially the larger ones in public domain, were often of lead; lead poisoning may have done a good deal to keep down the city population.) By the middle of the third century even the public buildings in a small Egyptian town had glass windows.

The city population was composed mainly of landowners, shopkeepers, artisans, and domestic servants (mostly slaves). Food came from the surrounding countryside; supply and variety varied from season to season. Manufacturing was by handicrafts and mostly for local consumption. Trade was a minor factor in the total economy because transportation was slow and costly. (Italy lost its pottery trade to the western provinces because it was cheaper to move the Italian potters than to ship the pots.) Apparent exceptions—for instance, the shipment of Egyptian and African grain to Rome or the import of perfumes, jewels, and silk from the east—had little influence on the economy of the average city, which remained one of local subsistence. The need of supplying grain to the big cities did, however, necessitate the development of bigger ships —up to 1,300 tons, a capacity not reached again by merchantmen until the nineteenth century. For this shipping, ports were expanded.*

As for intellectual life, the classics—Greek in the east, Latin in the west—were drilled into the boys in the gymnasium. Adults encountered them chiefly on the stage, where traveling companies of actors kept them alive. There were all sorts of itinerant entertainers, from philosophers or rhetoricians (difficult to distinguish) down to sleight-of-hand artists and men with dancing bears. But the main entertainments were indicated by the main buildings: the baths, the circus for chariot races, the amphitheater for gladiatorial shows. (The use of torture for public amusement increased through the second century.) Usually there was no bookstore, but larger cities did have public libraries, and some rich families had libraries in their villas.

The main religious concern of the city was the cult of the local gods. These had usually been identified with the Roman Jupiter, Juno, and Minerva, or with Mars-Apollo and Venus-Aphrodite, the patrons of the Caesarian house. Often their priests were elected annually. Rich men contested for these honors; there was no priestly class. Priesthoods of the imperial cult were similarly sought after. Augustus and some later emperors had been deified after death by the senate; their cults were now established everywhere as the common expression of loyalty, and the chief alien element in the religious life of the small city, which otherwise turned to its local gods for its daily needs.

The government of the city was principally local—an assembly, elected magistrates, and a system of courts. These the empire willingly recognized; it was reluctant to multiply and pay officials, and therefore it had no staff for local government. So it encouraged urbanization and left the cities to themselves, provided they paid their taxes and debts and maintained order. This limited local independence fostered local patriotism. Wealthy men competed for civic offices, although these carried no salaries and often obligated the incumbent to provide, at his own expense, municipal services or entertainments. Everywhere cities were enriched by private munificence with public buildings and lands.

Augustus' "constitution" was to provide the framework for two hundred and fifty years of this peaceful, provincial life* of the small cities* that made up the bulk of the enormous empire. It was a life of considerable comfort and elegance. An epigram of the time says that six hours of the day are for work, the rest, for life. A single Greco-Roman artistic style became common, producing innumerable artifacts—metalwork, pottery, carving—which still command admiration. The great public monuments—bridges, aqueducts, theaters, temples—continued the tradition of the republic and survived to be the wonders of the medieval world.

PHILOSOPHY IN THE AUGUSTAN EMPIRE

These practical achievements were matched by a practical philosophy, directed, as in the hellenistic world, to the achievement of "the good life." The upper and middle classes turned to Stoicism—desperately during the civil wars and reigns of terror, optimistically when good relations between the senate and the emperors were reestablished. Lower-class thought was permeated by the teaching of the Cynics, a school of vagrant preachers who made "philosophy" an excuse for rejecting ordinary social decencies. Preaching, indeed, was characteristic of all this "philosophy"; even the greatest Stoics of this time, Seneca, Epictetus, the emperor Marcus Aurelius, were mainly concerned to drive home familiar principles. The same is true of Plutarch, the outstanding Platonist, and Philo, an eclectic who sought to justify Judaism. "Philosophy" retained its hellenistic meaning: "the practice of a peculiar discipline in daily life." Jews, Egyptian priests,* and self-styled Indian sages all passed as "philosophers."

Homiletic Stoicism runs through all the literature of the period. The rhetoricians have little else to say. The most remarkable product of Stoicism in poetry was satire, in epigrams and versified diatribes, which enabled writers to combine morality with popular appeal; in attacking vice they could describe it with revolting and readable details. Martial and Juvenal used this technique to the full and are therefore famous. Petronius is more famous for his satirical picaresque novel, of verse and prose alternately, which has equally readable details, but none of the revolting morality; he was a favorite of Nero's,* and Stoicism appears in his works only in parody. The picaresque tradition was continued, with wide variations, by Apuleius and Lucian.

Stoic influence was stronger in the historians, of whom Tacitus was the greatest. A master of innuendo and understatement, Tacitus saw history as political intrigue and was determined to defend the senatorial party. The brilliance of his work, in spite of these limitations, makes the later Suetonius seem a scandalmonger and men like Appian, Arrian, and Dio Cassius, more compilers. But their works are often more reliable, in total effect, than Tacitus' special pleading. As artistic achievements, however—polished presentations of his sardonic view of the world—Tacitus' histories are unrivaled save by Thucydides.

From this peak literary history plunges into a sea of collectors and commentators, industrious men with mediocre minds. Nor is the history of the fine arts more rewarding. The early years of the empire saw some brilliant fresco painting and mosaics. Pompeii and Herculaneum preserve examples prior to 79. But this was decoration rather than fine art. Much sculpture was throttled by the dead hand of classicism, though Roman realism survived in vigorous portraits, and a new artistic form—

the narrative frieze with a historical subject*—became prominent. The great Roman architectural tradition lived on, and increased means made possible larger and larger buildings. All in all, however, the artistic output of the imperial age, like the literary and the philosophical, was mediocre. This holds, too, for scientific and technological thought. There was much collection of accepted results, and some application of known principles; but little was new.

In spite of this prevailing conservatism and the social stability it reflected and produced, major changes did come about in these two centuries and more from the death of Augustus to the death of Severus Alexander. Some have been mentioned: increase of population, of cities, and of wealth, especially in equipment, extension of agriculture, extension of membership in the senate to rich families from all parts of the empire,[1] establishment everywhere of cults of the deified emperors, extension of Stoicism and permeation of all classes by its basic suppositions.

TOWARDS A MORE LIBERAL SOCIETY

Connected with Stoicism was a far-reaching change in the privileges accorded persons of inferior social status. Stoics had long preached the brotherhood of man (including women), and contrasted natural rights with social privileges. Also, some rights of women had long been protected by law. Already in many states of the ancient Near East and in classical Athens, women, like men, had the right to divorce. These legal rights were now considerably extended: In 178 A.D. women were granted the right to inherit from their children without special testamentary disposition; forty years later Caracalla ruled that an adulterous husband might not prosecute his wife for adultery. But in spite of such occassional provisions the position of women as fixed by law remained low, from our point of view. However, in practice things were different. Many women, Roman and provincial alike, actively participated in social and economic life. Of preserved imperial answers to private petitioners, in questions of business, property rights, legal proceedings, and such, about 25 percent are addressed to women. This evidence is confirmed by the many references to women on statues, in honorary decrees, and in literature, all of which show them acquiring that liberty and higher status which, even in post-Roman times, would be characteristic of their position in the western world. Children and slaves were protected from

---

[1] At the end of the first century eighty percent of the senators were Italian, at the end of the second, only forty percent. There were 600 senators. The turnover was about twenty per year and the average life span seems to have been about fifty years.

arbitrary exercise of parents' and owners' authority. In the case of slaves, as of women, a considerable difference appears between their limited legal rights and their actual social position. In the honorary decrees of cities, when a man's civic virtues are listed, his "fairness and humanity" to his slaves is often mentioned. This change of attitude took place for economic as well as legal and humanitarian reasons. Suppression of piracy had cut down the supply of new slaves; the end of civil wars and conquests reduced it further; the common practice of manumission diminished the supply of existing slaves. So prices went up. It became more economical to work estates with free tenant farmers. One consequence of this was a decline in legal respect for the free man as such. The law now began to distinguish between free men of upper and lower class—*honestiores* and *humiliores*. The former were exempt from humiliating procedures and punishments to which the latter were subject. Peasants begin to replace slaves as the most exploited class. Yet even the peasants felt something of the pride engendered by social stability and well-being. On their tombstones* they often have themselves represented in their labors; a figure plowing, for instance, will proclaim to the passers-by—even to those who cannot read—the occupation of the deceased.

THE SPREAD OF NEAR EASTERN RELIGIONS, INCLUDING JUDAISM AND CHRISTIANITY

Equally important was the change in religion during the first two centuries. Cults of Near Eastern deities spread widely in the west: Isis* of Egypt and her son, Harpocrates;* Yahweh of Jerusalem and his son, Jesus;* Mithras, the Persian; Cybele of Phrygia, "the Great Mother of the Gods," and her consort, Attis. All these deities had, attached to their regular cults, special ceremonies which promised the participants blessing in this life and well-being in the life to come. Life after death now occupied much of the common worshiper's concern. These special ceremonies were commonly secret initiations called "mysteries"; they admitted one not only to future bliss, but also to the circle of fellow initiates who could be helpful connections. In a humdrum world the appeal of secret societies and occult knowledge was understandable. There had always been a large element of superstition in Roman culture; it increased in Antonine and Severan times. The Near Eastern cults, with magic and astrology, were symptoms of this increase; they supplied, then as now, the revelations, the certainties, needed in a world where rationalistic criticism had destroyed much of the faith in the native gods. Among these cults two, Judaism and Christianity, became the major religions of the western world.

The Judaism of the Greco-Roman world is a riddle. In the first place, where did the Jews come from? The Greek (and thence the Roman) word "Jew" looks like a geographical term and should mean "Judean," that is, resident of, or emigrant from, the tiny district around Jerusalem. But this poor hill country could never have supported a large population. Yet in 1 B.C. there were large "Jewish" populations in Palestine, Transjordan, Egypt, Cyrenaica, Cyprus, western Asia Minor, Syria, the Greek islands, Rome, south Italy, Tunisia, Arabia, Mesopotamia, Persia, and Armenia, perhaps a total of 3,000,000. That all these were descendants of the perhaps 50,000 inhabitants of Judea in 600 B.C. is unlikely.

Many certainly were converts or descendants of converts; probably more had been first called "Jews" by their neighbors because they worshiped the god whom the Jews worshiped. The syncretistic Judean worshipers of Yahweh—the majority during the Israelite monarchy—carried his cult with them into exile and taught it to their neighbors. This explains the syncretistic worship of Yahweh in fifth-century Egypt and Mesopotamia, and the prominence of Yahweh in the polytheistic magical papyri. With the rise of a Judean state in the second and first centuries B.C. many of these worshipers of Yahweh, including the descendants of the north Israelite exiles, probably came to be called by the name of the most prominent community of their god's adherents, and adopted Judean ways. Against this supposition, it must be said that Greek and Roman law paid no attention to a man's religion and used the term "Jew" as they did "Egyptian" or "Greek," primarily to mean a native of the territory, or a descendant of natives. But popular usage paid little attention to legal precision. The term "Greek" could be used, for instance, in Egypt for any non-Egyptian, in Christian circles for any pagan, and in Greek circles for anyone who spoke the common dialect as opposed to Attic. And Roman writers tell us that the term "Jew" was similarly extended to those who followed Jewish customs. On the other hand there is no conclusive evidence for large settlements of such converts by syncretism, nor for the common estimates of the size of the Jewish population in the Empire.

This rise of a Judean state began when quarrels between rival candidates for the Jerusalem priesthood and attempts to hellenize the cult led, in 168 B.C., to revolts against the city government and the Seleucid kingdom. A military leader, Judas "Maccabeus," turned the revolts into a guerrilla war. His brothers and their children eventually won the war, took over the high priesthood of Jerusalem (in violation of the Pentateuchal law), conquered most of Palestine and parts of Transjordan in the late second and early first century, and forcibly converted large bodies of the population to their brand of Judaism. They quarreled among themselves and were ousted in 37 by a Jewish politician named Herod who had been recognized as king by the Roman senate. Herod, like the Maccabees, made himself the patron of "Jews" all over the empire. He lavishly rebuilt Jerusalem, especially the temple, which he made one of the famous buildings of the Greco-Roman world. In his reign ancient Judaism reached the apogee of its power and prestige.

But what was it? A great variety of beliefs and practices which can best be called "the cult of Yahweh," since they were all regarded as obedience or worship of "the Lord," the god not to be named, whose greatest temple was that in Jerusalem. The official authority as to the religion there was the high priest, an appointee of Herod, for whom many Jews had little respect. There was a rival temple-in-exile in Egypt, staffed by descendants of the legitimate high-priestly line, but they, too, seem to have had little influence with most of the Jews. There were in Palestine at least three unofficial schools of legal interpretation—and consequently of religious practice—organized as sects: the Pharisees, in one dubious passage said to number 6,000, the Essenes, said on better authority to number 4,000, and the Sadducees, reportedly an even smaller group. These sects were sharply opposed to one another. The mass of the people belonged to none but followed their own traditional practices. They were also ready to listen to holy men whose teachings were often peculiar.

One of these holy men, named John, was called "the Baptist" because he introduced a new rite of immersion ("baptism") which, he claimed, would take away sin as well as impurity. Great crowds went out to him for baptism, and he preached to them against the vices of the rulers and prophesied the imminent end of the world. His preaching was so successful that one of the rulers, a son of Herod, had him executed about A.D. 30. His disciples persisted as a sect for some time after his death; some are said to have believed he was the Messiah—the "anointed" king whom "the Lord" was expected to send to save his people.

Another holy man was Jesus, who began his career by going to John for baptism. When baptized, he had a vision in which he saw a spirit coming down on him and heard a voice from heaven, presumably the Lord's, declaring him "my son." "The Spirit" then drove him into the desert, whence he returned to Galilee, began "to cast out demons" (that is, to quiet maniacs), and was believed to perform other miracles. He also preached on moral questions, and was criticized by the Pharisees for neglect of their religious law. From the large following thus attracted, he chose twelve assistants. To them he revealed that he was the Messiah and that the end of the world would come in their lifetime. With them he went up to Jerusalem for the Passover, and there, in a private meal, he gave them bread and wine which he said were his body and blood. (This rite had close parallels in magic practices.) Later that night he was seized by the temple authorities. The next day they handed him over to the Romans as a would-be revolutionary. The Romans had him crucified.

On the third day thereafter his disciples began to see him risen from the dead. Later they had a vision of his ascent to heaven, themselves received the Spirit, and began to preach a baptism "in his name" which not only took away the sins of the penitent, but also conferred the Spirit and assured salvation in the judgment to come at the end of the world. This preaching led to their persecution by the temple authorities, who did not wish to be blamed for Jesus' death, and also by the Pharisees, probably because the members of the new sect were no more observant of the Law than their teacher had been. Many fled the city. Thus the cult was carried to neighboring territories and eventually to Antioch, where the adherents first called themselves "Christians," that is, adherents of the "Christ" (Messiah). A Pharisee named in Hebrew Saul (in Greek, Paul), who had played a prominent part in the Jerusalem persecution, was converted by a vision of Jesus and, after adventures in Palestine and Syria, began a series of missionary journeys through Cyprus, Asia Minor, and Greece, leaving groups of converts in most of the cities he visited. He also occasionally returned to Jerusalem. There in the middle fifties he was involved in a riot in the temple, seized by the Roman authorities, sent to the procurator in Caesarea and eventually to Rome for trial, and—here the story, as told in the Acts of the Apostles, breaks off. Later tradition says that he was executed in Rome, probably in the early sixties.

For this account of the work of Jesus, his immediate disciples, and Paul, the sources are the four Gospels, written in the last quarter of the first century; the Acts of the Apostles, originally a sequel to the Gospel According to Luke; and the letters of Paul, dating mainly from the fifties. These sources disagree with one another, and sometimes with themselves, in many points—for instance, their stories of the resurrection. Further, they represent Christian tradition as it was after one or two generations of reflection, controversy, exaggeration, and invention. Finally, they are full of incredible stories of which some—those of the resurrection will again serve as instances—may be of historical value as reflections of subjective experiences. Consequently, no more than the main outlines of the history can be ascertained with certainty. The only *certain* facts about Jesus are that he was a Jew, crucified about A.D. 30, some of whose disciples came to think he had risen from the dead and to expect him to save them. Of the other events described above, Jesus' choice of the twelve and their role, his arguments with the Pharisees, and his teaching about himself are matters of particular dispute. The history given by Acts is full of riddles, and we know nothing of the history in areas Acts neglected, for instance, Alexandria and Rome.

Hence the early history of Christianity cannot be followed in detail.

We can see that there were at first conflicting interpretations of Jesus' teaching and career, and that gradually a consensus—a rudimentary church—began to be built up. Eventually many churches agreed on a list of authoritative books—the present Old and New Testaments. A standard organization for individual churches gradually developed: an overseer ("bishop") supported in questions of policy by a board of elders ("presbyters," eventually "priests"), and in matters of administration by several assistants ("deacons"). The bishop was the authority on the legal as well as the devotional tradition of his church. He held a court to which believers were expected to bring their claims against each other. Most important in the growth of his power was his control of the church's charitable funds and organizations and of its cemetery. Christianity spread largely as a mutual protective association of people of small means.

With this growth came separation from Judaism. Paul's practice in coming to a new city was to preach first in the synagogue. Usually he won over some Jews and more pagans who reverenced the Lord but were not prepared to observe the more painful requirements of Pentateuchal law—circumcision, for instance. Presumably other missionaries did likewise. Resultant disputes between converts to the new sect and the majority of the synagogue members led to the antithesis between "the Christians" and "the Jews." The Christians claimed—and still claim—to be "the true Israel," but in practice they came to be mostly of pagan background and ceased to think of themselves as Jews or to be recognized as such by other Jews. Thus by gradual fission Christianity changed from a Jewish sect to a "new" religion. In Palestine the fission was not complete at the beginning of the second century, when rabbinic authorities put a curse on Christians into the daily prayer to prevent them from attending rabbinic synagogues.

Since the "new" religion worshiped a man who had been crucified by the Romans for attempted rebellion and since the quarrels between its adherents and the Jews were frequent occasions of civil disorder, its members were often in trouble with civil authorities. When a great fire destroyed much of Rome in 64, Nero's officials put the blame on them. Since the scrupulous members would not participate in the worship of gods other than Jesus and the Lord, popular opinion stigmatized them, along with Jews and Epicureans, as "atheists," and popular imagination (aided by the practices of some libertines and the ritual words of the communion meal) turned their secret meetings into orgies of copulation and cannibalism. Consequently, local persecutions became more frequent. Nevertheless, by the end of the Severan period (235) there were Christians in every part of the empire and in every class of society. Though there was no empire-wide organization, most bishops were in approximate agreement on questions of doctrine and discipline, and this agreement had produced a sort of orthodoxy, the "Catholic"—that is, "universal"—Church.

During this same period the other forms of Judaism changed no less than Christianity. Jewish resentment of Roman rule in Palestine led to a major revolt in 66. This led in 70 to the capture of Jerusalem by Titus and the destruction of the temple, which put an end to the official sacrificial religion. (Titus was the most efficient reformer of ancient Judaism.) At the same time the temple in Egypt was closed to prevent disturbances. In this revolt most Sadducees, wealthy, pro-Roman, and concentrated in Jerusalem, were killed off by the rebels. The Essenes and other parties who supported the revolt were liquidated by the Romans. But a leading Pharisee, Yohanan ben Zakkai, is said to have escaped from Jerusalem, made his peace with the Romans, and got their permission to establish a court at Jabneh. With Roman approval his court became the chief authority in Palestine for the settlement of questions of religious law, numerous and important because of the destruction of the temple. It laid down the main lines for reorganization of Judaism around the existent synagogue worship, with almsgiving, penitence, and prayer replacing sacrifice. From ben Zakkai, leadership passed to a descendant of the famous teacher Hillel of Herodian times, whose family was said to have headed one wing of the Pharisaic party. The Hillelite court carried the reorganization of Judaism much further and brought into being the "rabbinic" form of the religion—that characterized by the role of the rabbi as its chief official. (Hitherto "rabbi" had been merely a term of respect used loosely of many teachers, Jesus, for instance.) Besides developing the official rabbinate, the Hillelite court did much for the collection, organization, and development of legal traditions; it revised the liturgy; and it settled the question as to which books should be considered sacred. (The list decided on, different from the Christian list, was taken over in the Reformation by the Protestants.) The diasporic Judaism of Cyrenaica, Egypt, and Cyprus rose in revolt against the Romans in 115–117. Cause and course of the revolt are obscure, but its end was the annihilation of Judaism in these provinces. Finally, control of Palestinian Judaism passed from the house of Hillel to anti-Roman rabbis of whom the greatest, Akiba, backed a Messianic pretender named bar Kosiba[2] in a revolt from 131–135 which ended with the wiping out of Judaism in southern Palestine.

For a short period the Roman government considered stamping out Judaism altogether—circumcision and teaching of the Law were prohibited. But soon the Hillelite court was reestablished, now in Galilee and supported by Roman soldiers. A Roman commission investigated

---

[2] Commonly called "bar Kokeba." The correct form of his name has recently been determined.

the Jewish law and suggested changes to diminish conflicts between Jews and gentiles. The revised law was codified and the code published under Rabbi Judah the Prince, head of the Hillelite court in the late second and early third centuries. His code, the Mishnah, became the basis of study in both Palestine and Mesopotamia, the commentaries on it being eventually collected in the Palestinian and Babylonian Talmuds. The Mishnaic type of Judaism spread gradually through the Greco-Roman diaspora, becoming dominant, it seems, only in the fifth and sixth centuries (about the time the Talmuds were completed). Thereafter, it remained the dominant form of the religion, though it, in turn, was dwarfed by Christianity.

The success of both was perhaps largely a matter of convenience. Prayer was cheaper than sacrifice, and the synagogue a more economical establishment than the temple. Accordingly the cut-rate righteousness that Judaism offered made many converts, the more because conversion carried admission to a mutual protective association, the comfort of belonging to something, and the privilege of looking down on one's neighbors. ("Blessed art Thou, O Lord our God, that Thou didst not make me a gentile, a woman, or a slave." Greek tradition ascribes to Thales and Plato similar thanksgivings for not being an animal, a woman, or a barbarian, and like formulas are attributed to Persian and Chinese sages. Snobbery is ecumenical.)

As the demands of the Law were extended with the extension of Pharisaic influence after 70, conversions diminished. Other factors were the Jewish revolts, which made Judaism unpopular, and the increased public financing of paganism, especially of the imperial cult, which at many festivals gave the worshipers shares of the sacrifices—meat was a luxury—and at some, wine or oil. Also Judaism now had to compete with Christianity, which stood to it as it did to paganism.

Christianity, too, offered righteousness, protection, and the sense of membership and superiority. But its price was lower—faith is cheaper than obedience. So Christianity won over most of the world, but thereby lost much of the prestige of exclusiveness and the consequent coherence and mutual care. In the Middle Ages poor Christians would generally be left to the chilly charities of ecclesiastical institutions, but the Jews' generosity to each other would be proverbial. Christian preaching could proclaim the superiority of the Church to paganism, Judaism, and Islam, but the average believer would find himself undistinguished and unprotected in a world where everybody else was Christian, too. The synagogue could say nothing in public against the Church, but its members could console themselves in private by relying on each other for help, reflecting with satisfaction on their own peculiarity, and blaming the gentiles for the consequences peculiarity entailed.

FOR FURTHER READING

J. Carcopino, *Daily Life in Ancient Rome*
S. Dill, *Roman Society from Nero to Marcus Aurelius*
E. Gibbon, *The History of the Decline and Fall of the Roman Empire*, chs. 1–6
N. Lewis and M. Reinhold, *Roman Civilization: Vol. II, The Empire*
H. Lietzmann, *The History of the Early Church*
G. Moore, *Judaism*
S. Neill, *The Interpretation of the New Testament, 1861–1961*
A. Nock, *St. Paul*
M. Rostovtzeff, *Rome*
A. Schweitzer, *The Quest of the Historical Jesus*
M. Smith, *The Secret Gospel*
A. Stenico, *Roman and Etruscan Painting*
M. Wheeler, *Roman Art and Architecture*
———, *Rome Beyond the Imperial Frontiers*

A.D.	
235	Murder of Severus Alexander, beginning of fifty years' chaos
249–251	Decius' persecution of the Christians
268–269	Goths defeated in the Balkans
270–275	Reign of Aurelian, Rome fortified, Dacia evacuated, Gaul and the east reconquered, currency reform
285	Defeat of Carinus; Diocletian in control
303–305	Diocletian's persecution of the Christians
306	Constantine proclaimed emperor at York
c. 320	Pachomius' first monastery
324	Constantine defeats Licinius and reunites the empire
325	The Council of Nicaea
330	Constantinople becomes the imperial residence
331	Pagan temples' properties expropriated
361–363	Julian the Apostate restores the privileges of paganism
391	Theodosius I prohibits pagan worship
406–429	Gaul and Spain overrun by Alans, Sueves, and Vandals
410	Rome sacked by the Visigoths; Britain abandoned
418	Visigoths settle in Gaul
429	Vandals invade Africa (Carthage taken 439)
441–453	Huns raid Danube provinces and Gaul
459–487	Ostrogoths loot the Balkans; Isaurians in Asia Minor and Syria; end of imperial succession in the west
488	Ostrogoths move into Italy
493	Bulgar invasions of Thrace begin
533	Beginning of Justinian's attempt to reconquer the west
540–561	War with Persia, reconquest of Italy
568	Lombard invasion of Italy; Avars along the Danube
572	Visigoths reconquer Spain
602	Maurice overthrown by the army; Phocas installed
610	Phocas overthrown by Heraclius
610–627	Avars attack Constantinople; Persians overrun Asia Minor, Syria, and Egypt; the Empire reorganized; Avars destroyed; Persians driven out
636	Battle of the Yarmuk; Syria lost to the Arabs
641	Death of Heraclius; Egypt lost to the Arabs

15
THE LATER ROMAN EMPIRE

THE COLLAPSE OF 235–285, CAUSES AND CONSEQUENCES

The fifty years from the murder of Severus Alexander in 235 to Diocletian's defeat of Carinus in 285 were a period of anarchy. Diocletian,* during his twenty-year reign, reestablished order and reorganized the empire, but his retirement in 305 was followed by another outbreak of civil war. Only Constantine,* after reuniting the empire in 324, developed a polity strong enough to prevent serious revolts, defend the frontiers, and secure regular succession to the throne.

The primary cause of the anarchy had been military insubordination, for which the reasons were complex. An important factor seems to have been the increased number of officers risen from the ranks. Formerly officers, drawn from the upper classes, had little in common with their men and, with little military experience, had neither the support nor the skill necessary for a revolt. The historian Dio Cassius, consul in 229, still favored this system, but he was a reactionary. Already advancement of men from the ranks, often of barbarian background, had begun to change the officer class. In 217 a North African named Macrinus, risen from the ranks to be chief of staff, murdered the emperor Caracalla and

186 The Later Roman Empire

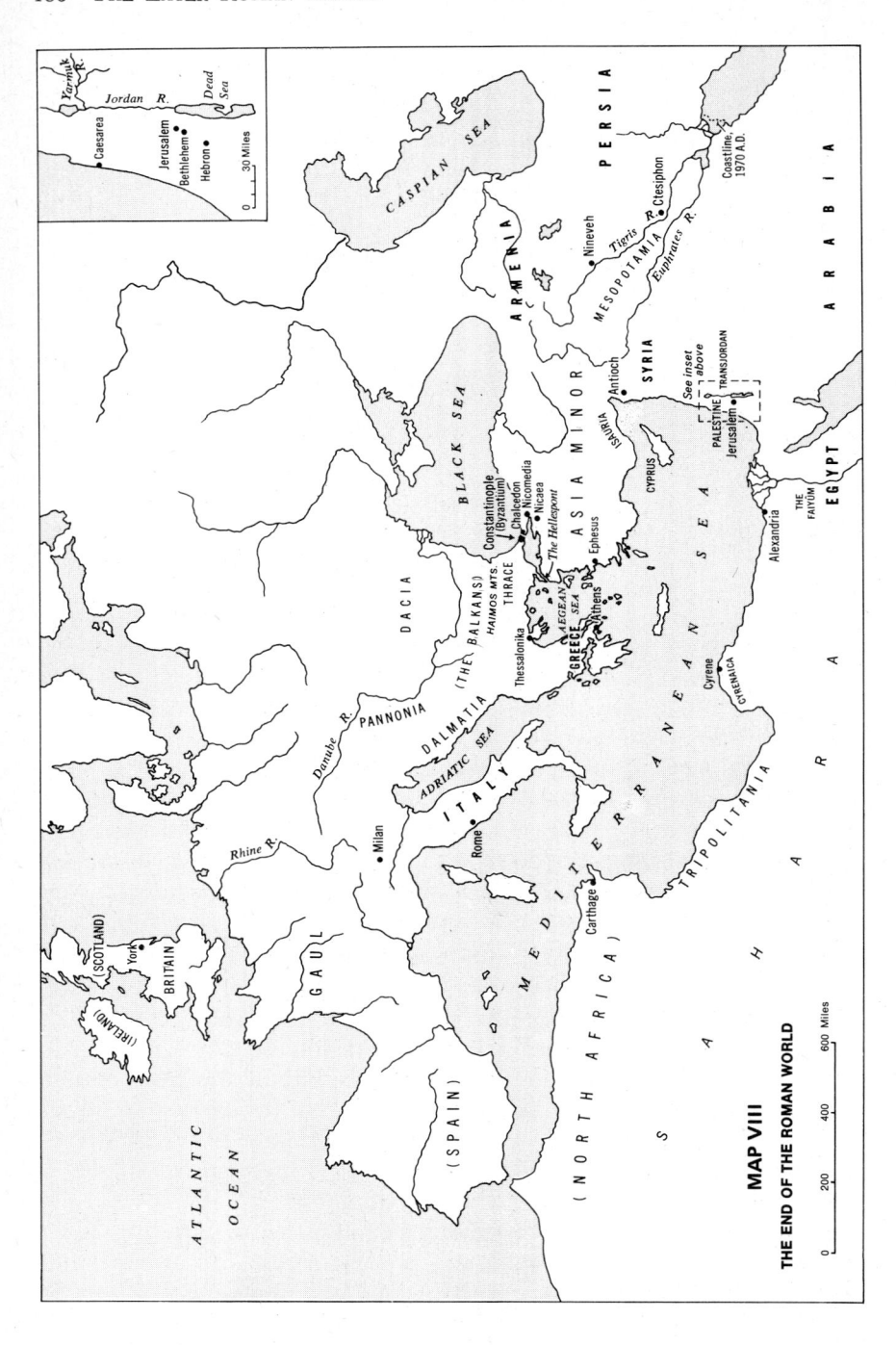

MAP VIII

THE END OF THE ROMAN WORLD

briefly usurped the throne. Maximinus, murderer and successor of Severus Alexander in 235, was a Thracian risen from the ranks to command of a legion. As the municipal upper classes withdrew from the army, their withdrawal opened the way for potential usurpers. Perhaps municipal life had become too comfortable; civilizations fail by succeeding too well.

Another important factor, however, was the extent of the empire. Dio Cassius observed that, because of the distances involved, the frontiers could not well be defended by Roman or Italian mobilization. But to give military training to the provincials, so that they could be mobilized when the barbarians threatened adjacent frontiers, was to risk civil war. Therefore the empire needed a standing army of professional soldiers (who served as long as they could fight—twenty years). This reasoning Dio probably got from an Augustan source; as historian rather than thinker, he repeated it without noticing what he had seen—that professional armies, too, pose the threat of civil war if they become more attached to their generals than to the central government, or even if they get the notion that they can profitably take over the empire or some large part of it. The local subsistence economy that made the parts relatively independent, encouraged such notions. Therefore, again and again, frontier troops mutinied and set up their commanders as emperors. The consequent chaos left the frontiers open to the barbarians. All the countries along the Rhine and Danube were ravaged. From the Black Sea, Gothic pirates sailing through the Hellespont plundered Aegean cities. In the east the new Sasanid Persian empire undertook reconquest of northern Mesopotamia and annexation of Armenia. Egypt and Africa were raided by savage tribes who had grown numerous along the fringes of Roman cultivation. These raids destroyed much property and many lives; the open countryside was laid waste; numerous cities were captured. Moreover, raids occasioned further insubordination in the army. Most divisions had strong local ties and wanted to defend their own districts, so many refused to be transferred to areas where they were more needed. They set up their commanders as local rulers and organized their own defense. Finally, movements of Roman armies to repel the raiders or fight civil wars were almost as hard on the countryside as the raids themselves.

All these military operations had to be financed, and money had to be raised to buy off barbarians who could not be driven off. Cities and temples became impoverished; private fortunes and charities diminished sharply. At site after site, the series of inscriptions honoring benefactors —series sometimes begun in or before the hellenistic period—now came to an end. As the ruin of the countryside and the breakup of trade cut down income from taxes, money had to be coined. There was copper for it, but silver was lacking, so the silver content of nominally silver coins was cut to a minimum, and, at the worst period, as now in the United

States, replaced by a thin silver plating. Prices soared. Eventually even the government could not live on its own money—the principal taxes had to be paid in kind.

THE RECOVERY AND THE NEW IMPERIAL STRUCTURE

Recovery began as the breakdown had begun, with the army. First the Goths were crushed in the Balkans in 268–269, then the emperor Aurelian in 271 pulled Roman forces back from Dacia (western Rumania) to the Danube. This shortened the frontier and made it more defensible. The forces thus released strengthened the provinces, depopulated by Gothic raids south of the river, while the evacuated territory gave the remaining Goths room to settle and reduced their pressure on the frontier. Aurelian could then withdraw troops from the Balkans to resubjugate the east and Egypt in 271–273 and Gaul in 274. This enabled the empire to survive another attack of military insubordination which ended with the triumph of Diocletian.*

In territory the new empire was almost identical with the old; only southern Scotland, the Rhine-Danube salient, and Dacia had been lost. Its primary concern, however, was one which had hitherto been minor: security from attack. All cities were now fortified. Rome itself, where the ancient walls had fallen into decay during the first century B.C., began to build new ones in 271. Moreover, walls and ditches, or strings of towers, and supporting military roads, were constructed around the entire frontier, even across the deserts of north Africa. But these physical fortifications were monuments to intellectual failure. The civilization had failed to develop devices that would give its men decisive superiority. Its defense was still, in the end, a man with a sword standing off another man with a sword. And the barbarians were bigger.

Concern for defense implies the primacy of the army. Under Diocletian its strength was raised to about 400,000. To make it efficient yet keep the units loyal was the fundamental problem for Diocletian and Constantine.

The background of many third-century revolts, especially in the western provinces, had been the local loyalties of the frontier troops, often stationed for their whole tour of duty in their native province. Consequently the army was now divided into first- and second-class troops, and only the latter were left in their own provinces, mostly as border guards. Further, to check ambitious generals, the civil government was almost everywhere separated from the military, and the provinces—all now governed by imperial appointees—were so fragmented that few could offer any considerable basis for revolt. At the same time the army units were fragmented, and command of the units was given mostly to men risen from the ranks who had no experience of civil government or ties with the civilian population. Finally, the first-class troops were commonly concentrated in cities somewhat back from the frontier, as mobile forces capable of striking an invasion at any point. For this purpose they were given special training and strengthened by enlarged cavalry units. Since all units, foot and cavalry alike, were of relatively small size, and the force in any city was made up of many units of different backgrounds, the chance of revolt by first-class troops was small, and these first-class troops kept the provincial forces along the frontiers in awe.

The chance of revolt by first-class troops was further diminished by the fact that many of them were foreigners. Because of the shortage of farm hands and the government's insistence that all cultivable land be taxed, many landowners obligated to provide recruits preferred to give money rather than a man. With the money the government hired barbarians individually, to serve in the regular army. Since these barbarians were picked for their fighting ability while the men sent by landowners were generally the worst who could pass muster, levies from the provinces went largely into the second-class frontier guards and the first-class troops got a large proportion of barbarians who, as isolated aliens, were not likely to revolt. The employ of whole tribes of barbarians as units under their own leaders was a different matter. This led to serious revolts by these tribes, but not by the regular army.

Both the loyalty and the efficiency of the army were directly dependent on its proper upkeep. This proved the most difficult problem Diocletian and Constantine had to face. Although agricultural production had improved since Augustan times—use of wind and water mills was extended, the silo, the cold cellar, and hay were discovered—yet deforestation, erosion, and exhaustion of soil and of mines and quarries had impoverished the empire. Still worse was the widespread destruction of property, especially farm buildings and livestock, orchards and vineyards. The rural population had no financial reserves, so a raid which carried off livestock or destroyed vineyards put the affected area out of production for a long time. Consequently the financial burden, which for the Antonine empire had been considerable, was worse for the Constantinian empire.

Most of this burden had to be borne by the peasantry, for the great majority of the empire's production was agricultural. But the peasants had already been paying almost all they could. A little more could be squeezed out of them, and traders and artisans and even senators could be made to pay something—and were. But this did not suffice. People gave up keeping accounts for fear of taxation. Therefore the government cut salaries by debasing the currency and then supplementing money salaries with payments in kind which sufficed only for subsistence. Moreover, it squeezed the well-to-do families of the small cities until many of them were reduced to poverty.

The earlier empire had made city councils responsible for collection of taxes from city territories. Similarly, it had held them responsible for maintenance of roads, bridges, and post stations in their territories, and had also imposed on them occasional levies in kind to meet extraordinary needs. With anarchy and inflation taxes had mostly become nominal, but levies in kind had become routine. Diocletian, unable to stabilize the currency, resorted to an annual tax in kind assessed on land. The city councilmen were made personally responsible for the total assessed on their city's territories. From them the produce went to the provincial governors for transport to officials specified by the paymaster general. By these officials it was paid out as rations to all government employees, military and civil alike.

This tax remained the chief source of imperial income down to the fifth century. It entailed considerable social changes. Land had to continue to be cultivated in order to yield its assigned quota. Therefore the farm laborers had to stay on it to cultivate it. Similarly the municipal councilmen had to remain in office to collect or make up for their quotas, and the officials of the provincial governor to transport the produce, and so on. Consequently a series of laws fixed these and more classes of the population, and their descendants, in their places and professions. Moreover, this system required a large secretarial staff to draw up the census, estimate the needs, make the allotments, certify the collection, check the transfers, investigate delinquencies, try the offenders, and so on. This was doubtless a major reason for the fragmentation of the provinces. Provincial governors now had so much supervision and adjudication on their hands that one was needed (with his staff, of course) for every small district. Besides the trebling of provincial administrations, the bureaucracy of the central government proliferated fantastic titles, and with every title went a state salary and the opportunity—which soon becomes a legally recognized right—of demanding fees from the public for performance of the prescribed service. Thus the taxpayer had to support both the army and the bureaucracy. The bureaucracy came to number thirty or forty thousand. This was only a tenth of the army, but bureaucrats were more expensive than soldiers. Besides their salaries and their fees were their bribes. And worst of all, the empire could not afford enough of them to do the paper work the system required—especially since every copy of every document had to be written individually. Without efficient filing systems the accumulation of documents became unmanageable and there were innumerable opportunities for evasion of the laws. Finally, with the proliferation of the bureaucrats, edicts proliferated defining their functions, revising the definitions, creating exceptions and then exceptions to the exceptions.

Since the regular recourse from bureaucratic injustice was through the law, the multiplication of lawsuits and lawyers and courts immediately complemented the multiplication of the bureaucracy and further increased the size and importance of the nonproductive population.

These luxuries ruined many city councilmen who had to make up the deficits of their districts. In the countryside the financial pressure fell hardest on the small landowners. The rich were able, through bribery and influence, to have the assessments on their holdings minimized and to avoid paying even the minimum. Therefore this period, especially in the west, saw a growth of great estates. The rich had already used the opportunities of the civil wars and invasions to buy up or appropriate the ruined or deserted farms of their neighbors. Now increased taxation led many peasants to make over their properties to the rich landlord of the neighborhood in exchange for protection from the city council's tax collectors and a guarantee of the right to live on and work the land. Thus the peasants were gradually transformed to serfs. Eventually law ratified the change; the great proprietors were given criminal jurisdiction over the territories of their estates. At the same time the law further developed its long-standing distinction between the upper and lower classes. Normally, upper-class individuals might not be tortured to secure evidence, or subjected to humiliating punishments, or compelled to labor on public works, or required to provide animals, housing, or other services for public officials. None of these exemptions held for the lower classes.

Most prominent among the rich landowners who profited from these developments were senators. Hostility between senate and army had been one of the main causes of the fall of the Severan dynasty in 235. Through the following period of anarchy and invasions the army necessarily gained in power and senators were eventually excluded from military commands. But no military leader had the time or the forces to suppress the senate thoroughly; it would have required a major civil war. When Diocletian and Constantine fixed their capitals in the east, the senate, remaining in Rome, was reduced to a city council. But the city was Rome; its prestige was still of great importance. Moreover, the senate was made up of the empire's richest landowners, protected by legal privileges and family connections. It escaped annihilation through subservience and serious taxation through bribery and influence. So senatorial wealth increased. Senators' villas now became villages, centers both of subsistence economy and of local government and defense, important links in the transmission of classical farming techniques to the Middle Ages.

On the other hand, in the imperial government the senate became merely an audience to which decisions might be announced for acclamation. All laws and important appointments were made by the emperor.

Decisions on policy were made in the imperial council (or bedchamber). The imperial council was composed of the two chiefs of staff, the commander of the imperial guards, the head of the provincial administration (who was also chief justice and paymaster general), the head of the imperial estates (the emperor owned almost a fifth of the arable land), the treasurer (who controlled coinage, receipts, and expenses in precious metals, and imperial monopolies, such as mines and arsenals), the secretary for legal affairs, and the head of the records office (who was also in charge of appointments, couriers, and intelligence). Not a member of the council, because a eunuch, the grand chamberlain of the imperial palace had great influence by reason of his access to and knowledge of the emperor, not to mention the empress.

The government thus reverted to the Oriental pattern—a despotism resting on an army and acting through a royal council composed of executives arbitrarily appointed by the king. The Greek experiment was abandoned. Even in law, trial by jury died out. All that survived was a literary tradition from which subsequent ages would draw inspiration.

The nature of the new government was reflected in the new titles, trappings, and rituals of the court. These, like the government, had their beginnings in earl'er periods, but only now were developed consistently. Everything that had to do with the emperor became "sacred"; he no longer wore the old Roman toga, but a purple triumphal robe, embroidered with gold and jewels, and a diadem, symbol of hellenistic kingship, studded with pearls or with the rays of the sun god; he was surrounded always by a military escort; his ministers and officials customarily wore military uniform; he was hailed as "King" and "Autocrat." As the court was predominantly military, and the army predominantly from the Latin provinces, so the language of the upper administration, even in the east, now became Latin, and remained so for more than a century.

The new monarch needed a new capital. Rome called up too many memories, and worse, the senate was there. Moreover, concern for defense demanded a capital nearer the dangerous frontiers. And since the court and central administration fed on taxes paid in kind, and transport, expensive by sea, was even more expensive by land, the court was best located at a seaport in the richest part of the empire—the east. Constantine's choice was Byzantium, which he renamed Constantinople. The situation was superb economically—controlling the crossroads between Europe and Asia, the Black Sea and the Aegean—and also strategically—a spacious, well-watered, easily fortified peninsula within striking distance of the lower Danube, where barbarian pressure was greatest, and with good communications to Antioch, the base for defense against the Persians.

THE NEW RELIGION: THE TRIUMPH OF CHRISTIANITY

One advantage of the new capital, in Constantine's eyes, was its lack of the religious establishment of ancient Rome. Fifty years of anarchy had made many converts to Christianity. Some turned to its promises of future life, or of immediate grace, for refuge from the present world. More found companionship and financial security in its communities and their charities, on which the disasters of the civil society made many dependent. The resultant combination of the growth of Christianity and the ruin of the state made the imperial policy toward the new religion an acute question. Both Christians and pagans believed that the gods would punish men who did not worship them properly.

While Christianity had been uncommon and the empire prosperous, the Christians' refusal to worship the pagans' gods had been generally ignored. But now Christians were everywhere, and the disasters of the empire proved that the gods were angry, presumably at the Christians' "atheism."

In 249 the emperor Decius decided to stamp out Christianity. Next year he was killed trying to stop an invasion of the Goths. This ended the persecution and probably persuaded many that the Christians were right—"the deaths of the persecutors" became a favorite theme of their propaganda. The two following reigns were equally brief and disastrous. Then Valerian renewed the persecution in 257 and was captured, with much of his army, by the Persians* in 259. His son, Gallienus, called off the persecution and officially permitted the practice of Christianity.

So matters stood until the end of Diocletian's reign, when in 303 Gallienus' edict was rescinded and persecution renewed. By this time Christians were so numerous that the decision to persecute involved a great economic sacrifice and administrative effort. This probably influenced Constantine,* when he seized power in the west in 306, to let persecution there lapse. His mother Helena's devotion to Christianity, his own belief that he was under the protection of the Christians' god, and the strength of Christianity in Italy and the east, which he hoped to conquer, also shaped his decision. After his conquest of Italy in 312 he arranged with his eastern co-emperor for toleration of all religions, but immediately began in his own domains to patronize Christianity. After eliminating his co-emperor in 324, he seized the treasures and estates of most pagan temples—the treasures he particularly needed to restore the supply of gold and silver currency*—but he gave vast sums to the Christians, especially for building. Bishops all over the east were authorized to draw on imperial funds for repairs of damages from the persecutions. Magnificent churches were built at Rome and in many cities of Italy, as well as Nicomedia, Antioch, Jerusalem, Bethlehem, and Hebron, while Constantinople received a whole choir. All these churches were lavishly endowed. Others throughout the empire received from the state annual subsidies of food for distribution to the poor. Christian clergy were exempted from service as city councilmen, a privilege which led to an epidemic of vocations among the well-to-do of the cities and cut down sharply the resources on which cities could draw to meet their expenses; finally Constantine had to prohibit ordination of councilmen. The bishops' powers were increased by increase of the funds they controlled. Civil and criminal law was also revised in Christian interest and more or less according to Christian standards. Sunday was made a holiday as "the day of the sun," so pagans as well as Christians would observe it. Celibates were permitted to inherit property. Divorce was made more difficult (for women, almost impossible), concubinage and pederasty outlawed, illegitimacy penalized. Gladiatorial games were prohibited—though they continued in the west until the beginning of the fifth century. Beside expropriation of the lands and treasures of pagan temples, animal sacrifice was prohibited, but this prohibition, too, remained a dead letter. A few temples were destroyed. Obstacles were put in the way of conversion to Judaism. Finally Christians were favored in appointments, benefactions, petitions, and appeals. The upper administration became largely Christian.

Christianity was not merely the cult of a new god (or gods—the Christians were not clear on this point). It was an *organized* cult in a way that none of the pagan cults had been. It was also an *intolerant* cult, not only intolerant of those who worshiped other gods without the state's permission (this paganism had often been), but intolerant, by inheritance from Deuteronomy, of anyone who worshiped any other god at all, and thence, by theological extension, of anyone who practiced Christianity "incorrectly." These two characteristics were complementary: the intolerance had done much to build up the organization; the organization made the intolerance effective.

In Constantine's time the organization was still loose. The bishops of large districts met as occasion required under the presidency of the bishop of the chief city of the district. There was no empire-wide church government. The bishop of Rome claimed a vague preeminence, but even in the west important bishops sometimes contradicted him. However, the members of the church thought of it as a unity, corresponded with one another, were concerned about the treatment of their fellow members in other parts of the empire, and were in approximate agreement on teaching and discipline. A man expelled from the organization in Alexandria or Antioch would usually find its doors closed to him in Rome or Carthage, and vice versa. Moreover, this organization had a tradition of independence from the civil government, indeed, of hostility to it.

Now, for the first time, there were two great powers within the empire—state and church. No longer were priests civil officials in charge of religious affairs, as they had been by Greco-Roman tradition. They now belonged to an organization essentially different from the civil government, one claiming a different (and higher) authorization. The bishops were happy to accept Constantine's patronage and willing, in return, to follow his directives. They would also use their influence in the service of the state—with the fourth century begins their condemnation of Christians who refuse to perform military service. But they did not become members of the imperial council, nor did they normally invite imperial officers to participate in their councils. From now on, these two organizations, civil and ecclesiastical, were to live side by side, through conflicts and alliances.

The alliance initiated by Constantine immediately involved him in difficulties. The Church was anxious to use him to implement its intolerance. The consequent treatment of pagans and Jews has already been mentioned. "Heretics," that is, minor Christian parties, were more energetically persecuted. And competing groups within the main organization now battled for government patronage, the victors using the power of the state to suppress their opponents. This policy backfired in Africa, where growth of great Roman estates had produced a large class of landless agricultural migrants who hated the Roman government and became violent supporters of the party the government decided to oppose (the "Donatists"). Constantine eventually gave up the struggle; persecution was a luxury he could ill afford.

In the east a dispute broke out between Alexander, bishop of Alexandria, and one of his presbyters named Arius, over the relation between the "Word" or "Son" of "God" which had been incarnate in Jesus, and "God" himself, now called "the Father"—his name, Yahweh, having generally gone out of use, except in magic. Practically all Christians now worshiped "Jesus, the Son of God" as a god, and would not consider giving up this practice. Were there then two gods? Or were the Son and the Father somehow one? Arius took the first position, making the Son an inferior god created by the Father. Alexander excommunicated him, but many neighboring bishops supported him. Constantine's ecclesiastical advisers at first backed Alexander, and Constantine summoned all the bishops of the Church to a council in 325 at Nicaea. Some three hundred showed up and adopted a creed to which all "orthodox" Christians were thenceforth required by the state to assent; it asserted belief in "God the Father," and in Jesus Christ "the Son of God" "of the same substance as the Father." All bishops were willing to sign this, except two who were deposed and banished, as was Arius. Later on, however, Constantine came under the influence of pro-Arian advisers and called other councils which readmitted Arius to communion and condemned his leading opponent, Athanasius, who had succeeded Alexander as bishop of Alexandria.

MONASTICISM, A NEW FACTOR IN THE SOCIETY

The situation in Egypt began to look like that in Africa. In Egypt, though, opposition to the government was centered in a new class of social institutions, the monasteries. Withdrawal from society had taken a variety of physical and psychological forms in antiquity. Most conspicuous had been that of the Cynics. But in the late third century Cynicism withered away. As anarchy and consequent poverty spread, there was less to spare for wandering preachers of anarchy; a man who rejected society now had to support himself, otherwise society would reject him, too. Yet as a heritage from the Psalms and from Cynic preaching, the belief that poverty was good and riches were wicked survived in wide sectors of the population (especially, of course, among the poor, who nevertheless hoped to escape poverty). In a Christian inscription of about 350 we read, "Either get rich now, or receive your wages in Paradise." A Jewish story, somewhat earlier, tells of a rabbi so desperate for a decent meal that he prayed to receive an advance on his destined reward. Immediately an arm came down from heaven and gave him a table leg of solid gold. But that night he had a vision: He saw the rabbis in Paradise eating from golden tables. All the rest had three legged tables, but his table had only two legs. So he prayed again and the arm came down and took back the leg.

From such beliefs, and from the social and economic conditions of the third century, came the Christian hermit. Diocletian's policies augmented the flight from society by persecuting Christians in the cities and by increasing and regularizing the tax on cultivated land. Land which would not yield enough to pay both the tax and the cost of cultivation was now, if possible, disowned, since if ownership were admitted the government would tax it anyhow. Much of this disowned land was good enough for subsistence farming. On it the hermits settled.

By the time of Diocletian's retirement (305) hermits were so thick near the Faiyûm that one of them, the legendary Antony, formed a loose organization of solitaries for mutual protection and common worship. About 320 in upper Egypt an ex-soldier named Pachomius founded a monastery—a community with a definite head, common residence, common discipline, common daily worship, and division of labor to meet its own needs, under the direction of the superior. By his death in 346 he had nine monasteries for men and one for women, with some three thousand inmates. By this time, too, there were many ascetics and possibly some beginnings of organization (whether native or imported from Egypt is uncertain) in Palestine, Syria, and Asia Minor.

The first monks were mostly social misfits, many of peasant stock. They usually hated cities and tax collectors, and had no appreciation for the higher aspects of classical culture: they perpetuated, with other elements of Cynicism, contempt for learning and identification of asceticism with virtue. The few more educated were often men from city families who had been ruined by taxation and had no love for the government. The first monasteries accordingly paid no taxes. Located in desert areas, they governed themselves. Politically they were bases for heretics and a consequent drain on the military forces of the government; economically they aggravated the shortage of labor both directly and by extension of celibacy; they cut down income from taxes, and, in this first period, contributed no important products or services to the surrounding society.

THE CONSTANTINIAN SYSTEM AND ITS SURVIVAL

Thus Constantine's empire was from the beginning a structure of mutually repellent elements. The monasteries were antisocial; the alliance with the organized Church entailed the hostility of discontented parties within the organization, as well as those expelled (the heretics) and rival religions. The "New Rome" (Constantinople) was in obvious rivalry to the old; its location in the eastern half of the empire would necessitate the creation of a practically independent center of command for the German frontier. The new imperial council and the old Roman senate (still the richest body in the empire) were barely on speaking terms. The government was composed of two separate structures, the army and the civil officials. The army was held in control by balancing the first-class troops against the frontier guards, and the first-class troops themselves were a mosaic of forces of different types from different backgrounds. Similarly, the civil officials were divided in half a dozen departments, each spying on the other.

The burden of this complex structure fell on the officials of the cities and the peasants from whom they had to squeeze the produce. The system reduced many officials to bankruptcy and many peasants to serfdom, and it further exacerbated the age-old hostility between city and countryside—a weakness of all Greco-Roman civilization. In Syria and Egypt, where the countryside still spoke Aramaic (Syriac) and Egyptian (Coptic) while the cities spoke Greek, this hostility was particularly serious. Finally, the whole structure was now surrounded on north, east, and south by enemies, ready at the first sign of weakness to invade and plunder. Nevertheless, the Constantinian structure survived for three hundred years.

Its survival was largely due to the fragmentation of the army and the solidity of the bureaucracy. Generals, whose men might revolt if they were removed, were always counterbalanced by other generals. The great bureaucrats had no militant following; beneath each was a line of lesser bureaucrats, every one anxious first to keep his own place, next, to advance. From 324 to 602 no emperor in the east was overthrown by a usurper. In the west, however, where the balance of elements in the military forces was not preserved, the emperors, falling more and more under the power of their generals, became mere puppets; at last (shortly before 500) the office disappeared.

The failure in the west to control the army was partly the result of geographical factors, partly of personality and chance. Until 375 the emperors were military men who kept strong holds on their armies; then the throne passed to Gratian, a bookish adolescent. Resultant revolts and civil wars produced a series of juvenile and incompetent emperors under whom central control rapidly disintegrated. They also stripped the northern frontiers of their best troops and left them open to barbarians. The Rhine frontier was overrun in 406–407 by Alans, Sueves, and Vandals; Rome was sacked by Visigoths in 410; Italy, Gaul, Spain, and North Africa were successively looted; Carthage fell in 439. Such fragments of the empire as could be patched up in the wake of the barbarians were necessarily dominated by the military. Since the military was now predominantly barbarian "allies," its leaders could not, themselves, take over the imperial office. The last emperor to reign in Rome was merely deposed; he was not important enough to be killed.

The survival of the empire in the east, like its fall in the west, was due to a combination of geographic factors, personalities, and chance. Geographically its dangerous frontier was shorter and more easily defensible, roughly 800 miles as against 1,300. Of these 800 dangerous miles, about 250 were on the eastern frontier bounded by Persia. The Persians normally observed treaties, and they had no intention of leaving their homes and moving en masse into the Roman territories, as the barbarians did. The major barbarian powers had to be faced only along the lower Danube, which was large enough to make a good boundary. South of the Danube a defensible mountain barrier ran across Thrace; south of that, the straits separating Asia Minor from Europe were impassable to barbarians who had no fleets. Consequently the rulers in the east were less dependent on their armies. Further, when the succession of strong emperors in the east was first broken, in 395, adroit ministers managed —after a few uneasy years—to secure a generation of comparative peace during which dangerous commanders were eliminated and the tradition of civilian administration was firmly established.

The army, now about 350,000 men in the east alone, had been split by the Constantinian tradition into some 250,000 second-class troops along the frontiers and about 100,000 first-class troops. These latter were now split into two classes and five armies, each with its own commander in chief, kept in check by his rivals. Below these came the regional commanders, *duces* and *comites*, whence the "dukes" and "counts" of the Middle Ages. At the same time the landward fortifications of Constantinople were strengthened. Thus when barbarian pressure again became acute the government, secure in its capital, could bargain with the barbarians, if necessary fight them, if defeated let them loot the northern provinces until the exhaustion of those forced them to move west. In such bargaining the eastern government could draw on money accumulated from the Greek islands, Asia Minor, Syria, Cyprus, Palestine, Egypt, and Cyrenaica which, though often disturbed by riots or border raids, were in the main secure. The same resources paid its troops and kept them quiet.

THE MILITARY HISTORY OF THE EAST TO THE RISE OF ISLAM

In spite of these advantages the history of the eastern empire was far from tranquil. The northern provinces were invaded in the early 400s by Visigoths, in the 440s by Huns, in the later 400s by Ostrogoths, in the early 500s by Bulgars, in the later 500s by Avars, not to mention lesser peoples. But Constantinople stood off all attacks, the straits barred progress to the south, and the waves of invaders spent their force, often in fighting each other. Wars with Persia ended disastrously in 363, but the Persians were content with the settlement then extorted and there was little more fighting until the sixth century. During the fifth century the government was repeatedly in danger of falling into the power of its Gothic "allies," forces which had been employed as units under their own leaders. To balance these the emperors depended chiefly on troops from Isauria (the southeastern nub of Asia Minor), mountaineers who took advantage of this dependence to raid their neighbors, striking as far as Palestine. Eventually, in 488, the Goths went west to the greener pastures of Italy and the government then crushed the Isaurians.

Internal security, thus restored, was the basis for Justinian's* attempt to reconquer the west, beginning in 533. His generals retook most of the north African coast, the southern coast of Spain, the western Mediterranean islands, Italy, and Dalmatia. This expansion frightened Persia, which began war in 540. Pressure on the northern front continued, too. Nevertheless Justinian held his conquests. His successors even survived another war with Persia, though it prevented them from doing much to stem the Lombard invasion of Italy or the Visigothic reconquest of Spain. What finally brought down the structure was not foreign defeat, but, as in the third century, loss of control of the army. Economies ordered by the emperor Maurice in 602 occasioned a revolt of the northern army, which killed him and installed one of its officers, Phocas, who proved a tyrant. The eastern army revolted. The Persians took the opportunity to overrun Syria and Asia Minor. In 610 Heraclius,* son of the exarch (governor general) of Africa overthrew Phocas. Now the Persians advanced into Egypt and the northern barbarians (this time, Avars) to the walls of Constantinople. But the city held out, the Avars were defeated, and after another year's fighting the Persians were forced to withdraw. The Roman and Persian empires, however, had both been exhausted and neither could now stop the Arabian tribes organized by Muhammad and his followers. Syria was lost in the 630s, Egypt, Cyrenaica, and Tripolitania in the 640s, and the Roman Empire was reduced to its Byzantine form.

FOR FURTHER READING

J. Bury, *History of the Later Roman Empire from the Death of Theodosius I to the Death of Justinian*

H. Chadwick, *The Early Church*

E. Gibbon, *The History of the Decline and Fall of the Roman Empire*, chs. 7–47

F. Lot, *The End of the Ancient World and the Beginning of the Middle Ages*

A. Nock, *Conversion*

P. Ure, *Justinian and His Age*

16
LATE ROMAN SOCIETY AND CULTURE

THE ECONOMIC REVOLUTION

For three hundred years from Constantine's death in 337 to the reign of Heraclius in the 600s the political structure of the Constantinian empire was preserved with only peripheral changes of its form, though its extent was altered by loss of the west in the fifth century, and its economic, social, and cultural character was altered by continued development.

Economically the most conspicuous characteristic of the period was the transfer of property. Cities and temples, well-to-do, landowning families of the cities, merchants, shopkeepers, and small landowners of the countryside, were stripped of their holdings. The barbarians, the emperor's estates, great landowners (especially Roman senators), bureaucrats, churches, and monasteries acquired some of this wealth, but much was destroyed in war and perhaps twenty percent of the cultivated land was abandoned because high taxation made it unprofitable to farm marginal tracts.

Most important in the transfer of property were conquests and raids, imperial confiscations, taxes, bureaucratic extortion, and private dona-

A.D.	c. 250	Plotinus, beginning of Neoplatonism
	325	The Council of Nicaea
	330	Constantinople becomes the imperial residence
	331	Constantine expropriates temple properties and endows churches; classical and Biblical historiographic traditions fused by Eusebius
	351	Apollo expelled from Daphne by the relic of St. Babylas
	381	Council of Constantinople, doctrine of the Trinity completed
	391	Theodosius I prohibits all pagan worship
	400	The Senate of Constantinople, mainly bureaucrats, has two thousand members; tax collectors need military escorts
	410	Sack of Rome by Visigoths, followed by Christian apologetics, notably Augustine's *City of God*
	431	Council of Ephesus, Nestorius condemned, half of Syria alienated from the imperial Church
	439	Capture of Carthage by the Vandals, the west completely overrun by barbarians, piracy rife in the western Mediterranean; the imperial administration in the east begins to use Greek
	451	Council of Chalcedon, the Patriarch of Alexandria condemned, Egypt alienated; the system of patriarchal jurisdictions completed
	496	Conversion of the Franks to Christianity
	500	Big landlords have private military forces and prisons
	529	Platonic Academy in Athens closed; all pagans ordered to become Christians; revolt of the Samaritans
	534	Completion of Justinian's law code
	560	Samaritans and Jews join in revolt
	641	Death of Heraclius; loss of Egypt to the Arabs; the Gospels have been translated into nine languages, Christian missionaries working in China.

tions. Most of the western empire changed hands by conquest in the fifth century and much again in the sixth. In the east no territory was officially lost, but repeated barbarian raids led to abandonment of much land in the northern provinces, Egypt, and Cyrenaica. The Vandals, after their conquest of North Africa in the 430s, reintroduced large-scale piracy to the western Mediterranean and raided the coasts for a century.

Within the empire Constantine's confiscation took the properties of the cities and temples; eventually cities were allowed a third of the incomes from their former lands for maintenance of their buildings. Confiscations, following occasional revolts and frequent trials for treason, sorcery, or heresy, brought a steady flow of lands to the imperial estates. Impoverishment of the middle class and the peasants by taxation led to transfer of their lands to estates of larger landowners and of the emperors, the largest of all.

What the emperors took with one hand they gave with the other, but not to the same people. Taxes went primarily to support army, court, and bureaucracy; these were the largest regular items in the budget. Extraordinary imperial grants vastly enriched churches and, later, monasteries, as well as great officials of the court and their families and favorites; thus political power was consolidated as economic power. Some taxes were repaid to the common people in government services. The government provided the courts, police, and military protection, now often needed; it made at least occasional grants for upkeep of roads, bridges, aqueducts, and other public buildings, and for the cost of public festivals; in a few big cities it paid for advanced instruction, maintenance of doctors, and free food. It also made grants following major disasters such as earthquakes or invasions. How far such benefactions reached into the countryside is unknown: recently published papyri have shown that sometimes there was regular distribution of grain even in small Egyptian towns. But overall, from the remains of the towns, the literature, and the documents, it seems that the upper classes of the small cities got much poorer, while army, court, bureaucracy, and churches got the bulk of the benefits.

Private giving, formerly to the towns for games, baths, gymnasiums, theaters, and the like, now went largely to churches for buildings, decoration and upkeep, salaries of the clergy, and support of the monks, also for alms to the poor, hospitals, orphanages, maintenance of widows and unmarried girls (in ecclesiastical terminology, "virgins"), and other charities. In the pagan world charity had been almost exclusively a concern of the rich and a means to civic honors; Christianity made it also a duty for the poor and a means to eternal salvation. The churches' income from donations was therefore more widely based than that of the cities had been. Ecclesiastical wealth made religious offices attractive, the more so because celibacy was not yet required. Both simony and sale of offices in the bureaucracy increased during the fifth century. By that time, too, the monastic movement had been taken over by polite society. Most monasteries lived on their endowments and paid taxes; manual labor by monks was exceptional. Clergy, monks, and bureaucrats were three new, or newly enlarged, groups whose labor, if any, was rarely productive, and whose care and feeding were an additional burden on the peasantry. If we had sufficient evidence we should probably find that neither trade nor industry figured among the most important forms of exchange of property in these three centuries; more capital changed hands through conquest and robbery, taxation and governmental expenditures, official corruption and private charity.

Important changes in social structure accompanied these movements of capital. Orientalization of the imperial court and of great households imitating the court increased the number and influence of eunuchs. Below the court circle, the higher bureaucrats, especially in the east, began to constitute a new hereditary aristocracy; son followed father into the administration, perpetuating family power and augmenting family fortunes. By the end of the fourth century the senate of Constantinople, largely composed from such families, had 2,000 members.

Great ecclesiastical families also began to spring up in the east, in spite of the rule that bishops, priests, and deacons might not marry after ordination. In the west the bishops of Rome, from the end of the fourth century, decreed that married men, if ordained, should abstain from intercourse. (The efficacy of this decree is difficult to estimate.) Since orthodox monasticism also required celibacy, church officials had to be replenished continuously from other classes.

While these privileged classes expanded, those which had to bear the burden of taxation steadily diminished in spite of repeated laws fixing their members in their callings. The well-to-do of the cities escaped into bureaucracy and the Church. Lesser provincial administrators, underpaid and overburdened, also found priesthood attractive. Lawyers, too, found the Church congenial; they contributed to the disputes about heresy. As the bourgeoisie thus shrank, tax revenues declined. Hence economies, finally fatal, in the upkeep of the army. Already in the fifth century inferior frontier troops had begun to be assigned plots of land to cultivate in lieu of salaries; their training and effectiveness suffered.

Finally the peasants, who bore the bulk of the burden, fled wherever they could. Many went into monasteries, some became migratory agricultural laborers, some got into the army, some into the Church, some into the cities where life was more lively. Even in little cities there were horse races, bear fights, visiting preachers or disputes about heresy, and, of course, the baths. A village bath house in Africa proudly proclaimed, "Here you can wash as they do in the city." Also, labor in the cities seems to have been better paid, perhaps because the government kept down the price of grain. An indentured servant in Egypt, in 569, would have to spend for a cloak a sum that would have kept him in food for three months. Accordingly the shortage of farm labor became more and more serious and the legal condition of tenant farmers, whom Constantinian polity had bound to the land as serfs, was reduced almost to slavery. They had to pay taxes as well as rent to the landlord; they could not sue him (except for overcharging in rent). They were forbidden to alienate property, be ordained, or enter a monastery without their landlord's consent. Since they were exempted from military service, even conscription could not set them free.

PEASANT RESISTANCE AND MILITARY INADEQUACY

Inevitably the peasants came to hate the government and the rich. Their hatred manifested itself in many ways. Sometimes, seizing on ecclesiastical quarrels, they supported whichever faction opposed the government. In Africa, Spain, and Gaul they supported political revolts. In Africa and Egypt they joined marauding tribes along the fringes of the cultivated land; these tribes became so populous that considerable military forces failed to contain them. Everywhere men took to mountains, woods, and deserts to live as bandits. The world became full of robbers.

Even when they remained on the land, the peasants violently resisted tax collectors; the collectors, in turn, made ever more use of torture. By the end of the fourth century collectors commonly had to be backed up by military force. Much of the army was tied down to garrison duty, preventing revolts and helping to collect taxes. This lowered its efficiency and raised the number of troops needed, but not the number that could be put in the field for a campaign. The last great army fielded by the empire was that of Julian the Apostate, about 65,000 men. Less than fifty years later the eastern emperor could spare only 4,000 men to save the west. Part of this decline was due to a general decline of population, probably to something between twenty and forty million: in city after city we find the new walls of the fourth or fifth century enclosing only a tiny segment of the area formerly built up. But other factors were apathy and alienation from the imperial government by rich and poor alike. The average man was interested in himself, the "public spirited" man in his city, the superior administrator in his province, but no more; and all accepted the agreeable axiom that the Roman Empire could not fall. Even the exceptional Rabbi Jacob, who, in the fourth century, predicted, "If the Germans go forth from their country they will destroy the whole world," was inspired by apocalyptic speculation and wishful thinking rather than military intelligence.

The central administration, isolated by public apathy and hostility, tried to meet the increasing barbarian pressure by increased conscription of citizens and recruitment of barbarians. So military expenditures rose, so taxes rose, so popular resistance to taxation, especially by the peasantry, kept rising. By the end of the fifth century landlords commonly needed their own illegal bands of armed retainers—and private prisons. This situation made effective resistance to the barbarians impossible. Large landowners and city authorities did not dare give arms and military training to the peasantry. They preferred invasion by a few barbarians rather than a peasant revolt. When barbarians did break in, the peasants either took the opportunity to revolt and plunder for themselves or joined the invaders; they rarely did anything to resist them. Not that they were unable to resist. For instance, the barbarians had no difficulty overrunning Spain, but forces sent to drive them from the country had less trouble with them than with peasant revolts. Moreover, when the Goths finally established themselves, their violation of a local martyr's shrine led to a popular rising in which they were defeated. Had there been any such popular support for the Roman government, it is inconceivable that barbarian tribes, which normally numbered about 20,000 fighting men, should have overrun Italy, France, Spain, and North Africa and dominated a population of at least 10,000,000. The Roman Empire in the west fell because most of its subjects would not fight to preserve it.

THE DECLINE OF THE EMPIRE AND
THE GROWTH OF CHRISTIANITY

This defeatism was fostered by Christianity. Pagan patriotism had taught men that the sun could see nothing greater than the city of Rome and that a Roman's highest duty was to live and, if necessary, die for his city. Christianity substituted for Rome the heavenly city above the sun, and taught that the earthly city was of little importance. When Augustine described the sack of Rome by the Goths, he worried most about the virginity of the nuns. After that disaster his younger contemporary, Melania, a lady of the highest Roman aristocracy, devoted her life and her enormous fortune—to supporting monks and nuns in Palestine. A little later Pope Celestinus I lectured the emperor on the theme: preservation of the faith is more important than that of the empire (whence it followed that the emperor, regardless of political consequences, should require all his subjects to subscribe to Celestinus' notion of the relation of the two natures of Christ). Yet worse, a number of emperors were willing to sacrifice internal concord for theological correctitude; their attempts to impose the latter almost tore the empire apart.

While the empire was going to pieces the Church was extending and consolidating its conquests. Conversions in northern Mesopotamia had perhaps begun in the first century; during the third and fourth they were extended to Persia and beyond. Official adoption of Christianity in the Roman Empire made it a suspect religion in the Persian; the church there had many martyrs. Armenia, converted about the time of Constantine, became a base for further conversion in the Caucasus. The fourth century saw the conversion of the Irish to "orthodox" (Nicaean) Christianity and of Goths and Vandals to Arianism. Conversion of Germanic peoples continued through the fifth century and thereafter; the grand prize was Clovis and his Franks, in 496. In the fourth century conversion of Ethiopia was begun; the Nubians adopted Christianity in the time of Justinian.

CHRISTIAN PERSECUTION OF OTHER RELIGIONS

Consolidation of Christianity within the empire was a complex process. Its three chief aspects were acquisition of adherents and property, organization of church government, administration, and discipline, and determination of doctrine. In these the Church relied on help from the state. Except for the brief restoration of paganism by Julian in 361–363, imperial patronage continued; this sufficed to convert the prudent. From the end of the fourth century pagan worship, whether public or private, was prohibited under severe penalties. All temples were closed; many were granted to individuals for destruction or to Christian communities for use as churches; more were destroyed by Christian vandalism which went unpunished. The Christians' fanatical hatred of other gods was in striking contrast to the tolerance of many pagans willing to accept Jesus as a new deity. Fanaticism proved an advantage; tolerance facilitated conversions and fanaticism made them profitable. In the fifth century pagans were gradually barred from the civil service and the army, then from legal practice, finally, under Justinian, from teaching. In 529 Justinian closed the Platonic Academy in Athens and ordered all pagans to become Christians. Those who refused were exiled, their property confiscated. Agents were sent out to destroy temples and forcibly convert the peasantry in districts still pagan. Monasticism had already been important in conversion of country districts; it would continue to be so beyond the imperial frontiers. Much had also been done by

Christian landowners who converted their tenants. These methods reduced paganism to unimportance, though in remote country districts all around the Mediterranean it survived the empire and still survives.

However, Christianity had competitors within the empire—its two half-sisters, Judaism and Samaritanism, and the strange religion founded by Mani, a Mesopotamian prophet, reportedly of Persian family, who during the middle of the third century had represented himself as the final revelator of whom the Buddha, Zoroaster, and Jesus had been forerunners. With adherents scattered from the Atlantic coast to China, Manicheism was an international religion; as such it was relentlessly persecuted by both Rome and Persia, the one intent on using Christianity, the other Zoroastrianism, to consolidate their realms.

Judaism and Samaritanism were dealt with more gingerly. They were protected by the tradition of Roman law, which authorized their practices. Also, the god they worshiped was recognized by the Christians as one of the "persons" of "the true God." Again, Paul had predicted that "Israel according to the flesh" would eventually be converted; this was part of God's plan; therefore some Jews (and Samaritans?) had to be kept on hand for conversion. Another factor may have been the separation of Church from state. While persecuted, Christians had preached tolerance; Tertullian, a distinguished apologist, had insisted that the civil government had no right to compel belief. Christian emperors forgot this doctrine in dealing with pagans, Manichees, and heretics; but it may have influenced their treatment of Jews and Samaritans. At all events, both cults remained licit, but only for persons born of Jewish or Samaritan parents. Conversion to them was prohibited. Christian vandalism, moreover, went beyond the laws; destruction of synagogues followed destruction of temples. Early in the fifth century erection of new synagogues was prohibited; thereafter Jews and Samaritans, like pagans, were expelled step by step from civil service and army, from all public dignities, and from practice of law. These measures were followed in the sixth century by others more severe. Many synagogues of the Samaritans, in particular, were destroyed. They revolted in 529 and 560, in the latter revolt being joined by the Jews. Both Jews and Samaritans welcomed Persian and Arab invasions of Palestine and took these opportunities to square accounts by destroying churches and massacring the Christians.

CHURCH DISCIPLINE AND ORGANIZATION;
POWER POLITICS AND HERESY HUNTING

The Church's growth complicated the problems of disciplining its members, administering its property, and governing its organization. Since the great persecutions, when many of the baptized had sinned by apostasy, postbaptismal sins had been deemed forgivable—the few who denied this became heretics. Practice required that those who had sinned after baptism should confess to their bishop or his deputy and be assigned penance, usually severe; after its performance they would be readmitted to communion. During the fourth century the increase of infant baptism and the flood of time-serving converts lowered the standard of Christian behavior and made penance both more common and easier. Finally a scandal in Constantinople in the late fourth century led to the abolition of the confessor's office and penance was left to the individual's conscience. The east thus temporarily gave up the task of disciplining the laity save for open scandal or heresy, for which the penalty was excommunication, but in the west penitential discipline was preserved and with it the power of the Church as an agency of forgiveness. Discipline of clergy was always in the hands of the bishop, who could order his clerics about as he chose. Monks vowed to obey the superior of the monastery, and Justinian put all monasteries under the jurisdiction of the bishops. Finally the bishop controlled administration and disposition of church property.

Thus the enormous growth of church property and personnel caused a corresponding growth in the power of the bishops. By Justinian's time the personal income of the bishop of a rich see was as great as that of the highest government officials, and patriarchs were in a class with senators. In a good-sized see the cathedral alone would have fifty to a hundred clergy; in a patriarchal see it would have three or four hundred—mostly in minor orders—to say nothing of monks and nuns. Bishops accordingly lived in grand style, and episcopal elections were often violently contested; one in Rome left 137 dead in a day's fighting. Therefore the rules were more sharply defined and the approval of the presiding bishop of the regional council, now "the metropolitan," was made prerequisite. Further organization and consolidation followed. Finally in 451 the Council of Chalcedon completed the process by which most imperial territories were subjected to five great sees—Egypt and Cyrenaica to Alexandria, Palestine to Jerusalem, Syria to Antioch, most of Asia Minor, Thrace, and Greece to Constantinople, and the west to Rome. The incumbents of these five sees came to be known as "patriarchs," by distinction from mere metropolitans, their subordinates.

This consolidation made conflicts between sees even sharper. Rome and Alexandria were jealous of Constantinople and tried to break its power by attacking the orthodoxy of its bishops. The fourth century offered little opportunity for this tactic. Constantine's successor in the east, Constantius, was Arian and his successor, Julian, pagan; subsequent emperors until Theodosius generally avoided religious controversies, and when Theodosius organized the Council of Constantinople in 381, to restore the Nicaean position, the opposition had disintegrated. (The council declared the Holy Ghost of the same substance as Father and Son and so completed the official trinity, "one God in three persons.")

In the fifth century, however, a controversy broke out over "Christology"—the relation of God the Son to Jesus the Christ, in whom the Son was incarnate. Since the physical Jesus had been born, suffered, and died, he had to be human. But since the Church worshiped "Jesus Christ the Son of God," Jesus had to be united with the Son. This much was at first admitted. But was the union merely one of agreement and cooperation, as partners are united in a company, or was it some sort of mixture or fusion?

Something like the former view was defended by Nestorius, Patriarch of Constantinople, who was so indiscreet as to attack, in consequence, the popular use of the term "Mother of God" as a description of Mary, whose cult was rapidly growing. This gave the Patriarch of Alexandria, Cyril, his chance. He allied with Rome and secured Nestorius' condemnation in the Council of Ephesus, 431. Constantinople was discredited and Antioch, where Nestorius had been very popular, was deeply divided.[1]

At Rome, however, the triumph of Alexandria produced uneasiness. In the next generation the Roman patriarch Leo allied with Constantinople, and the Council of Chalcedon in 451 condemned the Alexandrians for heresy because they taught that the two natures in Jesus Christ had been fused into one, the human lost in the divine as a wine drop in the sea. Leo declared the union was perfect, but the natures remained perfectly distinct; this apparent contradiction became the orthodox position. The monks and peasants of Egypt and populace of Alexandria supported their patriarch; when orthodox patriarchs were sent out they needed military guards. The "monophysite" (one-nature) position also won support in Syria, Asia Minor, and Armenia; the Armenian, Coptic, Ethiopic, and "Jacobite" Syrian churches still hold to modifications of it.

The imperial government supported the decisions of the councils, expelled heretical bishops and clergy, and made over their church properties to orthodox appointees. But heresies became matters of intense popular dispute, and adherents of heretics fought vigorously to defend their clergy and churches. These doctrinal squabbles damaged the authority of the eastern patriarchates, caused widespread violence, tied down large numbers of troops, and destroyed much property.

---

[1] Many of Nestorius' followers emigrated to Mesopotamia, where the Nestorian church eventually became the principal form of Christianity within the Persian empire and carried its missionary work as far as China.

SURVIVALS FROM CLASSICAL CULTURE

The triumph of the Church was thus a Pyrrhic victory, but a victory. All over the empire churches were erected from stones of former temples and a Christian culture from elements of the pagan world. The chief elements lost were the pagan cults and the amenities of small cities —games, gymnasiums, police and fire brigades, libraries, and so on. But these were not entirely lost. Athletic and gladiatorial games were replaced by chariot races as the great popular amusement, but not entirely: when the Devil tried to seduce St. Hilarion he showed him good food, naked women—and gladiators in combat. Christians and Jews often went from church or synagogue to the amphiteater—or straight to the amphiteater, without any devotional delay. Shows in which wild animals were killed continued popular. Baths long remained the major centers of relaxation, but eventually, in the west, Christianity destroyed the Greek ideal of cleanliness. "A clean skin means a dirty soul," said Saint Jerome (he probably stank). When Justinian's general, Narses, recaptured Rome he built a monastery, but did not repair the aqueducts. In the east, the pagan tradition was stronger; while the clergy fumed, the laity steamed. Larger towns still employed professors and doctors. Monastic and church libraries began to accumulate.

Techniques of classical culture continued with little change, though some things were taken over from the barbarians. (By 325 the wardrobe of a high Roman official in Egypt included breeches.) On farms the peasants perpetuated their traditional skills. Knowledge of engineering for irrigation and the like was still available when there were funds to employ it. By Julian's time, many houses in Paris (Lutetia) had central heating. At Trier even the enormous audience hall of Constantine's palace was heated by pipes running under the floor and twenty-four feet up the side walls; the system had an efficiency of eighty to ninety percent, good by modern standards. A Roman lighthouse in Spain is still in operation. Military techniques were extended by increased use of cavalry and missile weapons, although the old Roman training for infantry maneuvers and camp fortification was no more. In fine arts the chaos of the third century had produced a shortage of skilled craftsmen in the provinces and consequent breakdown of traditions, particularly in sculpture. Of the resultant untrained work some was brilliant, some merely gauche. The early fourth century saw a revival of the older skills; thereafter stylization set in and became, by the time of Justinian, grotesque. Some arts, however, particularly those *de grande luxe,* throve on stylization; for patterned silks, cloisonné enamels on gold, carved porphyry, and gold coinage,* the late empire is unrivaled. In villas and imperial churches mosaics,* with much more use of gold, glittered as never before. The churches were at first basilicas—elongated barns—but deforestation (to which their erection and the heating of the baths alike contributed) led to increased use of stone vaulting and eventually to the great domed churches of which Constantinople's St. Sophia* (Holy Wisdom), built for Justinian, is the supreme example—the most skillful, daring, breathtaking, magnificent achievement of ancient architecture.

Classical medicine was perpetuated with an increasing dosage of fantastic pharmacopoeia. The elements of classical law were collected and codified, the codification carried through under Justinian becoming the basis of most modern European legal codes. The pagan tradition of historical writing was continued by many writers and produced in Ammianus Marcellinus the second greatest historian in Latin literature. Of his account of the empire from Nerva to the death of Valens we have only the concluding books beginning with the later years of Constantius, but these deal with that history in which he participated as a high military official and of which his penetrating vision saw the tragedy.

In philosophy a revival of pagan scholarship and speculation produced important commentaries on Plato and Aristotle, and, in Neoplatonism, a heroic effort to reconcile the classics of pagan literature which everyone officially admired, the monotheism of Greek philosophy which everyone officially accepted, and the demons, magic, and astrology in which everyone actually believed. Plotinus, about 250, the earliest representative of Neoplatonism, was primarily concerned with philosophical thought as a means of ascent from the world to mystical union with "the One." His successors took over his way of salvation and made it a religion. Magical rites and pagan ceremonies served for sacraments; Greek classics were their sacred literature, which they rendered innocuous by allegorical exegesis, as Christians did the Bible. They lacked, for competition with Christianity, a simple story and a simple style capable of appealing to the common man. Already in Plotinus' day, it was said that only people with linguistic training could read Plato, but everybody could read Epictetus (the great Stoic teacher of the second century). Now the Christians—especially the monks—took over the simple Stoic and Cynic style, to spread their interpretation of the simpler Gospels, but the followers of Plotinus became more and more Platonic and archaic.

Stylistically they were bound by the tradition of classical rhetoric, the principal subject taught in the secondary schools. This rhetoric attempted to teach students to write in styles elaborated from those of Greek orators seven centuries dead. The resultant compositions were almost incomprehensible to anyone who had not gone through the training. Neoplatonism therefore never had a chance against the superior rhetoric of the Gospels. But classical rhetoricians had a firm hold on the professorships in the principal cities; training under them was the first step of a barrister's career. This was a public misfortune, for such training was likely to produce men incapable not only of leadership but even of clear, simple thought and expression. Moreover, it inculcated the ancient beliefs that practical questions, manual labor, manufacturing, and trade are vulgar, and that dialectic, not experiment, is the way to knowledge. One reason for the decline of the empire was classical education.

All these elements of classical culture—medicine, law, history, philosophy, rhetoric, and education—survived into Christian times and were appropriated by Christianity, thanks, largely, to conversion of the city councilmen and lower government servants. But the appropriation was superficial. Greek was now almost lost in the west; Latin survived in the east only for those going into the upper levels of government or legal interpretation, as distinct from pleading: its use by the central administration ended about 440. In the west there was considerable translation of Greek works into Latin. Greeks generally did not think Latin works worth translating.

CHRISTIAN IMITATION, DEVELOPMENT, AND DISSEMINATION OF CLASSICAL FORMS

As Christians with classical training increased, so did Christian works on classical models. Neoplatonic ontology had its counterpart in theological speculations as to Trinity, creation, and incarnation. Commentaries on philosophic writers and Homeric poems were matched by commentaries on the Bible using the same methods and reaching much the same conclusions. The rhetorical effusions of pagans were more than matched by rhetorical Christian sermons. The pagan tradition of historiography was continued by Christian authors like Procopius, who in Justinian's time almost equaled the classical historians—as a scandalmonger. Eusebius of Caesarea under Diocletian and Constantine, wrote the earliest preserved church history and made it, perhaps by laziness, a new type of history, the annotated source book with specification and purportedly exact quotation of the sources. (Classical authors had preferred to rewrite sources in their own style, generally without acknowledgments.) Another element in Eusebius' books, this derived from the Bible, is the intent to demonstrate that human history is the working out of a divine plan. This concern was sharpened after 410 when Christian writers had to answer the pagan argument that Rome had prospered while it worshiped pagan gods, and fallen when it started to worship Christ. The most successful answer, Augustine's *City of God*, was an elaboration (in twenty-two books) of the position: Who cares about Rome? All that matters is the (true) Church.

As Christianity perpetuated the forms of classical culture, it also extended them to lower classes within the empire and barbarians without. By the end of the sixth century the Gospels had been translated into Coptic, Nubian, Ethiopic, Syriac, Sogdian, Armenian, Georgian, Gothic, Latin, and perhaps Thracian. In all these languages except Sogdian, Latin, and Thracian, the translation was the first written literature; in almost all it was soon followed by translation of other Christian works of classical forms. From these beginnings a number of these languages developed native literatures of some classical coloration. Both inside the empire and beyond it monasteries converted many rustics and educated some.

THE BARBARIZATION OF IMPERIAL SOCIETY

While culture was extended to the lower classes, lower-class elements became prominent in the culture. Many emperors had military training but little cultivation. They surrounded themselves with men of their own type in the high military and legal offices. In part from the influence of this circle, laws became appallingly brutal. Savage penalties like burning alive became frequent, tortures atrocious beyond description were commonly used on all but persons of the highest classes, and sometimes even on them. But these changes were too widespread to be explained solely by the influence of the uppermost court circle. Much was probably due to the cumulative effect of the prominence of torture through centuries of popular entertainment, more to brutalization of the people by poverty, taxation, and barbarian inroads. To poverty and the pressure of taxation must be attributed much of the corruption and oppression at all levels of government.

With these changes came a fantastic growth of superstition and credulity in all classes. Origen in 250 recognized that the eclipse reported by Matthew as occurring at the time of the crucifixion (the day before a full moon) could not have happened; he concluded that the statement in Matthew was an interpolation. Augustine, 150 years later, said the impossibility of an eclipse proved the occurrence of a miracle. Yet Augustine, before his conversion, held the state professorship of rhetoric at Milan. And he was no worse than Neo-Platonists in Rome, Alexandria, and Athens who by this time were deep in "practical" magic. Christian and pagan alike evidence the failure of Greek rationalism to hold intellectuals. In the west the scientific tradition was almost wholly lost; in the east it lived on among a few specialists, who did little to advance it. This failure is a mystery. It is often blamed on the ancient aristocratic attitude and the consequent neglect of experiments. But few important theories could be proved by the experiments possible to the ancients (or to the men of the Renaissance and later). Galileo's law of falling bodies "works" only in a vacuum; in air a ball of lead falls faster than a sheet of paper. Newton's laws of motion contradict experience and "work" only when there is no resistance. The "Copernican" hypothesis—that the earth and the other planets revolve around the sun—was advanced in antiquity but "refuted" by "experiment," that is, by the "observable fact" that the sun goes round the earth. That "scientific theory must agree with observable facts" was an ancient principle deadly to science, which proceeds, like religion, by faith in things unseen—atoms, for instance. More deadly, perhaps, was the stability of ancient society, particularly in the Roman empire; it relieved men of the need for technological advance, and got them out of the habit of thinking about it. With this stability went a shift of interest from the physical world to theology, a shift that had begun already in the first century A.D. when Seneca apologized for writing about scientific topics by saying we need science to discover how much the deity can do and to demonstrate the smallness of all things in comparison to it.

THE GENERAL PREVALENCE OF SUPERSTITION

Another aspect of the problem was a general decline of mental as well as physical health, due to increase of poverty and of military, economic, and governmental pressure. This decline was reflected not only in the terrible tortures, but in the fanaticism and violence of religious conflicts about incomprehensible formulas, and in the universal atmosphere of suspicion that makes this age seem one of mass paranoia. Outright insanity seems to have become more frequent; many forms of it were revered as evidence of peculiar holiness. Psychotics who mutilated or starved themselves or went naked in the cold of Aegean winters or the heat of the Egyptian sun were commonly supposed to be saints. Not the least important achievement of the Church was the sanctification of nonsense. To be a fool had always been possible, but henceforth one could be "a fool in Christ." Those types of insanity that could not be sanctified —those that resulted in violence or obvious physical malfunctions— were usually understood as the results of demonic possession. Demons were everywhere; every church had a staff of exorcists, and they were kept busy; rabbis and saints were famous for their abilities to command spirits; all philosophers believed in the efficacy of magic; many considered it the most important branch of philosophy. Reasoning, but reasoning from fantastic premises, increased, while the rationalistic attitude (the most precious legacy of classical Greece), which is largely a matter of common sense in the choice of premises, survived only in books. Medicine was overrun with recipes for amulets.*

Better than amulets were relics of holy men, especially martyrs, whose cults had grown up everywhere since the persecutions of the fourth century. Such relics were sovereign against demons; the expulsion of Apollo from Daphne (a suburb of Antioch) by the relics of St. Babylas was world famous. Besides the relics of martyrs were those of Biblical worthies; these were constantly being "discovered"; the most famous such discovery was that attributed to Helena, Constantine's mother, of "the true cross."* Special churches, built to house the most effective relics, became centers of pilgrimage and famous for their miraculous cures. In the pagan world the sick had gone to shrines of Asclepius and Sarapis for similar cures, but now the actual going, the pilgrimage, became a religious exercise; healthy pilgrims outnumbered the sick, and centers of pilgrimage, especially Jerusalem, were thronged. Holy men, most often monks, were honored no less than martyrs, and this in their lifetimes. Everywhere saints took over the old gods' functions: they sent rain, averted storms and blight, drove away pestilence and enemies, and so on. An oceanic literature recounted their lives and miracles. But the cult that emerged as most important was that of Mary, the all-holy Mother of God.* The government's patronage of these cults was recompensed by the saints' and the Virgin's protection of the empire, that is, by transfer to it of the loyalty of their believers. Mosaics in St. Sophia showed Constantine offering the city of Constantinople to the Virgin. Later, when the city was besieged, even a "fool in Christ," a Christian beatnick, would encourage the defenders by seeing the Mother of God drawing her cloak around the walls.

THE ANTITHESIS BETWEEN THE CHURCH AND THE WORLD

Even such protection was not sufficient to keep away sin. Extension of the consciousness of sin was a major result of the triumph of Christianity. This consciousness was less an awareness of individual transgressions than a perception of the necessary imperfection of life in the physical and particularly in the social world. "The world [that is, lay society], the flesh, and the devil" were almost three aspects of man's fallen condition, from which Christianity was primarily a means of escape. Escape was salvation. A life lived "in the world" could hardly lead to salvation, and the further a man was involved in the world, the worse his chances. Even permitted physical relationships were viewed with suspicion. The last Latin nuptial poem until the Renaissance was written about 530 in north Africa, but a century earlier a Christian poet, in his poem for a newly wed couple, discreetly suggested abstinence in marriage. "The delights of passion and the poison of curiosity," said Augustine, "are products of the mind's morbidity"; and he declared that a Christian should love his wife as he should love his enemy—merely as a human being. "God," he said, "hates copulation."

Because of such assumptions the Church was not primarily concerned to provide guidance for government, nor even for life in the world; its concern was to get men out. Men who did live "in the world" accepted the prevailing conception of this world as a vestibule to an eternal life. The quality of that life, whether bliss or torment, would be determined by a man's relation to the Church and its all-sufficient sacraments. But for a Christian the sacraments were only the beginning. Beyond them lay the wilderness of the spiritual life. Even those who physically fled from the world had the flesh and the devil to cope with. Introspection, hitherto the luxury of a few philosophers, now became a major concern of millions of baptized Christians. And the officially approved orientation of western man was shifted from the world without to the world within.

Official approval did not entail universal practice. The peasants continued to be concerned primarily with getting food from the soil. Had they not, society would have collapsed and the religious would have had no leisure for introspection. The hundreds of thousands in the army, the tens of thousands in the civil government, the innumerable laity who accepted Christianity because it was the best way to get on, all continued their customary mundane concerns. But the new orientation was now represented by an organization larger than the civil government, and the government officially recognized and supported that organization's claims. From now on, western history would be one of continuous adjustments between the demands and representatives of the new orientation and of the old. The ancient world had ended, the Middle Ages had begun.

FOR FURTHER READING

S. Dill, *Roman Society in the Last Century of the Western Empire*
E. Rand, *Founders of the Middle Ages*
I. Richmond, *Roman Britain*
H. Taylor, *The Emergence of Christian Culture in the West*

17
THE CHARACTERISTICS OF ANCIENT CIVILIZATION

THE BASIC PATTERN OF ANCIENT CIVILIZATION

We have come a long way. From the clustered huts of prehistoric Jericho to the palaces of Byzantium is a journey of more than eight thousand years in terrestrial time, and seems longer in psychological time. The changes of ancient civilization during these eight thousand years should not conceal its basic "pattern," the persistent characteristics that set it off from the new world created in the past two centuries by the scientific and industrial revolutions. Let us now try to describe these characteristics.

LIFE OUT OF DOORS

As a growth of Mesopotamia, Egypt, and the eastern Mediterranean basin, ancient civilization was shaped by the generally dry and sunny climate of those lands, and kept many of its original traits, even when transplanted to the colder, wetter basins of the western Mediterranean and Black Sea. Much of life was lived out of doors; business transactions, law suits, public meetings, civil and religious ceremonies, and festivals commonly took place in the open or, at most, under colonnades—an architectural form then common. The monumental, many columned halls of Egyptian temples were the most spectacular developments of this form, intended primarily for protection from the sun. They may have inspired the deep porches of some Greek temples, for instance, at Ephesus, and the similar halls of Persian palaces. Many shops had open fronts. The most common form of house was that built around a courtyard, though in very hot countries like Egypt the yard would be shaded by a high roof. Much family life took place in this courtyard or on the flat roof. King David, for instance, strolling on the roof of his palace, noticed an officer's wife bathing on the roof of her house; she became the mother of King Solomon.

SPARSITY OF POPULATION

Sunshine and drought, then as now, made many areas of the Near East almost uninhabitable, but even in those which supported life, man was a comparatively rare animal. The population of the Roman empire at its acme—England and Wales, all of Europe south of the Rhine-Danube line, all Africa north of the Sahara, Turkey, Syria, Jordan, and Israel—was substantially less than 100,000,000. It is now above 430,000,000.

When man was a rare animal, there was always room for expansion. From the Near East to the Mediterranean basin, to Europe, to the world, western civilization has lived for ten thousand years by expansion into new territories and development of new resources. Freedom to expand enabled the powerful to secure good lands and leave the worse unoccupied. Thus the ancient world was one of "antres vast and deserts idle," offering refuge to dissidents from the cities. Such dissidents, their settlements and adventures, are a form of ancient history that has continued to the present, but will probably not continue much longer.

LIFE IN SMALL CITIES AND VILLAGES

In the ancient world most people were concentrated in cities or large villages. (The difference between the two is obscure and fluctuating; we shall use *city* to refer to both.) Rarely was a countryside cut up into farms with a house on each. The core of the city was commonly the owners of the surrounding land: Only a "son of Nippur" (native of the city) could own land in the territory of Nippur. From the city, workers walked out to their land in the morning and back at night—it was a cause of revolution in one Greek city that the older settlers kept the nearby land for themselves and gave latecomers that farther away. Until the eighteenth century A.D., a city was customarily walled; only the development of heavy artillery, which made walls useless, and the increase of population, which overflowed them, ended this fashion. Walls gave sharp, picturesque definition, the more so because suburbs were uncommon and, when they did exist, usually small. Commonly the open country lay just beyond the wall, so the city dwellers were in close touch with it, especially because the city was a tiny place. Alexandria, with perhaps the largest population in the ancient world, was a bit under three and a half miles long by a mile and a quarter wide. A mile is only fifteen minutes' walk. So you could have walked the length of Alexandria in less than an hour, have walked across it in twenty minutes, and have got to the wall, from any place inside, within ten minutes. One can walk across ancient Rome* in an hour and a half. In the smaller places, often, you could stand in the center of an ancient city and see all the gates. Only in the very biggest places, such as Rome, could city dwellers get out of touch with the countryside. Poetic metaphors continued till the eighteenth century to be drawn chiefly from country life.

Moreover, the average city depended for its food on the surrounding fields. To this rule there were early exceptions. Wine from Syria was imported by the Sumerians—no doubt as a luxury—and Ur, by the end of the third millennium B.C., seems to have relied on grain imported from farther up the Euphrates. But outside the river valleys transportation was so slow and expensive that cities usually had to live on what their men could grow in their own territories and their women and children could pick, dry, salt, and otherwise preserve. Refrigeration was a luxury of no practical importance (the rich sometimes had snow brought down from the mountains to cool their drinks). The average man's diet of fresh foods was seasonal. When some fruit or vegetable "came in" you ate all you could for three or four weeks, then saw no more of it fresh until next year. Consequently the religious year was normally agricultural, its high spots were connected with the planting, growth, harvesting, and preparation of the major crops.

Sharply defined by its walls, the city as a visible entity was a natural center of loyalty for its inhabitants and profited from their benefactions, often commemorated by inscriptions or legends. In the ancient Near East, building of walls, temples, and such, was usually a royal prerogative; in Greco-Roman times rich citizens vied to distinguish themselves by beautifying their cities. The civic devotion of the Greeks is famous, but was not peculiar. The fall of Ur before 2000 B.C. produced a famous lament. Later the Psalmist wrote, "If I forget thee, O Jerusalem, let my right hand forget its skill." And Horace, "O Sun, thou canst see nothing greater than the city of Rome." Christianity preserved this attitude in its

Scriptures; the Apocalypse represents the goal of human life as "the city of God."

Since the city was so small the citizens knew each other pretty well. The poor man could smell the roast in his rich neighbor's kitchen, an Athenian poet said. Five hundred years later, a Roman imperial writer remarked in passing that if someone makes money fast he buries it to avoid popular envy. The city, as an architectural unit, had an egalitarian tendency. To counteract this, kings and gods (that is, priests) often fortified their palaces and temples as "inner cities," forbidden to the average citizen. Others moved out. Ikhnaton left Thebes for Tell el Amarna; the Assyrian kings built a series of private capitals; Tiberius retired to Capri. But Nero,* after the fire of 64, seized the damaged area to build a palace. He said, "At last I shall live like a human being," and some months later lost his throne and his life. Famous variants are "the forbidden city" in Shanghai, Versailles and Petrograd, the Kremlin and the Pentagon.

Yet the city's small size also worked against egalitarianism. The differences between men were made apparent, while poverty made the poor dependent on the rich and increased the latter's influence. Thus when the government was not in the hands of a single ruler the rich were usually the most influential citizens and held the highest offices—professional politicians were not common. Accordingly, a king or tyrant would regard the rich with particular suspicion. One tyrant gave a famous lesson in practical politics: As he walked through a field he cut off the heads of the tallest plants with his stick (he was remembered as one of "the Seven Sages").

Since extensive slums, segregating social classes, were rare, the proximity of rich and poor sharpened their hostility and provided excuses for the "sadism" characteristic of human beings (which has deeper roots than the political circumstances that enable it to find expression). During a civil war in Miletus the poor had the children of the rich trampled to death by oxen; when the rich won, they smeared the children of the poor with pitch and burned them alive. But while such class conflicts, and reigns of terror by tyrants, became famous, the usual pattern of government was a monarchy with its staff of royal officials, or an oligarchy in which the wealthier citizens controlled the government, but were themselves controlled, to an extent now uncommon, by public opinion. In these small communities, where everybody knew everything, public surveillance of private life was detailed. Hebrew law regulated even the fringes on garments; Spartan law prohibited finished woodwork in private houses; Solon prohibited a woman's wearing more than two undergarments; the tyranny of the New England town meeting perpetuated antiquity. From such surveillance the masses fled, with the coming of the modern world, to the blessed anonymity of the metropolis.

SHORTAGE OF MANPOWER, USE OF WOMEN, CHILDREN, AND OTHER ANIMALS

The smallness of ancient cities limited manpower and projects. Irresponsible historians wrote of armies numbering millions, but the forces of Rome at its greatest numbered about 500,000, and this for an army in the field (not counting settled militia) was not surpassed till modern times. Perhaps 100,000 men were organized for the building of the great pyramid, but it was one of the wonders of the world. Many less ambitious projects had to be abandoned for lack of means: the canal through the Isthmus of Corinth, the temple of Zeus in Athens, the temple of Apollo in Selinus, and so on.

In default of manpower, the labor of women, children, and other animals was important, and small farmers tried to increase their stock. Accordingly girls were trained to expect motherhood and to bring up children. Until the nineteenth century, marriages, commonly decided on by the parents of the bride and groom, united families, not merely individuals. In Athenian marriage the bridegroom received his bride "to plow" in order "to beget legitimate children." Only legitimate children could perpetuate the family and the city (since only they could become citizens); therefore antiquity generally punished a wife's adultery with death, but took no such serious view of a husband's adultery, which did not threaten the family's identity.

Like other female farm animals, women could be used for work as well as for breeding. Work included, for lower-class women, the light field and farm labor, for upper class women it was mainly management of the house. Working indoors such a woman was pale, "just like a cobbler," who also worked indoors. In Egyptian and primitive Greek paintings women are white, men, brown. In the house she commonly did the housework, and might manage some household industry—spinning thread and weaving* remained the work of women to the eighteenth century A.D. "The good woman" of the Book of Proverbs clothed her family. Perhaps the commonest remains of classical Greek civilization, after building stones and sherds of pottery, are the weights used on domestic looms.* When Greeks recommended homosexuality because it made possible "love without fear" and so a greater *élan*, the fear they had in mind was that which haunted ancient marital relations: If the wife conceived she might die in childbirth, and she was a very valuable possession. Augustus* tried to give the senators an example of economy and domestic discipline by wearing togas woven by the women of his family. Still at the end of the Middle Ages the state of nature was conceived as that "when Adam delved and Eve span."

Children, too, could be useful in the parent's business as well as in house and field work. The father of the Greek orator, Aeschines, was a school teacher's servant, so Aeschines' opponents report with glee that as a boy he had to go to school with his father, grind the ink, wash the benches, and sweep the schoolhouse. And even when he was grown he had to help his mother, who gave religious initiations: He read the book, managed the props, led the processions, and so on. If father had a shop or practiced a trade, the boys began to help as soon as they were old enough; little girls were put to helping mother. Defoe, in his *Tour of England* (1727) enthusiastically reports that in Yorkshire, where much cloth was spun at home, the children work beside their parents and there is "hardly anything above four years old, but its hands are sufficient to (support) itself." Such training was the basic form of most ancient education; the ancients were generally too poor to afford the modern fashion, which wastes the labor potential of children, separates them from adults from whom they might learn, and segregates them in a workless world of fantasy, idleness, and irresponsibility.

With women and children, the lower animals were pressed into service. They were of course used for food and clothing as today. Meat was a luxury; lack of refrigeration limited the use of milk and butter, but cheese was perhaps the most important protein food. Wool and linen were the only woven fabrics in common use. Accordingly leather was much used. Beside providing raw materials, animals were the sole means of overland transport, they pulled plows (it is forbidden by Jewish law to yoke your wife and donkey together), they pulled boats upstream, they pulled irrigation wheels, when circular mills were introduced they pulled mills.* Since they played so large a role in the economy, they were important in religion. Above all they were the messengers of the gods; their movements, cries, and the appearance of their organs after they were sacrificed, were universally recognized as omens and constantly consulted. A king of Assyria was informed by an official letter that a fox had entered Ashur. Even in rationalistic Greece they were, in the fables of Aesop, the masks of proverbial wisdom (and folly). In Egypt they were worshiped as embodiments of supernatural powers. In Assyria their embodiment of the wild and demonic was dramatized: Kings were shown killing lions* (as pharaohs were shown killing hippopotami and crocodiles), and lions were rounded up and released so that the kings could pursue and kill them.

This was not idle sport. Men had nothing but bows, arrows, and spears with which to resist animals' violence. A dangerous animal—an unusually large and savage boar, for instance—could pose a serious problem. When new settlers in eighth-century Samaria did not worship the local god he sent a plague of lions. Because men were so few and the country so large, destruction of "varmints" was both duty and pleasure of the upper class. For this, man's animal ally, the dog, was of value; he was also the earliest burglar alarm. Women's war on domestic vermin was carried on by the cat, age-old in Egypt, domesticated in Athens by the fifth century B.C. Conspicious subjugation of wild animals—putting lions, for instance, to draw a chariot—as well as the use of wild animals for torture, was common in Roman entertainment. Zoos appeared in Assyrian times, if not earlier. Tiglath-pileser III received a crocodile as a gift from the Pharaoh. We have a full account of how natives of central Africa trapped a forty foot python and shipped it to Alexandria for the delectation of King Ptolemy.

PRIMITIVE STATE OF SCIENCE, ESPECIALLY MEDICINE

Lack of manpower and dependence on animals resulted from the primitive condition of science and technology. This was important everywhere, but most of all, perhaps, in medicine. The best thing to be said for ancient medicine was that, in its earlier stages, it was usually rationalistic when, with the means available, rationalism would help. An Egyptian medical papyrus of the eighteenth dynasty prescribes rational treatment for forty-seven different injuries of which the causes are observable; only for illnesses of which the cause was unknown did the physician resort to charms. Similarly in Babylonia the doctor, who used mostly rational means, was distinguished from the priest and the magician. In Greece, it was only the development of "scientific" medical theory in the hellenistic world and later that divorced much medicine from common sense and made doctors really dangerous. But even before that time the ignorance of the true causes of diseases and consequently of infection—ignorance which continued till the 1890s—kept the infant mortality rate extremely high, perhaps fifty percent (in New York in 1970 it was two percent). The ancient death rate for women in childbirth was perhaps thirty or forty percent. There was also a high death rate throughout childhood and adolescence; perhaps only one of every four children lived to have children of his own. In Egyptian Thebes during the Roman period the average boy of fifteen would be dead before thirty. Even the tough survivors of this rigorous selection could not escape the plagues that doctors could neither understand nor prevent, and that also remained common until the nineteenth century. These might destroy as much as a third of a city's population. By comparison with later, as well as earlier, populations, Greek men were probably healthier because of their regular exercise and bathing. In Roman times, exercise for adults gradually died out, baths came to include heated communal tubs that probably did much to spread disease, and increased water supply and larger sewers were probably balanced by extensive use of poisonous lead piping. At all events, the mortality rate was high.

Thus most inhabitants of the ancient world were saved from a fate worse than death, old age, by our standards dreadful and premature. Lack of mechanization made the physical weakness of old men and women much more important than it is in our society. There is no word for "middle age" in Greek; as soon as a man ceased to be "young," he was "old," that is, at fifty (when, in Athens, his liability for military service usually ended). A woman was "old" at forty or forty-five. Eyeglasses were practically nonexistent until the fifteenth century A.D., hearing aids and false teeth were rudimentary, inefficient, and uncomfortable till the twentieth. It was so rare to find an adult with a complete set of teeth that Aristotle was led to believe men had by nature more teeth than women. For most phenomena of physical degeneration, as for the slow diseases of the old, there was nothing to be done. Hospitals appear in the Greco-Roman world, mainly for men without families, like soldiers. With Christianity came hospitals for the poor. Until their appearance, care of the old, sick, and insane fell on their families. Madness, disease, and death were familiar sights; the basic facts of "the human condition" could not be so easily forgotten as in the modern world.

The impact of old age was increased by general poverty. Because the means of production were rudimentary most men could not accumulate substantial savings, therefore the average man's old age insurance was his family. Family coherence, obligations of children to care for parents and of parents to bring up children carefully, were instilled by self-interest and enforced by the law. That family connections were far more important in the ancient world (and until World War I) than at present, resulted from religious and social factors too, but economic concern for security shaped religious teaching and social practice.

IGNORANCE OF CHEMISTRY

Hardly less important than ignorance of bacteriology was ignorance of chemistry which until the late nineteenth century affected almost every side of life. Experiments with plants, stones, minerals, and men gradually led to pharmaceutical knowledge, but as to *why* different ingredients acted as they did, there was only speculation. Consequently little could be done against diseases or personal parasites—lice, fleas, etc.—which were common. More serious was the inability to fight diseases of crops and insect plagues. Local disasters, given the high cost of transportation, made famine always a possibility. And even when the crops flourished and the locusts did not come, there was only natural fertilizer and not much of that. Therefore much of the soil—commonly thirty to fifty percent—had to be left fallow each year to recuperate its fertility, and the rest was none too rich. Only the flooded river valleys were exceptions to this rule.

While ancient chemistry could not increase the food, it could not prevent the increase of the population. Rubber and its vulcanization, to say nothing of hormones, were unknown. Contraceptive practices of varying efficiency were current, but the only reliable methods of population control until the present century were abortion, infanticide, and homosexuality, of which the last was customary only in the Greco-Roman world. Greeks simply "exposed" unwanted children, abandoning them outside the city (which should not be polluted by burials); Phoenicians and their neighbors sacrificed them, making an economical virtue of necessity. Along the Palestinian coast and in Mesopotamia it was common to bury unwanted children under the dirt floors of the houses; when a new building was going up, one or more might be buried under the foundations, to protect or secure protection (as sacrifices) for the structure. Nothing was wasted. Exposure continued common until the nineteenth century; a Parisian church register for 1777 shows that more than 20 percent of the children baptized in that year had no known parents.

Beyond these basic considerations, it is impossible to enumerate the aspects in which chemistry has transformed modern life and made it difficult for us to imagine the ancient world—a world without, for instance, plastics, synthetic fabrics, sugar (the ancients used honey), soap, and paper. And no distilled beverages!

LIMITED KNOWLEDGE OF ENGINEERING

Equally far reaching was the ignorance of engineering, though in the course of antiquity new principles, and new applications of familiar principles, were discovered, the most spectacular being extensive use of the arch, by which the Romans transformed architecture, though arches had been used occasionally ever since the Bronze Age. Mechanization, begun with the sling, lever, and bow, went on, but at a snail's pace. Potter's wheel, sail boat, and pulley are prehistoric, siphon and bellows date from the Bronze Age, with hellenistic and Roman times came pumps of several sorts, the Archimedian screw, wind, water, and animal driven mills, multiple stamps for coins, tiles, bricks, and pottery, catapults powered by twisted ropes, and so on. Most of this development was based on analogy and experiment, not on scientific understanding of principles or prior calculation of forces involved; such understanding and calculation became common only in the late nineteenth century.

Moreover, even in hellenistic times and later, when there was some interest in the principles, engineering rarely had practical results. (Archimedes was almost alone in using pure science for important technological discoveries.) There was no pressing need for them. The natural products and resources of the land, as produced and improved by manual labor, sufficed to support the limited population at the relatively low standard to which most of its members were accustomed and resigned. Indeed, the introduction of new techniques was sometimes prohibited by Roman emperors as likely to cause unemployment. Also the hellenistic and Roman notion of progress was influenced by Aristotle, who, because of his biological studies, thought of "progress" as that of an organism advancing from immaturity to a limited maturity that remains constant at best, at worst is followed by decline. (Thus a child progresses to manhood, but no further; once a man, the best he can do is maintain maturity; ahead lies death.) The statesmen of the Roman Empire liked to think of themselves and the empire as mature, so they were not anxious for progress.

POVERTY, STABILITY, AND VARIETY

Without engineering and mechanization, the ancient world was mainly one of farmers, fishers, hunters, and handicraftsmen. Productivity was therefore low and poverty, by modern standards, general. Hence an almost universal simplicity of life. A creditor who has taken the borrower's garment as a pledge, says the Book of Exodus, must return it to him every evening, whether or not the debt has been paid, "for it is his (one) garment to (cover) his skin. In what (else) will he sleep?" A lawyer in an Athenian murder case could argue that the motive had not been robbery—because, the victim's clothes were not taken.

With poverty went stability. In Greek "new things" is a term of abuse; "to think new things" means to plot a revolution. Those lucky enough to have farms or shops clung to them; sons were trained in the handicrafts or farming skills of their fathers; daughters in the housekeeping of their mothers. The main business of life was to make a living and build up, if possible, a little reserve against the next drought or plague of locusts or passing army. "Acts of God" and acts of the government, beginning with taxes, were always to be feared.

Manufacture by craftsmen, not by machines, and lack of transportation made the ancient world one of enormous variety. Each district had its skills and specialties—things found nowhere else—its peculiar religious beliefs, laws, customs, coinage, dialect, wine, and so on. Even in Roman times, when certain statue types, pottery shapes, and the like became fashionable through most of the empire, the individual examples of these types were manufactured in different places with different materials, details, and skills. Rarely could one find two objects almost identical, except for the few things produced by stamping from molds—coins, bricks, tiles, certain types of pottery. Similarly, there were few large companies selling the same wares through wide areas. Very early Mesopotamia and Egypt saw something remotely like "socialism," but once private industry and trade developed, the general pattern became one of small entrepreneurs, with state control of certain monopolies, most often mining. The result was a world of infinite variety—for those who could travel.

RARITY OF TRAVEL AND MINOR ROLE OF TRADE

Travel, however, was limited by the mountainous terrain of most Mediterranean countries and by the lack of engineering. Overland, the fastest conveyance was a riding horse or, in the east, a camel. In rough terrain news might be carried more quickly by runners. Anything weighty or bulky had to go by caravan, usually of donkeys. A donkey caravan moves slower than a man on foot. Hence the importance of rivers. They were moving roads, the fastest, easiest, cheapest means of transport across their lands. Any stream large enough to carry a rowboat was used. The tiny Tiber (formerly fordable at Rome) played so large a role in provisioning the city that there is still, beside it, a little hill composed of scraps of packing jars. This in spite of the fact that the Tiber's current was so strong that the boats coming upstream had to be pulled by oxen. Almost every large city was located on and fed by a river.

Because travel was slow and expensive, most people stayed home. Even in the first centuries of the Roman Empire, when shipping was relatively secure and some tourist trade developed, seventy or eighty percent of the population never went more than a day's journey—twenty-five or thirty miles—from their homes. Nor were they able to see or hear the rest of the world by pictures or recordings. Transmission of sound was simply nonexistent; pictures and sculpture, rarely historical, at best represented only a few main figures and some sketchy background.* (This made pictures on coins important; they were much used in Roman propaganda.)* Most people knew only what was to be known in their home towns. The largest comparatively mobile class of the population was the military, but in imperial times before 200 the army made up less than .02 of the adult population, and many soldiers spent all their lives in one district!

Hence, the importance of local connections—the family, the guild, the religious association, the city. These directed and limited their members but also protected them. Family fights were frequent, but a family would commonly stick together against outsiders, protect its members when threatened, and help when necessary. And so would other local associations. The resultant society was extremely conservative and offered great resistance to external coercion. A government had to deal, not with individuals, but with members of groups who could rely on their fellows for intercession, support, concealment. An inscription from Anatolia tells us that the local god punished with sickness a man who appealed to external, probably Roman, authorities about a village affair; Paul thought it disgraceful that some Corinthian Christians had gone to law in the pagan courts. Moreover, with the communication and transport available, the government could collect information and send orders only very slowly. A decree of the Seleucid king, Antiochus III, issued at Antioch in March, reached his governor in central Asia Minor in early May, and his governor in Iran, in June! An urgent letter of the emperor Gaius (Caligula) to his legate in Syria was held up for three months en route. To discover whether or not orders were obeyed, took more time, and to enforce obedience, yet more—not to mention manpower and expense. Consequently central governments customarily let subject localities do much as they pleased, and contented themselves with tribute, military right of way, services to high officials in passage, perhaps quartering a governor and garrison in the territory, but little more. Tyrannies and persecutions were commonly intracity phenomena; the larger totalitarian state was made possible only by modern technology.

Another consequence of the lack of rapid transport was the general unimportance of trade. From early times basic materials—especially metals—were shipped considerable distances. So were small luxury items: gold, silver, turquoise, crystal, lapis lazuli and similar semiprecious stones and pigments, fine timber (for Mesopotamia and Egypt), amber from the north, incense and condiments from the east, fine manufactured goods from the Mesopotamian and Mediterranean cities. Slaves were valuable but perishable; trade in them was mostly with adjacent countries until Greeks and Phoenicians developed maritime transport. Trade in foodstuffs was limited by lack of refrigeration. Grain, fish (dried, pickled, or salted), wine, olive oil—things that would keep if sealed in big jars ("amphorae")—were the only foods shipped in quantity. Hence came the local, seasonal diet, danger of famine, importance of the agricultural year for religion—all mentioned above, as was the fact that workmen could be exported more cheaply than their products. The cost of shipping wine to the north explains the development there of vines resistant to cold and humidity. At first fine Greek pottery was exported, later it lost the overseas market to cheaper local imitations. In Roman times something similar happened to Arretine pottery, but here the businesses and artisans were exported to start new production in the countries (Spain, Gaul, Rhineland) to which trade had formerly gone. Glassmaking moved in the same way from the Rhone valley to that of the Rhine.

SIMPLICITY OF LIFE

The relative unimportance of trade contributed to the simplicity of ancient life. Many materials now common were then exotic or unknown. Silk was an enormously expensive luxury imported from China (not until Byzantine times were silkworms smuggled to the west). Cotton, from India, was almost as expensive as silk. Pepper, cinnamon, nutmeg, and many other spices were semiprecious imports. Bananas, pineapples, grapefruit, potatoes, tea, coffee, tobacco, and many such products of the Americas, the South Seas, and the hybridization of the present century were unknown.

As the difficulty of transport shaped culture by restraining trade, it shaped political life by restraining troop movement. Armies generally had to walk, as they would until the development of railways in the 1850s. Few armies were transported by sea; major naval campaigns were even fewer, probably because of the unreliability of sea transport, at the mercy of the weather and without reliable instruments for navigation. (A kind of astrolabe appears in the hellenistic age; the central rudder turned by an axis is of the same age or later.) The Carthaginians were among the best sailors of antiquity, yet in 205 a Carthaginian fleet to relieve Hannibal set out for southeast Italy but arrived in Sardinia.

LARGE EMPIRES AND SMALL LOYALTIES

The difficulty of moving troops favored the growth of large political units: It hampered the cooperation of small states to withstand a big one, which could take over its little neighbors singly. So we find a succession of large states—the early Mesopotamian, Egyptian, and Hittite empires, Assyria, the neo-Babylonian and Median empires, Persia, the Macedonian kingdoms, and Rome. Most of these were bigger than any states now located in the same territories; Persia and the brief kingdom of Alexander rank among the largest achieved in southwestern Asia; the Roman Empire was the most extensive and enduring political structure that western Europe has seen.

Yet difficulty of transporting troops and slowness of communications made these superstates inefficient in controlling their components. Imperial organization was balanced by the intense parochialism of the city states. Even the power of Rome occasionally failed to prevent the cities of Asia Minor and Syria from going to war with their next door neighbors. Within the Persian empire many cities and temples became practically self-governing. Thus unification without uniformity, which modern political theorists desire in vain, resulted from lack of transportation.

SILENCE AND THE IMPORTANCE OF SONG AND SPEECH

The rudimentary state of science and technology affected psychological, no less than physical, life. One consequence must have been the silence of the ancient world—no subways, trolleys, busses, automobiles, horns, sirens, engines, radios, telephones. Noises were made only by human beings, other animals, moving waters, or winds—no wonder the winds were important deities! And each sound vanished when it ceased—there was no recording, no broadcasting. The average resident of a city knew only the sounds produced there; "music," for him, was what the local performers sang and played.

Accordingly, what sounds there were, were noticed. Ancient literature delights to specify the sounds of humans, animals, even reptiles and insects—the cicadas creak in the trees, the frogs croak in the marshes. And by contrast with the silence of the countryside, the ancients found their cities noisy—metal workers and stone cutters hammering, shouting hucksters, whining beggars, street musicians, fights, braying donkeys, barking dogs. The Babylonians thought the noise made by mortals decided the gods to send the flood. Juvenal's description of the noises of Rome is famous.

Where all sounds were noticed, human utterance commanded attention. Song, especially choral music, played an even larger role in ancient than it does in modern society, but it was decentralized. In Rome and a few other cities popular performers might count their followers by the hundreds of thousands, but even they, even when they travelled, could sing only for one city at a time. Accordingly local singers were of greater importance than at present. Choral performances were the main feature of many public ceremonies; private or professional singing was probably the commonest form of after-dinner entertainment. Modern business and industry plays background music; ancient craftsmen and laborers sang at their work—women at the loom, sailors as they rowed, shepherds as they watched their flocks. When the walls of Thebes were building, legend said, the songs were so good that the stones seemed to move by themselves. Military actions began and ended with songs; children in school memorized their texts to tunes.

Speech, like song, profited from silence. The ancient and medieval worlds were oral ones; the age of communication mainly by reading began with Gutenberg (about 200,000,000 books were published between 1550 and 1700); now, with radio and television, we may come back to the predominance of speech. In the ancient world, that predominance was unquestioned. Speech was the primary means of mass communication; men with loud voices were employed to make public announcements and, in war, to give commands, or communicate with the enemy by shouting at them. The town crier was still the public newspaper in most small cities of the eighteenth century. In the second place, to hear a good speaker was a form of entertainment, so, from early Egyptian times on, we hear praises of men who can plead a case well ("the eloquent peasant"). Pleadings in law courts, both as performances when given and, when reported, as literature, became widely popular. The same was true of speeches made in assemblies, or even to bypassers in the marketplace. Speeches in the Roman senate sometimes ran to seven hours. In Greek and Roman times, both speech writers and speakers became professional classes from which some individuals rose to the highest honors. Finally, written works, when read, were commonly read aloud; many persons of wealth owned or regularly employed readers. Even literary works were perceived as speech.

HOMEMADE ENTERTAINMENT

The importance of speaking points up the problem of entertainment. To meet his needs man had learned to restrain himself and pursue consistently a single purpose. He had thus ceased to be a mere stimulus-response mechanism like the other animals; he had taught himself to imagine remote goals, choose between them, and work for them; he had come to think it normal and desirable for a man to "have something to do." When he did not have something to do, he was "at leisure." Thus "leisure" became a peculiar state, something different from normal, and having learned to be occupied, he now needed something to occupy his leisure. The more stable society became, the further technology advanced, the more pressing this problem.

In the ancient world technology sufficed to make the problem important, but not to do anything of importance for its solution. Mechanization of entertainment by printing, motion pictures, radio, and television has reshaped modern leisure. In the ancient world almost everybody wanted to live in a city, not only for protection—though that was important, especially before Roman times—but also for company and entertainment.

The principal entertainment offered by city life was that of watching your neighbors. This was done more openly in antiquity than at present.

In early days the best observation post was the city gate, since all who came in or went out had to pass scrutiny there. As long as the city was a small, fortified place with only one main entrance, the most honored and influential citizens were "those who sat in the gate." As cities became bigger and gates more numerous, the center of observation shifted to the marketplace, the courts, the main temple, and the like. Religious ceremonies, especially processions, played a much larger part in ancient cities than in most modern ones—those who have been in a Mediterranean city for Holy Week will have some notion of the ancient spectacles. The government, too, was a frequent source of public shows —their occasions and natures differed from one country and time to another, but they usually involved processions and sacrifices. Sacrifices were popular because the public often got a share of the meat, for most a rare luxury. Other food and wine might be provided. Apart from these big shows, however, the citizens were mostly on their own. There was a lot of amateur singing at parties, and a considerable population of singers, dancers, pantomime artists, storytellers, acrobats, men with performing animals, and so on. Egyptian temples staged "dramatic" representations of myths—with actors who represented the different persons and who said and did the appropriate things—but we find no strictly theatrical performances or competitive athletic contests before Greek times, and only in Greek and later architecture do we find buildings such as theaters and concert halls designed to make a performance visible and audible to the largest possible audience.

LACK OF ARTIFICIAL LIGHTING

Entertainment and many other activities of life were limited by the lack of good, cheap lighting (never available till the nineteenth century). Until late Roman times the ancients never got beyond the oil lamp—a fuel basin with an exposed wick—both expensive and ineffective. The rhythm of life was determined by natural illumination. Almost everyone awoke as soon as the sky began to get light. In the grey dawn the farmers would start walking from the city out to their fields. Shops and markets opened at sunrise, by Greek and Roman reckoning the beginning of "the first hour." An "hour" was one-twelfth of the period from sunrise to sunset; it varied from place to place and day to day. By the end of "the sixth hour" (noon) business was mostly done in Greece and Rome and the Greeks were off to the gymnasium, the Romans to the baths. These institutional solutions to the problem of leisure were peculiar to the Greco-Roman world; how men of earlier antiquity spent their afternoons is unknown. Probably business went on somewhat longer. Almost everybody dined before sunset; few stayed up long after dark. "To burn the midnight oil" (of the lamp) was to leave yourself only four or five hours for sleep, since you would be up again well before dawn. The time available for reading was thus limited and few were widely read.

Another consequence of the lack of lighting was that, even in cities, nights were black. Street lighting was rare and at best rudimentary. There were no illuminated signs or store fronts. Windows in ancient houses were usually in upper stories; those on the ground floor were relatively few and small; most internal lighting came from courtyards. Since nights were so dark, men were more aware of celestial bodies—sun and moon were of greater practical importance and stars more conspicuous. Night was a great goddess of whom Zeus stood in awe. Sun and moon were major deities. Stars and planets were believed to determine human destinies by their movements. Nocturnal rituals were awesome things. Our midnight masses of Christmas and Easter are isolated survivals of the ancient mysteries, as lizards of the dinosaurs.

BELIEF IN A SUPERNATURAL POPULATION

Ordinary religious ceremonies, then as now, were diurnal, but differed vastly from their modern descendants. So did the suppositions behind them. The ancients almost universally believed that the world was full of supernatural beings, gods and demons* of varying characters, more powerful than men. Many were localized in objects or areas, but they also moved about, usually invisible, on, over, and under the earth. They could hear when called, often would come, and sometimes appear. Their powers, though vague, were vast. They could cause storms, calms, or earthquakes, blight or protect crops, send plagues and heal diseases, terrify enemies or inspire them. (Christianity replaced the gods with saints and angels, but left the demons; most died out in the eighteenth century; a few still survive.)

SACRIFICIAL WORSHIP

It was almost universally believed that the best way to solicit these supernatural beings was by appropriate sacrifices (each had his or her peculiar tastes, which were usually "known"). Every city provided regular sacrifices for the deities with which it had most to do; it marked off considerable areas as sacred to them and built them temples as residences and centers for worship. The normal religious ceremony of antiquity, whether public or private, was a sacrifice that consisted of pouring out or burning something, normally on or by an altar (or in a pit, if the deities worshiped were those of the underworld). On important occasions the sacrifice was usually an animal, killed, skinned, and cut up on the spot before portions of it were burned. In festivals the courtyards of the temples became vast slaughterhouses, stinking and alive with flies. Yet few philosophers denied the value of sacrifices and virtually nobody opposed the practice. Judaism still laments its enforced interruption, and even the Christian author of the Epistle to the Hebrews can write, "Without the shedding of blood"—by which he meant, sacrifice of an animal—"there is no forgiveness of sins." Why did men continue to believe this, let alone practice it?

For the ordinary worshiper, the ordinary sacrifice was a private one performed in his home at the shrine of his household gods. On special occasions—for requests or thanksgivings of particular importance, when he had made and had to perform some vow, or the like—he would go to a temple, but there too his worship would be private. When the city celebrated a festival he would watch the procession, if there was one, and might even march in it, or go to the temple to see the sacrifices, hear the singing, and join in the public acclamations, but that was usually the full extent of his worship. The type of service now common in Judaism, Christianity, and Islam, consisting of prayer, praise, and reading and exposition of some sacred text, began relatively late in antiquity, possibly about 500 B.C., as a peculiarity of Judaism. In Judaism it remained a supplement to the sacrificial worship of the Temple, until the Temple was destroyed in A.D. 70. Only with the great expansion of Christianity did nonsacrificial worship become common. But Christianity did not limit itself to this form; its principal service, in antiquity, was a sacrifice in which bread and wine were offered to the deity, transformed into the body and blood of Jesus, and then eaten (as parts of ancient sacrifices were commonly eaten) by the worshipers. As in other ancient sacrifices, prayers or hymns might be said or sung, and the occasion might be used for reading sacred texts or public instruction, but none of these was essential. The essential, "the thing done," was the sacrifice which in Christianity, as in many magical sacrifices, had to be accompanied by the recitation of a holy story containing certain sacred words. The notion that bread and wine can be transformed by such a ceremony into the body and blood of a god also comes from ancient magic.

MAGIC AND OTHER COMMUNICATION WITH THE GODS

"Magic" was the term used in later antiquity for several sorts of prayers and sacrifices to diverse deities and demons, and also for operations performed by use of little known powers of celestial bodies, plants, minerals, or parts of animals. The term was a sort of general, pejorative label for procedures, mostly intended to have sensible effects, and many prohibited by law. There was no single concept or type of action that all "magical" operations had in common; the sense of the term was fixed by arbitrary and inconsistent social usage, but it did refer to an extensive religious and scientific underworld. Probably most of the lower classes —particularly women—occasionally tried their hands at magic. There were also a good many professional or semiprofessional practitioners, probably more often influential in ancient society than such persons are today. Ancient literature in this respect is misleading, the product of a rationalistic upper crust, not representative of the superstitions of the masses. Thus the Attic orators do not speak of magic, but some curse tablets found in Athens contain the names of persons mentioned by the orators.[1]

Magic and other forms of ancient religion had in common not only sacrificial worship (which made real death a familiar, everyday fact to men of antiquity), but also the belief that worship might be expected to get perceptible results. The gods were in constant communication with men. They made their opinions known by shaping the viscera of the sacrificed animals (interpretation of the resultant shapes was a discipline in which there were recognized professionals, often hereditary), by omens and portents (appearances of sacred animals or birds in significant situations, "unnatural" events such as misshapen births, thunder and lightening), by dreams and visions, and through recognized oracles—certain holy places each of which had its own technique for discovering what its god wanted to say.

The difference from the modern world is mainly one of extent and status. Prophets are still at large, but those that claim divine inspiration are usually of little influence. In antiquity, however, all important official actions began by sacrifice and examination of the viscera, by consideration of omens and consultation of prophets who were on hand in every city as recognized officials. In classical Greece, if any action of special importance were contemplated, one or more oracles would also be consulted. Oracles dwindled away in Roman times, but prophets and professional interpreters of viscera and omens still accompanied every army, and tactical decisions were based on their advice. This might be disastrous: It destroyed the Athenian force at the siege of Syracuse. To

---

[1] "Curse tablets" are tablets, usually of lead, on which a would-be magician has written the names of persons to be injured or killed by the underworld powers. Often they also contain prayers to the underworld powers, telling them what is wanted. Such "letters" were commonly "mailed" by being buried in graveyards, thrown into wells or springs, or sent underground in some other fashion. Thus they were preserved and are now among the most important sources for the history of Greco-Roman magic.

neglect their advice might also be disastrous. One Roman admiral who wanted to engage the enemy was directed by his accompanying augur to avoid an encounter—the sacred chickens would not eat. "Then let them drink," said the admiral. He threw the chickencoop overboard, proceeded to attack, was defeated, and became an example of the perils of impiety. Most commanders were well aware of the importance of prophecy for the morale of their men. Alexander the Great, the pupil of Aristotle, was accompanied throughout his campaigns by selected prophets, more complaisant than the sacred chickens, but probably more influential than the chaplains of a modern army.

The gods did not limit their communications to civic and military officials. They gave messages to individuals through sacrifices, omens, prophets, oracles, and appearance in dreams and visions. Innumerable statues, altars, and other objects (often decorative elements in temples, sometimes even the temples themselves) carry inscriptions declaring they were erected by individuals "at the command of the god." Yet the known examples must be a small proportion of those once erected. And how many things of which no tangible record could remain were done "at the command of the god"?

THE PECULIARITY OF GREEK RATIONALISM

One philosopher said, "The world is full of gods"; another declared there were gods even in a kitchen stove. Given such statements, the emergence of Greek rationalism is amazing. It is also the supreme achievement of antiquity and the foundation of the modern world. Too often, it is taken for granted. Consider the civilizations in which this scientific approach to the world did *not* emerge and which therefore, in spite of great achievements in government, architecture, the arts, speculative philosophy, and mystical religion, attained at most plateaus from which they could go no further, and on which they remained, limited by the limited possibilities of repetitive learning and manual labor, until the flood of modern civilization overwhelmed them. It was thanks to the Greeks that western learning did not merely collect and repeat data, but analyzed, understood, speculated, tested, and so found the way from the ancient poverty supported by manual labor to the comparative plenty of the mechanized world.

THE STABILITY OF CULTURES UNDISTURBED BY RATIONALISM: EGYPT

Something of the greatness of the Greek achievement can be seen if we contrast the history of the millennia after the Greek cultural revolution, when rationalism was at work, with that of the millennia before.

Take the case of Egypt. From 2600 B.C. to 600 B.C. Egyptian civilization was essentially static. If the first pharaoh of the pyramid age had returned to his country 2,000 years later he would have found many superficial changes: The power of the pharaoh would have declined, the pharaohs themselves would have become Libyans (!), the number of mercenaries from across the Great Green Sea would have much increased and they would now have weapons of iron, a metal that in his day had been precious. He would have found many monumental buildings—some of them beautiful—that had not been there in his day, and he could have learned from the inscriptions on them (which he could have read, with difficulty) the names of his royal successors, their military conquests and religious donations, during two thousand years of history. But that history would have had nothing to teach him except a few lessons about military tactics and technology (chariots, composite bows, etc.) and the dangers of overexpansion. Similarly in religion he would have found many new (or newly prominent) cults, and he would have been furious at the disappearance of many he had endowed, especially those for his own divinity. If he had talked with the priests at Memphis he might have learned some theological speculations of no practical importance, and some detailed accounts of the afterlife. In this life, however, he would have found a general decline of good taste and good workmanship. The objects made by craftsmen and represented by the arts, and the general style of the representations, would have changed little, usually for the worse. No one, now, was making the exquisite stone tableware they made in his time. The arts and crafts were full of claptrap and vulgarity; the elegance, simplicity, and grandeur of his day were no more. Even in the work of the best craftsmen—and he would have had to admit there were still some very good ones—there was a striving for effect that spoiled the effect. And in sculpture they actually had the impertinence and vulgarity to produce lifelike portraits! He would certainly have concluded that since his day the country had gone down hill. But he would have found no fundamental change. The basic economic life, the techniques used by the peasants and craftsmen, the social structure, the government, the sort of stuff that constituted "learning," the fundamental religious beliefs, the general attitudes, practices, and institutions would almost all have been familiar or readily understandable. He would have come back to, essentially, the world he had left.

But what if Cicero, murdered in 43 B.C., had come back to Rome in 1957? Everything would have been strange but the hills and the Tiber. To enumerate the economic, political, technological, and social changes would be impossible; the important change, however, the cause of most of the others, would be the new understanding of the physical world, including man. And the root of this new understanding is Greek rationalism, the ultimate source of the scientific and industrial revolutions that replaced the ancient by the modern world.

FACTORS THAT LIMITED THE EFFECTS OF RATIONALISM

These revolutionary consequences of the new tendency were not, however, immediately apparent. By contrast with the modern world, the ancient was a culture of extraordinary intellectual, as well as economic, stability, not to say stagnation. After the Greek "Renaissance" of the eighth to fifth centuries B.C., the momentum of intellectual change steadily diminished and society drifted back toward the pattern of the great nonwestern civilizations. Poverty, the consequent dependence of parents on their children for support in old age, the early integration of most children into the family's economic life, and their training to follow parental patterns, have already been noted.

The consequences of these practices were not wholly unfortunate. For instance, there was no such gap as there is now between the play world of children and the work world of adults. Most children never had to face the terrible question, "What do you want to do?" There was no painful readjustment at the end of adolescence and "identity crises" were rare. But so was originality of thought and novelty in action.

Practically all girls brought up by free parents became mothers and housewives; a few exceptions became priestesses. In Greco-Roman times we hear of a very few skilled ladies who practiced professions—usually literature, but also medicine, and occasionally even athletics. Girls of slave parents and those sold into slavery had more varied careers, as did slave boys. Many were used as prostitutes while their looks lasted, beyond that usually lay domestic service or, for the men, farm work, though unusual ability (or the master's favor) might lead to important careers. One man who began life as a slave rose to be prefect of Egypt. Marcus Aurelius was descended from a slave. Free boys normally were taught their fathers' trades and went on to practice them; working groups were largely hereditary. Craftsmen knew what they had learned from their fathers and had practiced from childhood on. They were not open to change. They had learned by doing, without explanations; their knowledge was of techniques, not principles; they were mechanics, not engineers. Even those who went into some trade other than their fathers' were taught by apprenticeship, which had the same stultifying effect.

The consequences are clear in sculpture, because the evidence is unusually well preserved. Even after the achievements of classical and hellenistic Greece, the majority of sculptors went on copying types. Instead of learning, from the masterpieces of Praxiteles and Scopas, how to produce realistic, moving, three-dimensional figures, they made those masterpieces into new types and continued to copy them as mechanically as their predecessors had copied sphinxes.

Besides this inherent conservatism, ancient education suffered from the deficiency of technical knowledge. Ignorance of optics and of lense-grinding meant that there were generally no eyeglasses (Nero used an emerald as a monocle, but it probably was not cut as a lens to correct his vision). Most children with poor vision were never able to become learned, and science lost the discoveries they might have made. Astronomy never went much beyond calculation of the movements of the celestial bodies and speculative theories to explain these; notions of the solar system, to say nothing of the universe, were frequently false, with far-reaching effects in religion and philosophy. (The highest god was located above the "sphere" of the fixed stars.) At the other end of the scale the lack of magnification prevented understanding of the cellular structure of living tissue, the role of bacteria, and so on. Less fundamental, but important, was the failure to develop printing, which made books extremely expensive. This limited learning, for the most part, to families of means, and also limited the number and accessibility of books absolutely. Much that was written circulated in a few copies and disappeared or was inaccessible to the man to whose thought it would have been important. Another handicap was the use, until the second or third century A.D., of scrolls rather than books of modern form ("codices"). To read a scroll takes two hands, note taking and cross-references are difficult. The introduction of the codex made information more quickly discoverable and misinformation more quickly detectable. Again, ancient books, before the end of the Roman period, were not commonly illustrated, and illustrations, when they did occur, were imaginative or diagrammatic, not accurate. Lifelike representation of absent objects became common only with engraving, in the eighteenth century. Except for verbal information, the ancient scholar was practically limited to what he could see and hear for himself.

Given these obstacles, the emergence of Greek rationalism is truly amazing. The development of a body of thought neither hereditary, nor utilitarian, nor connected with any technique, nor to the interest of any authority, nor backed by any, would have been, in itself, a marvel. But rationalism was not merely a body of thought, it was a way of thinking, a way that drew consequences, and so led to understanding from which further consequences could then be drawn, and so on. It was the beginning of an intellectual progress of which the conclusion lay far beyond anything its initiators could foresee—or anything we can.

Yet, marvelous as the Greek achievement was, it was not unparalleled. In the late stone age, the development of civilized life had resulted from a series of revolutionary innovations. Again, most of the great technological discoveries that precipitated the emergence of modern civilization were not made by scientists or engineers, but by intelligent mechanics. Watt, who produced the first efficient steam engine, was the apprentice of an instrument maker. Arkwright, who invented the spinning machine, was a barber. Studebaker was a coach maker; Opel made bicycles, so did the Wright brothers. There are many more such examples. By contrast, it has been shown that in England the Royal Society played no significant part in the industrial revolution. Indeed, professional intellectuals and scientists have often been prominent in obstructing scientific progress. Pasteur was hated by the doctors of his time. Edison, when he displayed his phonograph to the French Academy of Sciences, was accused of being a ventriloquist. The famous physicist Arago opposed the introduction of railways into France because he was convinced that if a passenger happened to lean out of the window the wind would blow off his head. Another physicist, Biot, was more open to experiment. He wrote in the *Journal des Savants* of 1816 that steamships might someday be useful for passenger travel on rivers, but of course would never be important as cargo boats. All this goes to confirm the observation of Cicero: "The greatest obstacle for those who wish to learn is the authority of those who teach."

FOR FURTHER READING

S. Dill, *Roman Society from Nero to Marcus Aurelius*

S. Dill, *Roman Society in the Last Century of the Western Empire*

T. Frank, ed., *An Economic Survey of Ancient Rome*

W. Jaeger, *Paideia*

M. Rostovtzeff, *The Social and Economic History of the Hellenistic World*

M. Rostovtzeff, *The Social and Economic History of the Roman Empire*

18
WHAT HAPPENED IN ANCIENT HISTORY

Now that we have described the course and characteristics of ancient civilization, we may try to summarize its achievements. What happened in these 8,000 years?

LIFE, THE MOST IMPORTANT HISTORICAL EVENT

First of all, men lived. "Dead matter" (as matter is commonly conceived) or even profound sleep (our model for the concept) differs so far from human consciousness that every occurrence of the latter is a unique historical event that would be thought a miracle were it not a commonplace. The two fundamental events of history are the occurrence and recurrence of this miracle. The ancient Near East and the Greco-Roman world were the product of less than twenty billion lives, about five times the present population of the world (roughly 3,700,000,000). But of these twenty billion, almost half died within a year, and perhaps another quarter in childhood. Only about five billion reached maturity, and of these at least a fifth died early, mostly in childbirth. So the total number of men and women who lived what we should consider full, normal lives, through the 8,000 years of antiquity, was little more than the number of human beings now living.

PRIVATE HISTORY

Each human being has his own history. If "What happened in history?" means, "What was of most importance to the people who lived?" then history consists in the main of a pattern: birth, infancy, childhood, learning, work, social relationships, sex, family life, senility. At every moment, examples of this pattern are begun by birth and broken off by death, some earlier in the sequence, some later. This constitutes personal history, which is, to a considerable extent, independent of political and cultural history. Even in concentration camps men fall in love. However, personal history generates demands—for food, shelter, and the like—that sometimes occasion the events of political history and always serve as a semiobjective control for the course of politics.

DEVELOPMENT OF A BASIS FOR A PUBLIC HISTORY

Far back in the prehistoric period, moreover, human awareness, interest, and memory were extended beyond this personal pattern to social groups as well as individuals. With this extension came the ability to control and direct the environment, and with this the gradual civilization of man. Of the techniques basic to civilization—use of shelter, clothing, fire, tools, domestication of vegetables, of men and other animals, cooking, weaving, pottery, mining and smelting, glassmaking, and so on—most were developed before writing, so history proper, the account of civilizations from which we have written records, begins after man's greatest achievement, the development of civilized life.

HISTORY OF CULTURE AND TECHNOLOGY

The first two millennia after the appearance of writing—roughly 3200–1200 B.C.—saw the expansion of this basically agricultural civilization from the centers in Mesopotamia and Egypt to all the lands of the eastern Mediterranean, while many of its elements were carried far beyond these limits. At the same time there was a great increase in the material of civilization—the numbers of trained humans and domesticated animals, of tools and buildings, the amount of cleared land suitable for agriculture. With this went a complementary destruction of vermin—not only snakes, crocodiles, bears, lions, and such, but also savage and criminal men. The environment, too, was made over. Woods were cleared, useless plants destroyed, swamps drained, and deserts irrigated, all with the elimination of their original "ecologies" and the creation of new ones more useful to man. Man was learning to cultivate his garden (as Voltaire said, referring to Genesis), and the first step of cultivation is to root out the weeds.

This pattern of expansion and enrichment was interrupted by the barbarian invasions that began in the late 1200s, but the interruption was temporary and progress resumed in all respects. The geographical area of civilization was extended, the material basis increased, and new materials and techniques were developed, some of them very important —iron smelting, alphabetic writing, glass blowing, the use of lime plaster, cement, arches, wind and water mills, the domestication of the camel. This gradual, but eventually enormous, growth and diversification of what may be called the embodiment of civilization was probably the most important physical change that took place between 3000 B.C. and A.D. 650. (The necessity, here, of brief description should not conceal the meaning of this development in terms of human experience. Even a single beautiful object is an incalculable power. To have created, not the pyramids or the Parthenon, but even one perfect vase, is to have changed the possible experience of mankind.)

POLITICAL HISTORY

This general change was not, of course, what the people who "made history" thought they were making. The rulers and rebels, soldiers and statesmen, whom the development of states had brought into being and whose doings are recorded by most "historical monuments," rarely had much to do with the advance of civilization. Their squabbles about political control of this or that area seemed to them often more important than life itself, but often seem to us matters of indifference, as did, to them, the private lives of their subjects. At the same time, the infinite complexity of historical causation makes it impossible to be certain how the change of any detail will affect subsequent events. It is easy to think of details, even of personal history, that had enormous consequences—some time about A.D. 30, for example, an obscure Palestinian Jew came to think himself the Messiah.

Tangled in this network of incalculable causes, historians first followed the lead of epic poets, who sang of what most interested their audiences: kings and love affairs and battles and "deeds of derring-do." These fill the earliest of preserved histories. From then on most political history has been merely personal history writ large, which accounts for its perennial interest to the young, but also its eventual monotony.

Plus ça change, plus c'est la même chose: The more numerous the varied incidents, the more clearly they can be seen to follow certain general patterns.

THE EMERGENCE OF GREEK CIVILIZATION

These patterns of civilized life as a whole underwent in antiquity two major changes. The first was that extraordinary enrichment and diversification produced by the interaction of the Greek genius and the physical circumstances of Greek history. The years from 800 to 400 saw the emergence in Greece and the Greek colonies of a new sort of life that offered the ordinary citizen far more opportunities, and opportunities of a different sort, than had ever been known before.

The citizen of Athens in the year 400 could participate in his own government and speak his mind freely. If tried, he would be tried not by a royal appointee, but by a jury of his fellow citizens, in public and according to the published laws. He would not be tortured. He would have the opportunity to confront his accusers, hear and answer their accusations. He had the privilege—and he knew it was a privilege, as well as a duty and a burden—of serving both in the offices of the government (including most of the priesthoods) and in the ranks of the army. He was trained to use arms, owned them, and could carry them when on military duty. In sum, he was a free man, nobody's subject. He might be happily married and also be carrying on a love affair with a lady of pleasure or an adolescent boy. He spent much of his free time at the gymnasium, regular exercise did a good deal to keep him clean and healthy. The gymnasium also helped him get through the hot Greek summer, when clothes are burdensome. If he got sick, he could consult a doctor whose approach, at least, would be rational.

So long as he was healthy, his city offered the Athenian a variety of pleasures hitherto unparalleled. At the great dramatic festivals, twice a year, he could see the plays of Aeschylus, Sophocles, Euripides,* Aristophanes, and a score of other dramatists. For choral music and lyric poetry there was the Odeum of Pericles. In the law courts and the assembly there were sometimes brilliant speeches, sharpened by argumentative techniques learned from rhetoricians who demonstrated their skills in public lectures and private debate. For understanding of the past and of the world around him the average Athenian, since he was literate, could draw on the works of many historians and geographers, including Herodotus and Thycydides. His general knowledge was improved, too, by conversation with sailors and merchants from Greek cities as far afield as Spain, Russia, and Egypt. If he had money he might himself travel and devote his life to learning, as did Herodotus. There were public recitations of parts of Herodotus' works and of the poems of Homer at Panathenaic festivals, and in these and many minor feasts there were contests of singers, dancers, and athletes, as well as choral music and processions. Apart from such occasional pleasures, the buildings and artifacts of his everyday life were often of extraordinary elegance, and from any part of the city he could look up to the Acropolis* with its magnificent gateway and crown of temples. Finally, if this beauty, or problems of human nature and political life, moved him to wonder, he could hear questions of philosophy discussed in marketplace or gymnasium by Socrates.* Such were the possibilities of life in Athens.

ATHENS COMPARED WITH BABYLON

Compare these with the possibilities of life in Babylon during the last years of its greatness (the time of Nabonidus, about B.C. 550). The difference will make clear the nature and extent of the Greek achievement. The Babylonian was a subject of the king and had no say in political decisions that might determine the course of his life. He lived under a government of officials appointed by the king. The only balances to the king's power were the traditional privileges of the city of Babylon and those of the great temples and their hereditary, privileged priesthoods. His sexual life was legally limited to heterosexual relationships, others were criminal. He got no more exercise than he had to. If he was a man of position, dignity demanded that in public he be swathed from neck to heel, regardless of Mesopotamian climate. If he got sick, he might consult not only a doctor, but also, and perhaps by preference, a magician or priest who would try to drive out the demon. (Rational medicine existed, but was inferior to the Greek; Persian kings would soon be importing Greek doctors.) Drama, properly speaking, did not exist; there were a few religious pageants of fixed content, mostly performed in the temples by and for the clergy. No doubt there was lyric poetry and choral music; what we know of it is cultic or in praise of the king; there is no trace of lyrics so poignant, powerful, or personal as the Greek. Rhetoric was nonexistent; geography, rudimentary; history was limited to brief chronicles, bare lists of kings, and brief reports of their wars and buildings; philosophy, to repetition of proverbs and laments about the vanity of life. There was no coherent rational inquiry of any extent. The intellectual scene was dominated by superstition, pseudolearning, and philology: lists of animals, minerals, and vegetables, omens and their significance, dreams and their interpretations, astrological observations and the events that followed them, endless texts for religious and magical ceremonies, interminable collections of proverbs, dictionaries, and dictionaries for dictionaries; all brute factual information, never an attempt to explain rationally *why*. Finally, these dismal documents were almost wholly in the hands of the courts, the scribal schools, and the temples; the average man was almost illiterate. The utensils he had to use were commonly lumpish and drab, and the city he lived in was mainly a collection of mud brick boxes. The only public buildings were palaces, military installations, and temples, at best ostentatious rather than elegant. The physical, as well as the intellectual, atmosphere was stifling.

THE DISSEMINATION AND STAGNATION OF GREEK CULTURE

The new Greek culture spread from Greece, through the colonies, around the Mediterranean and Black Sea basins. It first infiltrated and then, by Alexander and his successors, was imposed on Egypt and on the east as far as India. Above all it was appropriated by Rome and carried to the limits of the empire. But while Greek civilization thus gained the world, it lost its life. The Roman Empire reached its farthest limits under Trajan in 116; two centuries later, under Constantine, little was left of its culture save the shell. City assemblies had become moribund, the city magistracies and membership in the city senates were financial burdens imposed on the rich. Effective control of most cities was in the hands of overseers imposed by the emperors. The Roman voting assemblies were long gone and the powers of the senate itself would soon be reduced to municipal administration. The imperial government was of the ancient Near Eastern pattern: an absolute ruler installed by the army, and a circle of ministers who were his appointees. Citizen participation was practically nil. Criminal trials were frequently in the hands of royal officials and not open to the public. The accused, even if a citizen, might be tortured to obtain evidence; barbarous punishments were increasing. The professional, standing army was sharply distinct from the rest of the citizen body and only its members might bear arms. Some sexual liberty would last for another century and more, but the old close relationship between men and boys was gone. Most gymnasia were now secondary schools; the center for recreation was the bath and the habit of exercising was fast dying out. Gymnastic "games" were still staged, but only professionals competed and popular interest went to horse races. Rational medicine survived, but was rapidly sinking in a slough of fantastic remedies—baboon's blood, pigeon's dung, and anything else imagineable, all supposed to have peculiar "powers." Even doctors who rejected such superstition were often uncritical adherents of pretendedly "rational" theories, which made them more dangerous than diseases. Exorcism was thriving.

Even for the healthy, the range of possible pleasures was sharply reduced. Classical drama was dying, driven out by mimes and vaudeville. Lyric poetry was a literary antiquity. Literacy was still general, the works of classical literature were widely accessible, and the rhetorical tradition flourished, but philosophic discussion was fast giving way to preaching by missionaries of diverse oriental deities. Even the artifacts of daily life had become crude by comparison with the Athenian, and architecture was undergoing a transformation that would mirror the change of intellectual attitude, from the extrovert porches and colonnades of the classical world to the walled and domed chambers of Byzantine introspection.

Thus after 1100 years (800 B.C.–A.D. 300) the Greek revolution seemed to have run its course and in many fields ancient Near Eastern patterns, with more or less modification, had reappeared. They were easier to follow. It is easier to submit to a ruler than to participate in a democratic government, to bribe a judge than to persuade a jury, to pay for an army than to serve in one, to lounge in the baths than to exercise in the gymnasium, to watch sports than to participate, to hope for some magical cure than to practice a rational regimen, to laugh at vaudeville than to follow (let alone, reflect on) a tragedy, to believe and be saved than to analyze a philosophic argument and act on the consequences of the analysis. It was not only plagues, exhaustion of soil, forests, and mines, social conflict, military insubordination, and barbarian invasion that brought down classical culture; behind and beyond these were sloth and stupidity. Political and intellectual liberty require intelligence and hard work.

EMERGENCE OF THE WORLD RELIGIONS AS COUNTER CULTURES

Yet the new pattern of late imperial life which emerged about A.D. 300 as a result of all these factors, differed no less profoundly from that of the ancient Near East than from that of classical Greece. And the difference was not merely one of greater extent, wealth, and variety of techniques and of products, nor of the survival of many important elements of classical culture—the alphabet, literacy and much classical literature, the rhetorical, scientific, legal, and philosophical traditions, and so on. Such survivals of material, of techniques, and of intellectual traditions were undeniably important, but more important was something more difficult to define. Roughly one may call it a new orientation and say that the ancient Near East and the classical world were extrovert, late antiquity, introvert; the older cultures were this-worldly, late antiquity was mainly concerned about the invisible world (of the individual's "spiritual" life), the next world (that one would enter after death), and the world to come (after the last judgement).

Roughly, these statements are defensible, but enormous exceptions come to mind at once. What people were more concerned about the next world than the ancient Egyptians? What author is more introvert than Sappho? On the other hand, the Roman Empire did not survive by mere inertia. The endless wars and constant labor necessary to maintain it testify to the survival of this-worldly interests as major concerns of the culture. It would be naive to take religious literature at face value, even as evidence of the lives of the writers, to say nothing of the total life of the community.

But it can be said that a number of patterns of life—possibilities open to men—that had been comparatively rare and unimportant in the classical world, now became common and important, and these newly important patterns were in the main other-worldly. Most of them, too, involved membership in a religious organization other than the regular state cults. Whether one became a Christian, Jew, Manichaean, initiate of Mithras, or whatever, one commonly joined a private organization, consciously distinct from "the world" and "the government," more or less selective of the persons it would admit, to some extent secretive, a mutual benefit society, whose members could count on each other, or on their common fund, for assistance in crises or even in daily needs. Such new organizations, in effect, offered insurance, more needed as the empire became more troubled. But they also offered assurance—the assurance of being something (a Christian, a Jew, an initiate, or the like) and of belonging to something (the church, the synagogue, the brotherhood). Which of these services was more important?

Furthermore, the needs of these newly powerful organizations created a newly important set of careers—priest, monk, missionary, martyr, and so on. These offered new means for the expression of ancient ambitions, and also shaped new types of personality: The Roman aristocrat with a gift for administration and a genius for politics now became a bishop—Cyprian of Carthage or Ambrose of Milan; the brilliant rhetorician became a famous preacher and perhaps even a patriarch—John Chrysostom; the sharp-tongued Cynic became a monk—Jerome—or a wandering "fool in Christ"; the soldier with a subconscious need to die as a hero became a martyr; the Neoplatonist a theologian; and so on.

As the "Catholic" Church gradually distanced competitors and won over the vast majority of the population of the empire, a new world of careers within the Church was built up to match the career structure of the old, imperial world. At the same time, that old structure continued, and continued independent. Vast though the influence of the Church may have been, it never completely controlled the State. Vice versa, though emperors often made or broke patriarchs and sometimes dictated decisions to councils, the life of the Church—the life of the myriad Christian communities—was always beyond government control: The government never had the means of communication or the personnel to enforce its dictates.

CONSEQUENT PLURALISM OF WESTERN SOCIETY AND SURVIVAL OF THE POSSIBILITY OF RATIONAL INQUIRY

Thus if we look back from the court of Justinian, in 550, we can see that the last great achievement of ancient civilization was the development of these more or less extensive "countercultures"—Christianity, Judaism, Manichaeanism, and the various heretical sects. These institutionalized concerns with various forms of the spiritual life, presented men with a new set of careers and loyalties, thus increased the range of possible choice and, in this respect, of freedom, and, finally, constituted a social power capable of resisting both civil government and rational criticism. The resultant pluralism of western society has, until today, been the most important condition of individual liberty, of which a major element is the right to believe and practice nonsense.

Yet this last achievement of antiquity, important as it was, cannot be our conclusion. The ancient world did not issue merely in the barbaric kingdoms of the west, the imperial autocracies of Byzantium and Persia, and the institutionalized religions that offered refuge from the rulers of this world. There was a little leaven in the lump. If we compare the Constantinople of Justinian with the Babylon of Nabonidus we are at first struck by the similarities: absolute ruler, appointed ministers, bureaucracy, abstract, mostly symbolic, art, enormous endowed temples and a huge priesthood busy with ineffectual ceremonies and sterile speculations. But Babylon was sand, Byzantium was seed. Beneath its hieratic husk was a kernel, the art and literature of ancient Greece, and at their core the tradition of systematic inquiry, the habit of asking Why?, a child's question that would eventually break the bonds of the administrative and theological systems and launch mankind on a new and perpetual adventure, that of following rational investigation to its yet unknown conclusions.

FOR FURTHER READING

G. Childe, *What Happened in History*
C. Cochrane, *Christianity and Classical Culture*
H. Kitto, *The Greeks*
H. Saggs, *The Greatness that was Babylon*
W. Tarn and G. Griffith, *Hellenistic Civilization*, 3 ed.
T. Webster, *Life in Classical Athens*

PICTURE CREDITS

1 Stela of Eannatum, from Telloh. Photo Maurice Chuzeville. By courtesy of the Louvre Museum, Department of Oriental Antiquities. 2 Palette of Narmer, Cairo Museum. Photo Hirmer Fotoarchiv München. 3 The Nile in flood, private photograph. 4 "The Mosaic Casket of Ur." By courtesy of the Trustees of the British Museum. Museum photo. 5 The Lion Gate, Mycenae. Photo Alison Frantz. 6 The Ziggurat, Tchoga Zambil. Photo R. Ghirshman, by courtesy of E. Porada. 7 Fertility figurine from Jerusalem. By courtesy of Prof. N. Avigad of the Institute of Archeology of the Hebrew University, Jerusalem. 8 Aphrodite of the "Cnidian" type, Vatican Museum. Photo Columbia University slide collection. 9 Pharaoh Mycerinus and his Queen, from Giza. Courtesy, Museum of Fine Arts, Boston. Museum photo. 10 "The Anyvassos Kouros," National Museum, Athens. Photo Deutsches Archäologisches Institut, Athens, Neg. no. Nat. Mus. 4262. 11 Stela of Baal with thunder, from Ras Shamra. Photo Maurice Chuzeville. By courtesy of the Louvre Museum, Department of Oriental Antiquities. 12 Zeus hurling thunder, from Dodona. By courtesy of the Ehemals Staatliche Museen, Berlin, Antikenabteilung. Photo J. Luckert. 13 Seated goddess from Ras Shamra. Photo Maurice Chuzeville. By courtesy of the Louvre Museum, Department of Oriental Antiquities.

252 PICTURE CREDITS

14 "The Demeter of Cnidus." By courtesy of the Trustees of the British Museum. Museum photo. 15, 16, 17 Wall paintings from the tomb of Nakht, Thebes. Photos by the Egyptian Expedition, the Metropolitan Museum of Art, N.Y. 18 Tomb model of weavers, Cairo Museum. Photo by courtesy of the Metropolitan Museum of Art, N.Y. 19 Egyptian woman grinding meal, Florence, Archeological Museum. By courtesy of the Soprintendenza alle Antichità d'Etruria, Firenze. 20 Black figured Lekythos, women working wool. The Metropolitan Museum of Art, N.Y., Fletcher Fund, 1931. Museum photo. 21 Roman grain mill, Vatican Museum. Photo Deutsches Archaeologisches Institut, Rome, Inst. neg. 7170. 22 Olive harvest, black figure vase by the Antimenes painter. By courtesy of the Trustees of the British Museum. Museum photo. 23 Women drawing water, black figure hydria. The Metropolitan Museum of Art, N.Y., Rogers Fund, 1906. Museum photo. 24A Heterosexual dinner party, red figure kylix made by Hieron, painted by Makron, 490–480 B.C. The Metropolitan Museum of Art, Rogers Fund, 1920. Museum photo. 24B Homosexual dinner party, red figure kylix by the Marlay painter, 450–430 B.C. The Metropolitan Museum of Art, Rogers Fund, 1941. Museum photo. 25 Egyptian model fishing skiff, from the tomb of Meket-Re, Thebes. The Metropolitan Museum of Art, N.Y., Museum Excavations, supplemented by contribution of Edward S. Harkness and Rogers Fund, 1920. Museum photo. 26 Theseus and companions arriving at Delos, detail from the "François Vase" by Clitias, Florence. Photo Hirmer Fotoarchiv, München. 27 Relief showing Tiglath Pileser III besieging a city, from Nimrud. By courtesy of the Trustees of the British Museum. Museum photo. 28 Relief showing Ashurnasirpal II's camp, from Nimrud. By courtesy of the Trustees of the British Museum. Museum photo. 29 Troops of Ramses III on a hunting party, from Medinet Habu. Photo, Center of Documentation and Studies on Ancient Egypt, Cairo. 30 Persian royal guards, Persepolis, from F. Schmidt, *Persepolis* I, plate 50. By courtesy of the Oriental Institute, University of Chicago. 31 Gold ring from Mycenae. National Museum, Athens. Photo, Deutsches Archäologisches Institut, Athens, Neg. num. N.M. 4856. 32 Sarpedon carried by Thanatos and Hypnos, red figure crater by Euxitheos and Euphronios. The Metropolitan Museum of Art, N.Y., Bequest of Joseph H. Durkee, gift of Darius Ogden Mills, and gift of C. Ruxton Love, by exchange, 1972. Museum photo. 33 Ashurnasirpal II hunting lions, from Nimrud. By courtesy of the Trustees of the British Museum. Museum photo. 34 Cylinder seal showing Darius the Great hunting lions. By courtesy of the Trustees of the British Museum. Museum photo. 35 Footrace, black figure amphora. The Metropolitan Museum of Art, N.Y., Rogers Fund, 1914. Museum photo. 36 Ground plan of the mortuary temple of Ramses III at Medinet Habu. From U. Hölscher, *The Mortuary Temple of Ramses III*, III, ii, fig. 1. By courtesy of the Oriental Institute,

PICTURE CREDITS 253

University of Chicago. **37** Athens. The Acropolis from the southwest. Photo Alison Frantz. **38** Ground plan of the Parthenon. From D. Haynes, *An Historical Guide to the Sculptures of the Parthenon*, p. 18, fig. 6. By courtesy of the Trustees of the British Museum. Museum photo. **39** Gold stater of Croesus, King of Lydia. Confronting forequarters of lion and bull. Collection of the American Numismatic Society. Photo by courtesy of the Society. **40** Gold daric. Darius running with bow and spear. Collection of the Am. Numismatic Society. Photo by courtesy of the Society. **41–42** Stater of Aegina. Silver. Obverse, turtle; reverse, punch mark. Collection of the Am. Numismatic Society. Photo by courtesy of the Society. **43–44** Stater of Corinth. Silver. Obverse, head of Athena; reverse, Pegasus. Collection of the Am. Numismatic Society. Photo by courtesy of the Society. **45–46** Athenian tetradrachm. Silver. Obverse, head of Athena; reverse, owl. Collection of the Am. Numismatic Society. Photo by courtesy of the Society. **47** Cuneiform tablet with Aramaic docket, from Nippur. The University Museum, University of Pennsylvania, CBS R5160. Museum photo. **48** A section from the papyrus of Nebseny. British Museum no. 9900. By courtesy of the Trustees of the British Museum. Museum photo. **49** The Phoenician, Hebrew, and Greek alphabets. Drawing. **50** Limestone statue of a seated scribe, from Saqqarah. By courtesy of the Louvre Museum, Department of Egyptian Antiquities. Museum photo. **51** Boys being tutored, red figure kylix by Douris, from Cervetri. By courtesy of the Ehemals Staatliche Museen, Berlin. Museum photo. **52** Diorite head of Gudea, from Telloh. By courtesy of the Metropolitan Museum of Art, N.Y., Fletcher Fund, 1949. Museum photo. **53** Head of Alexander the Great, "the Azara Herm," from Tivoli, now in the Louvre. Photo Columbia University slide collection. **54** Head of Socrates. Bust from the Farnese collection, now Naples, National Museum, Inv. no. 6129. Photo Deutsches Archäologisches Institut, Rome, Inst. neg. 36.896. **55** Head of Euripides from the Farnese collection, now Naples, National Museum Inv. no. 6135. Photo Hirmer Fotoarchiv München. **56** Head of Cleopatra VII on a bronze coin from Egypt. Collection of the Am. Numismatic Society. Photo by courtesy of the Society. **57** Silver denarius with head of Augustus. Collection of the Am. Numismatic Society. Photo by courtesy of the Society. **58** Bronze coin of Alexandria showing Isis Pharia and the lighthouse, reign of Antoninus Pius. Collection of the Am. Numismatic Society. Photo by courtesy of the Society. **59** Bronze sestertius of Nero, showing Temple of Janus. Collection of the Am. Numismatic Society. Photo by courtesy of the Society. **60** The Roman aqueduct at Segovia, Spain. Photo Prof. Frank Brommer. **61** Model of ancient Rome. Museo della Civiltà Romana, Rome. Photo Deutsches Archäologisches Institut, Rome, Neg. No. 68.1042. **62** The Roman Theater at Timgad. Private photo. **63** The ruins of Timgad. Private photo. **64** Bronze sestertius of Nero, showing the port of Ostia. Collection of the Am. Numismatic

Society. Photo by courtesy of the Society. **65** Funerary stela of L. Erennius Praesens, Avignon, Museum Calvet. Photo by courtesy of the Museum. **66** Monument of M. Vergileus Eurysaces, Rome. Photo E. Bickerman. **67** Terracotta statuette of a gladiator, from Córdoba. Madrid, Museo Arqueológico Nacional. Photo by courtesy of the Museum. **68** Sleeping hermaphrodite, marble. From Rome. Museo Nazionale Inv. 1087. Photo Columbia University slide collection. **69** Mosaic with skeleton and motto, Rome, Museo Nazionale Inv. 1025. Photo Deutsches Archäologisches Institut, Rome, Inst. neg. 75.1296. **70** Scene from the Column of Trajan, Rome. Photo Deutsches Archäologisches Institut, Rome. Inst. neg. 41.1640. **71** Relief carved in a cliff, Naqsh-i-Rustam, Persia. A Roman emperor kneeling to a Persian king. Private photo. **72** Bronze sestertius of Nero, with his portrait. Collection of the Am. Numismatic Society. Photo by courtesy of the Society. **73** Bronze head of Trajan, from Ankara, Turkey. By courtesy of the Archaeological Museum of Ankara. Museum photo. **74** Coin of Diocletian, with his portrait. Collection of the Am. Numismatic Society. Photo by courtesy of the Society. **75** Colossal bronze head of Constantine (formerly identified as Constantius II). Rome. Palazzo dei Conservatori. Photo Deutsches Archäologisches Institut, Rome, Inst. neg. 59.1721. **76** Herm of Lucius Cecilius Iocundus, from Pompei. Naples, Museo Nazionale. Photo Alinari, Scala New York/ Florence. **77** Marble head of "Eutropius," from Ephesus. Vienna, Kunsthistorisches Museum. Photo by courtesy of the Museum. **78** Bronze head of a philosopher, from Anticythera. Athens, National Museum. Photo Alison Frantz. **79** Marble head of a priest (?), from Egypt, Berlin, Ehemals Staatliche Museen, Antiken Abteilung, Inv. 1810. Photo by courtesy of the Museum. **80** Mosaic from Tabarka, Tunisia, showing a country house. Museum of the Bardo, Tunis. Photo by courtesy of the Museum. **81** Reconstruction by E. Hébrard of the palace of Diocletian in Split, Jugoslavia. Old print. **82** Terracotta statuette of Isis nursing Horus. The Antiquarium of Herculaneum. Photo by courtesy of the Soprintendenza alle Antichità della Province di Napoli e Caserta. **83** Haematite amulet showing Egyptian gods on womb, in ouroboros. British Museum, G 440. By courtesy of the Trustees of the British Museum. Photo M. Smith. **84** Green jasper amulet with anguipede, B.M. G. 153. By courtesy of the Trustees of the British Museum. Photo M. Smith. **85** Haematite amulet with six-winged Moses, B.M. G. 470. By courtesy of the Trustees of the British Museum. Photo M. Smith. **86** Orange jasper amulet with crucifixion, B.M. G. 231. By courtesy of the Trustees of the British Museum. Photo M. Smith. **87** Inscribed limestone plaque from Medinet el Fayoum, Egypt; the Virgin nursing Jesus. By courtesy of the Staatliche Museen zu Berlin, D.D.R. Museum photo. **88–89** Gold coin (solidus) of Justinian. Obverse, the emperor; reverse, angel holding Christogram and orb with cross. Collection of the American Numismatic Society. Photos by courtesy of the Society. **90–91** Gold solidus of Heraclius. Obverse, Heraclius and sons; reverse, the Cross on a four-stepped pyramid. Collection of the American Numismatic Society. Photos by courtesy of the Society. **92** St. Sophia, Constantinople (Istanbul), interior, the nave from the west. Photo Columbia University slide collection. **93** St. Sophia, cross section. Photo Columbia University slide collection. **94** St. Sophia, exterior. Photo Columbia University slide collection.

MAP INDEX

The numbers refer to pages. This index is mainly intended to locate cities, territories, and minor items of physical geography. These are located in relation to the nearest term in heavy print, or major area, on the map on which they *first* occur. Knowledge of the general location of major items is presupposed, and for these reference is given only to the pages on which they are shown.

A

Abila (Seleucia) 136 in Transjordan
Abyssinia 18
Acragas 116 in Sicily
Actium 148 inset B
Adriatic Sea 92, 116, 136, 148, 186
Aegean Sea 18, 60, 78, 92, 116, 136, 148, 186
Afghanistan 116, 136
Africa (province) 148 in Tunisia
Akkad 18 S. of Assyria
Alalakh 18 in Syria, 60
Aleppo 18 in Syria
Alexandria 136 N. of Indian Ocean (two)
Alexandria (Alexandretta) 136 in Syria
Alexandria by Egypt 136, 148, 186
Alexandria (Herat) 136 in Afghanistan
Alexandria (Kandahar) 136 in Afghanistan
Alexandria (Khodzent) 136 E. of Aral Sea
Alexandria (Merv) 136 E. of Caspian Sea
Alexandria on the Helmand 136 in Afghanistan
Alexandria on the Indus 136
Alexandria on the Persian Gulf 136
Algeria 142
Alps, the 148
Amarna 60 in Egypt
Amman (Philadelphia) 136 in Transjordan
Anatolia 18, 60, 92, 116, 136
Ankara 60 in Anatolia
Antioch 136 in Anatolia
Antioch (Edessa) 136 in Syria
Antioch (Gerasa) 136 in Transjordan
Antioch on the Orontes 136 in Syria, 186
Apennine Mts. 148

Map Index

A

Aquileia 148 inset A
Arabia 18, 60, 78, 92, 116, 136, 186
Aral Sea 116, 136
Arcadia 116 inset
Armenia 92, 116, 148, 186
Arno R. 148 inset A
Ashur 18 in Assyria, 78
Asia Minor 60, 78, 116, 148, 186
Asia (province) 148, on W. coast of Asia Minor
Assyria 18, 60, 78, 92
Athens 60 inset, 92, 116, 136, 148, 186
Atlantic Ocean 148, 186
Azerbaijan 116 W. of Caspian Sea

B

Babylon 18 in Akkad, 60, 92, 116, 136
Babylonia 78 N.E. of Arabia
Bactria 116
Balearic Islands 148
Balkans, the 78, 116, 186
Belgium 148
Bethlehem 186 inset
Bithynia 116 in Anatolia, 136, 148
Black Sea 18, 60, 78, 92, 116, 136, 148, 186
Boghaskoy 60
Britain 186
Byblos 18 in Syria, 60
Byzantium 116 on Sea of Marmara, 186

C

Caesarea 148 inset C, 186
Cannae 148 inset A
Cappadocia 18 in Anatolia
Carchemish 92 in Syria
Caria 116 in Anatolia
Carthage 92 on N. African coast, 116, 136, 148, 186
Caspian Sea 18, 60, 78, 92, 116, 136, 148, 186
Çatal Huyuk 18 in Anatolia
Cataracts of the Nile, see First, etc.
Caucasus, the 92, 148
Chaironea 116 inset
Chalcedon 186 on Sea of Marmara
Cilicia 148 in Asia Minor
Cisalpine Gaul 148 inset A, 186
Cnossus 60 in Crete
Constantinople 186 on Sea of Marmara
Corinth 60 inset, 92, 116, 148
Corsica 148
Crete 60, 78, 148
Ctesiphon 186 on the Tigris
Cumae 92 in Italy
Cyprus, 18, 60, 78, 92, 116, 136, 148, 186
Cyrenaica 92 on N. African coast, 116, 136, 148, 186
Cyrene 186
Cythera 60 inset

D

Dacia 148 N. of the Danube, 186
Dalmatia 148, 186
Damascus 60 in Syria
Danube R. 92, 116, 136, 148, 186
Dead Sea 18 in Palestine, 92, 148, 186
Delos 116 inset
Delphi 92 inset A, 116, 148
Delta, the 18 N. of Egypt, 60
Diyala R. 18 S. of Assyria
Dneiper R. 116 N. of Black Sea, 136
Don R. 116 N. of Black Sea, 136

E

Ebro R. 92 in Spain
Ecbatana 116 in Media
Edessa (Antioch) 136 in Syria
Egypt 18, 60, 78, 92, 116, 136, 148, 186
Elam 18, 92, 116
Elea 116 in Italy
England 148
Enkomi 60 in Cyprus
Ephesus 186 on W. coast of Asia Minor
Epirus 116 N.W. of Greece
Eridu 18 S. of Sumer
Etruria 116 in Italy, 148
Euphrates R. 18 E. of Syria, 60, 78, 92, 116, 136, 148, 186

F

Fayyum, the 18 in Egypt, 148, 186
Fertile Crescent 60 from Palestine, through Syria and Assyria, to Babylon, 78, 92
First Cataract 18 in Egypt
Fourth Cataract 18 in Nubia
France 92, 148

G

Galatia 136 in Anatolia
Galilee 18 in Palestine, 148
Gaul (France) 148, 186 (Cisalpine Gaul, see Cisalpine; Narbonnese Gaul, see Narbonnese)
Gerasa (Antioch) 136 in Transjordan
Germany (ancient) 148
Greece 18, 60, 78, 116, 148, 186

H

Haimos Mts. 186 in Thrace
Halys R. 92 in Anatolia
Hebron 186 inset
Heliopolis 18 in Egypt
Hellespont 92 inset A, 148, 186
Herat 136 see Alexandria
Herculaneum 148 inset A
Hermus R. 92 inset A
Himera 116 in Sicily
Hittites 60 in Anatolia

I

Indian Ocean 116, 136
Indus R. 116 in Pakistan, 136
Ionia 78 W. coast of Asia Minor, 92, 116
Iran 18, 136
Ireland 186
Isauria 186 in Asia Minor
Israel (ancient) 78 N. of Jerusalem, 92
Issus 116 in Anatolia
Isthmus of Suez 18 N.E. of Egypt
Italy 92, 116, 186
Ithaca 78 in Greece

J

Jabneh 148 inset C
Jericho 18 in Palestine
Jerusalem 78, 92, 116, 148, 186
Jordan R. 92 inset A, 148, 186
Judah 78 S. of Jerusalem, 92
Judea 92 inset A, 116

K

Kandahar 136 see Alexandria
Karnak 18 in Egypt
Khodzent 136 see Alexandria
Kish 18 in Akkad

L

Lagash 18 in Sumer
Latium 148 inset A
Lesbos 92 inset A
Lydia 92 inset A, 116
Lyons 148 in Gaul

M

Macedon 116 N. of Grece, 136, 148
Marathon 116 inset
Mari 18 E. of Syria
Meander R. 92 inset A
Media, 92, 116, 136
Mediterranean Sea 18, 60, 78, 92, 116, 136, 148, 186
Megara 116 inset
Megiddo 92 inset B
Memphis 18 in Egypt, 60
Merv 138 see Alexandria
Mesopotamia 18 W. of Assyria, 60, 78, 92, 116, 136, 148, 186
Milan 186 N. of Italy
Miletus 116 inset
Mitanni 60 in Mesopotamia
Moesia 148 S. of the Danube
Morocco 148
Mt. Mycale 116 inset
Mycenae 60 inset, 78

N

Nabateans 148 S.E. of Palestine
Narbonne 148 in S. France
Narbonnese Gaul 148 in S. France
Nicaea 186 S. of Sea of Marmara
Nicomedia 186 on Sea of Marmara
Nile R. 18, 60, 78, 92, 116, 136
Nineveh 60 in Assyria, 92, 186
Nippur 18 S. of Akkad
Noricum 148 S. of the Danube
Nubia 18 S. of Egypt

O

Olympia 92 inset A
Opis 136 see Seleucia
Oxus R. 136 S.E. of Aral Sea

P

Paestum 116 in Italy
Pakistan 116
Palestine 18 S. of Syria, 60, 92, 116, 136, 148, 186
Pannonia 148 at Danube bend, 186
Panticapaeum 116 N. shore of Black Sea
Paros 92 inset A
Pasargadae 116 in Persia
Peloponnese, the 60 inset, 78
Pergamum 136 E. of Aegean Sea, 148
Persepolis 116 in Persia
Persia 92, 116, 148, 186
Persian Gulf 18, 60, 78, 92, 116, 136
Pharsalus 148 inset B
Philadelphia (Amman) 136 in Transjordan
Philippi 148 in Thrace
Phoenicia 92 inset B
Phrygia 148
Plataea 116 inset
Po R. 92 N. of Italy, 116, 136, 148
Pompeii 148 inset A
Pontus 116 in Anatolia, 136, 148
Punt 18 N.E. of Abyssinia
Pylos 60 inset

R

Raetia 148
Red Sea 18, 60, 78, 92, 116, 136
Rhine R. 148 in Germany, 186
Rhodes 78 S.W. of Asia Minor, 116, 136, 148
Rhone R. 92 in S. France
Rome 92 in Italy, 116, 136, 148, 186
Rubicon R. 148 inset A
Russia 148

S

Sahara, the 148, 186
Saïs 92 in Egypt
Salamis 116 inset
Samnium 148 inset A
Samos 116 inset
Sardinia 148
Scotland 148, 186

Sea of Marmara 92 inset A, 116
Second Cataract 18 in Nubia
Seleucia 136 in Anatolia (two)
Seleucia (Abila) 136 in Transjordan
Seleucia (Opis) 136 in Mesopotamia
Seleucia (Susa) 136 N. of Persian Gulf
Selinus 116 in Sicily
Sicily 92, 116, 148
Sinai 18 E. of Egypt, 60, 78, 148
Sogdiana 116
Spain 92, 148, 186
Sparta 92 inset A, 116, 136, 148
Suez, *see* Isthmus of Suez
Sumer 18 S. of Akkad
Susa 18 in Elam, 60, 116, 136 (*see* Seleucia)
Switzerland 148
Syracuse 116 in Sicily, 136
Syria 18, 60, 78, 92, 116, 136, 148, 186

T

Tagus R. 92 in Spain
Taima 92 in Arabia
Tell el Amarna 18 in Egypt
Thebes in Egypt 18, 60
Thebes in Greece 60 inset, 116
Thessalonika 186 on N. coast of Aegean Sea
Third Cataract 18 in Nubia
Thrace 116 W. of Black Sea, 136, 148, 186
Tiber R. 148 inset A

Tigris R. 18 in Assyria, 60, 78, 92, 116, 136, 148, 186
Transjordan 60 E. of Palestine, 148, 186
Trasimene 148 inset A
Trevia R. 148 inset A
Tripolitania 148 on N. African coast, 186
Troy 60 W. coast of Asia Minor
Tunisia 148
Turkestan 116 E. of Caspian Sea
Turkey 148
Tuscany 92
Tyre 92 inset B, 116
Tyrins 60 inset
Tyrrhenian Sea 92, 148

U

Ugarit 18 in Syria, 60
Ur 18 S. of Sumer
Urartu 92 S. of Armenia
Uruk 18 S. of Sumer
Uzbekistan 116 S.E. of Aral Sea

V

Volga R. 116 N. of Caspian Sea, 136

W

Wales 148

Y

Yarmuk R. 186 inset
York 186 in Britain

SUBJECT INDEX

Numbers following the word "Photo" are the numbers of the photographs. All other numbers are those of pages.

A

abortion, 226
Abraham, 60, 80f.
Abrasax, *Photo 84*
Absalom, 80
Academy, Platonic, 132, 202, 207
accounting, 16
Achilles, 80
Acragas, 120
Acropolis, the, 246
  Photo 37
Actium, battle, 156, 164
Acts of the Apostles, 179
Adapa-Oannes, 39
adultery, punishment, 222
Aegean, the, 65, 77, 80, 86, 96
Aegina, coinage
  Photos 41, 42
Aeschines, 223
Aeschylus, 114, 126, 245

Aesop, 223
Afghanistan, 134
Africa, 86, 146, 166, 187, 195, 199, 205
  circumnavigation, 102
  country house in, *Photo 80*
afterlife, 44, 46, 49ff., 56, 238
Agade, 32
Agamemnon, 66
agriculture, 19–21, 225
  and religion, 220
  Bronze Age, 25, 35, 43f., 46, 56
  early Iron, 84
  Greek, 98, 106
  hellenistic, 143f
  Punic, 160
  Roman, 157, 171
  Photos 15–17, 22, 80
Agrippa, M., 159
Ahura Mazda, 115
Ajax, 80
Akiba, 181

Subject Index 261

Akkad, Akkadians, and Akkadian, 16, 32–39, 62
Alalakh, 37
Alans, 184, 198
Alasia, 66f.
alchemy, 143
Aleppo, 36
Alexander, bishop of Alexandria, 195
Alexander of Macedon, 130, 134, 137, 143, 230, 237, 247
   Photo 53
Alexander (Severus), 164, 184f., 187
Alexandria by Egypt, 130, 135, 141, 195, 220
   lighthouse, 143; *Photo 58*
   Patriarch, 202, 209
alphabet, 64f., 86
   Photos 47, 49
Alps, annexed by Rome, 164f.
Amarna, 57, 221
   Amarna Age, 42, 58
Amasis of Egypt, 105, 110
amber, 66
Ambrose of Milan, 249
Amenhotep III, 55
Ammianus Marcellinus, 212
Ammonites, 81
Amon, 69f., 72, 74
Amos, 90, 96ff.
amphitheater(s), 159, 171, 173, 211
   See also Colosseum
amulets, 215
   Photos 83–86
anarchy, impossibility of, 23
Anath, 60, 97
Anatolia, 91
ancient civilization, characteristics of, 218–241
ancient history, what happened in, 242–250
ancient world, emptiness 219
angels, *Photo 88*
animals, 16, 19ff., 160, 222f., 243
   See also donkeys; horses; lions; agriculture; hunting; etc.
Antioch, Patriarch of, 209
Antiochus III, 146f., 150, 229
Antoninus Pius, 164, 170
Antony (Mark), 146, 156
Antony, Saint, 196
Anubis, *Photo 83*
Anyvassos, youth from, *Photo 10*
Aphrodite, hymn to, 87
   statue of, *Photo 8*
Apollo, 87, 93, 96, 105, 121, 202, 216
Apollonius Rhodius, 138
Appian, 164, 174
Apuleius, 164, 174

aqueducts, 146, 158f., 171
   Photos, 60, 61
Aquileia, founded, 153
Arabia, 77, 81, 103, 109
   Roman province, 164, 169
Arabs, 81, 184, 200
Aramaeans, 76f.
Aramaic language, 81, 115, 197
   Photo 47
Arcadian League, established, 130f.
arch, use of, 158, 226
   Photos 60, 63, 92–94
Archilochus of Paros, 102, 105
Archimedes, 138, 143, 227
architecture
   Athenian, 123f.
   Doric, 120
   Egyptian, 48, 53
   Mycenaean 66
   Roman, 158ff., 173ff., 248
   Sumerian, 27
   Photos 5, 6, 23, 27, 36–38, 58, 59–64, 66, 80, 81, 92–94
archives, 37
Argos, 67
Arinna, 73
Aristarchus of Samos, 138, 143
Aristophanes, 95, 114, 126, 245
Aristotle, 130, 133, 212, 225, 227
Arius and Arianism, 195, 207
Armenia, 90, 109, 146, 164, 187, 207, 210
armies, 222, 230
   Akkadian and Sumerian, 31f.
   Assyrian, 78, 99, 101
   Egyptian, 58, 61f.
   Greek, 106, 120, 122, 245
   Persian, 115
   private, 202
   Roman, republican, 151f., 154f.
      Caesar's, 156
      Augustus', 163, 165
      early empire, 169f., 185, 187
      reorganization of, 284–337 A.D., 188f.
      late empire, 197–200, 205, 247
   Photos 1, 4, 27–32, 70
Arrian, 164, 174
art
   Assyrian, 85, 99
   Egyptian, 103
   Greco-Roman, 173
   Greek, 94
   Persian, 117
   Roman, 158f., 211
   See also painting; portraiture; sculpture
Artaxerxes II, 129
artifacts, 246, 248
Asa of Judah, 76, 97
asceticism, 107, 215f.
Asclepius, 132, 216

262 Subject Index

Ashera, 97
Ashur, city state, 16, 78
Ashurbanipal of Assyria, 90, 99, 102
Ashurnasirpal II of Assyria, *Photo 33*
Asia, province, 146, 153
Asia Minor, 77, 90, 117, 141, 164f., 184, 200, 210
asses (quadruped). *See* donkeys
Assyria, 16, 26, 33, 36, 76–79, 85–90, 99–102
    Photos 27, 28, 33
astrology and astronomy, 143, 176, 240, 246
Astyages of Media, 114
Athanasius, 196
Athena, 67, 93
    Photos 43, 45
Athens
    culture, 93, 102, 105, 107, 123–127, 245f.
    foundation, 65
    political history, 67, 108f., 114, 120–123, 127–131, 146f., 153
    Photos 20, 22–24B, 26, 32, 35, 37, 38, 45f., 51, 54, 55
athletics, 93, 233
    Photo 35
Attica, size, 107
Attis, 176
Atum, 73
Augustine, 87, 202, 206, 213f., 216
Augustus (= Octavius = Caesar Octavian), 146, 156, 163–169
    Photo 57
Aurelian, 184, 187
Avars, 184, 199f.

B

Baal, 59, 97
    Photo 11
Babel, tower, 27
babies
    baptism, 209
    sacrifice, 226
    sale, 140
Babylon, 27, 33–36, 62, 65, 77, 81, 90, 99, 101ff., 109, 134, 246f., 250
Bactria, taken by Alexander, 130
Balearic Islands, 146, 153
Balkans, looted by Ostrogoths, 184
bandits, increase, 205
banking, origins, 26, 141
baptism, infant, 209
bar Kosiba, revolt, 164, 181
barbarians, 189, 198f., 206
    Photo 70
barbarization, of later Roman Empire, 214
barbers, 156
barley, 35, 46

barter, 47
basalt, 26
basilicas, 211
bathing and baths, 94, 171, 173, 204, 211f., 224, 233
    Photos 61, 63
bathrooms, 46
battering ram, 76, 89
    Photo 27
Bau, 73
beauty, in Greek culture, 86f., 246
beer, 46
Belgium, Caesar's conquests in, 146, 155
bellows, 42
ben Zakkai, Yohanan, 164, 181
Berossus, 138, 144
Bible, New Testament 180
    Old Testament, 60, 80ff., 111f., 130, 180
biography, 76
bishops, 180, 194, 204, 209
Bithynia, 141, 146, 155
Black Sea, 86, 96
bleeding, practice, 143
boats, 16, 28
    See also shipping
    Photos 25, 26, 64
body, the, in Greek culture, 93f.
    Photos 8, 10, 12, 24A, 35, 68
books, 240
bourgeois, Roman, 152f., 166, 170
    Photo 76
bows, 32, 58, 61, 238
boys, careers, 239
"bread and circuses," 159
breeches, dissemination, 211
bridges, Roman, 171
Britain, 164, 184
bronze, 26, 29, 46f., 144
Bronze Age, 26–74, 79
brotherhood of man, 175
Buddha, 144, 208
building, Roman, 171
Bulgars, 184, 199f.
bull-fighting, 159
bureaucracy, hellenistic. 142; Roman, 190ff., 204
Byblos, 42, 47, 54, 59, 73
Byzantium, 192
    See also Constantinople

C

Caesar, Julius, 146, 155ff., 160
Caesar, Octavian. *See* Augustus
calendar, 160
Cambyses of Persia, 113f.
camels, 64, 76f.
Cannae, battle, 150
capitalism, **35**
capitals, away from cities, 221

Subject Index 263

Capitol, the, of Rome, *Photo 61*
Cappadocia, 26, 36
Caracalla, 164, 170f., 175, 185
caravans, 26, 64
Carchemish, battle, 102
careers, religious, 249
Carians, 131
Carinus, 184f.
Carthage, 86, 91, 114, 120, 131, 146, 150, 153, 184, 198, 202
Çatal Huyuk, 16, 21
"Catholic" (Church), meaning of, 181
Cato, 146, 157
cats, 224
Catullus, 146, 157
causation, 6f., 13, 119, 244
cedar wood, 47
Celestinus I, Pope, 206
celibacy, of clergy, 204
Celts, 141, 150. *See also* Galatians
cement, Roman, 146, 160
cereals, cultivated, 16, 20f.
Chaironea, battle, 130, 134
Chalcedon, Council, 202, 209f.
Chaldeans, invasion of Babylonia, 77
charity
 classical vs. Christian, 203
 to cities, 187, 220
chariot(s), 58, 61f., 173, 211, 238
 Photo 4
cheese, 223
chemistry, 225
childbirth, 222, 224
children, 175, 222f., 226, 239
"children of Israel," 81
China, 16, 202
Chnum, *Photo 83*
Christianity, 176
 beginnings, 179
 characteristics, 194, 206, 212, 235, 249f.
 competitors, 208
 development and organization, 180, 182, 193–196, 202, 204, 206–209, 211, 213f., 216
 persecuted, 180, 184, 193
 persecuting, 207f.
Christology, controversy, 210
church/state, dichotomy, 195, 217, 249
church/world antithesis, 216f.
churches
 buildings, 193, 211f.
 wealth of, 203
 Photos 92–94
Cicero, 146, 157f., 161, 238
Cilicia, 109, 146, 153
Cimmerians, 90, 101f.
circumcision, 81, 180
circuses, 159, 171, 173
cisterns, 22, 58, **64**

cities
 beginnings, 21
 characteristics, 67, 79, 83ff., 144, 197, 219ff., 232f.
 Greek and hellenistic, 96, 140, 142, 144
 late Bronze–early Iron, 77, 84f.
 planning, 96
 Rome and Roman, 147, 158, 166, 170ff., 187f., 201, 203f., 247
 Sumerian, 27
 Photos 37, 61, 63
citizenship
 Athenian, 109, 245
 Roman, 149f., 154, 170
city-country relations, 197, 220
"city of God," the, 213, 221
city states, described, 84
civilization, ancient
 characteristics, 218–241
 development, 243f.
classes, distinctions and conflict, 153f., 176, 191, 221
classical culture, survival, 211–214, 248
Claudius, 159, 164
cleanliness, 171, 211
Cleopatra VII, 6f., 146, 156
 Photo 56
clothing, 227, 246
Clovis, conversion, 207
Cnidus, Demeter of, *Photo 14*
codex, form of book, 240
coinage, 103, 115, 122, 143, 187, 189, 211, 228
 Photos 39–46, 56–59, 64, 72, 74, 88–91
colonies
 Greek, 90, 95f., 122
 hellenistic, 140
 Roman, 151, 170
colonnades, 219
Colosseum, 159
 Photo 61
combat, *Photo 31*
comedy, 139, 157
Commodus, 164, 170
communications, 228f., 232
 with gods, 236f.
concert halls, 233
Condorcet, 3
Constantine, 184f., 188f., 193, 195, 197, 202f.
 Photo 75
Constantine, age of, 247
Constantinople, 184, 192, 197, 199, 202, 204, 209, 216, 250
 Council, 202
 Patriarch, 209
 St. Sophia, *Photos 92–94*
Constantius II, 209
 Photo 75 (?)

264 SUBJECT INDEX

constitutional law, Greek, 93
contraception, 226
copper, 16, 21, 26, 29, 37, 42, 46f., 61, 66
Corinth, 65, 104, 122, 146, 153
    Photos 43, 44
cotton, 144, 230
countryside, 197, 219f.
    Photo 80
courtyards, 219
covenant at Sinai, 82
Crete, 58, 65f., 77, 146, 153
Croesus of Lydia, 104, 113f.
    Photo 39
"Cross, the true," 216
    Photo 91
crucifixion, the, 179f., Photo 86
Cumae, 90, 96
cuneiform, 28
    Photo 47
cures, miraculous, 216
Cynics and Cynicism, 139, 174, 196f., 212
Cyprian of Carthage, 249
Cyprus, 37, 61, 65f., 77, 86, 91, 110, 164, 181
Cyrene and Cyrenaica, 96, 109, 113f., 117, 146, 153, 164, 181, 200
Cyril of Alexandria, 210
Cyrus the Great of Persia, 102, 113f.
Cyrus "the Younger," 129

D

Dacia, 164, 169, 184, 188
    Photo 70
daily round, 233
Dalmatia, 164f., 199
Damascus, 101
Danube frontier, 198
Darius I the Great, 113ff., 120
    Photos 34, 40
Darius III, 130, 134
"dark age," of Greece, 68
David, 76, 80f., 83
deacons, 180
dead, the, 44
Death, deity, Photo 32
Decius, persecution of Christians, 184, 193
decorum, 167
deforestation, 189, 212
deification, 49ff., 167, 173
Delian League, 113, 120f., 123
Delos, 121
Delphi, 93, 96, 105, 153
Demeter, Photo 14
democracy, 14, 108, 121, 127f., 152
Democritus, 114, 125
demons, 215, 234
Demosthenes, 130, 132, 134
Deuteronomic school, 110f.

Deuteronomy, 102, 110, 112
"diaspora," 111
dictionaries, 246
Digests, Justinianic, 162
Dio Cassius, 14, 174, 185
Diocletian, 184f., 188ff., 193
    Photos 74, 81
Diogenes, 130, 139
Dionysius I, tyrant of Syracuse, 131
diseases
    of crops, 225
    of men. See medicine
divination, 37, 70, 84, 223, 236f.
doctors, Greek 246
dogs, 19f.
Domitian, 164, 169
donatives, Augustus', 166
donkeys, 26, 31f. Photo 21
Dorians. See Greece; invasions; culture
Draco, 102
drama, Greek, 126, 245, 248
    Photos 55, 62
dreams, 237, 246

E

Eannatum of Lagash, Photo 1
Ecbatana, 115, 130, 134
ecology. See environment
economy
    ancient, 103, 222–230
    Egyptian, 46
    Greek, 96, 104, 108, 121, 123, 132
    hellenistic, 137, 140f.
    Roman, republic, 151ff., 155, 158
        early empire, 171, 187
        late empire, 189, 197, 203–206
Edomites, 81
education, 222f., 239
    Bronze Age, 29, 37f., 53
    Greek, 94, 107, 124
    hellenistic, 144 n. 1
    Roman, 172f., 212ff.
Egypt, 36, 41–57, 237f.
    agriculture and economy, 43, 46, 143
    art and culture, 19, 44–51, 53f., 56, 103f., 140, 147, 160, 176, 237f.
    geography, 41ff.
    Jews and Christians, 164, 181, 195f., 202, 210
    political and military history
        Bronze Age, 42, 45, 47, 51f., 54–57, 60, 62, 76ff.
        Iron Age, 81, 90, 99, 101f., 109f.
        Persian period, 113f., 130f., 184, 200
        hellenistic, 134ff.
        Roman, 156, 166, 184, 187f., 200, 202
    Photos 2, 3, 9, 15–19, 25, 29, 36, 48, 50, 58, 79, 82, 83
El, 97

Elagabalus, 164
Elam, 32, 90, 99, 102, 115
    Photo 6
Elamite writing, 36
elegance, Greek, 123
Eleusis, mysteries, 51
Elijah, 97
Elisha, 97
emmer, 144
emperor(s), Roman, in general, 156, 169f., 192, 198, 214
empire, as a governmental form, 16, 230
enamels, 211
engineering, 226
Enkidu, 23
Enlil, 69
entertainment, 173, 224, 232f., 246, 248
    Photos 24A, 24B, 35, 55, 62, 67, 68
environment, made over by man, 244
Ephesus, citizen of, *Photo 77*
    Council, 202, 210
Epictetus, 164, 174, 212
Epicurus and Epicureanism, 138, 139, 157
    Photo 69
Epirus, 131
eponymous ancestors, 81
"equestrians," Roman, 152, 166
Eratosthenes, 138, 143
erosion, 189
Esarhaddon of Assyria, 90, 99
Essenes, 178, 181
Ethiopia, conversion, 207
Etruscans, 103, 131, 150, 159
Euclid, 138, 143
eunuchs, 192
Euripides, 114, 126, 245
    Photo 55
Eusebius of Caesarea, 202, 213
exchange, bill of, 26
    media of. *See* barley; copper; gold; silver
exercise, 94
Exodus, 145, 227
exorcism, 215, 247
experimentation, 86, 214f.
exploration, 86
Ezekiel, 102, 105, 110, 112

F

fabrics, 104, 223
faïence, 66
family coherence, 225
farmers, tenant, 176, 205
Fertile Crescent, 76f., 91
fertility, *Photo 7*
fertilizer, 225
fire signals, 115
fires, in Roman cities, 172

fish, trade in, 229
fishing, *Photos 17, 25*
"five good emperors," the, 164
Flavian dynasty, 164, 169
flint, 46
food, 20, 160, 211, 220, 223, 229
    Egyptian, 46
    Greek, 107, 122
    hellenistic, 139
    Roman, 154, 166, 172
    Sumerian, 25
    Photos 15–17, 19, 21–25, 28, 29, 65, 66, 80
"fools in Christ," 215f., 249
fortifications, 16, 29, 55, 188, 220f.
    of Athens, 122
    of Constantinople, 199
    of Rome, 188
    Photos 27, 70
forums, Roman, 171
    Photo 61
fowling, *Photo 17*
France, 96, 146, 155, 202, 207
freedom, 245, 248
funerary practices
    Egyptian, 44
    hellenistic, *Photo 65*
    Roman, *Photo 66*

G

Gaius (Caligula), 164, 229
Galatians, 138, 141
Galilee, 178
Gallienus, 193
"games" (Olympic, etc.), 93, 116, 169, 211, 247
    Photo 35
Gaugamela, battle, 130, 134
Gaul, 184, 188, 198, 205
    See also Narbonnese Gaul
Genesis, 79
    Genesis to II Kings, 80, 82
geography, 245f.
Germany, 146, 155, 164f.
Geta, 164
Gilgamesh, 39, 87
girls, 222, 239
gladiators and gladiatorial shows, 159, 173, 194, 211
    Photo 67
glass, 104, 146, 160, 230
    windows, 172
globe, *Photo 88*
God, the Father, 195
    hates copulation, 217
gods, 69–74, 97, 195, 217, 234, 236f.
    Photos 7, 8, 11–14, 32, 53, 56–58, 73–75, 82–87
gold, 47

266 SUBJECT INDEX

goldsmiths, 139
good life, how conceived, 139
Gospels, 164, 179, 202, 214
Goths, 184, 187f., 199, 206f.
government, 23f., 91, 142f., 221, 229f.
   Assyrian, 78, 99
   Babylonian, 246
   Egyptian, 51
   Greek, 96, 104f., 106, 108, 123, 127f., 245
   Persian, 115
   Ptolemaic, 140
   Roman, republican, 151ff., 155, 167
     imperial, 166–173, 190ff., 195, 197, 203, 247
Gracchi, 146, 154
grain, processing, *Photos 16, 19, 21, 66*
   trade, 95, 104, 108, 166, 172, 220, 229, 205
   Photos 64, 66
   See also barley; emmer; wheat
grapes, 46
Gratian, 198
Greece, 65, 76, 95
   agriculture and economy, 85f., 95, 104, 132
   invasions, political history and government, 66, 76f., 81, 90f., 106, 129, 138
   Photos 20, 22, 23, 45, 46
   See also cities' names
Greek culture and religion, 65, 82, 86, 93–96, 98, 103, 105f., 125, 140, 142, 237–240, 245, 247f., 250
   Photos 5, 8, 10, 12, 14, 24, 31, 32, 35, 37, 38, 51, 54, 55
Greek colonization, emigration, diaspora, 80, 96, 130, 132, 137, 150
   See also colonization
   Photo 26, 58, 65
Greek, language, 67, 86, 142–145, 197, 202
   Photo 49
"Greek," meaning of term, 177
Gregory of Nyssa, 87
Gudea of Lagash, *Photo 52*
gymnasium, 94, 173, 233, 245, 247

H

Hadrian, 164, 170
Hammurabi of Babylon, 16, 33ff.
Hannibal, 146, 150
Haran, 73, 109
harbors, Roman, 172
   Photo 64
Harpocrates, 176
Hatshepsut, 47
hay, discovered, 189
heating, central, 211
Hebat, 73
Hebrew, 59, 81
   Photo 49

Helena, mother of Constantine, 193, 216
Helios, 141
hellenization and hellenistic culture, 131, 141–145, 156
   Photos 14, 56, 58, 65, 78, 82f.
   hellenized states, 131, 141
Hellespont, 96, 108
helots, 106
Heraclitus, 119
Heraclius, 184, 200, 202
   Photo 90
Herculaneum, 174
Hercules, children of, 81
heretics and heresies, 195f., 202, 210
hermits, 196
Herod the Great, 165, 177f.
Herodotus, 114, 126f., 245f.
heroes, cults of, 93
"heroic" cultural elements, 76, 79f., 83
Hesiod, 90, 98
heterosexuality, in Greece, 94f.
   Photo 24A
hieroglyphs, 45
   Photos 2, 48
Hillel, 181
Himera, battle, 114, 120
Hippocrates, 114, 125
historiography, 244, 246
   Christian, 213
   Greek, 126f., 245
   Hebrew, 76, 126
   hellenistic, 144
   Roman, 174, 212
history
   ancient, 11ff., 75, 97, 218
   divisions and varieties, 10, 75, 243f.
   Marxist, 4, 7
   nature and functions, 1–8, 10–15, 19, 117
Hittites, 36, 58, 61, 63f., 76f.
holidays, Roman, 166
Holland, 16, 146, 155
Homer and Homeric poems, 79f., 83, 87, 90, 246
homosexuality, 94f., 22, 226
   Photos 24B, 68
honestiores, 176
honey, 226
honor, concern for, 85, 93
hoplites, 90f.
Horace, 164, 168
horses, 61f.
   Photo 28, 44
Horus, 73
   Photo 82
Hosea, 90, 97
hospitals, 225
housing, 160, 172, 219
humiliores, 176

SUBJECT INDEX

Huns, 184, 199
hunting, 19f., 223f.
  Photos 29, 33, 34
Hyksos, 42, 55, 58

I

Iao. *See* Yahweh
Ice Age, 16
Ictinus, 114
Ikhnaton, 42, 56ff., 221
Iliad, 90
imperator, 156
imperial council, 192
incense, 103, 229
India, 156
individuals and individualism, 85, 105, 119
Indus Valley, 16, 113, 117, 130, 135
infanticide, in population control, 226
inquiry, systematic, 250
insects, 225
"intelligence" (espionage), 115
intolerance, religious, 111f., 194, 207
introspection, 217
invasions, barbarian
  of Roman empire, 187, 198f., 200, 206
  of 1200–900 B.C., 75, 77, 79, 247
Ionian coast, 114, 122
Ireland and the Irish, 16, 207
iron, 58, 64, 84, 144
Iron Age, 75–77, 80, 84f., 91
irrigation, Egyptian, 25, 43, 56, 171
Isaac, 81
Isaiah 40–55, 102, 112
Isaurians, 199
Ishmaelites, 81
Ishtar, 62
Isis, 176
  Photos 58, 82, 83
Isocrates, 130, 133
Israel and Israelites, 76f., 81ff., 90, 97ff., 101
Issus, battle, 130, 134
Italy, 86, 96, 137, 146, 150, 184, 198f.
ivory, 104

J

Jabneh, 164, 181
Jacob, 80f.
Janus, temple of, *Photo 59*
Jeremiah, 102, 110
Jericho, 16, 21f.
Jerome, 211, 249
Jerusalem, 83, 102, 118, 164, 176, 178, 209, 216, 220
  Photo 7
Jesus, 73, 164, 176, 178f., 195, 208, 210
  Photos 86f.
"Jew," meaning of term, 177

jewels, 172
Jewish revolts, 164, 181, 202
Job, Book of, chapters 3–26, 118
John Chrysostom, 249
John "the Baptist," 178
Jonathan, son of Saul, 83
Joshua, 82
Josiah of Judah, 102, 110
Judah, 76
Judaism
  history, 110, 118, 177f., 180ff., 208
  origin and characteristics, 111, 177f., 235, 249f.
  varieties, 177f., 181
  Photos 84–86
Judas "Maccabeus," 177
Judea and Judeans, 105, 110, 112, 164
Julian the Apostate, 184, 205, 209
Julio-Claudian dynasty, 169
Julius Caesar. *See* Caesar, Julius
Juno, 173
Jupiter, 173
jurisprudence, Roman, 161f.
justice, in Greek and Israelite religion, 98
Justinian, 132, 184, 199, 202, 207, 211f., 250
  Photo 89
Juvenal, 164, 174, 231

K

Karnak, 55
kingdom, the, of a god, 115
kingdoms, hellenistic, 140
Kish, 32
knives, with flint blades, 16
Knossus, 66

L

labor 24, 48, 56, 205, 222
  Photos 15–20, 22, 23, 25, 28, 30
Lagash, 31, 73
  Photos 1, 52
lamps, 233
land
  abandonment, 196, 201f.
  ownership, 142, 152, 154, 191f., 203
lapis lazuli, 26, 229
Latin, language and literature, 157, 192, 213
  See also Rome; literature
Latium and Latins, 146, 150
latrines, public, 171
law(s), 16, 104, 110, 221, 232
  Bronze Age, 30, 34, 59
  Greek, 96, 105, 107, 122, 141, 221
  Jewish, 102, 110, 161, 182
    Photo 85
  Persian, 161
  Roman, 161f., 194, 212, 214

SUBJECT INDEX

lead poisoning, 172, 224
leisure, 232f.
Leo, Pope, 210
Lepidus, 156
lesbianism, 106
letters, to the dead, 50
Leuctra, battle, 130
libraries, 99, 141, 173, 211
Libyans, in Egypt, 78
Licinius, 184
life, 242
  expectancy, 19, 224
lighthouse(s), 143, 211
lighting, artificial, 233f.
Lion Gate, of Mycenae, 66
  Photo 5
lions, 31, 223
  Photos 5, 23, 33, 34
literacy, 30, 64f., 247
literature
  ancient Near Eastern, 79, 99
  Greek, 126, 145
  hellenistic, 144
  Roman, 157, 168, 174
Livy, 164, 168
Lombards, 184
"Lord," the, 178
loyalty, to cities, 220
Lucian, 164, 174
Lucretius, 146, 157
Lycurgus, 107
Lydia and Lydians, 101ff., 109f.
  Photo 39
lyric poetry, 105f., 126, 248
Lysistrata, 95

M

Maccabees, 142
Macedon, 16, 113f., 117, 131, 134–140, 146, 150, 153
  See also Alexander; Philip
machines, 29, 46
Macrinus, usurpation, 185
magic, 22, 49f., 176, 212, 214f., 224, 235f.
  Photos 83–86
Magnesia, battle, 147
man
  prehistoric, 19
  domestication of, 23
managerial class, development, 140
Manetho, 138, 144
Mani and Manicheanism, 208, 249f.
manpower, shortage, 222
manufacture, 172, 227
Marathon, battle, 114, 120
Marcus Aurelius, 164, 170, 174, 239
Marduk, 109f.
Mari, 16, 32, 36, 65
Marius, 146, 154f.

marriage, 222
Mars-Apollo, 173
Martial, 164, 174
martyrs, 215f., 249
Marxism, 4, 7, 48
Mary, "Mother of God," 210, 216
  Photo 87
mathematics, 38, 143
Maurice, 184, 200
Maximinus, usurpation, 187
meals. *See* food
meat, a luxury, 223
mechanization, examples, 226
Media, 90, 99–103, 109, 115
medicine, 38, 125, 143, 212, 224, 245ff.
Megara, 122
Megiddo, battle, 102, 110
Melania, 206
Memphis, 45, 65, 73
Menelaus, 80
Menander, 138
mental health, 215
mercenaries, 93, 132, 238
Mesopotamia, 17–40, 164, 187
Messiah, the, 178, 244
metals, trade in, 104, 229
  See also bronze; copper; etc.
Micah, 98
Miletus, 221
military service, Christian approval, 195
mills, 160, 172, 189; *Photo 21*
Minerva, 173
Minoans, 65f.
Mishnah, the, 164, 182
missionaries, Christian, 202
Mitanni, 58
Mithras and Mithraism, 176, 249
Mithridates VI of Pontus, 146, 155
Moabites, 81
mobs, 142, 159, 166, 169
Moesia, 164
monarchy and monarchies, 91, 96, 142, 221
monasteries, monks, and monasticism, 196f., 204, 207, 214, 216
money, 104. *See also* coinage
monophysite heresy, 210
monotheism, 57, 98, 112, 114, 119
moon, 234
morality, 73
mortality, 224, 242
mosaics, Roman, 174, 211
  Photos 69, 80
  from Ur, *Photo 4*
Moses, 80ff., 110
  Photo 85
"Mother of God." *See* Mary
Mount Mycale, battle, 114, 120
Muses, cult, 132, 141

Museum of Alexandria, 141
"music," meaning of, 231
music, structures for, 233
Mycenae and Mycenaeans, 58, 65-68, 76f., 86
 Photos 5, 31
Mycerinus, Pharaoh, *Photo 9*
mysteries (religious), 51, 176
mythology, 46, 48, 71, 98

N

Nabonidus of Babylon, 73, 103, 105, 109, 113f., 246
Nabu, 73
Nakht, tomb of, *Photos 15-17*
Naramsin, 32, 69f.
Narbonnese Gaul, 146, 153
Narmer, 45
 Photo 2
Narses, 211
Naucratis, 110
navy, Athenian, 109, 122
Near East, history and culture, 17, 19, 96, 109
 See also names of component areas
Nebuchadnezzar II, 102f., 109f.
Necho, 101
Necho II, 102, 104, 110
Neolithic Age, 75
Neoplatonism, 202, 212, 214
Nero, 164, 174, 180
 Photo 72
Nerva, 164, 169
Nestor, 80
Nestorius and Nestorianism, 202, 210
Nicaea, Council of, 184, 195, 202
Night, a goddess, 234
Nile River 41ff.
 Photo 3
Nile Valley, 41, 43, 47
Nineveh, 62, 101f.
Ningirsu, 73
Nippur, 33, 69
nocturnal rituals, 234
nonsense, 250
 sanctification of, 215
Noricum, 164f.
Nubia, 42, 47, 54f., 57f., 64, 109, 207
nudity, Greek, 94, 106, 245

O

obsidian, 16, 21
Octavian and Octavius. *See* Augustus
Odeum, the, 245
Odysseus, 80
Odyssey, the, 79, 90
office equipment, Sumerian, 37
officers, Roman, 185

oil, trade in, 104, 229
old age, 87, 225
oligarchy and oligarchies, 91, 93, 109, 221
olives, 108
 Photo 22
Olympic Games, 90, 93
omens, 236, 246
optics, 240
oracles, 236
orientalization, of Roman court, 204
Origen, 214
Orpheus, 105
Osiris, 72
Ostia, *Photo 64*
Ostrogoths, 184, 189
out-of-doors life, 218
overpopulation, 95
Ovid, 146, 164

P

Pachomius, 184, 196
Paestum, 120
paganism, 98, 208
painting, 174
 Photos 15-17, 20, 22-24B, 26, 32, 51
Pakistan, 130, 133
palaces, 117, 221
 Photos 61, 81
Palestine, 59, 76f., 91, 109, 164, 177f., 180f.
Panathenaic festivals, 246
 Photo 35
Pannonia, 164f.
Panticapaeum, 131
papyrus, 43
 Photos 48, 50
parasites, personal, 225
parchment, 141
parents, dependence on children, 239
Parmenides, 114, 119
Parthenon, 114, 122
 Photos 37, 38
parties, dinner, etc. *See* pleasure
Parsargadae, 117
past, altered by history, 1
"patriarchs"
 Biblical, 81
 Christian, 202, 209
patriotism, local, 173, cf. loyalty
Patroclus, 80
patterns of life, 249
Paul (Saul), 164, 179
peasants, 176, 197, 204ff., 217
Peleshet. *See* Philistines
Peloponnesian War, 114, 122f.
penance, 209
Pepi II, 52
perfumes, in Roman trade, 172
Pergamum, 138, 141, 146f., 153
Pericles, 122

270 SUBJECT INDEX

persecutions, 229
  by Christians, 194f., 207f.
  of Christians, 179f., 193, 197, 208
  by Jews, 179, 208
  of Jews, 181, 208
  of pagans etc., 194, 207f.
Persepolis, 117, 134
Persian Empire, Achaemenid
    characteristics, 113ff., 230f.
    history, 113–117, 120, 129f., 134
    Sassanid, 184, 187, 198ff., 207
    Photos 30, 34, 40, 71
Petronius, 164, 174
pharaoh(s), 42, 44f., 49, 52–56, 238
  Photos 2, 9
Pharisees, 178f., 181
Pharsalus, battle, 146, 155
Phidias, 114
Philadelphia, 140
Philip II of Macedon, 130f., 133
Philip V of Macedon, 146f.
Philippi, battle, 146
Philistines, 58, 76f., 83
Philo of Alexandria, 164
philosophy
  Greek, 94, 96, 107, 114, 118ff., 125, 130,
    132f., 212, 246
  hellenistic, 139f., 157
  under Rome, 157, 174, 212, 248
  Photos 54, 69, 78, 79
Phocas, 184, 200
Phoenicia and Phoenicians, 85f., 91, 101f.,
    104
  Photo 49
physical exercise, 94, 247
  Photo 35
physical sciences, 39, 118f., 125, 143, 214f.,
    224–227, 240f.
pilgrimage, 216
Pindar, 114
piracy, 86, 141, 187, 202f.
Pisistratus of Athens, 102, 108, 114
plagues, 224
plaster, 58
Plataea, battle, 114, 120
Plato and Platonism, 7, 96, 107, 130,
    132ff., 174, 202, 207, 212, 214
Plautus, 146, 157
pleasure, *Photos 24A, 24B, 62, 67–69*
  See also entertainment
Plotinus, 202, 212
plow(s), 16, 25, 37, 46, 64
  Photo 15
pluralism, of western society, 250
Plutarch, 15, 164, 174
Po Valley, 153
poetry, 30, 39, 80, 98, 105, 112, 118,
    126, 157, 168
politics and political theory, 94, 107, 142f.

Pompeii, 164, 174
  Photo 76
Pompey "The Great," 146, 155
Pontus, 117, 141, 146, 155
poor, care for, 50, 98, 104, 111, 154, 166,
    194, 203, 225
population, 19, 43, 123, 219, 226, 242
porphyry, 211
portents, 236
portraiture, 158, 174, 238
  *Photos 1, 2, 9, 10, 16, 17, 27, 33, 34,
    52–57, 71–79, 89, 90*
Portugal, 164
Poseidon, 67
pottery
  beginnings and Bronze Age, 16, 22, 25,
    29, 37, 42, 46, 66, 79
  Greek, 103f., 108, 114
  hellenistic, 139
  in the Roman Empire, 172, 229
  Photos 20, 22–24B, 26, 32, 35, 51
poverty, 196, 225, 227, 239
  See also poor
praetor, urban, 161
praetorian guard, 166, 169f.
prayer, 72
Praxiteles, 130, 132
  Photo 8
prehistory, and history, 17
"priestly material" in Pentateuch, 112
priests and priesthoods, 84, 93, 180, 195,
    245f.
princeps, title, 164
principate, the, 163, 167, 169
printing, approaches to, 38
privacy, modern, 221
Procopius, 213
professionalism, 143
progress, notion of, 227
prophets and prophecy, 96ff., 105, 110,
    112, 236f.
prostitution, 239
  Photo 68
proverbs, 246
provinces, Roman, 151, 167f., 172, 187,
    190
Psalms, 118, 196
Psammetichus I, 101f.
Ptah, 73
Ptolemies, 140, 144, 146f., 156
  See also Cleopatra
  Photo 56
Punic Wars, 146, 150
Punt, 47
purity, ritual, 105
Pylos, 58, 66ff., 76
  palace burned, 77
pyramids, 16, 42, 45, 47f., 158
Pythagoras and Pythagoreanism, 114, 119f.

Q

quarrying, 21, 46

R

Rabbi Jacob, 205
Rabbi Judah the Prince, 164, 182
Raetia, 164f.
Ramses II, 58, 60, 63, 69, 74, 81
Ramses III, *Photo 29*
rationalism, Greek, 214, 237–240, 250
reading, aloud, 232
recitations, public, 246
refrigeration, 220
"relevance" of history, 4
relics, 215f.
relief, "temporary," 154
religion(s)
　characteristics and social role, 48, 220, 223, 233ff., 240, 248ff.
　Egyptian, 238
　Greek and hellenistic, 124, 142
　Roman, 167
　Roman imperial, 176–182
　See also gods; paganism; Christianity; Judaism; etc.
revolts, 78, 104, 117, 122, 149f., 164, 177, 181, 185–189, 198, 200, 206, 208
rhetoric, 124, 212f., 245
Rhine-Danube frontier, 165, 198
rhinoceros, 159
Rhodes, 77, 138, 141, 147
rich, the, 221
rivers, economic importance, 41ff., 228
roads, 33, 158, 171
Roman Empire
　to A.D. 235: 163–182
　　culture, 166, 168, 170, 172–175, 187
　　extent and economy, 165, 170f., 176, 219, 230
　　government and politics, 163–167, 169f.
　A.D. 235–285: 185–188
　A.D. 285–640: 188–217
　　culture and society, 194, 201–217, 247ff.
　　extent and economy, 187, 189, 198, 203–206
　　government, 189–192; 197f., 201, 203
　　political and military history, 188, 192f., 198ff., 202, 206, 249
　Photos 21, 57–64, 66–77, 79–94
Roman Republic, 137f., 146–162
　culture and society, 147, 149, 156–162
　government, 146f., 149–155
　political and military history, 137f., 146f., 149f., 153ff.

Rome
　bishops of, 194, 204
　city of, 164, 166, 180, 184, 188, 220
　cult of, 168
　grain supply, 166
　Photo 61
roofs, life on, 219
rulers, and gods, 72
ruling, a skill, 117
runners, 228
　Photo 35

S

sacraments, 217
sacrifice, 233ff.
　of children, 226
Sadducees, 178, 181
sailboats, 16
St. Babylas, 202, 216
St. Sophia, 212
　Photos 92–94
saints, replace gods, 216
Saïs, 103
Salamis (Cyprian), 68
Salamis, battle, 114, 120
sale. *See* exchange
Sallust, 146, 157
Samaria and Samaritans, 202, 208, 223
Samnites, 150
Samson, 40
sanctity, and psychoses, 215
Sappho, 102, 105
Sarapis, 216
Sardinia and Corsica, 146
Sargon I of Agade, 16, 30, 32
Sargon II of Assyria, 90
Sasanid Empire. *See* Persian Empire
satraps and satrapies, 115
Saul, 81, 83
　See also Paul
"savior of the world" (title), 168
schools. *See* education
science. *See* physical sciences
scribes, 29f., 37f., 52ff., 64, 96
　Photo 50
scrolls, 240
sculpture
　Assyrian, 85
　Egyptian, 44, 52, 54, 103, 238
　Greek, 94, 106, 124, 133
　hellenistic, 139, 141, 143f.
　Persian, 117
　Roman, 158, 174f., 239
　Photos 1, 2, 5, 7–14, 18, 19, 27–31, 33, 50, 52–55, 65, 67, 68, 70, 71, 73, 75–79, 82
Scythians, 90, 101f., 109
Sea of Marmara, 96
"sea peoples," 58, 63f., 76f.

272 SUBJECT INDEX

"Second Isaiah," 102, 112, 114
Segovia, aqueduct, *Photo 60*
Seleucid empire, 137f., 140
Selinus, 120
senate, Roman
    republican, 152, 155
    Caesar's, 156
    Augustus', 165ff.
    imperial, 169f., 191, 232
senators, Roman, 152ff., 167, 175, 191
Seneca, 164, 174
Sennacherib, 144
Septimius Severus, 164, 170
Septuagint, 87, 136
serfdom, 191, 197
Sesostris I, 53, 55
Severan dynasty, 164, 170, 184f., 187
Severus Alexander. *See* Alexander
    (Severus)
sewers and sewage, 37, 66, 146, 159, 224
sex, in Greek culture, 87, 94f.
    See also heterosexuality; homosexuality;
    etc.
shadoof, the, 42
sheep and cattle, domesticated, 16, 21
shipping, 66, 121f., 143, 172
    See also boats; harbors
    Photo 64
Sicily, 86, 96, 146, 150, 152
siege warfare, 76, 122
    Photo 27
silence, general, 231
silk(s), 172, 211, 230
simony, 203
simplicity, of life, 227, 230
Sin (the deity), 73
sin, 209, 216
Sinai, 81f.
silver, 35, 47, 109
slaves and slavery
    Bronze Age, 31, 34
    in Greece, 104
    Roman, 152, 154, 157, 168, 175f., 229, 239
Sleep, deity. *Photo 32*
sloth, 248
snobbery, religious, 182
social classes, 34f., 53, 84, 93, 104, 121ff.,
    149, 151–154, 165ff., 175f., 191,
    203ff., 221ff., 239, 249f.
social structures, 30f., 79f., 91ff., 106f.,
    108f., 115, 117, 121, 141, 152ff.,
    163–168, 190ff., 197, 203ff., 220,
    227ff., 239, 244–250
Socrates, 114, 125, 130, 132f., 246
    Photo 54
Sogdiana, 130
soil, exhaustion, 189
Solomon, 76, 80, 83
Solon, 102, 108, 221

Son of God, the, 195, 210
song, in ancient society, 231, 233
sophists, 114, 124
Sophocles, 114, 126, 245
Spain, 96, 146, 153, 164f., 184, 198f., 205
Sparta, 106f., 122, 129f., 153
specialization, professional, 132, 143
speech, speeches, and speakers, importance, 231f., 245
    See also rhetoric; sophists
spices, trade in, 229f.
spinning, 222
    Photo 20
stability, social and cultural, 215, 227, 237f.
stamps, substitute for writing, 38
stars, importance, 234
state/church, dichotomy, 195, 249
Stoicism, 157, 169f., 174f., 212
stone, 21f., 46, 238
stupidity, 248
suburbs, uncommon, 220
Suetonius, 164, 174
Sueves, 184, 198
Suez, 55
Sulla, 146, 155
Sumer and Sumerians, 16, 24–33, 37, 47, 234
sun, importance, 234
Sunday, made a holiday, 194
supernatural population, the, 234
superstition, 214f.
Susa, 115, 117, 134
Syria, Syrians, and Syriac, 58–62, 76f., 81,
    89, 91, 109, 146, 155, 184, 197, 200,
    202, 210
Switzerland, 146, 155

T

Tacitus, 164, 174
Taima, 103
Talmuds, the, 182
taxation and tax collectors
    Ptolemaic, 140
    Roman, republican, 146, 151, 155
    early empire, 168, 190
    later empire, 188–206, 214
Tchoga Zambil, Ziggurat, *Photo 6*
technology, 226f., 232, 238, 240f.
    prehistoric, 20ff., 243
    Bronze Age, 25–29, 31f., 37f., 46, 55f., 61, 64
    Iron Age, 75f., 85f., 89
    Greek, 91, 120, 132
    hellenistic, 143
    Roman
        republican, 158–162
        early empire, 171–175, 189
        late empire, 211
    Photos 1, 4, 15–21, 23, 25–30

SUBJECT INDEX 273

temples, 26ff., 31, 55, 71f., 84, 90, 114, 120, 164, 181, 193, 203, 221
  Photos 36–38, 59, 61, 63, 92–94
Ten Commandments, anticipated, 73
tenements, 172
Terence, 157
terra-cotta statuettes, 139, 143
Tertullian, 208
Thales, 114, 118
theater(s), 159, 171, 233
  Photo 63
Thebes (Egyptian), 59, 62
Thebes (Greek), 129ff.
Theocritus, 138, 141
Theodosius I, 184, 202, 209
theology, 72f., 97f., 110f., 119, 180f., 195, 208ff., 212, 215ff., 234ff.
Theophrastus, 138, 143
Thoth, 73
Thrace, 113f., 117, 138, 164f., 184, 198
Thucydides, 14, 114, 126f., 245
Thutmoses I, 58, 60
Thutmoses III, 55
Tiber, the, 228
Tiberius, 164
Tiglath-pileser III, 90, 99
  Photo 27
Tigranes of Armenia, 146, 155
timber, trade in, 229
Timgad, *Photos 62, 63*
time
  and causation, 7
  division of, 233
  See also calendar
tin, 26, 46
Titus, 164, 169, 181
tombs and tombstones, 47–52
  Photos 3, 15–17, 65, 66
torture, 78, 205, 245, 247
trade
  Bronze Age, 26, 46, 62, 66
  Iron Age and Greek, 84ff., 95f., 109, 115, 117, 122, 131
  Roman, 172
  unimportance of, 220, 228f.
tradition, and history, 19, 30
Trajan, 164, 169f.
  Photo 73
Transjordan, 177
transport, 227–230
Trasimene, battle, 150
travel, 137, 227–230, 245
Trevia, battle, 150
trial by jury, 192, 245
tribute, Roman provincial, 151
Trinity, the, 202, 210
Tripolitania, 146, 153, 200
Troy, 58, 76, 80
turquoise, 229
Tutankhamen, 55

tyrants, 104, 108, 229
Tyre, 86, 103, 109, 130, 134

U

Ugarit and Ugaritic, 59, 64, 97
  Photos 11, 13
unemployment, and Roman policy, 227
Ur, 16, 31f., 69, 220
  Photo 4
Urartu, 90, 99
Ur-Nammu of Ur, 16, 30
utopias, their background, 117
Uzbekistan, 134

V

Valerian, 193
Vandals, 184, 198, 202f., 207
variety, of the ancient world, 227f.
Ventris, Michael, 67
Venus-Aphrodite, 173
Vergil, 164, 168
Vespasian, 164, 169
Vesuvius, eruption, 164
villages, 84, 98, 219
villas, 160, 171, 173, 191
vines (grape), 171, 229
  Photo 17
Virgin, the. *See* Mary
"virtue," Spartan, 107
visions, 237
Visigoths, 184, 199, 202
vital statistics, 224

W

war, 31, 55, 89, 127, 149
water, 22, 24, 41–44, 118, 172, 189, 228ff.
  See also agriculture; baptism; baths; navies; etc.
  Photos 3, 17, 23, 25, 26
wealth, 123, 139, 196, 201, cf. poverty
weaving, 16, 22, 222
  Photos 18, 20
wheat, 144. *See also* grain
wheels, 16, 29, 37, 42
winds, 189, 231
wine, 46, 104, 220, 229
winnowing, *Photo 16*
"wisdom"
  Babylonian, 246
  Church of the Holy. *See* St. Sophia
womb, the, in magic, *Photo 83*
women, 30, 34, 106, 159f., 175, 211, 217, 222, 239
  Photos 7–9, 13, 14, 18–20, 23, 24A, 43, 45, 56, 58, 65, 82f., 87
Word, the (deity), 195
world/church, antithesis, 216f.
worship, 72, 111, 234f.

writing, 16, 27
  alphabetic, 58, 86, 90
  Bronze Age, 27f., 36, 38, 43, 45, 67
  loss and revival, 79, 86
  Photos 2, 47–51

X

Xenophanes, 102, 114, 119
Xenophon, 95, 128
Xerxes, 114, 120

Y

Yahweh, 76, 81, 90, 97f., 110, 176ff.
  Photo 84
Yahweh-alone "party," 97, 110
Yarmuk, battle, 184
youth, Greek concern for, 87

Z

Zeno, the Stoic, 138, 139
Zeus, 67, 98
  Photo 12
ziggurats, 27
  Photo 6
zoos, 224
Zoroaster, 115, 208